Jim Fobel's
Big
Flavors

Other Books by Jim Fobel

The Stencil Book

Big Book of Fabulous, Fun-Filled Celebrations and Holiday Crafts

Beautiful Food

Jim Fobel's Old-Fashioned Baking Book

Jim Fobel's Diet Feasts

Jim Fobel's Whole Chicken Cookbook

Jim Fobel's

Big

Flavors

Clarkson Potter/Publishers
New York

Published by Clarkson Potter/Publishers, 201 East 50th Street, New York, New York 10022. Member of the Crown Publishing Group.

Random House, Inc. New York, Toronto, London, Sydney, Auckland

CLARKSON N. POTTER, POTTER, and colophon are trademarks of Clarkson N. Potter, Inc.

Manufactured in the United States of America

Design by Richard Ferretti

Library of Congress Cataloging-in-Publication Data
Fobel, Jim.
  [Big flavors]
  Jim Fobel's Big flavors / by Jim Fobel.
    p. cm.
  Includes index.
  1. Cookery, International. I. Title. II. Title: Big flavors.
TX725.A1F556 1995
641.59—dc20   94-19390
                                                  CIP

ISBN 0-517-59095-6 hardcover
     0-517-88356-2 paperback

10 9 8 7 6 5 4 3 2 1

First Edition

For my **big** brothers—John, Bob, and Eddie—with love.

Acknowledgments

I am especially grateful to all of my old friends and new friends who have helped this book to take on a life of its own. I give heartfelt thanks to: Jean Anderson, Michael and Ariane Batterberry, Carole Berglie, Tom Bernardin, Pam Bernstein, Bonnie Lee Black, Amy Boorstein, Betty and Anthony Borge, Roger Bourget, Michael Carlisle, Maddie Chevlin, Julia Child, Craig Claiborne, Tina Constable, Brown Cranna, Joan Denman, Cathy and Rus DePriest, Marlene Diaz, Tom Eckerle, Denise Ferguson, Richard Ferretti, Roy Finamore, Reiko and Jim Fobel, Bob Fobel, Dawn and John Fobel, Tina and Eddie Fobel, Leta Jo Goddard, Willie Griffin, Dr. Alan R. Hirsch, Hannah Joyce, Barbara Kafka, Michael Kalmen, Diana Kennedy, Paul Kergoat, Sue Kirby, Kathleen Holmgren Krichmar, Jere Kupecky, Reid Larrance, Florence Lin, Michael and Monica McGlade, M. A. McQuade, Steve Magnuson, Barbara Marks, Leyla Morrissey, Lynn Neavling, James Paltridge, Nancy Pollard, Peter Prestcott, Dr. Robert W. Ramsey, Brenda and Nancy Regan, Mardee and Gary Regan, Nicole Routhier, Sharon Sanders, Elizabeth Schneider, Arthur Schwartz, Michelle Sidrane, Bernadette and Bob Simms, Nina Simonds, Paul Sylvester, Michelle Tessler, John Thomas, Jane Treuhaft, Barbara Tropp, Myra Wahlstrom, Bill Weinberg, Ann Wilder, Paula Wolfert, and Eileen Yin-Fei Lo.

Special thanks to The James Beard Foundation, *Bon Appétit, Cooking Light, Family Circle, Food & Wine, Food Arts, Gourmet,* IACP, La Cuisine, Pitchfork Ranch, 6666 Ranch, Restaurant Mesón del Caballo Bayo, Bar del Jardin, Smell & Taste Treatment and Research Foundation, Ltd., and Vann's Spices.

And, finally, I want to thank all of the food writers, cookbook authors, and editors, too numerous to list individually, that have gone before me and paved the way, contributing so enormously to the evolution of good food.

Contents

Introduction

This book of recipes is an exploration of my lifelong love affair with flavor. Even as a young boy I insisted on adding more flavor to my food. I recall Easter Sundays during my childhood in the 1950s; while my three brothers preferred to eat the hard-cooked eggs from their Easter basket sprinkled with salt, I headed to the kitchen and deviled mine. Even back then my little taste buds wanted *big flavors!*

Around the same time I invented a chunky hot dog relish that had a big flavor—even though I didn't call it a big flavor, and I hadn't consciously attempted to *invent* anything. The relish just evolved as I experimented in the kitchen, combining flavors and textures that I liked. I had forgotten about that relish until now, but I can clearly picture myself as a kid in the kitchen concocting it. I think it went like this: I'd coarsely chop dill pickle, sweet pickle, and raw onion—say a quarter cup of each—and combine them with brown mustard and mayonnaise. That was it, I think. I might have added chopped green olives as a variation once in a while. And most likely I experimented by adding ketchup, but that probably made it murky and led to the discovery that, to me, ketchup tasted best along one side of a hot dog with the relish spooned generously over the other.

Thinking about it now, that simple hot dog with its toppings was a complex combination of aroma, taste, and texture, from the smoky hot dog with its snappy, juicy bite to the sweet-and-spicy ketchup complemented by that bold relish and framed in a soft bland bun. But all I did was combine a few ingredients so I could enjoy a more exciting experience than eating a plain hot dog. The ingredients I chose were simple on their own. They worked in harmony and added up to bigger flavor. I gained self-confidence as I successfully dabbled in the kitchen, and have continued to experiment with food and flavor ever since.

Old school textbooks and science books tell us that there are four basic flavors: sweet, salty, bitter, and sour. Most of the foods that we eat are a combination of several or all four. Although it is generally agreed that these are flavors our taste buds easily recognize, more recent studies[1] have shown that to adequately describe a broader range of complex flavors, at least four secondary flavor sensations must be added: pungent, cool, astringent, and flavor enhancers. *Pungency* includes ingredients like chili and black pepper that *enrage* the taste buds. *Cool* comes from menthol and causes a fresh, light numbing sensation in the mouth. *Astringency* is contributed by tannin, found in such ingredients as cocoa, tea, spinach, and unripe fruit. And the category of *flavor enhancement,* called *unami* by the Japanese, includes ingredients like MSG. Some would add metallics and alkaloids to that list.

New information is being learned every day, and perhaps even more classifications of flavor will be added in the future, enabling us to more accurately describe, analyze, and appreciate flavor.

Yet with all this talk of taste, it is amazing to learn that only 10 percent of any flavor is actually "tasted" by our taste buds; 90 percent of all flavor comes from the aroma of food. Our sense of smell is much more discriminating than our taste buds.[2] It is because of aroma that we can, for example, distinguish between chicken salad and tuna salad, tell the difference between olive oil and peanut oil, or "taste" the smoke in smoked foods. It is also interesting to note that not all aroma is sniffed through the nose. As we chew food, aromas travel from the back of our mouth, to be analyzed and appreciated from within.

Although the inseparable sensations of aroma and taste evoke the overall flavor of food, the consistency—from watery or bubbly to thick and creamy—affects the release of flavor. Did you ever wonder why flat Champagne or beer tastes different from bubbly? Or why orange juice tastes one way when sipped from a glass and another when made into gelatin and spooned? Consistency.

To understand consistency we can compare skim milk, low-fat milk, and whole milk. They are all the same cow's milk, but their consistency—and therefore flavor—varies greatly depending on the fat content. The butterfat in milk coats the tongue, holding and releasing flavor. Skim milk tastes watery compared to whole milk because it contains less fat. Continuing up the scale in butterfat richness are half-and-half, light cream, and heavy cream. Temperature and melting qualities also affect flavor, and that is why we perceive some ice creams to be richer than others.

We get the most pleasure and passion from food when we savor a wide range of aroma, flavor, and texture. When I create a recipe, I want to intoxicate and seduce you with aromas that start your mouth watering before you open it, then tease, tingle, tantalize, and please your taste buds in ways that make you want more. I am always exploring new flavor combinations and fresh ways to combine ingredients. And, of course, my goal is to leave you feeling content and well-nourished.

But what are *big* flavors? To me, big flavors are bold, complex, aromatic, assertive, and always exciting and varied. You definitely know that you are eating something when it has a big flavor.

Many ingredients have big flavors on their own. Who would deny that garlic, basil, mint, cilantro, chili pepper, lemon, or anchovies have big flavors? They are at once fragrant and assertive—not the flavors you would feed to a baby. But these ingredients are relatively simple and become even more exciting when treated as components to create more complex dishes with even bigger flavors, similar to notes that are combined as chords in a larger composition.

In fact, we might compare cooking to playing the piano. Fragrance, flavor, and texture would be the keys. If a simple tune is produced by hitting just three or four keys, it can be pleasant, but not nearly as fascinating nor as compelling as when the entire keyboard is used. The rest of the keys on the board make the sounds that let us more fully appreciate that original tune. Some notes offer background, foreground, or subtle nuance; others, punctuation or drama. A few of the keys might be touched just once or twice, but the contrast shows off the full range and holds our interest, adding excitement and enticing us to hear more.

So it is with food. Big flavors are created when many taste sensations and aromas are combined with a variety of textures and consistencies. But food notes are more complex than musical notes. Each ingredient already has a certain complexity of aroma *and* taste. When I create a dish I try to excite as many taste buds as possible, perhaps awakening some that you didn't know you had, from the tip of your tongue all the way down your throat, offering aromatic bouquets along the way.

How big is *big*? Flavor is always relative to the other ingredients in a recipe, or to other food on your plate. Combining garlic, olive oil, and salt can make a big basic flavor, but when the mixture is tossed with spaghetti, the blandness of the pasta will diminish the flavor. To counteract this and make it bigger, you could increase the garlic, taking into consideration that how you treat the garlic will change its flavor (raw, sautéed, and roasted garlic all taste different). However, the flavor will remain relatively simple. To add dimension you could sauté a hot chili pepper in the olive oil and strike a high note. Add a few juicy sweet tomatoes and a handful of fragrant fresh basil, and you create a bigger flavor that explores a wider range. You can make the flavor fuller by adding a splash of dry white wine and round it out with nuances of black olive, lemon, or anchovy. Or give it a smoky accent by adding bacon. If I had a few sprigs of fresh oregano, I'd add them for depth of flavor, but not in quantity large enough to take center stage or interfere with the basil. If freshly grated Parmesan cheese is added at the last moment, to release its great burst of aroma, you have created something close to a culinary symphony, striking many pleasant notes as a big flavor crescendos.

This orchestration of taste sensation brings us to the importance of proportion and balance. Just how much of any ingredient is enough? Everyone will have his or her own idea about what tastes best because each of us has a unique sense of taste and smell as different, I am told, as our fingerprints.

You may want to add more garlic and less basil to *your* sauce, or no garlic at all. You might like the hotness of raw garlic or prefer to tame it by sautéing. The character of the pasta sauce will vary depending on the flavor you feature. You can make a basil sauce with a garlic nuance, or a garlic sauce with a note of basil. It could become a hot chili sauce with a background of tomato, basil, and garlic, or an anchovy sauce, robust with black olives. The ingredients would be the same, but the end result is totally different because of proportion and balance. If you were to use all ingredients in the same proportion, they would cancel out one another and you'd end up with a muddled, confused flavor, not interesting at all.

As a final note, I want to discourage you from eating foods that are artificially flavored or sweetened. Unfortunately, this is difficult to do as we are fast becoming a nation that seems to prefer big *artificial* flavors. Today, chemists come up with artificial flavors that try to fool us into thinking how, for example, a grape *should* taste. But this happens mostly to the untrained palate, and the sooner you get rid of all those artificial flavorings, the sooner you will appreciate the subtleties and complexities of *real* flavor.

Paying close attention to the fragrance, taste, and texture of food will actually sharpen your senses and increase your eating pleasure.

This collection of recipes for dishes with *big flavors* is for everyday home cooking and for entertaining. My taste is but one taste; the recipes are meant to be guidelines for your own culinary improvisations. Experiment with these recipes and find the balance and proportion of flavors that suits *your* taste. Remember, the possibilities are endless.

[1] Karl Heinz Ney, *Aromagrams—A New Approach to Flavor Classification and Descriptions, Flavors and Off-Flavors*, Elsevier, Amsterdam, 1990.

[2] Alan R. Hirsch, "Flavor and Aroma: A Study of 10 Chefs (Are Their Olfactory and Gustatory Abilities Better Than Ours?)," The Smell & Taste Treatment and Research Foundation, Ltd., Chicago, Ill.

Big Flavor Pantry

I hope that you are not frightened by the length of these lists. I have included my favorite ingredients for adding flavor to foods because they are helpful for inspiration. Do not feel as though you must go out and buy everything. You can create a big flavor from ingredients you already have on hand; for example, salt, pepper, mustard, and perhaps an herb are all you need.

Salt

Salt is one of the four basic flavors. It draws out flavor and aroma, making food taste richer and fuller; it enhances herbs and spices and most other ingredients, bringing their fullest flavors forward; it deepens color, so foods become more appealing. And, quite frankly, you cannot obtain as much flavor from food when you omit one of the four basic flavors. That would be like trying to make a rainbow without one of the primary colors.

I like to think of salt as a spice, to be used judiciously as a flavoring to enhance other ingredients. It is a very important building block to creating big flavors.

The three most popular forms of cooking salt are coarse (kosher), sea, and table. **Coarse (kosher) salt** is my favorite all-purpose salt. I always choose the coarse variety because it is light and fluffy and easy to feel between your fingers when measuring by the pinch. This salt has a pure, light, bright, clean salt flavor that tastes of nothing else. You will need to use a little more than the same volume of denser table salt.

Sea salt is an excellent salt for cooking and flavoring. It has a fuller, more intense flavor than coarse salt. Sea salt has a definite sea flavor all its own and tastes "saltier." I find sea salt to be an excellent finishing salt, best added just before serving. It is also an excellent choice for a salt to use at table.

Table salt is the ordinary round carton of fine salt so common in every kitchen across America. Often this salt has iodine added but even the boxes that do not contain iodine have other ingredients added, such as *sodium silicoaluminate* and *tricalcium phosphate*. I encourage you to conduct a little salt tasting on your own. First, touch a moist finger to coarse salt and taste it on your tongue. Rinse with water, then repeat with sea salt, then with table salt. I think that you will be shocked to discover just how awful common table salt tastes compared to the other two.

There are two other salts worth investigating. In India there are several varieties of natural *"black" salt* (*kala namak*) in colors that actually range from pinkish tan to dark brown. They have a slight smoky fragrance and tangy sour flavor accent. You can buy them in lumps or ground.

Korean bamboo salt (chugyom) is sea salt that has been packed into large stalks of bamboo and baked nine times to temperatures as high as 2730° F. It is claimed to have many health benefits and is extremely expensive. It has such a strong saltiness that I can still taste it in the air 30 minutes after I have worked with it! It is available in powder, granules, and tablets.

Note: Although I use coarse (kosher) salt for virtually all of my cooking, the teaspoon measurements for salt quantities in this book were calculated with ordinary table salt (unless otherwise noted). There were several reasons for this: 1. That is what most people use in their kitchen; 2. It is denser and heavier so you won't accidentally add too much if substituting another kind; and 3. The food will only taste better if using kosher or sea salt instead. Even so, I encourage you not to use the table salt in your cooking.

Peppercorns-Black, White, Green, and Pink

As often as I reach for the peppermill, I never lose sight of the fact that pepper was once so precious that it was used as money. Today it is as common as salt, but I still give it the respect it has earned.

Piper nigrum, the pepper plant, produces the world's most important spice. The berries—whether black, white, or green—grow in clusters on the same climbing evergreen vine. Early colonists from India introduced pepper to Indonesia around 100 B.C.

Black peppercorns are picked green about nine months after flowering. They are fermented in mounds and then dried in the sun until they turn black and wrinkled. Black pepper gives a strong penetrating fragrance that is very familiar to all of us. It gives a pleasant numbing sensation to the tongue and leaves us with a burning aftertaste.

The United States imports ten times as much black pepper as white. The peppercorns are named for the regions where they are grown or for the ports from which they are shipped. The best ones include Lampong, Malabar, Tellicherry, Sarawak, and Brazilian.

White peppercorns are the fully ripe berries—yellow with tinges of green and beginning to turn red—that are soaked for a week in flowing water to soften. The hulls are rubbed off and the berries are dried in the sun until creamy white. The procedure tames some of the harshness that the skin gives but renders them fragrant and pungent enough to contribute full pepper flavor. White pepper has a more refined or well-rounded flavor than black pepper. It is often added to light-colored dishes, such as mashed potatoes and white sauces, where black specks might detract.

In the perfectly stocked kitchen, one should keep separate peppermills for black and white peppercorns. Buy whole peppercorns and store them in a jar in a cool, dry place, and they will keep for several years. Grind the pepper, from fine to coarse, as you need it. Preground pepper loses its potency quickly.

At one time, green peppercorns were available only where they grew. Now they are canned and sold packed in brine or vinegar, or treated with salt and packed in water. Green peppercorns are firm, but soft and moist enough to bite into. They have a fresher, more fragrant flavor than dried and give a good burst of pepper heat to the back of the tongue. Store them in their packing liquid in a jar in the refrigerator, and they will keep for at least a year.

Pink peppercorns are not related to the true peppercorn. They have a sweet peppery flavor without the hot, numbing sensation of black and white peppercorns.

Fresh Ingredients

Fresh ingredients give such vital fragrance and taste that we should utilize them whenever possible. This is just a partial list of big flavor fresh ingredients. I'm sure that you have some favorites of your own. The suggestions here can help to inspire you when wondering which ingredient to choose to make a flavor bigger. Some ingredients have a simple big flavor while others are more complex. Often, several will be used in combination, such as ginger, garlic, and scallions for cooking Oriental dishes, or cilantro and chilies for Mexican cooking. Most frequently, fresh ingredients will be combined with dried and bottled ingredients to explore and expand flavors.

arugula	garlic	pineapple
bananas (very ripe)	ginger	raspberries
basil	grapefruit	rosemary
chili peppers, such as de arbol, habañero, jalapeño, poblano, serrano	horseradish	sage
	lemongrass	scallions
	lemons	shallots
cilantro	limes	sorrel
citrus zest	mint	sour cherries
coconut	onions	tamarind
currants	oranges	tangerines
dill	oregano	tarragon
epazote	passion fruit	thyme

Dried Ingredients

Often, dried ingredients have more intensity than fresh because the moisture has evaporated and the flavor becomes more concentrated. What they may lack in freshness is made up for in strength. In general, you will use less dried than fresh of the same product. For example, a very general rule for substituting dried herbs for fresh is 1 to 3; that is, 1 teaspoon of dried herb in place of 3 teaspoons fresh. And, while just ½ ounce of dried porcini will add a wallop of wild mushroom flavor to a pasta sauce, a full pound of fresh porcini will contribute a wonderful woodsy flavor and double as a vegetable, without overpowering.

chili peppers, such as ancho, cascabel, cayenne, chipotle, guajillo, mulato, pasilla

chili powders and flakes, such as aleppo, ancho, cayenne, paprika (hot and mild), pasilla, chili powder blends

cocoa

coffee

flowers, such as hibiscus

fruit, such as apricots, blueberries, cherries, cranberries, currants, peaches, pears, prunes, raisins

herbs

mushrooms, such as cèpes, morels, oyster, porcini, shiitake

nuts

salt and pepper

seafood, such as shrimp and scallops

seaweed

seeds

spice blends, such as crab boil, curry, garam masala, pickling spice, poultry seasoning, quatre epices

spices

tomatoes, dried and sun-dried

vanilla beans

Dairy Products

With the exception of a multitude of strongly flavored cheeses and tangy yogurt, most dairy products do not have a big flavor all their own. They do, however, contribute creaminess and richness, and they are an important vehicle for making flavors bigger.

butter

cream, light and heavy

cream cheese

crema

crème fraîche

fresh cheeses, such as cottage, farmer, ricotta

half-and-half

melting cheeses, such as fontina, Monterey Jack, Muenster, raclette

milk; rich, whole, 2%, and 1%

sharp-flavored cheeses, such as blue, cheddar, Emmentaler, feta, goat, Gruyère, Parmesan, provolone, Romano

sour cream

yogurt

yogurt cheese

Bottled, Canned, and Packaged Ingredients

So many condiments that can add a big flavor in a flash keep well on the pantry shelf and in the refrigerator. I try to keep practically all of the ingredients on this list on hand at all times. In fact, I feel most secure when I have at least a dozen varieties of vinegar in my kitchen cupboard. The same goes for bottled chili sauces, prepared mustards, pickles, relishes, and bottled Chinese sauces.

anchovies and anchovy paste

artichoke hearts, canned, frozen, or marinated

barbecue sauces and marinades

bean sauces, such as Chinese black bean, sweet or hot, Japanese, Korean

beans; black, Chinese salted or fermented

bitters, Angostura and others

capers and caper berries

caramel

chilies, canned, in adobo sauce, pickled

chili sauces, such as Cajun, Caribbean, Chinese, Heinz, hot pepper, salsa, Tabasco, Tex-Mex

chocolate

chutney, such as Major Grey's, mango and other fruit varieties

clam juice

distilled flavor essences

extracts

fish sauce

fruit juice concentrates, frozen or bottled

fruit syrups

hoisin sauce

honey

horseradish (prepared)

jams, jellies, marmalades, and preserves

ketchup

kim chee

maple syrup

miso, such as brown, red, yellow, etc.

mustards

nectars

nut butters

orange flower water

pickled onions and other vegetables

pickles

relish

rosewater

salad dressings

salsas and spicy sauces

sardines

sesame paste and tahini

sour cherries

soy sauces, such as Chinese light (thin), dark, black, thick

steak sauces

tartar sauce

tomatoes; crushed, paste, puree, sauce, whole

vegetable juice

vinegars, such as Balsamic, black Chinese (Chinkiang), cider, fruit, herb, malt, rice, etc.

Worcestershire sauce

Smoked Foods

We invented many smoked foods—like chicken, turkey, and trout—in this country. Nowadays, to my great delight, we seem to smoke everything in sight. Today you can even buy smoked shrimp, sea scallops, vegetables, and cheeses.

There have always been smoked ham bones to flavor split pea soups and baked bean casseroles, but now we can save that smoked chicken or turkey carcass and add a big flavor to a stock. Adding smoked meat or bones to foods is the easiest way of adding smoke flavor without actually smoking. Something so simple as a slice of hickory-smoked bacon added to a recipe will strike an extra note of flavor, while adding one dried chipotle chile to your spaghetti sauce will elevate it to the sublime. And quite inexpensively you can give a smoky dimension to stock or sauce by adding a smoked ham hock or smoked neck bones.

bacon and bacon fat	fish, such as chub, salmon,	seafood, such as oysters,
beef	trout, whitefish	scallops, shrimp
bones	ham and ham hocks	tasso
cheese	pastrami	turkey
chicken	pork necks and bones	vegetables
chipotle chilies	sausages	

Spirits

Cooking with spirits greatly expands your flavor range. I would be at such a loss if I didn't have wine to add to foods—and of course the stronger spirits too, like Cognac, brandy, and whiskey. They add a big flavor in an instant. When foods are cooked with spirits much of the alcohol is burned off, leaving behind a special essence of flavor. In cold and frozen desserts the alcohol remains, adding even more flavor and dimension.

ale	gin	Scotch
aquavit	liqueurs	sherry
armagnac	Madeira	tequila
beer	marsala	vermouth
bourbon	mirin	vodka
brandy	port	wines
Chinese rice wines	rum	
Cognac	sake	

Big Flavor Techniques

Instead of repeating many of the basic cooking techniques over and over again in specific recipes, here they are explained in detail. Of course many cooks won't need to refer to this chapter at all, while others, I hope, will gain self-confidence in the kitchen by learning basic procedures.

Adding Smoke

In this country we invented foods like smoked turkey, chicken, and trout. And staples like smoked hams and bacon go back to early America. Nowadays we can buy a tremendous variety of smoked foods—from poultry and pork to seafood and vegetables. The hardwood that they were smoked over will affect the flavor.

You can add mouthwatering smoky flavor to foods with any of these smoked ingredients. If you have a smoker, you can experiment and make really big flavor. To smoke food over charcoal, soak some hardwood chips in water, then add them to the glowing coals just before placing your food on the grill. Cup loosely with a sheet of aluminum foil to hold in the aromatic flavor.

Cooking with Garlic

There is no right or wrong way to use garlic, and there are no rules saying how much or how little to use. Raw, sautéed, roasted, toasted, and fried garlic all taste different. And they will taste different still depending on whether you leave them whole or decide to slice, mince, puree, or squeeze.

When you add forty whole cloves of garlic to make that famous chicken recipe, the flavor will be less garlicky than if you were to squeeze four or five cloves of garlic directly over the chicken.

Mideastern cooks roast whole heads of garlic directly in the glowing charcoal embers of a barbecue until the outside is charred and the garlic inside is soft and brown. All you have to do is break off a clove and squeeze out the luscious paste over bread, meat, or vegetables.

Mexican and Indian cooks fry garlic in fat until it is dark brown and crisp, resulting in a strong nutty garlic flavor that contributes boldness to sauces, stews, and rice. In Oaxaca, whole unpeeled cloves of garlic are toasted on a griddle until the outside is charred and the inside becomes a soft mellow paste.

Add minced or pureed raw garlic for a strong garlic flavor and hotness, a flavor that some find addictive. I prefer to sauté garlic very gently in oil or butter to tame the heat and play up the pure garlic taste. I do this even for dishes usually associated with raw garlic, such as French aioli and pistou, Italian pesto, and Mideastern hummus.

By the way, the younger the garlic the milder the flavor.

Degreasing Stocks and Sauces

After stocks have simmered for the specified time, they must be degreased. There are many ways to do this; choose the technique best suited to you.

The stock must first be strained. It is most efficient in my kitchen to work directly in the sink; not only is it near the stove, but any spills are easy to handle. Place a colander in a large bowl. Using a slotted spoon, remove the largest ingredients from the stock and place them in the colander. Press lightly to extract any liquid and discard the solids. Pour the rest of the stock through the colander, again pressing lightly on the solids. Discard the solids. Strain the stock through a medium sieve and then a finer one, or through dampened cheesecloth, if desired.

All of the fat in the stock will rise to the top. To remove it, you can:

1. Let it cool to room temperature, chill it so the fat solidifies, and then scrape it off with a spoon.

2. If you want to degrease it right away, simply skim off as much of the fat as possible with a large spoon, and then blot off the last traces of fat by floating a paper towel on the surface. Lift it off along with the fat; repeat, if necessary.

3. There is a special brush that is shaped like a large pastry brush, made of a material that attracts fat. This can be passed over the surface several times and it will collect the fat. Rinse it under hot tap water after each collection.

4. Get a special gravy strainer, usually a cup with a strainer set into the top and a trap door at the bottom. Since the fat rises to the top, you can reverse-siphon off the degreased stock or pan drippings from the bottom.

To degrease pan drippings, after the roast, turkey, chicken, or meat loaf has cooked, remove the meat and tilt the pan. Depending on the quantity, the fat can be spooned off or a shallow layer can be removed by blotting with a paper towel.

Hard-Cooking Eggs

Contrary to the old term "hard-boiled eggs," eggs should never be boiled; it toughens the protein. What you really want to do is cook them gently in barely simmering water. First, eggs cook best when they are at room temperature. If you are in a hurry and your eggs are cold, put them in a bowl of warm tap water for 10 to 15 minutes.

Put the eggs in a saucepan just large enough to hold them in a single layer without crowding and add cold water to cover by an inch. Place over moderately high heat and bring almost to a boil; watch carefully so the water does not come to a full boil. Immediately reduce the heat and keep at a bare simmer. Cook for 10 to 12 minutes; large eggs should take only 10 minutes, while extra-large might take 12.

Drain the eggs and rinse them under cold water. Put the eggs in a bowl of cold water to cook completely, changing the water as it loses its chill.

Here's a hint for centering yolks if you want to make perfect slices or deviled eggs: As soon as you reduce the heat, carefully stir the eggs in a circle, using a large spoon, spinning them faster and faster for about 10 seconds so centrifugal force pushes the yolks to the centers.

Making Ginger Juice

Fresh ginger juice adds ginger's concentrated aromatic essence without adding the bulk and fiber of the ginger itself.

To make ginger juice, choose the firmest, shiniest fresh ginger you can obtain (old and shriveled will not yield much juice or flavor). The yield will vary depending on the juiciness of the ginger, but 3 ounces will give approximately 2 tablespoons of juice. Coarsely grate the ginger through the largest holes of a cheese grater onto several layers of dampened cheesecloth or a linen napkin. Roll up tightly and wring out the juice by twisting and squeezing over a bowl to catch the juice.

Marinate or Macerate

Marinate and macerate are similar terms, loosely interchangeable, though marination most often refers to meats, seafood, and poultry that have been soaked or pickled in strongly flavored liquid, while maceration usually describes fruit or vegetables that have been soaked and softened in spirits, juice, or brine. Both contribute flavor and texture. These processes can be done for short periods of time or as long as several days.

Some ingredients, such as yogurt, tenderize through enzymatic action, and meats left too long in the marinade will become soft and pasty. Poultry and seafood soften quickly so it's not a good idea to leave chicken in such a marinade for more than a couple hours, and seafood just thirty to sixty minutes. Beef and lamb, however, will hold up for twenty-four hours.

A word of caution: Don't rely on marinade to tenderize meats. Instead, choose meats that will be tender naturally and use marinades to add flavor rather than tenderness.

Experiment. Be inventive and try making marinades from tangerine juice, grapefruit juice, or Valencia orange juice. Try passion fruit juice, or layer slices of star fruit with your ingredients. Sour cherries are perfect in a marinade for pork, poultry, and shrimp. Yogurt adds great tang. Combine it with lemon or lime juice or rice vinegar to emphasize this quality.

Take a look at the marinade that I used for the Crunchy-Spicy Fried Chicken (page 208) and notice that I have stirred in huge quantities of hot pepper sauce and cayenne. That way, enough is absorbed by the meat to make a big flavor after it has been coated and fried (techniques that tend to tame the spice). Of course, you could not add ingredients like that in such a huge quantity directly to a dish; it would simply overwhelm and become inedible. But in a marinade, the flavor is absorbed and then the solids discarded.

You can add enormous quantities of fresh or dried herbs to marinades so at least some of their flavor will be absorbed. Ditto for aromatics like ginger and garlic. Try adding ½ cup grated fresh ginger to a marinade for poultry; the flavor and fragrance will absorb beautifully without overpowering.

I like to macerate sliced tomatoes in balsamic vinegar with fresh basil leaves. You might want to try them with cilantro leaves and garlic. Some vegetables, such as cucumbers or eggplant, can be lightly salted to draw out some of the liquid before macerating, then the brine will be absorbed and replace the extracted liquid.

Melting Chocolate

Over hot water. This can be done in the top of a double boiler or in a stainless-steel bowl that fits over a saucepan. Pour about 1 inch of water in the pan and bring it to a boil. Reduce the heat and keep the water at a bare simmer. It is important that not one drop of water or moisture get into the chocolate or it will seize and become stiff and impossible to melt smooth. Chop the chocolate and place it in the top of the double boiler or in the bowl. Let stand without stirring over barely simmering water for a few minutes and then stir occasionally until melted and smooth. Remove the top of the double boiler or bowl and dry the bottom before removing the chocolate.

In a microwave. Choose a small microwavable dish that is perfectly dry. Add 1 to 3 ounces coarsely chopped chocolate. Do not cover. Microwave at medium power for 2 minutes. Check and stir the chocolate and microwave for 1 to 2 minutes longer, if necessary. Stir until smooth.

Note: *If you are microwaving chocolate with butter, shortening, or liquid, microwave at full (100 percent) power for 1 minute, then stir and microwave 1 minute longer, if necessary.*

Peeling and Seeding Tomatoes

There are two good ways to peel tomatoes: dip them into boiling water, or run them over a gas flame. When I have a large quantity, I usually use the water technique. When I need just a couple, I choose the flame.

For the water method, bring a large pot of water to a boil over high heat. Drop in 3 or 4 tomatoes and time them for 10 to 15 seconds. If the skin should burst before that, take them out. The timing will vary with the ripeness of the tomato. Some thick-skinned ones will take 30 seconds to loosen and some may not loosen at all. In general, ripe summer tomatoes will take just 10 seconds. Remove them with a slotted spoon and drop them into a bowl of cold water to quickly cool and stop the cooking.

For the flame method, you will need a gas flame (or small torch). Jab a tomato onto a long fork and hold it directly in the flames. When it blisters and the skin cracks or bursts, slowly twirl it around to loosen the skin all over. Set aside to cool.

To peel tomatoes, grasp the skin between thumb and paring knife and pull off the skin. When tomatoes are very ripe, the skin will practically fall off in one piece. Use a paring knife to cut out the core from the stem end.

Some recipes require tomatoes to be seeded. This is a refinement that is not absolutely necessary. The seeds do, however, add bitterness and texture. When I seed tomatoes I do so over a sieve placed over a bowl to catch all of the juice. Cut the tomato in half crosswise and gently squeeze out the seeds into the sieve. That's all there is to it. Rub the seeds in the sieve to remove any juice and then discard them. Some recipes do not require additional liquid. In those cases, reserve the juice for another purpose, such as a sauce or soup, or drink.

Note: When served raw, tomatoes are great with skin, seeds, and juice intact. It is only upon cooking that the skin toughens.

Peeling Peaches

As with tomatoes, the skin of a peach can sometimes be objectionable. Some people don't mind it when eating a peach out of hand, but peaches are almost always peeled when used in desserts.

The best way to peel peaches is by dipping them in boiling water. Bring a large pot of water to a boil over high heat. Add 2 or 3 peaches and time them for 10 to 15 seconds (or even a little longer if the skins are thick and stubborn); remove with a slotted spoon and place in a large bowl of ice water until cool. To peel, hold a paring knife between thumb and forefinger and pull off the skin. Peaches darken quickly because of their low acid content. To counteract this, toss them (whole or cut up, as you wish) with a little lemon juice.

Preparing Dried Beans

Dried beans, with the exception of pinto beans, should be soaked before cooking. First, put them into a large bowl of cool water and swish them around to dislodge any sand or grit. Place a colander and the bowl of beans in the sink. Pick up a few beans, inspect for grit, and rinse under slowly running water, working over the colander to catch any beans that fall. Transfer to another bowl. This procedure actually moves very quickly.

There are two ways to soak beans: quick and slow. I prefer the slow way, soaking them in cold water to cover generously, for about 8 hours. However, you can also put the rinsed beans in a pot, cover generously with cold water, and bring it to a boil over high heat. Let boil for 1 minute, remove from the heat, cover tightly, and let soak for 1 hour.

Rinsing and Cooking Spinach

Spinach can be very sandy or dirty, so special care must be taken to clean it. Fill a large bowl or the sink with cool water and add the spinach. Swish it around to dislodge any sand or grit. Have a colander nearby. Pick up each stem, one by one, and rinse again under slowly running water. Pull off any tough stems or roots, if present; medium stems and tender stems can be left on. Drop the cleaned leaves in the colander. Most of the bagged varieties are prewashed and need only a quick rinse.

Put the wet leaves into a large nonreactive pot; the pot can be packed quite full. Cover and place over high heat for 1 minute. Uncover and use 2 large spoons to turn over the entire mass. Cover and cook for 1 to 2 minutes, or until wilted down. Uncover and toss for 1 minute. Drain in a sieve placed over a bowl to catch the juices. Reserve the juices for a sauce or soup.

Roasting and Peeling Chilies and Bell Peppers

To roast a pepper, place it directly in the flames of a gas burner turned to high, or about 3 inches below an electric broiler. Turn the pepper frequently until it is blistered and charred all over. This technique cooks the pepper, and the natural sugars add flavor as they caramelize. Let the pepper cool for a minute or two. Place in a plastic bag. Twist the top closed and set aside to cool to room temperature.

The skin can be simply rubbed away with your fingers, or (with some loss of juice and flavor) rubbed away under gently running water. Use a paring knife to cut out the stem (except, of course, if you are roasting whole poblanos for Chilies Rellenos [page 152]; you'll want the stems intact for those). Pull out the seeds and ribs. Cut the peppers or leave whole, depending on the recipe you are following.

The peppers can be roasted a day or two ahead, covered, and stored in the refrigerator. They begin to sour quickly so a day or two is as far in advance as I recommend, unless you are marinating them in lemon juice or a vinaigrette or oil.

Segmenting Citrus

Removing the membranes improves the texture (and therefore, the flavor) of citrus fruits. Remove the membrane between each segment. First remove the rinds and white pith from the whole fruit: use a sharp knife to slice off the top and bottom just beneath the pith. Then with fruit upright, cut downward, removing strips of rind all around, just below the pith. After the rind and pith have been cut away, hold the fruit in one hand over a bowl and use a paring knife to cut down along one side of each segment's membrane and then up along the membrane on the other side to free the segment. Do this with each segment. With practice, the chore progresses swiftly and you will cut down along one side and up with lightning speed. When all the segments have been removed, you will have left in your hand a sort of accordionlike membrane, which you should squeeze over a bowl to extract any juices before discarding.

Shaping Wontons and Chinese Dumplings

Wonton skins and eggroll wrappers are a great convenience; they are sheets of pre-rolled pasta ready for filling. Wonton skins come in thin, medium, and thick, though the specification is usually written in Chinese. Eggroll skins are always thicker than wonton skins. When I want a thicker wrapper or one to use for ravioli, I buy the eggroll skins and cut them into quarters (each large wrapper will make 4 wonton skins). Keep the skins covered with a damp towel while you work, or they will dry out. (If you work fast, as I do, you don't need to bother with this.)

For sealing the wontons or dumplings, stir 1 egg yolk and 2 teaspoons cold water together in a cup. Place 1 square (wonton skin or quartered eggroll wrapper) of dough in front of you and rotate it 45 degrees so that it is a diamond shape. (I do this entirely in my left hand but you might want to assemble and shape on a plate until you get the knack of it.) Spoon about 2 teaspoons (or up to 1 tablespoon) of filling onto the center. Dip a finger into the egg yolk and moisten the top 2 edges of the dough. Fold up the bottom point, enclosing the filling and making a triangle, but fold it so the 2 top points are slightly askew. Pinch to enclose the filling and seal the edges, squeezing out any air as you pinch around the edges. Dab a little of the egg on the right point and bring the left and right points together, overlapping them by about ½ inch. Pinch together. The dumpling will resemble a nurse's cap. As they are shaped, place on a sheet dusted with cornstarch. If making ahead, cover and chill for 1 to 2 hours.

Toasting Herbs and Spices

Herbs and spices create mystery, and they animate food. Herbs and spices taste best after a brief toasting or sautéing. They become more fragrant and flavorful. That is why it is a good idea to sauté curry powder in fat when making curry. I often add spices and herbs to a skillet when I am sautéing meat or vegetables. If you want to add these herbs and spices dry to a dip or a dressing, simply toast lightly in a small dry skillet over low heat—15 to 30 seconds should do it—just until fragrant. It is always a good idea to toast whole spices lightly before grinding.

Toasting Nuts and Seeds

Nuts and seeds develop a bigger flavor when they are toasted. This happens naturally during baking when you sprinkle them over muffins or cakes, but other times you will want to toast them before adding them to a recipe.

To toast nuts, preheat the oven to 325° F. Scatter whole shelled nuts or large pieces on a baking sheet. Toast, tossing or stirring occasionally, until lightly browned and fragrant, about 15 minutes for 4 ounces and about 30 minutes for a pound. If the pieces are finely chopped they will take slightly less time to toast.

You can toast sesame seeds in a small, heavy skillet over a low heat or in a special Japanese screened skillet especially designed for this purpose. Shake them until they toast and turn light golden and begin to pop. Immediately turn them out of the hot pan or they will continue toasting and become dark and bitter.

Other whole seeds, such as cumin and coriander, benefit from a light toasting in a dry skillet to bring out their fullest flavor. They need just a minute or two and should turn just light golden, otherwise they will become bitter.

Using Onions

Similar to garlic, onions develop different flavors depending on how they are treated. Raw onions are juicy and range from sweet and gentle to very hot with qualities similar to tear gas. A gentle sauté tames onion and renders it sweet and luscious and mellow; it almost becomes another vegetable entirely. Lightly browned, the onion takes on a toasted richness. In Indian brown-frying, a huge quantity of onions are sautéed until they are deep caramel brown and reduced to a pasty essence; it is this rich bittersweet nuttiness that adds distinction and depth to many Indian sauces and curries. Onion rings can be fried until brittle and brown and used to garnish meats and vegetables.

Appetizers and

Barbecued Bacon-Wrapped Shrimp

Mesquite-Grilled Stuffed Jalapeños

Seafood Cocktail

Cheese and Tomato Crostini

Hors d'Oeuvre

Tapenade

Stuffed Mushrooms

Mediterranean Stuffed Zucchini

Fresh Vietnamese Spring Rolls

Crunchy Vietnamese Spring Rolls

Chicken-and-Rice-Stuffed Grape Leaves

Flaky Pesto-Tomato Tart

Mexican Tartare

Chunky Guacamole

Spinach Dip

Lemon-Dill Dip

Bacon-Horseradish Dip

Pumpkin Seed Dip

Roasted Red Pepper Puree

Totopos

Oaxacan Peanuts with Chilies and Garlic

Marinated Greek Olives

Bonus Recipes

Bruschetta   Vampiro   Sangrita   Frozen Mango Daiquiri

Flor de Jamaica Spiced Tea   Margarita

Four-Blossom Iced Tea   Potato Skins

Barbecued
Bacon-Wrapped Shrimp

These jumbo shrimp are tangy, sweet, and sour with a thick, spicy marinade that clings after grilling. A slice of smoky bacon is wrapped around each shrimp to keep it moist and add more flavor during grilling. Marination can be complete by the time the grill is ready to go, or you can assemble them up to a day ahead and hold them in the refrigerator.

MAKES 6 FIRST-COURSE OR 3 MAIN-COURSE SERVINGS

2 teaspoons imported sweet paprika
½ teaspoon cayenne pepper
½ teaspoon curry powder
½ teaspoon ground cumin
½ teaspoon ground coriander
½ teaspoon salt
½ teaspoon black pepper
1 tablespoon olive oil
2 tablespoons sugar
2 tablespoons fresh lemon juice
18 jumbo shrimp (1½ pounds), shelled and deveined
9 slices lean hickory-smoked bacon (about 8 ounces)

1. In a medium bowl, combine the paprika, cayenne, curry powder, cumin, coriander, salt, and black pepper; stir in the olive oil, sugar, and lemon juice. Add the shrimp and toss to coat. Set aside to marinate at room temperature for 30 to 60 minutes.
2. Cut the slices of bacon crosswise in half. In a large heavy skillet, partially cook the bacon over moderate heat to render some of the fat, until limp but not crisp, 1 to 2 minutes on each side. Remove the slices as they are done and drain on paper towels.
3. Meanwhile, prepare a barbecue grill and preheat, if necessary. To achieve maximum flavor, soak a handful of hickory or mesquite wood chips in cold water for 20 to 30 minutes.
4. Remove the shrimp from the marinade and reserve the marinade. Wrap a piece of the bacon around each shrimp and secure the ends with a toothpick. Toss in the marinade to coat.
5. Set the grill rack about 5 inches above the heat source and preheat it for about 5 minutes. Drain the wood chips and scatter them over the heat source. Place all of the shrimp on the grill and brush with a little of the marinade; grill for 4 minutes. Turn, brush with some of the remaining marinade, and grill for about 3 minutes longer, or until the shrimp are just opaque throughout. Serve hot or warm.

Mesquite-Grilled
Stuffed Jalapeños

The first time I tasted grilled stuffed jalapeños was at a chuck-wagon cookout on the 6666 Ranch in Guthrie, Texas. It was a hot, clear day and the sky was as big and blue as could be. I was thirsty and hungry, and I must have eaten more than a dozen of 'em, washed down with three huge glasses of lemonade. I loved them so much that I barely recall the rest of the menu.

Mesquite covered the ground as far as the eye could see, and that's the fuel the chuck-wagon cook used. When I asked why, he said, "It's free." It's also big on flavor. I have to buy mesquite here in New York, but I don't mind too much. The flavor just can't be beat.

MAKES 40 (10 APPETIZER SERVINGS)

> 1 **pound thin-sliced lean bacon, slices halved crosswise**
> 20 **large fresh jalapeño chilies (about 1 pound)**
> 8 **ounces cream cheese, at room temperature**

1. Put the bacon in a large, heavy skillet and partially cook over moderate heat to render some of the fat and until limp but not crisp, 1 to 2 minutes on each side. Remove the slices as they are done and drain on paper towels.
2. Chilies irritate the skin so you might want to wear plastic or rubber gloves when you work with them. Cut off the stem end from each jalapeño. Halve each chili lengthwise. With a paring knife or tiny spoon, scoop out most of the seeds and ribs. (The more you leave in, the hotter the chilies will be.)
3. Fill each jalapeño half with some of the cream cheese, smoothing it level. Wrap a piece of the bacon around each and secure the ends with a toothpick. (The chilies can be prepared to this point up to a day ahead. Cover and refrigerate.)
4. Prepare a barbecue grill and preheat, if necessary. Soak about 3 cups of mesquite shavings or chips in a large bowl of warm water for 20 to 30 minutes.
5. Drain the mesquite chips and scatter them over the heat source. Arrange the jalapeños 4 to 5 inches from the heat and grill until nicely browned, 2 to 3 minutes on each side. If the fire flares up, spritz it with a little water. Serve hot or warm with cold drinks.

VARIATIONS

Substitution: **Use soft goat cheese in place of cream cheese.**

Bigger flavor: **For an extra kick, stir chopped fresh cilantro into the cream cheese.**

Seafood Cocktail

Although this luscious seafood cocktail is a specialty of Campeche on the Gulf of Mexico, it is served throughout Mexico and is equally at home at my table. The oysters are added raw, but the shrimp are cooked.

MAKES 4 TO 6 SERVINGS

> 1 **pound small to medium shrimp in their shells**
> 1 **large garlic clove, halved crosswise**
> 1 **pint freshly shucked oysters, preferably small (36 to the pint)**
> 2 **California avocados, preferably Haas**
> 3 **to 4 tablespoons fresh lime juice, plus wedges for serving**
> 3 **tablespoons extra-virgin olive oil**
> ¼ **cup chopped fresh cilantro**
> **Salt and pepper**
> **Hot pepper sauce**

1. Put the shrimp in a medium pot and add cold water to cover. Place over moderate heat and bring to a bare simmer. Remove a shrimp and cut it in half. When opaque to the center, the shrimp are done. Do not let boil and do not overcook. Rinse under cold water. Shell. Devein, if necessary.
2. Rub the interior of a large bowl with the cut side of garlic; discard the garlic. Add the shrimp and oysters (if they are very large, cut in half). Cover and chill until serving time.
3. Halve and pit the avocados; cut the flesh into ½-inch dice and add to the seafood. Sprinkle with the lime juice and toss gently. Spoon the olive oil over the ingredients and sprinkle on the cilantro and salt and pepper to taste. Toss gently. Serve cold, in cocktail glasses or on lettuce leaves with lime wedges and hot pepper sauce.

VARIATION

Presentation: **For a fancier dish, instead of adding diced avocado, serve the seafood in halved avocado cups. Or, stir in 2 to 3 tablespoons minced white onion or sliced scallions.**

Limes

Really a big berry with leatherlike skin, the lime is more aromatic and slightly more acidic than the lemon, and its delicate flavor is decidedly different—exotic and tart with seductive perfume.

The *flavedo* and *albedo*—that is, the green zest and white pith of the lime—contain essential oils. When zest is grated or sliced and/or steeped in liquid, this pungent oil is released.

Although both sweet and acid limes do exist, the acid type is the only kind grown on a commercial scale in this country. Of this category, the Tahiti lime and the Mexican lime are the two principal types. The Tahiti lime (sometimes called Persian) is large, juicy, and seedless and is the type found commonly on supermarket shelves. The most popular of the Mexican limes is the Key lime, made famous by Florida's Key lime pie. Grown mainly in the Florida Keys, the Key lime is small, yellowish, seedier, and more acidic than the Tahiti lime. The *limone* of Mexico is of this type.

Generally speaking, limes are plentiful all year long, though usually most affordable during their peak season in June, July, and August. When shopping for limes, look for smooth shiny skin, deep green color, and fruits that are heavy for their size. At home, limes should be stored in the refrigerator.

LEMON AND LIME HINTS AND TIPS

• For the highest juice yield, have lemons and limes at room temperature before squeezing. Roll them on a hard surface, pressing firmly, before squeezing.

• Grate or slice off the zest (the outermost colored surface of the rind) *before* squeezing out the juice.

• One medium lemon yields 2 to 3 tablespoons of juice and 1 to 1½ teaspoons grated zest. One medium lime yields 1½ to 2 tablespoons juice and ½ to 1 teaspoon grated zest.

• Lemons will keep for up to 6 weeks or more in the refrigerator and a week or 2 at room temperature. Limes will keep for 3 to 4 weeks in the refrigerator and about 1 week at room temperature.

• Both the juice and grated zest from lemons and limes freeze well.

• When buying lemons and limes, look for heavy, firm fruits with smooth skin.

• A bowl of lemons or limes in the kitchen is a marvelous, natural air freshener.

• Keep white vegetables white by adding 2 tablespoons lemon or lime juice to the cooking water.

• Rub low-acid foods—avocados, artichokes, peaches, and bananas—with lemon or lime to heighten flavor and prevent darkening.

• Place slices of lemon or lime in the cavity of a whole fish or chicken before poaching or roasting.

• Freshen up commercially prepared mayonnaise by adding a few drops each of lemon or lime juice and olive oil.

• Freshen store-bought barbecue sauce by adding lemon or lime juice.

• Add lemon or lime juice to soups and float thin slices on top to garnish.

Cheese and Tomato Crostini

Crostini and *bruschetta* are closely related slices of sturdy Italian bread. *Crostini* are slices of bread that are brushed with garlic oil and toasted in the oven, while *bruschetta* are more often than not grilled over charcoal or toasted under the broiler for a lightly charred effect. If you choose to prepare them ahead of time, reheat the crostini in a 250° F. oven for about 10 minutes just before serving.

MAKES 16

     3 tablespoons extra-virgin olive oil
     2 large garlic cloves, minced or crushed through a press
    16 slices firm, slightly stale Italian bread (3 to 4 inches in diameter),
          each cut ¼ inch thick
    16 slices mozzarella cheese (about 8 ounces total), each cut ¼ inch thick
    16 slices fresh Italian plum tomatoes, each cut ¼ inch thick
     8 flat anchovy fillets, halved (optional); or 8 oil-cured black
          olives, halved and pitted
     3 tablespoons freshly grated Parmesan cheese
    16 tiny fresh basil leaves, for garnish (optional)

1. Preheat the oven to 400° F. Lightly oil a large baking sheet.
2. Warm the olive oil in a small, heavy skillet over low heat. Add the garlic and sizzle until fragrant, 1 to 2 minutes. Let cool.
3. Arrange the slices of bread close together on the baking sheet. Lightly brush the tops with the olive oil–garlic mixture, reserving 2 teaspoons. Top each with a slice of mozzarella and a slice of tomato. Dot with the anchovies or olives and sprinkle each with about ½ teaspoon of the Parmesan. Drizzle the reserved 2 teaspoons garlic oil over the tops.
4. Bake the *crostini* in the top third of the oven for about 10 minutes, until the cheese is bubbly and the toast is golden brown. Top each with a basil leaf and serve hot.

VARIATION

Substitution: **Red Pepper Crostini**—You will need ⅔ cup of Roasted Red Pepper Puree (page 45) to make 16 Red Pepper Crostini. Brush the bread with the garlic oil and toast for 10 to 12 minutes, or until deep golden brown and crisp. Meanwhile, heat the Red Pepper Puree. Spoon about 2 teaspoons of the puree over each bread slice just before serving. Top each with a small basil leaf or a tiny sprig of fresh oregano.

Bruschetta

Bruschetta—charcoal-grilled or broiled bread rubbed with garlic oil—is probably the original "garlic bread." In Tuscany, *bruschetta* is called *fettunta.* Choose a loaf of good, sturdy Italian bread and cut it on an extreme angle into ⅓-inch-thick slices. Brush it lightly with the garlic oil used to make the *crostini* (3 tablespoons oil for each 2 garlic cloves).

If grilling over a barbecue grill, preheat the grill rack and toast the bread until crisp and slightly charred, 5 to 10 minutes depending on the heat. Otherwise, preheat the broiler and broil the toast for 1 to 1½ minutes, or until lightly charred. Turn and broil for 30 to 60 seconds longer, until deep brown. Serve the *bruschetta* with Roasted Red Pepper Puree (page 45), Tapenade (below), or with slices of fresh tomato, slivers of Parmesan cheese, and fresh basil leaves.

Tapenade

Here is a purple-black olive spread with big, bold flavor. It is at once salty and tangy on your tongue with an earthy, bold, robust, ripe olive flavor. For parties you'll want to double, triple, even quadruple the recipe. Serve it with chunks of crusty French bread or crisp raw vegetables or with the *Bruschetta* or *Crostini* above and at left.

MAKES ABOUT ¾ CUP

- ½ cup pitted black oil-cured olives (see Note)
- 4 flat anchovy fillets, drained and chopped
- 2 tablespoons drained capers
- 1 tablespoon Dijon mustard
- 2 teaspoons fresh lemon juice
- ½ teaspoon dry mustard
- ¼ teaspoon black pepper
- ¼ cup extra-virgin olive oil

Note: These olives are easiest to pit by squeezing or tearing each olive in half and prying out the pits. Measure after pitting.

1. In a small food processor or chopper or in a mortar, combine the olives, anchovies, and capers; process or pound to a coarse puree.
2. Add the Dijon mustard, lemon juice, dry mustard, and black pepper and blend briefly. Gradually add the olive oil and process to make a paste. Cover and store in the refrigerator for up to 2 weeks, or use right away.

Stuffed Mushrooms

These deliciously moist stuffed mushrooms sport the big flavors of ham and Parmesan cheese. They make a great hors d'oeuvre or an important antipasto, and they're simple to put together.

MAKES 16 TO 20

> 16 to 20 medium to large fresh mushrooms
> 3 tablespoons olive oil
> 1 tablespoon butter
> $\frac{1}{2}$ cup finely chopped onion
> $\frac{1}{2}$ cup minced smoked ham
> 1 garlic clove, minced or crushed through a press
> $\frac{1}{2}$ teaspoon dried oregano, crumbled
> $\frac{1}{4}$ teaspoon salt
> $\frac{1}{8}$ teaspoon black pepper
> $\frac{1}{4}$ cup dry white wine
> $\frac{1}{4}$ cup chopped fresh parsley
> 3 tablespoons plain dry bread crumbs
> 4 tablespoons freshly grated Parmesan cheese

1. Move an oven rack to the top third of the oven, and preheat to 375° F. Have ready a shallow 12 × 8-inch baking dish or pan.
2. Pull the stems off the mushrooms and reserve the caps. Trim and finely chop the stems.
3. Combine 1 tablespoon of the olive oil and the butter in a medium skillet over moderate heat. Add the onion and sauté until soft, about 3 minutes. Add the ham and cook for 1 or 2 minutes longer. Add the garlic, oregano, salt, and pepper and cook for 1 to 2 minutes. Add the chopped mushroom stems and cook for 2 minutes more. Pour in the wine and cook until it boils away and the mixture starts to sizzle. Turn the mixture into a bowl and stir in the parsley, bread crumbs, and 3 tablespoons of the grated Parmesan.
4. Brush the edges of the mushroom caps all over with the remaining 2 tablespoons olive oil. Stuff the caps, mounding the stuffing slightly. Arrange the mushrooms in the baking dish. Sprinkle the remaining 1 tablespoon Parmesan over the tops. The mushrooms can be covered with plastic and refrigerated for up to 3 hours. Bake for 8 to 10 minutes, or until lightly browned. Serve hot or warm.

Mediterranean Stuffed Zucchini

Bake these hors d'oeuvre when it's convenient for you and then chill. They're sure to transport you to whichever Mediterranean coast suits you best.

MAKES ABOUT 3 DOZEN

2	pounds (6 to 8 medium) zucchini
1	cup soft, fresh bread crumbs, made from firm white bread
1	can (2 ounces) flat anchovy fillets, drained and chopped
1	cup finely chopped pitted black olives
½	cup chopped fresh parsley
4	tablespoons fresh lemon juice
¼	teaspoon black pepper
	Pinch of salt
¼	cup plus 1 tablespoon olive oil
1	large garlic clove, minced or crushed through a press

1. Trim the ends from the zucchini and cut the zucchini into 1-inch lengths. Using a melon baller, scoop out some of the flesh from one cut side of each. Finely chop enough of the scooped-out pulp to measure 1 cup.

2. Bring a large pot of lightly salted water to a boil. Drop in the zucchini cases and cook for exactly 2 minutes from the time they hit the water. Remove the zucchini and refresh under cold running water. Drain thoroughly.

3. Preheat the oven to 450° F. Scatter the bread crumbs over a small baking sheet and bake, tossing once or twice, until lightly toasted, about 10 minutes. Remove and set aside. Leave the oven at 450° F.

4. In a large bowl, combine the anchovies, olives, and ⅓ cup parsley and mash together with a fork. Stir in 1 tablespoon of the lemon juice, the pepper, and salt. Set aside.

5. Combine ¼ cup of the olive oil with the garlic in a heavy medium skillet. Sizzle over low heat for 1 to 2 minutes, until softened. Add the mixture to the bowl with the olives and anchovies. Add the remaining 1 tablespoon olive oil to the skillet along with the chopped zucchini pulp. Sauté over moderately high heat until lightly browned and most of the liquid has evaporated, 3 to 5 minutes. Add the mixture to the olives and anchovies; stir in the bread crumbs.

6. Oil a 13 × 9-inch baking pan. Fill the zucchini cases by hand, mounding the stuffing slightly, and place the zucchini close together in the pan. Bake in the top third of the oven for 10 to 12 minutes, or until lightly browned.

7. Remove the zucchini to a platter and let cool to room temperature. Cover and chill. Spoon ¼ teaspoon of the remaining lemon juice over each stuffed zucchini and top with the remaining parsley. Serve cold.

Fresh Vietnamese Spring Rolls

These soft spring rolls—sometimes called summer rolls—are magnificently light and refreshing. There's no frying involved. All you do is dip edible rice paper rounds into water for a moment, add the filling, and tightly roll up. The wrapping becomes translucent and you can see the ingredients inside.

These spring rolls can be an appetizer or a main course. Be sure to make the dipping sauces (*Nuoc Cham* and *Nuoc Leo*) at least a day ahead.

The Vietnamese edible rice-paper wrappers (*banh trang*) come in 6-inch rounds, 8½-inch rounds, 10- to 12-inch rounds, and also in triangular quarter rounds. For this recipe you will need the 8½-inch rounds, although in a pinch you could use any of the other sizes and adjust the ingredients accordingly.

MAKES 16

> Nuoc Cham (page 369)
> Nuoc Leo (page 370)
> 1 skein (4 ounces) dried fine rice noodles
> 1 large skinless and boneless chicken breast (8 to 10 ounces), poached and cooled
> 32 medium shrimp (about 12 ounces), cooked, shelled, and deveined
> 16 sheets 8½-inch dried rice paper rounds (*banh trang*)
> 8 Boston, red leaf, or other soft lettuce leaves, halved
> 1 cup sliced whole scallions
> 1 cup coarsely shredded carrots
> 48 small mint sprigs
> 32 small cilantro sprigs

1. Have the dipping sauces ready. Put the dried rice noodles in a medium pot of boiling water and boil just until tender but firm to the bite, about 2 minutes. Drain in a strainer and rinse with cold water. Drain again and set aside in the strainer for at least 30 minutes to firm up. Toss the noodles occasionally. Using kitchen shears or a knife, cut the mass into smaller pieces. You will have about 2 cups of rice noodles.
2. Meanwhile, cut the chicken breast across the grain into 16 thin slices, each about 1 inch wide and 3 to 4 inches long.
3. Cut each shrimp in half lengthwise.
4. Spread out a clean cotton towel on your work surface. Have ready a large bowl of warm water. Working with 2 sheets of rice paper at a time, dip 1 sheet into the water for 5 to 7 seconds to soften; spread it out flat on the towel. Add the second sheet to the water and soften for 5 to 7 seconds; spread it out next to the first one.

5. Assemble the rolls. Place 4 pieces of shrimp, pink side down, in a horizontal row toward the lower third of a softened rice paper sheet. Top with 1 chicken slice and ½ lettuce leaf. Spoon on 2 tablespoons of the chopped noodles, 1 tablespoon of the scallions, 1 tablespoon of the carrots, 3 mint sprigs, 2 cilantro sprigs, and 1 teaspoon of the *Nuoc Cham*. Fold up the lower third of the rice paper over the ingredients. Fold the sides inward. Roll up from the bottom, burrito-fashion, into a tight roll. Place, seam side down, on a serving plate. Repeat with the remaining softened rice paper round. Dip 2 more rice paper rounds and continue assembling the spring rolls in the same manner. If making ahead, cover the spring rolls with a damp towel and refrigerate for up to 2 hours. Serve cold with the *Nuoc Leo* for dipping.

FISH SAUCE

Fish sauce is an acquired taste, and I think the sooner you acquire it, the happier you will be. A clear amber to dark brown liquid, it is the basic background flavoring for the cooking of Vietnam, Thailand, Laos, and most of the rest of Southeast Asia, where it is used as we use salt or as the Chinese or Japanese use soy sauce. But fish sauce is more than a condiment; it acts as an important source of dietary protein as well.

The flavor of fish sauce is somewhat reminiscent of soy sauce but richer and more complex. Although both are salty and full flavored, the former is made from fish and the latter from soybeans. Vietnamese fish sauce, *nuoc mam,* can be stronger than the Thai version, *nam pla,* but I use them interchangeably.

The strong fermented aroma and flavor of fish sauce diminishes and mellows during cooking. Usually it is used twice, in cooking and just before serving, one use boosting the other.

To manufacture the sauce, small fish (usually anchovies but often a combination of fresh and saltwater fish) are layered in a huge vat with sea salt and left to ferment for several months. Then the clear liquid is drawn off, poured into ceramic crocks, and matured in the sun. The first drawing is always the clearest, lightest, and best—and commands the highest price; even so, it is not very expensive.

The best fish sauce has a rich, mellow—not harsh—flavor, a clear amber color, and is not excessively salty. Successive drawings are darker, saltier, and less expensive.

Hundreds of variations of this sauce are made and each manufacturer has its favorite blend. You will have to sample several before you know which you prefer. Favorite brands to look for include Squid, Ruang Tong, and Three Crabs.

Crunchy Vietnamese Spring Rolls

These are crunchy little morsels of meat, noodles, and shrimp wrapped in rice paper. Unlike the larger Fresh Spring Rolls, these are fried. Serve them with the accompaniments listed below. The dipping sauce tastes best when made at least a day ahead.

MAKES 48

- 1 skein (2 ounces) dried cellophane noodles (bean threads)
- 8 to 10 medium (½ ounce) dried Chinese black or
    shiitake mushrooms
- 8 ounces ground pork or beef
- 8 ounces raw shrimp, shelled, deveined, and minced
- ½ cup minced whole scallions
- 1 large egg
- 2 tablespoons Vietnamese or Thai fish sauce (*nuoc mam* or *nam pla*)
- 2 tablespoons fresh lemon juice
- 1 teaspoon Oriental sesame oil
- ½ teaspoon black pepper
- ¼ cup sugar
- 48 sheets 6-inch edible rice paper rounds (*bahn trang*)
    Vegetable or peanut oil, for frying
    Nuoc Cham (page 369)
- 24 romaine lettuce leaves, halved crosswise, for serving
- 48 small mint sprigs, for serving
- 48 cilantro sprigs, for serving (optional)

1. Put the cellophane noodles in a medium bowl and add enough hot water to cover generously. Let soak for 30 to 60 minutes to soften. Drain and chop.
2. Meanwhile, place the mushrooms in a small bowl and add about 1 cup hot water. Let soak for about 30 minutes, until soft. Drain, discard the stems, and chop the caps.
3. Crumble the pork into a large bowl. Add the minced shrimp, scallions, egg, fish sauce, lemon juice, sesame oil, pepper, chopped noodles, mushroom caps, and 2 tablespoons water. Mix until thoroughly combined; you will have about 3 cups of filling.
4. The rolls can be assembled and kept covered with a damp towel in the refrigerator for up to 8 hours before frying. Combine the sugar and 2 cups hot water in a pie pan or shallow dish and stir to dissolve. Spread out a clean cotton towel on your work surface. Dip 1 sheet of rice paper into the sweetened water and let soften for about 10 seconds. Place on the towel. Soften a second sheet of rice paper and place it next to the first. (The sheets will

continue to soften—don't worry.) Fold up the bottom third of each round as soon as it is soft enough to bend. Place 1 tablespoon of the filling in the center of the folded-up portion and shape the filling into a skinny 2-inch-long log. Fold the sides in over the filling, roll up tightly, and place seam side down on a paper towel. Repeat the filling and rolling, arranging the rolls without touching each other (or they may stick together). Cover with a damp paper towel. If making ahead, refrigerate.

5. Pour ½ inch of vegetable or peanut oil into a heavy large skillet. (Since these take somewhat longer to fry than other tidbits—because they cook at a lower temperature and because you shouldn't crowd the pan or they might stick together—consider cooking them simultaneously in 2 skillets.) Heat the oil over moderately low heat to 325° F. If the oil is hotter, the rolls will brown too much and the rice paper will not be crunchy. Gently fry the rolls in batches, turning several times, until golden brown and shiny, 10 to 12 minutes. Do not fry more quickly. Drain on paper towels. Repeat until all the spring rolls are cooked. Keep hot in a 250° F. oven until needed.

6. To serve, spoon the *Nuoc Cham* into small dishes for dipping. Arrange the lettuce leaves, mint, and cilantro on a large platter or individual plates. To eat, place a spring roll on a half lettuce leaf, add a sprig of mint and a sprig of cilantro, and fold one end of the leaf over the ingredients. Fold in the 2 sides, dip the bundle into the *Nuoc Cham*, and eat from the hand.

VARIATIONS

Substitutions: **Use ground chicken or turkey in place of the beef or pork. Crabmeat is often added to these rolls; consider using 4 ounces crab and 4 ounces shrimp.**

Serving: **For a small get-together you might want to make only 24 of these rolls and save the remaining filling. The next day you can make 24 more and add them to any salad.**

Chicken-and-Rice-Stuffed Grape Leaves

During my art-school days in California in the 1960s, I used to pluck tender young leaves from a neighbor's grapevine and braise them in orange juice before stuffing, and they always turned out tasty and tender. If you have a grapevine, you can do the same. Nowadays I have to buy brined grape leaves in a jar. These appetizers take time and patience, but they can be made a day or two ahead and chilled. In fact, the flavor just gets better.

MAKES 50 TO 60

- ½ cup olive oil
- 1 large onion, finely chopped
- 2 large garlic cloves, minced or crushed through a press
- 1 teaspoon ground allspice
- 1 cup long-grain white rice
- 4 cups Chicken Stock (page 73) or canned broth
- ¼ cup dry white wine
- 8 ounces ground chicken
- 6 tablespoons fresh lemon juice
- ½ cup sliced whole scallions
- ½ cup chopped fresh mint
- ¼ cup chopped fresh parsley
- 2 tablespoons chopped fresh dill
- 1 teaspoon salt
- ¼ teaspoon black pepper
- 1 jar (16 ounces) grapevine leaves in brine, drained, rinsed, and drained again

1. Spoon 2 tablespoons of the olive oil into a 2-quart nonstick saucepan and place over moderate heat. Add the onion and sauté until softened, about 5 minutes. Add the garlic and allspice and sauté for 1 to 2 minutes. Add the rice, toss, and cook until lightly toasted, 2 to 3 minutes. Pour in 1 cup of the stock or broth and the white wine and bring to a boil. Lower the heat, cover, and simmer over low heat until the broth is absorbed, 5 to 8 minutes. Remove from the heat, cover tightly, and let stand for 10 minutes. Uncover, turn out into a large bowl, and let cool to room temperature.

2. When the rice is cool, crumble in the ground chicken. Add 2 tablespoons of the olive oil, 2 tablespoons of the lemon juice, the scallions, mint, parsley, dill, salt, and pepper. Mix thoroughly with your hands to combine.

3. Preheat the oven to 350° F. Lightly oil 2 shallow casseroles or baking dishes (approximately 12 × 18 inches).

4. Separate the grape leaves and arrange them in a stack. Working with 1 leaf at

a time, place a leaf, shiny side down, in front of you. Shape 1 to 1½ table-spoons of the filling into a log and place it across the lower third of the leaf. Fold up the bottom of the leaf over the filling, then fold in the sides and firmly roll up. As they are assembled, place the stuffed leaves, seam side down, close together in a single layer in the prepared casseroles. Continue stuffing the grape leaves. Pour 1½ cups chicken stock over each casserole to almost cover the leaves. Sprinkle 2 tablespoons of the remaining lemon juice over each pan; cover tightly with foil. Bake for about 50 minutes, until heated through and tender. Let cool to room temperature.

5. When cool, arrange the stuffed grape leaves in a deeper pan (a bread pan or some other deep container), making several layers. As you build up the layers, drizzle on the remaining ¼ cup olive oil. Cover and chill for at least 6 hours or overnight. Serve cold with more lemon, if desired.

Flaky Pesto-Tomato Tart

Inspiration for this simple pizzalike tart, made with layers of store-bought filo pastry as a base, came from a recipe that I saw in *Gourmet* magazine several years ago. Be sure to make it in the summertime when tomatoes are sweet and juicy and basil is fragrant and plentiful. And since you *buy* the pastry, there's not much fuss at all in the kitchen. This makes an exciting hors d'oeuvre, appetizer, or first course. Make the pesto ahead of time.

MAKES 6 SERVINGS

- 4 tablespoons (½ stick) butter
- 8 sheets (17 × 12 inches) filo dough, thawed if frozen
- ⅔ cup freshly grated Parmesan cheese
- ¼ cup Pesto (page 361)
- 3 large ripe tomatoes, halved and thinly sliced
- 1 teaspoon dried oregano, crumbled
- ¼ teaspoon salt
- ¼ teaspoon black pepper

1. Position an oven rack to the lower third of the oven and preheat to 375° F. Lightly oil a 15 × 1-inch jelly roll pan.
2. Melt the butter in a small pan over low heat. Unroll the sheets of filo and keep them covered with a damp towel while you work, so they won't dry out and become brittle.
3. Place 1 sheet of filo in the pan and press the edges up to conform to the sides

of the pan. Use about ½ teaspoon of the butter and a pastry brush to dab it all over. Do not paint it on: You want evenly spaced dabs with other areas uncoated. Sprinkle with 1 tablespoon of the Parmesan. Repeat, making 8 layers. Spoon on the pesto in ½ teaspoon dabs all over. Arrange the tomatoes over the pesto and sprinkle with the oregano, salt, and pepper. Sprinkle on the remaining 1⅔ tablespoons Parmesan. Bake for 30 to 35 minutes, or until deep golden brown.

4. Cut the tart into small rectangles and serve hot or warm. The pastry bottom actually crisps a little upon standing for a few minutes.

Vampiro, A Bloody-Cold Drink

Named for legendary vampires who haunt the Sierra Madre Sur in Mexico, this formula comes from Mexico City's Restaurant Mesón del Caballo Bayo at 360 Avenida del Conscripto. They use the Viuda de Sanchez (Widow Sanchez) brand of bottled Sangrita ("little blood"). You can also make your own (page 39). They also add Squirt brand citrus soda, but Collins mix, grapefruit soda, or Mountain Dew will work if you add an extra squeeze of lime.

To make 1 tall cocktail, rub the rim of a tall glass with a wedge of lime and dip it in salt as for a Margarita. (When I do this in advance for a party, I dip the glass rims in lightly beaten egg white, then in salt, and set them aside to air-dry so the salt hardens in place.)

Fill the glass with ice cubes and pour in 1½ ounces (3 tablespoons) of gold tequila. Add 2 tablespoons fresh lime juice, 3 or 4 drops of Tabasco or other hot pepper sauce, and ¼ cup Sangrita. Stir and then pour in enough Squirt or other grapefruit soda to reach the top. Serve with a swizzle stick and a straw.

Mexican Tartare

This is my Mexican version of steak tartare. The perfectly lean raw beef is marinated in lime juice the way seafood is for ceviche. The combination of rich ripe California avocados with sweet tomato, fragrant cilantro, perky picante peppers, and juicy beef is one of my favorites. Be sure to marinate the beef ahead of time.

MAKES 4 SERVINGS

  8 ounces very lean beef steak, such as flank, sirloin, or fillet
¼ cup plus 1 tablespoon fresh lime juice
¼ cup extra-virgin olive oil
  1 cup seeded and drained coarsely chopped fresh or canned tomatoes
½ cup finely chopped white onion
¼ cup chopped fresh cilantro
  1 fresh jalapeño chili, minced (partly seeded if less heat is desired)
½ teaspoon salt, or more to taste
¼ teaspoon black pepper
  2 ripe California avocados
¼ cup thinly sliced whole scallions

1. Thinly slice the beef across the grain. Using 1 or 2 large sharp knives, finely mince until the texture is slightly coarser than ground beef. Transfer the beef to a glass bowl and add ¼ cup of the lime juice. Toss, cover, and refrigerate for 6 to 8 hours.
2. Uncover the beef and stir in the oil, tomatoes, onion, cilantro, jalapeño, salt, and pepper. (This recipe can be prepared a day ahead to this point and stored, tightly covered, in the refrigerator.)
3. Taste the steak tartare for seasoning and add a little more salt, if needed. Halve the avocados lengthwise and remove the pits. Brush with the remaining 1 tablespoon lime juice and place on salad plates. Divide the steak tartare among them, mounding it in the center. Sprinkle each with 1 tablespoon of the sliced scallions and serve while the steak is still chilled.

Chunky Guacamole

This is my favorite formula for making guacamole. It is rich and chunky and totally addictive. Made from perfectly ripe California avocados, it's good enough to fill fresh corn tortillas, making guacamole tacos that need no adornment at all. I like heat, so I leave some of the seeds in the jalapeños.

I have never found that burying the avocado pit in guacamole does anything but make a mess. The guacamole still turns dark and you have to dig out the slippery pit. Instead, use a tablespoon of lemon or lime juice and make the guacamole just before serving. (If you must do it ahead, cover it with plastic placed directly on the surface, store it in the refrigerator, and toss well before serving.) Serve this with the Totopos on page 46.

MAKES ABOUT 2½ CUPS

> 1 teaspoon salt
> 1 large garlic clove, halved crosswise
> 2 medium jalapeño chilies partly seeded and minced
> ¼ cup finely chopped fresh cilantro
> 2 tablespoons finely chopped white onion
> ¼ teaspoon ground cumin (optional)
> ¼ teaspoon black pepper
> 1 tablespoon fresh lemon or lime juice
> 2 large (8 to 10 ounces each) firm-ripe California avocados
> 3 or 4 plum tomatoes, finely diced

1. Put the salt in a large bowl or Mexican *molcajete* (a mortar made of lava). Rub the cut sides of both garlic pieces in the salt against the sides of the bowl to extract some of the garlic juice. Discard the pieces.

AVOCADOS

For Mexican and Southwestern U.S. cooking, I've found that California avocados are best because they are buttery-rich in flavor and texture. I tend to reserve the larger, blander Florida varieties for tropical salads and Caribbean cookery.

The choicest of the pear-shaped California varieties are Pinkerton, Haas, Fuerte, Bacon, and Zutano. The best of the round ones include the Reed and Gwen varieties. In Mexico there are many more rich and creamy varieties—from small as Seckel pears to big as grapefruits.

Always keep avocados at room temperature. They are a tropical fruit and do not like the cold. To ripen hard ones, put them in a brown paper bag for a couple days. To find out if they are ripe, push gently with a fingertip at the stem end.

2. Add the jalapeños, the seeds and ribs, the cilantro, onion, cumin, and black pepper to the bowl or mortar; pound with a pestle or the back of a spoon until watery. Stir in the lemon juice.

3. Halve the avocados lengthwise and remove the pits. Spoon out the avocado flesh and add it to the bowl. Mash slightly with a fork, leaving it chunky. Fold in the tomatoes. Taste for salt and lemon and add a bit more if needed, to taste. Serve right away.

Sangrita

Sangrita ("little blood") is not to be confused with sangria, the spiced wine beverage. Sangrita is the fresh, sweet-tart, spicy, tangy, potent little concoction that you down as a chaser to a shot of tequila.

To make 1½ cups of Sangrita, stir together ¾ cup tomato juice, ½ cup fresh orange juice, 3 tablespoons fresh lime or lemon juice, 1 tablespoon grenadine syrup, ½ teaspoon Tabasco or other hot pepper sauce, and ½ teaspoon salt. To add that authentic depth of flavor that I find so addictive, grate ½ small onion onto a double layer of dampened cheesecloth. Gather up the edges and squeeze the juice into a small bowl. Add 1 teaspoon of the onion juice to the Sangrita.

Be sure to check out the Sangrita Sorbet on page 314, which, of course, contains no onion.

Spinach Dip

Tart and tangy with lemon and sour cream, and extra-creamy from the cream cheese, this bold dip is great when scooped up with raw vegetables, corn chips, pita crisps, or potato chips. Since lemon juice makes spinach turn a dull green, decide whether you want to serve it the same day or a day later. The flavor will be better on the second day, after the tarragon and nutmeg blossom, and you can add the lemon juice just before serving.

MAKES ABOUT 2½ CUPS

- 1½ pounds fresh spinach
- ½ cup sour cream
- ½ teaspoon dried tarragon, crumbled
- ½ teaspoon grated nutmeg
- 1 teaspoon salt
- ½ teaspoon black pepper
- 8 ounces cream cheese, at room temperature
- 1½ tablespoons fresh lemon juice

1. Carefully rinse the spinach in a large bowl or sinkful of cool water to remove any sand. Pluck off and discard the tough, thick stems. Put the wet spinach in a nonreactive large, heavy pot or Dutch oven (it can be packed quite full since it will cook down dramatically), cover, and set over high heat. Cook for 3 to 5 minutes, turning the mass once halfway through cooking, until wilted down. Place a strainer over a bowl, and pour in the spinach to drain and cool.

2. Squeeze out any excess juice from the spinach with your hands. Chop the spinach and measure 1 cup, packed. Reserve any remaining for another use.

3. In a food processor, combine the spinach, sour cream, tarragon, nutmeg, salt, and pepper. Process to a puree. Add the cream cheese and process until smooth. If serving the same day, blend in the lemon juice. Otherwise, cover and chill. Let come to room temperature and stir in the lemon juice just before serving.

VARIATIONS

Lower calorie: **To cut some calories, replace the sour cream with low-fat plain yogurt.**

Substitutions: **For a flavor change, use dried dill in place of the tarragon, or if fresh dill is available, use 2 tablespoons chopped.**

DILL AND DILL SEED

I love dill's clear, fresh aroma and dominant, well-rounded tangy flavor so much that sometimes I just chew on it. Both the seeds and leaves flavor America's favorite dill pickles, and I'm wont to throw a handful into salads—especially during the summer. Snipped fresh dill has an affinity for seafood and lemon, cold salads, and cool creamy sauces. The French like to flavor pastries and sauces with dill, while the Scandinavians add it into practically everything—from pastries, breads, and potatoes to vegetables, soups, and salads. The seeds are high in essential oils.

A member of the parsley family with cousins caraway, coriander, cumin, anise, and fennel, dill is a beautiful plant with feathery, dark green leaves; it is very easy to grow.

Lemon-Dill Dip

This fresh dip for vegetables, chips, and crisps is tart and tangy, cool and creamy. Make it a day ahead so the flavors can develop in the refrigerator.

MAKES ABOUT 1¼ CUPS

- 1½ cups low-fat plain yogurt
- ¾ cup sour cream
- 2 tablespoons snipped fresh dill, plus 1 sprig, for garnish
- 2 teaspoons grated lemon zest
- 1 tablespoon fresh lemon juice
- 1 teaspoon salt
- ½ teaspoon black pepper

1. Stack 7 or 8 layers of paper towels on a kitchen towel. Spread the yogurt over the top sheet and let drain for 30 minutes.
2. Invert the yogurt into a bowl and peel off the paper. Stir in the sour cream until smooth. Stir in the dill, lemon zest, lemon juice, salt, and pepper. Cover and refrigerate for 8 hours or overnight.
3. Mix the dip again and turn into a small serving dish. Garnish with a dill sprig.

Bacon-Horseradish Dip

The smoky bacon flavor comes through this creamy dip's background tang of yogurt, and there's a good horseradish kick. It is particularly good with sweet carrot sticks, potato chips, and Totopos (page 46). Make it a day ahead for bigger flavor or two days ahead for a more pronounced smoky flavor.

MAKES ABOUT 1½ CUPS

- 1 **cup low-fat plain yogurt**
- 8 **slices hickory-smoked bacon, cut into ¼-inch bits**
- ¾ **cup sour cream**
- 2 **tablespoons prepared horseradish, drained**
- ½ **teaspoon Worcestershire sauce**
- ½ **teaspoon salt**

1. Stack 7 or 8 layers of paper towels on a kitchen towel. Spread the yogurt over the top sheet and let drain for 20 minutes.
2. Meanwhile, put the bacon in a heavy medium skillet and cook, stirring frequently, over moderate heat until crisp and deep golden brown. Drain well on paper towels.
3. Invert the yogurt into a bowl and peel off the paper. Stir in the sour cream until smooth. Reserving 2 teaspoons for the garnish, stir in the bacon. Stir in the horseradish, Worcestershire, and salt. Cover and refrigerate for 1 to 2 days.
4. Stir the dip and turn it into a serving dish. Sprinkle the reserved 2 teaspoons bacon over the top and serve at once.

WORCESTERSHIRE SAUCE

Generically speaking, Worcestershire sauce is a dark brown, aromatic liquid sauce that has a pungent, sharp-sweet, complex flavor.

Lea & Perrins's benchmark formula for their Worcestershire sauce is a closely guarded, proprietary secret. It is said to include vinegar, molasses, anchovies, tamarind, onion, garlic, mushrooms, shallots, mace, chili peppers, and coriander seeds, and is aged for six months or longer. After its creation, we end up with a tasty product that will keep indefinitely on a cupboard shelf at room temperature.

A splash of Worcestershire is mandatory to correctly season a Bloody Mary or tomato juice cocktail or for browning a roast beef my mother's way. It also adds depth to cocktail sauces and salad dressings.

Frozen Mango Daiquiri

The original daiquiri was invented in Cuba and is named for a town on the east coast of the island. The frozen version of the drink evolved in this country, imitating what we did to the original Margarita when it, too, turned frozen. The result is something like fluffy, whipped sherbet made fresh and fragrant with mango.

You'll have to plan ahead to make my version. Instead of adding ice, which dilutes the drink and doesn't contribute any flavor or richness, here you combine milk and light cream and freeze it in an ice-cube tray.

To make about 3 cups of the drink (2 to 3 servings), combine 1 cup of milk with $\frac{1}{3}$ cup light cream and pour into an ice-cube tray. Freeze until solid.

Cut enough flesh from a large, ripe mango to yield 1 cup and put it in a food processor or blender. Add the frozen milk mixture, $\frac{1}{4}$ to $\frac{1}{3}$ cup dark rum, 2 tablespoons sugar (preferably superfine, but any will do), 2 tablespoons fresh lime juice, and $\frac{1}{4}$ teaspoon ground cinnamon. One teaspoon vanilla extract can also be added, if desired. Process to a fluffy puree and mound into stemmed glasses. Serve with a tropical swizzle stick, a lime wedge, and a slice of mango.

VARIATIONS

Substitutions: **Substitute 1 cup sliced strawberries, papaya, banana, diced peaches, or mixed berries for the mango.**

Pumpkin Seed Dip

Serve this rich, earthy dip of Mayan inspiration with cold shrimp, vegetables, and Totopos (page 46).

MAKES ABOUT 1¼ CUPS

 8 ounces hulled raw pumpkin seeds
 2 tablespoons olive oil
 1 fresh jalapeño chili, minced with the seeds and ribs
 1 large garlic clove, minced or crushed through a press
 ½ teaspoon ground cumin
 ½ to ¾ cup chicken broth or cold water
 3 to 4 tablespoons fresh lime or lemon juice
 ½ teaspoon salt
 ¼ teaspoon pepper

1. Scatter the pumpkin seeds in an ungreased medium skillet and place over moderate heat. Toast, stirring frequently, until the seeds begin to pop and swell and turn light golden brown, 4 to 5 minutes. Turn out onto a plate and let cool. Remove and reserve 2 tablespoons for garnish.

2. Meanwhile, spoon the olive oil into a small skillet set over low heat. Add the jalapeño, garlic, and cumin and sizzle for 1 to 2 minutes, or until the garlic is soft and fragrant but not browned. Pour the mixture over the toasted pumpkin seeds.

3. Scrape the seeds and chili mixture into a food processor or blender. Add ¼ cup of the chicken broth, 3 tablespoons of the lime juice, the salt, and the pepper. Process, stopping occasionally to scrape down the sides, and gradually add enough of the remaining broth to make a thick puree that is slightly thinner than chunky peanut butter. Taste for seasoning and add 1 tablespoon lime juice, if desired. Transfer to a container, cover, and refrigerate.

4. To serve, mound the dip in a small bowl and sprinkle with the reserved pumpkin seeds.

Roasted Red Pepper Puree

Roasting red bell peppers over a flame adds sweetness and intensifies flavor. Use this puree as a dip, to top *crostini* (page 26), or as a sauce for pasta (see Variations at the end of this recipe).

MAKES ABOUT 2 CUPS (ENOUGH FOR 48 *CROSTINI*)

  1½ pounds red bell peppers (about 4 large)
  ½ cup mashed cooked potatoes
  2 tablespoons olive oil
  1 large garlic clove, minced or crushed through a press
  ½ teaspoon dried oregano, crumbled
  1 tablespoon finely chopped fresh basil
  1½ teaspoons balsamic vinegar or fresh lemon juice
     About ½ teaspoon salt

1. Roast the peppers by placing them directly in the flames of a gas range or 3 inches below an electric broiler, turning frequently until blistered and black all over. Let cool for 1 to 2 minutes. Put the peppers in a plastic bag and twist the top to enclose. Let cool to room temperature. Scrape off the charred skin and cut out the stems and ribs. Discard the seeds. (This step can be done in a colander under very slowly running water, but some of the juices will be lost.) Coarsely chop the peppers and put them in a food processor along with the mashed potatoes.
2. Combine the olive oil, garlic, and oregano in a small skillet and place over low heat. Sizzle gently until fragrant but not browned, 1 to 2 minutes. Add to the food processor along with the basil, vinegar, and salt. Process to a smooth puree. Taste and add a pinch more salt, if needed. This can be served hot or cold. If making ahead, cover and store in the refrigerator.

VARIATIONS

Other uses: **To make a delicious pasta dish, cook 1 pound of dried penne until al dente and heat the roasted pepper puree. After draining the pasta, toss it with the puree, ¼ cup dry white wine, and ¼ cup snipped fresh basil. Toss in ½ cup freshly grated Parmesan and serve right away. It's enough for 4 to 6 servings.**

Totopos

Totopos (*Toh-TOH-Pohs*) are the quintessential Mexican corn chips. They bear little resemblance to commercial corn chips, so I suggest you buy some good stone-ground corn tortillas and make your own. Serve them with guacamole or beans or any of the dips in this chapter. They're best served the day you make them, but you can prepare totopos a day or two ahead and store them in an air-tight container.

MAKES 4 SERVINGS

> 1 **dozen corn tortillas**
>   **Vegetable oil, for frying**
>   **Salt**

1. Stack 6 of the corn tortillas. Using a large, sharp knife, cut the stack in half. Then cut each half into thirds, making 6 equal wedges. Repeat with the other 6 tortillas.
2. Pour ½ inch of vegetable oil into a large, heavy skillet or pour about 1 inch of oil into a deep-fryer. Heat the oil to about 375° F. Working in batches, fry the tortilla wedges, turning and stirring occasionally, until crisp and deep golden brown, about 1½ minutes. Remove with tongs and drain on paper towels. Lightly sprinkle with salt. Continue frying the remaining Totopos in the same manner.

Flor de Jamaica Spiced Tea

Throughout the Caribbean, especially in Trinidad, dried jamaica (a type of hibiscus) are used to make a tangy, bright red beverage that is especially popular at Christmastime, when the flowers are fresh. The rest of the year, and in this country, it is made from dried *flor de jamaica* (available in Latin American and Mexican food stores).

To make about 2½ quarts, put 2 ounces dried *flor de jamaica* (1½ to 2 cups) in a large bowl. Using a paring knife, cut the zest from 1 lemon and 1 orange into ribbons and add them along with three 3-inch cinnamon sticks, 12 whole cloves, 1 tablespoon whole allspice, and ¾ cup sugar. Pour in 12 cups of boiling water and let stand for 12 to 24 hours, stirring occasionally. Strain, pressing down on the solids. Chill. Serve in tall glasses over ice cubes.

Margarita

Here you have the classic flavors of lime, orange, tequila, and salt all in one potent, refreshing drink.

Coat the rims of 4 glasses with coarse (kosher) salt or use egg white and salt, as described in the Vampiro recipe on page 36. To make 4 cocktails, stir together ½ cup tequila añejo, ½ cup Cointreau or Triple Sec, and ½ cup fresh lime juice. Taste for sweet-sour balance and add 1 to 2 tablespoons more lime juice or orange liqueur if desired. Shake with ice cubes, then strain and serve on the rocks or straight up.

Oaxacan Peanuts with Chilies and Garlic

These salty, spicy, crunchy delights are just like the ones they put on your table during afternoons at the Bar del Jardin on the square in Oaxaca.

Deep toasting in peanut oil intensifies the flavor of all three main ingredients—peanuts, chilies, and garlic. You will need shelled raw peanuts to make this recipe, but don't be alarmed by the frying; any oil that is not drained off is blotted off with paper towels. These are not very spicy-hot because the chilies are left whole. But if you bite into one, watch out!

MAKES ABOUT 5 CUPS

⅓ cup peanut or other vegetable oil
⅓ cup small dried hot chilies
7 garlic cloves, sliced
1½ pounds shelled raw peanuts (about 4½ cups)
1½ teaspoons sea salt or coarse (kosher) salt

1. Preheat a large, heavy wok or skillet over moderate heat. When very hot, pour in the oil and heat until it shimmers. Add the chilies and garlic and cook, stirring, for 10 seconds. Add the peanuts, increase the heat to moderately high, and toss frequently until deep golden brown, 5 to 7 minutes. Stir more frequently during the last minute or two. Place a metal colander over a heat-proof bowl and pour in the peanuts and oil. Let drain for a few minutes.
2. Line a baking sheet with a large brown paper bag and top with several layers of paper towels. Pour on the peanut mixture and let drain, tossing occasionally. Blot with paper towels. Sprinkle with the salt and toss again. Serve warm or at room temperature. Store airtight for serving later on.

Four-Blossom Iced Tea

For this fresh approach to cool summer sipping, you'll need: dried Chinese chrysanthemums, chamomile, rose hips, orange blossom honey, and spices.

To make about 2 quarts, pour 2½ quarts of water into a large pot and bring it to a boil over high heat. Add ½ cup dried chrysanthemums, ½ cup chamomile, ½ cup slightly crushed rose hips, 1 tablespoon whole fennel seeds, and 1 teaspoon whole cloves. Reduce the heat and simmer gently for 5 minutes. Add ½ cup orange blossom honey and 3 large strips of orange zest. Let cool to room temperature.

Strain, pressing down on the solids to extract the liquid. Chill. Taste and add 1 or 2 tablespoons lemon or lime juice and more honey, if desired. Serve cold over ice cubes in tall glasses.

Marinated Greek Olives

Large black Greek olives are marinated in olive oil and vinegar with plenty of Greek oregano and other herbs to produce a deep, spicy flavor. Put these out for a party or serve them with lunch or dinner. Make them at least one day ahead, preferably two or three.

MAKES ABOUT 3 CUPS

> 1 pound large black Greek olives, such as Kalamata
> ⅔ cup extra-virgin olive oil
> 2 tablespoons dried Greek oregano, crumbled
> 2 large garlic cloves, minced or crushed through a press
> 2 bay leaves, halved
> 1 teaspoon dried thyme, crumbled
> 1 teaspoon dried rosemary, crumbled
>   Zest of ½ orange, cut into strips
> ½ teaspoon black pepper
> ⅓ cup red wine vinegar

1. Rinse and drain the olives. Place in a large bowl, top with about 2 quarts cold water, and let soak for 1½ to 2 hours to draw out some of the salt. Drain the olives as well.

2. Pour ⅓ cup of the olive oil into a small, heavy skillet and place over low heat. Add the oregano, garlic, bay leaves, thyme, and rosemary. Sizzle gently until the garlic is soft and fragrant but not browned, about 2 minutes. Turn

into a medium bowl. Stir in the remaining ⅓ cup olive oil, the orange zest, pepper, and vinegar. Add the olives and toss to coat. Cover loosely with plastic wrap and marinate at room temperature, tossing twice a day, for at least 1 day or as long as a week or two. Serve at room temperature.

Potato Skins

Crisp strips of potato skins make wonderful inexpensive hors d'oeuvre. They take on a bigger flavor when you brush them with Tabasco Butter (page 293) or Tarragon Butter (page 293) and you can add a burst of flavor by topping them with caviar.

To make 2 dozen Parmesan-crisped potato skins, scrub 6 medium russet baking potatoes (2 pounds). Prick them several times with a fork and bake in a 375° F. oven until tender, 40 to 50 minutes. Let cool to room temperature. You can bake them a day ahead.

Quarter the potatoes lengthwise and use a teaspoon to scoop out the soft centers, leaving a ⅛- to ¼-inch-thick shell. (Reserve the soft centers for a soup or a salad.)

Arrange the potato skins close together on a baking sheet. Melt about ¼ cup of Tabasco Butter or Tarragon Butter in a small pan over low heat. Brush generously over the skins. Sprinkle with about ¼ cup freshly grated Parmesan cheese and a little salt and pepper. Bake in the top third of a preheated, very hot (475° F.) oven until deep golden brown and crisp, 25 to 30 minutes.

To serve, spoon about 1 teaspoon sour cream onto one end of each. Add about ½ teaspoon caviar or a pinch of parsley or paprika and sprinkle with minced scallion. Serve hot.

Soups and Chowders

Bonus Recipes

Gazpacho

Here is a great big, cool, and refreshing soup that's made well ahead of time and kept cold. In Spain, ice cubes are often served in Gazpacho, and I think it's a good idea here at home, too, especially on a hot day. (Just add one or two; they won't dilute the soup too much.) Be sure to make this recipe with juicy, vine-ripened tomatoes during the hot summer months, and use canned broth because a well-made chicken stock will set as gelatin when cold.

This soup is best two days after it's made. Since I don't happen to like raw garlic, I sauté it, but if you like raw garlic, skip that step and add it raw. Make the croutons well ahead of time; even the day before is fine.

MAKES ABOUT 8 CUPS

- ¼ cup extra-virgin olive oil
- 1 large garlic clove, minced or crushed through a press
- 1 cup torn-up bits of firm white bread
- 2 pounds ripe tomatoes, quartered and cored
- 1 large green bell pepper, cored and cut up
- 8 whole scallions, cut up
- 1 large cucumber, peeled and cut up
- 2 tablespoons white wine vinegar or tarragon vinegar
- 1 tablespoon fresh lemon juice
- ¼ teaspoon dried tarragon, crumbled
- 2 teaspoons salt
- ½ teaspoon sugar
- ⅛ teaspoon black pepper
- ¼ to ½ teaspoon Tabasco or other hot pepper sauce
- 2 cups degreased canned chicken broth
- 1½ cups canned tomato juice
- ¼ cup dry white wine

For Serving
- ½ cup finely diced ripe tomato
- ½ cup peeled, seeded, and finely diced cucumber
- ½ cup finely diced green bell pepper
- Garlic Croutons (page 101)

1. Combine the olive oil and garlic in a small, heavy skillet set over low heat. Sizzle gently until the garlic is fragrant but not browned, 1 to 2 minutes.
2. Place the torn-up bread in a food processor, pour in the garlic oil, and add the tomatoes. Puree. Add the bell pepper, scallions, cucumber, vinegar, lemon juice, tarragon, salt, sugar, black pepper, and ¼ teaspoon of the Tabasco. Puree.

3. Pour the soup into a medium-mesh sieve placed over a large bowl. Force the puree through with a stiff whisk or the back of a spoon. Discard any solids that remain. Stir in the chicken broth, tomato juice, and white wine. Taste for heat and add ¼ teaspoon more Tabasco, if desired. Cover and chill the soup for several hours or up to 2 days.

4. To serve, ladle the cold soup into large, shallow bowls and pass the garnishes separately, or sprinkle each serving with 1 tablespoon each of the tomato, cucumber, and bell pepper. Pass the bowl of croutons. Serve right away.

GARLIC

In my kitchen I use more fresh garlic than anything else. Like onions, garlic belongs to the lily family.

Garlic should *always* be used fresh; powders, granules, salts, and prechopped in jars contribute a harsh, unnatural flavor to foods. Some people are so used to bombarding their taste buds with processed garlic that they can scarcely appreciate the subtleties of fresh garlic. I suggest that you clear out your cupboards right now and rid yourself of any such products.

It goes without saying that garlic has a big flavor all by itself. Its bold, vibrant fragrance and taste are familiar to all of us. Raw garlic is hot and potent—sensations that many of us relish. If you find raw garlic unpleasant, sizzle it gently in olive oil, butter, or another fat until softened but not browned. This cooking will tame the flavor considerably.

Roasted garlic has a nutty flavor. To roast a whole head of garlic, set it unpeeled on a sheet of aluminum foil in a 400° F. oven and bake for about 30 minutes. Remove the dry husks, then use it to flavor foods or squeeze it from the cloves onto toasted Italian bread as a good complement to soups and stews.

When shopping for garlic, choose heads that are hard. Soft or dented garlic will be weak and oddly flavored. Sprouted garlic will be bitter but still can be used, though it is a good idea to split each clove and take out the sprout. Store garlic in a cool, dry place. (I keep it with my potatoes and onions.) Peel, crush, slice, or chop garlic just before using it.

Cheddar Cheese Soup with Roasted Poblanos

Two of my favorite flavors—cheddar cheese and roasted poblano chili peppers—are brought to the foreground against a background of fine chicken stock thickened with potatoes and enriched with a little cream. And it's amazing how far a little cream can go. The roasted, slightly charred flavor of the poblanos comes through in a wonderful way.

One way I judge a new recipe is whether or not I want to eat more and more after I first taste it. With this soup, I had one bowl, then another, and before I knew it, half the soup was gone—a quick lunch all by myself!

MAKES ABOUT 8 CUPS

    8 ounces fresh poblano chilies
    1 pound russet baking potatoes (3 medium or 2 large)
    1 tablespoon butter
    1 tablespoon olive oil
    1 medium onion, finely chopped
    1 large garlic clove, minced or crushed through a press
    $\frac{1}{2}$ teaspoon ground cumin
    $\frac{1}{2}$ teaspoon dried oregano or thyme, crumbled
    $\frac{1}{8}$ teaspoon cayenne pepper
    $\frac{1}{4}$ cup all-purpose flour
    4 cups Chicken Stock (page 73) or canned broth
    $\frac{1}{2}$ cup heavy cream
    $\frac{1}{2}$ cup dry white wine
    6 to 8 ounces sharp cheddar cheese, grated ($1\frac{1}{2}$ to 2 cups)
    $\frac{1}{2}$ to 1 teaspoon salt
       Pinch of black pepper

1. Roast the poblanos by placing them directly in the flames of a gas range or about 3 inches from an electric broiler and turn frequently until black and

VARIATIONS

Substitution: In a pinch, substitute a 4-ounce can of whole roasted peeled green chilies, drained and chopped.

Lower calorie: To cut some of the fat, substitute light cream or milk for the heavy cream.

Presentation: Garnish with chopped fresh cilantro and/or Garlic Croutons (page 101).

charred all over. Let cool for a minute and then enclose in a plastic bag to cool completely. Pull out the stems and rub off the charred skin. Take out the seeds and cut the chilies into ½-inch squares.

2. Meanwhile, pour 2 cups of cold water into a medium saucepan. Peel the potatoes. Cut into 1-inch chunks and drop into the water as they are cut. Add a big pinch of salt and bring to a boil over high heat. Partially cover, reduce the heat slightly to prevent boiling over, and boil until very tender, 15 to 20 minutes. Uncover, but do not drain. Mash with a potato masher or electric mixer and reserve.

3. In a large, heavy saucepan or soup pot, combine the butter and olive oil over moderate heat. Add the onion and sauté until softened but not brown, 3 to 5 minutes. Add the garlic, cumin, oregano, and cayenne and cook for 1 minute. Stir in the flour and cook, stirring, for 2 minutes longer, or until very dry. Stir in the mashed potatoes and chicken stock and cook, stirring constantly, until thick and simmering, about 3 minutes. Pour in the cream and wine and simmer over low heat, stirring frequently, for 5 minutes. Add the reserved chilies and bring to a full boil, stirring over moderately high heat.

4. Remove the soup from the heat and stir in 1½ cups of the cheese, ½ teaspoon of the salt, and the pepper. Stir until the cheese melts. Taste and add more cheese and/or salt, if desired. To reheat, place over very low heat and stir frequently until heated through. Serve hot.

POBLANO CHILI PEPPERS

Without question, poblanos are my favorite fresh chilies. They are the biggest, meatiest, and mildest of all the "hot" peppers, resembling a flattened, pointed green bell pepper but usually a darker green and sometimes with a blush of orange. They turn red when fully mature, and when dried, are known as ancho chilies. In some parts of the country they are erroneously called pasilla chilies, a completely different chili altogether.

When raw, poblanos have a full, juicy-herbal flavor and heat intensity that can range from very mild to moderately hot (you occasionally get one that is very hot). Roasted and peeled, the chili takes on a deep, full, earthy flavor with a certain richness and tenderness.

Poblanos are the best chili choice for making Chilies Rellenos (page 152) and rajas (strips of roasted, peeled chilies). Store fresh poblanos in a paper bag in the refrigerator for up to a week. After roasting, the chilies can be frozen for 6 months or longer.

Mushroom and Smoked Chicken Soup

Smoked chicken complements earthy mushrooms in a wonderful way, and I like to use the very ripe, dark brown mushrooms because they have more flavor. This is a simple soup to put together when you have good broth on hand and some leftover smoked chicken.

MAKES ABOUT 8 CUPS

- 2 tablespoons butter
- 8 ounces fresh brown, cremini, or portobello mushrooms, thinly sliced
- 2 tablespoons all-purpose flour
- 6 cups Chicken Stock (page 73) or canned broth
- ½ cup dry white wine
- 1 large boiling potato, peeled and cut into ½-inch dice
- 8 ounces smoked chicken breast, sliced and cut into 1-inch cubes
- 1 bay leaf
- ¼ teaspoon dried thyme, crumbled
- 2 tablespoons chopped fresh parsley, ¼ cup freshly grated Parmesan cheese, or ½ cup Garlic Croutons (page 101), for garnishes

1. Melt the butter in a nonreactive large, heavy soup pot or saucepan over moderate heat. Add the mushrooms and sauté until lightly browned, 3 to 5 minutes. Sprinkle on the flour and cook, stirring constantly, for 1 or 2 minutes. Stir in the chicken stock and wine and bring to a boil. Add the potatoes, chicken, bay leaf, and thyme. Simmer until the potatoes are very tender and have absorbed the smoky flavor, about 30 minutes.
2. Serve the soup hot, sprinkled with the parsley, cheese, and/or croutons.

VARIATION

Substitutions: **You can add ½ cup heavy cream to the soup and/or about 4 ounces of fine egg noodles, cooked until al dente, in place of the potatoes.**

Asparagus and New Potato Chowder

You want to use large, fat, fresh asparagus spears to make this deliciously creamy and chunky chowder. Save the pencil-thin asparagus for other presentations.

MAKES ABOUT 12 CUPS

8 slices hickory-smoked bacon, finely chopped
3 leeks, trimmed, well-washed, quartered lengthwise, and sliced
½ cup finely diced celery heart
1 carrot, peeled and finely chopped
½ teaspoon dried thyme, crumbled
½ teaspoon dried tarragon, crumbled
1 bay leaf
3 tablespoons all-purpose flour
6 cups Chicken Stock (page 73) or canned broth
2 cups light cream or half-and-half
1½ teaspoons salt
1 teaspoon celery salt
1½ pounds small red-skinned new potatoes, peeled and halved or quartered (if tiny, leave whole)
1½ pounds large, fat asparagus spears, bottom ends peeled and asparagus cut diagonally into 2-inch lengths
2 teaspoons Worcestershire sauce

1. Put the bacon in a large, heavy soup pot or Dutch oven and cook, stirring frequently, over moderate heat until crisp and golden brown. Push the bacon

THYME

"When in doubt, use thyme," says the "Grass Roots Herb Society Newsletter." It's sound advice because thyme will make just about any plain food taste better.

Thyme has a distinctive warm and friendly aroma and a flavor that suggests oregano, citrus, and resin. It contributes an agreeable bitterness and a delicate fresh pungency with a subtle undertone of clove.

Thyme, a relative of mint, has tiny flowers that honeybees love. In fact, the honey from Mount Hymettus in Greece is incomparable in flavor and sweetness because the bees dine on the nectar of thyme blossoms. Of the more than 100 known varieties, French thyme and lemon thyme are the most popular.

Thyme is an important part of the French *fines herbes* mixture and an essential flavoring for clam chowder, sausages, meat and poultry stews, soups, cheeses, and Bénédictine liqueur.

to one side and tilt the pan; spoon off and discard all but 1½ to 2 table-spoons of the fat.

2. Stir in the leeks, celery, and carrot and sauté until softened and lightly browned, about 10 minutes. Add the thyme, tarragon, and bay leaf and cook for 1 minute. Sprinkle on the flour and cook, stirring constantly, for 1 to 2 minutes. Pour in the chicken stock and cream, and bring to a simmer, stirring constantly. Add the salt, celery salt, and potatoes, and simmer, stirring occasionally, until tender, 15 to 20 minutes.

3. Add the asparagus and simmer until tender, about 10 minutes. Stir in the Worcestershire sauce and taste for seasoning. Add a pinch more salt, if needed. The chowder will taste best if made several hours ahead and reheated gently over low heat.

4. Ladle the hot soup into soup plates or bowls and serve.

Manhattan Clam Chowder

There are a few dishes that feature the combination of clams and tomatoes, from linguini with red clam sauce to *cioppino* and—of course—a classic Manhattan clam chowder.

It's a good idea to make this chowder a couple of hours ahead. When ready to serve it, reheat over low heat for the biggest flavor.

MAKES ABOUT 12 CUPS

24 large chowder clams, such as Quahog or cherrystone, scrubbed and rinsed
6 slices lean smoked bacon, diced
3 leeks, trimmed, well-washed, quartered lengthwise, and sliced
1 medium onion, finely chopped
1 green bell pepper, trimmed and finely chopped
¾ cup finely chopped celery
¾ cup finely chopped peeled carrots
1 large garlic clove, minced or crushed through a press
1 bay leaf
½ teaspoon dried thyme, crumbled
½ teaspoon dried oregano, crumbled
3 boiling potatoes (4 ounces each), peeled and cut into ½-inch dice
1 cup dry white wine
1 can (28 ounces) peeled whole tomatoes

¼ **cup tomato paste**
2 **teaspoons sugar**
1 **teaspoon celery salt**
¼ **teaspoon black pepper**
⅓ **cup chopped fresh parsley**
   Salt, if needed

1. Combine the clams and 1 cup cold water in a large, heavy pot. Cover and place over high heat, stirring to tumble the clams once or twice, until they open, about 5 minutes. As they open, remove the clams with tongs to a large bowl. If they open slightly, just pry the shells apart. Discard any that will not budge. Reserve the cooking liquid in the pot.

2. When cool enough to handle, scoop the clams from their shells and put them into the cooking liquid. Discard the shells. Swish the clams around in the juice to rinse them, and transfer to a cutting board. Coarsely chop the clams and reserve them in a bowl. Pour the reserved juices through a fine sieve into a measuring cup or bowl and reserve.

3. Put the bacon in a nonreactive large, heavy soup pot or Dutch oven and cook over moderate heat until crisp and golden brown, about 5 minutes. Spoon off and discard all but 2 tablespoons of the fat. Add the leeks, onion, bell pepper, celery, and carrots and sauté until softened and lightly browned, 7 to 8 minutes. Add the garlic, bay leaf, thyme, and oregano and sauté until soft and fragrant, about 1 minute. Add the potatoes, wine, and clam juice and bring to a boil. Reduce the heat to low and simmer until the potatoes are barely tender, about 10 minutes.

4. Meanwhile, place a medium-mesh sieve over a bowl. Pour in the tomatoes and their juices and force through the mesh with a spoon. Discard the seeds. Add the strained tomatoes to the chowder along with the tomato paste, sugar, celery salt, and pepper. Simmer for 5 to 10 minutes.

5. Stir in the chopped clams and ¼ cup of the chopped parsley and simmer for 1 to 2 minutes. Taste for seasoning and add a pinch of salt if needed (the clams are salty, so be careful). Serve hot in large shallow bowls. Sprinkle with the remaining 1⅓ tablespoons parsley. The chowder will have a better flavor if allowed to cool to room temperature and reheated gently.

Fragrant Vietnamese Chicken-Noodle Soup

The beauty of this big soup is in its mouthwatering fragrance and flavor combination of fresh mint, cilantro, citrus, ginger, and smoke. It is an exotic, fulfilling meal all by itself, or can be served in smaller portions as a prelude to even bigger flavors. The chicken can be grilled a day or two ahead, over charcoal or under the broiler. The special ingredients are available from Asian grocers.

MAKES 4 MAIN-COURSE OR 8 SOUP-COURSE SERVINGS

Chicken and Marinade

- 3 tablespoons Vietnamese or Thai fish sauce (*nuoc mam* or *nam pla*)
- 3 tablespoons fresh lemon or lime juice
- 2 tablespoons minced fresh ginger
- 1 tablespoon sugar
- 1 large garlic clove, minced or crushed through a press
- 1 pound split skinless and boneless chicken breasts
- 1 tablespoon vegetable oil

Soup

- 8 ounces thin dried rice noodles or rice sticks ($\frac{1}{16}$ inch)
- 8 cups Chicken Stock (page 73)
- About $\frac{1}{4}$ cup Vietnamese or Thai fish sauce (*nuoc mam* or *nam pla*)
- 5 large, thin slices fresh ginger
- 1 large garlic clove, minced or crushed through a press
- 8 whole scallions, cut into $1\frac{1}{2}$-inch lengths
- 4 cups fresh bean sprouts (12 ounces), rinsed and drained
- 2 cups finely shredded romaine lettuce (preferably the small inner leaves)
- $\frac{1}{2}$ cup coarsely chopped fresh mint, plus small sprigs, for garnish
- $\frac{1}{2}$ cup coarsely chopped fresh cilantro, plus small sprigs, for garnish
- $\frac{1}{4}$ cup chopped unsalted roasted peanuts
- 1 lemon or lime, cut into 8 wedges
- Vietnamese chili-garlic sauce

1. Marinate the chicken. In a large, shallow glass dish, stir together the fish sauce, lemon juice, ginger, sugar, and garlic. Add the chicken, turning to coat all over. Cover and marinate in the refrigerator for 1 to 2 hours.

2. Preheat a charcoal grill or the broiler. Take the chicken from the marinade and pat dry with paper towels; discard the marinade. Lightly coat the chicken with the vegetable oil. Grill or broil for 3 to 5 minutes on each side, or until cooked to the center. Let stand until needed. If making ahead, when cool, cover and refrigerate. Tear into $\frac{1}{2}$-inch-wide shreds. If the chicken is cold, reheat in a small amount of the soup broth.

CILANTRO

I love cilantro so much that I could eat it by the bowl. It is one of my favorite big flavors. I vividly recall the day I first learned what it was. I was in high school at the time, and I had relished a certain fragrant flavor in restaurants many times before, but didn't know what it was. Then one day at home I was eating a chicken taco that my mother had made, and there it was: that undeniable aroma and taste. I quickly exclaimed, "That's *it!* That's the flavor I've been looking for. What did you put in this?" She told me that it was cilantro, and the mystery was solved. I was so relieved to find out that I could buy some anytime I wanted (we lived near Los Angeles, where Mexican ingredients are popular and plentiful).

Cilantro is the young coriander plant; its leaves resemble flat-leaf parsley in shape, though they are smaller, lighter, softer, and more delicate. The leaves are heavily aromatic and contribute a bright, herbal flavor to foods, especially when added just before serving. Although the flavor of cilantro blossoms when added to soup at the last minute, much of its fragrance and charm diminish upon cooking. Besides the abundant use of cilantro in Mexican cooking, it is favored in the cooking of China, Southeast Asia, the Caribbean, and Portugal. Cilantro also goes by the names fresh coriander, Chinese parsley, *culantro,* and *coentro.*

When shopping for cilantro look for bunches with bright perky leaves, preferably with roots intact. The leaves wilt and perish quickly. Do not rinse them until ready to use. As soon as you get the cilantro home, stand the roots or cut ends of the bunch in a small glass of tepid water for half an hour. Take the bunch from the water and wrap a wet paper towel around the roots or stems, place in a plastic bag, and refrigerate. Cilantro will stay fresh for 2 or 3 days, or slightly longer if it was quite fresh and not wet when you bought it.

3. Make the soup. Drop the rice noodles into a large pot of boiling water over high heat. After the water returns to a boil, cook for 1 minute. Drain in a colander and rinse under cold water. Let air-dry in the colander, tossing occasionally, for at least 30 minutes or as long as 2 hours.

4. In a nonreactive large saucepan or soup pot, combine the chicken stock, ¼ cup of the fish sauce, the ginger, and garlic. Bring to a boil over moderate heat. Reduce the heat to low and simmer for 5 minutes. Cover and keep warm until serving time.

5. Just before ladling into bowls, bring the soup to a boil. Remove the ginger slices and add the scallions. Taste and add more fish sauce, if desired.

6. For main-course servings, choose 4 large (6-cup) bowls. Into each, arrange one-fourth of the noodles (they will heat in the broth), one-fourth of the

shredded chicken, 1 cup of the bean sprouts, ½ cup shredded lettuce, 2 tablespoons chopped mint, 2 tablespoons chopped cilantro, and 1 table-spoon of the chopped peanuts. Ladle in about 2 cups of the scalding hot broth, putting some of the scallions in each. Serve hot, garnished with mint, cilantro sprigs, and lemon wedges. Guests should spoon in a little of the chili sauce to taste. For soup-course servings, use large shallow soup plates and halve the quantities given above.

VARIATIONS

Substitution: **Twelve ounces of fresh thin egg noodles can be used in place of the rice noodles; simply boil until tender but firm to the bite, 2 to 3 minutes. Drain and add to the bowls before ladling in the broth.**

Substitution: **Cooked shrimp and thin slices of roast beef can be used in place of the marinated chicken, or even added along-side the chicken for a big festive soup.**

Additions: **Sliced mushrooms can be added to the broth along with the scallions, as can slender asparagus spears, thinly sliced zucchini, or shredded napa cabbage.**

Tipsy Corn Chowder

The unusual addition of bourbon brings depth to this chunky corn chowder that's garnished with bacon-fried croutons or bacon bits. The chowder will be best if made ahead, cooled, and then reheated 2 to 3 hours later at serving time.

MAKES ABOUT 9 CUPS

- 3 **tablespoons butter**
- 1 **medium onion, finely chopped**
- 1 **cup diced celery, preferably from the heart**
- ½ **cup chopped red bell pepper**
- ½ **cup chopped green bell pepper**
- 3 **cups fresh or frozen corn kernels**
- ¼ **cup all-purpose flour**
- 2 **cups light cream**

2 medium red-skinned potatoes, peeled and cut into ½-inch dice
2 cups Chicken Stock (page 73) or canned broth
3 tablespoons bourbon
1 teaspoon sugar
1 bay leaf
¼ teaspoon curry powder
¼ teaspoon ground allspice
¼ teaspoon grated nutmeg
1½ teaspoons salt
¼ teaspoon black pepper

1. Melt the butter in a large, heavy soup pot or casserole over moderate heat. Add the onion, celery, and red and green bell peppers and sauté until softened, 7 to 10 minutes. Add 2 cups of the corn, increase the heat to high, and brown lightly, about 2 minutes. Stir in the flour and cook, stirring, for 1 minute.

2. Puree the remaining 1 cup corn with 1 cup of the cream in a blender or food processor. Add to the pot along with the potatoes and the remaining 1 cup cream. Stir in the chicken stock, bourbon, sugar, bay leaf, curry powder, allspice, nutmeg, salt, and pepper. Bring to a boil over moderate heat. Reduce the heat and simmer, stirring occasionally, until the potatoes are tender, about 30 minutes. Serve hot, topped with Garlic Croutons (page 101) or another salty topping.

BOURBON

The rich, full flavor of all-American bourbon comes from distilling a mash of grains that must contain at least 51 percent corn. It is aged in charred white-oak barrels for at least two years while it mellows and takes on its characteristic woody flavor. The alcohol content ranges from 80 to 125 proof.

Bourbon's name comes from Bourbon County, formerly in Virginia but now a part of Kentucky.

Moonshine was made at night under the moonlight to hide the illegal activity during Prohibition.

Sichuan Hot and Sour Soup

This bold Sichuanese soup—full of big flavor and contrasting textures—has been a very popular Chinese restaurant choice for the past two decades. But it turns out best when made at home. When buying the dried tree ears, look for those as small as flakes; otherwise they will expand too much and lose their delicacy.

MAKES ABOUT 12 CUPS

- 8 ounces lean boneless center-cut pork loin
- 2 teaspoons thin soy sauce
- 2 teaspoons dry sherry
- 1 teaspoon cornstarch
- 1/2 teaspoon dried red pepper flakes
- 1/2 teaspoon crushed Sichuan black pepper or black peppercorns
- 1/2 teaspoon sugar
- 1/2 teaspoon Oriental sesame oil
- 1/2 cup dried tiger lily buds (about 50)
- 10 large dried Chinese black or shiitake mushrooms
- 2 tablespoons dried small tree ears or wood ears

Soup

- 6 cups Chicken Stock (page 73) or canned broth
- 1/2 cup dry sherry
- 3 large, thin slices fresh ginger
- 1 garlic clove, minced or crushed through a press
- 1 to 1½ cups thinly sliced small fresh mushrooms
- 2 cups diced fresh firm bean curd (tofu) (2 to 3 cakes, 1/2-inch dice)
- 3 tablespoons light soy sauce
- 2 tablespoons dark soy sauce
- 2 tablespoons clear rice vinegar
- 1 tablespoon dark Chinkiang rice vinegar or additional clear rice vinegar
- 1 tablespoon Oriental sesame oil
- 1/2 teaspoon salt
- 1/3 cup firmly packed cornstarch
- 3 large eggs
- 1 tablespoon vegetable oil
- 6 whole scallions, thinly sliced
  Crushed Sichuan pepper or other black pepper, for topping

1. If desired, to facilitate slicing, partly freeze the pork just to firm up. Cut the pork into slices between 1/8 and 1/4 inch thick, then into matchsticks about 1½ inches long. In a medium bowl, combine the soy sauce, sherry, corn-

starch, red pepper flakes, black pepper, sugar, and sesame oil. Add the pork, toss well, and marinate in the refrigerator for 30 to 60 minutes.

2. Meanwhile, put the tiger lily buds, dried mushrooms, and tree ears into 3 separate small bowls. Pour 1 cup of very hot water into each bowl and let the ingredients soak until softened, 30 to 60 minutes. Drain, reserving the mushroom soaking liquid; discard the others. Keep the ingredients separate. One at a time, feel each lily bud and then cut off the hard stem end. Cut the buds crosswise in half. Cut off and discard the stems from the mushrooms. Cut the caps into $\frac{1}{4}$-inch strips. Feel the tree ears and cut off any hard parts. Cut the tree ears into $\frac{1}{8}$-inch slivers.

3. Make the soup. Pour the chicken stock into a nonreactive large soup pot or saucepan. Add the reserved mushroom-soaking liquid, the sherry, ginger slices, garlic, and slivered tree ears and bring to a boil over moderate heat. Reduce the heat to low, cover, and simmer for 5 minutes. Scoop out the ginger and discard.

4. Add the lily buds, soaked mushroom strips, and sliced raw mushrooms to the soup. Cover and simmer for 3 to 5 minutes. Remove a ladleful of the hot broth and stir it into the pork mixture. Stir to separate the pieces, add to the soup, and cook for 2 minutes. Add the diced bean curd, cover, and simmer for 3 minutes. Add the light soy sauce, dark soy sauce, clear rice vinegar, Chinkiang vinegar, sesame oil, and salt. Simmer for 2 minutes.

5. Meanwhile, in a bowl, dissolve the cornstarch in $\frac{1}{3}$ cup cold water, stirring until smooth. The soup should be barely simmering; pour in the cornstarch mixture in a big circle as you stir.

6. In a bowl, whisk the eggs with the vegetable oil. Pour in one-third of the egg mixture and heat for 10 seconds before stirring. Add the remaining egg mixture in 2 parts, allowing it to cook briefly before stirring. Serve hot, sprinkled with the sliced scallions and a pinch of the pepper over each portion.

VARIATIONS

Substitution: **Julienned bamboo shoots can be substituted for the lily buds.**

Substitution: **Chicken or beef can be substituted for the pork.**

Substitution: **For a seafood variation, marinate small butterflied shrimp for 30 minutes. Then add about 6 thinly sliced squid when you thicken the soup.**

Mexican Shrimp and Meatball Soup

Inspiration for this exciting and fragrant soup came from a small restaurant in Papantla in the state of Veracruz, Mexico, where it was made with a bouquet of cilantro. The total big flavor comes from chilies, lemon, chicken broth, beef, shrimp, scallions, and cilantro-saturated potatoes. The soup is also big on texture and totally addictive.

MAKES 6 SERVINGS

- 1½ **pounds small red-skinned potatoes**
- 1½ **tablespoons vegetable oil**
- 8 **cups Chicken Stock (page 73) or canned broth**
- ¾ **teaspoon salt**
- ⅔ **cup chopped fresh cilantro**
- 8 **ounces lean ground beef, such as sirloin or round**
- 1 **small zucchini, finely grated (¾ cup)**
- 1 **large egg**
- 1 **tablespoon plain dry bread crumbs**
- 1 **tablespoon tomato paste**
- 1 **tablespoon fresh lemon juice**
- ½ **teaspoon dried oregano, crumbled**
- ¼ **teaspoon ground cumin**
- 2 **large dried Mexican hot chilies, such as guajillo or mulato**
- 1 **pound medium shrimp, shelled and deveined**
- 12 **whole scallions, cut into 1½-inch lengths**

1. Peel the potatoes and cut them into ¾-inch cubes, dropping them into a large bowl of cold water as they are cut. Drain the potatoes thoroughly and pat dry on all sides.

2. Spoon the vegetable oil into a large, heavy skillet or sauté pan and place over moderate heat. Add the potatoes and sauté, shaking and tossing, until lightly browned all over, 8 to 10 minutes. Add 1 cup of the stock and ¼ teaspoon of the salt and bring to a boil. Reduce the heat to low, partly cover, and simmer until the potatoes are tender, 10 to 12 minutes.

3. Uncover the pot and boil over moderately high heat until only 2 tablespoons of the stock remain, about 5 minutes. Remove from the heat, stir in ½ cup of the cilantro, and keep warm until needed.

4. Crumble the beef into a large bowl. Add the zucchini, egg, bread crumbs, tomato paste, lemon juice, oregano, cumin, and the remaining ½ teaspoon salt. Mix thoroughly with your hands until well blended.

5. Pour the remaining 7 cups chicken stock into a heavy medium saucepan. Pull off and discard the stems from the chilies; tear the chilies lengthwise in half

and shake out the seeds. Add the large pieces of chili to the stock and bring the mixture to a boil over moderate heat. Lower the heat and keep the stock at a simmer.

6. Using a tablespoon to measure, scoop out level tablespoon-size portions of the meat mixture onto a plate. Roll them into smooth balls between the palms of your hands and drop into the simmering stock as they are shaped. Simmer the meatballs until tender, about 20 minutes. Remove the pieces of chili. Using a butter knife, scrape off the soft interior flesh and return it to the broth; discard the skins.

7. Add the potatoes and their liquid and bring the stock back to a simmer. Add the shrimp and scallions and cook gently, stirring frequently, until the shrimp are just cooked to the center, about 2 minutes.

8. To serve, ladle the soup into each soup bowl, making sure each portion gets some shrimp, some potatoes, and about 6 meatballs. Sprinkle each with a generous teaspoonful of the remaining cilantro. Serve hot.

VARIATIONS

Substitutions: **Lean ground pork can be used in place of the beef and ¾ cup chopped well-drained cooked spinach can be used instead of the grated zucchini.**

Substitutions: **If the dried chilies are not available, add ½ teaspoon dried red pepper flakes to the stock or eliminate entirely for a milder soup.**

Serving: **Serve with hot soft corn tortillas or chips, if desired.**

Hearty Tuscan Minestrone

Although this is a substantial soup for fall and winter, you can enjoy it all year long. I cooked this up on March 13, 1993, the day of New York's big blizzard, and it nourished my friends and me over a three-day snowed-in weekend. The base is thick and creamy with pureed white beans and potato, and chunky with vegetables, chicken, beef, and macaroni. This soup has a great big flavor, big texture, and *makes a big batch*. Cannellini (white kidney beans) are slightly larger and meatier than great northerns, but the two can be used interchangeably. If you are starting with homemade chicken stock, make it a day ahead.

MAKES 22 TO 24 CUPS

- 1 pound dried white kidney beans (cannellini) or great northern beans; or 3 cans (each 16 to 20 ounces) cannellini
- 2 bay leaves
- 2 large garlic cloves, minced or crushed through a press
- 2 teaspoons vegetable oil
- 12 ounces lean beef chuck or bottom round, cut into ½-inch cubes
- 2 cups full-bodied dry red wine
- 1½ tablespoons olive oil
- 2 leeks, trimmed, well-washed, halved lengthwise, and sliced; or 1 onion, chopped
- 1 medium onion, chopped
- 1 teaspoon dried oregano, crumbled
- 1 teaspoon dried basil, crumbled
- ½ teaspoon dried thyme, crumbled
- 2 teaspoons salt
- 6 to 8 cups Chicken Stock (page 73) or canned broth
- 1 can (14 to 16 ounces) tomatoes with juice, cut up
- 2 cups chopped green cabbage (½-inch pieces)
- 4 carrots, peeled and thinly sliced
- 1 large russet baking potato
- 1 cup diced celery (½-inch pieces)
- 1 cup chopped fresh green beans (½-inch pieces)
- 8 ounces fresh spinach, rinsed well, trimmed of large tough stems, and coarsely chopped
- 6 ounces small macaroni (1 to 1¼ cups), such as ditalini or elbow macaroni
- 1½ cups diced chicken (cooked or uncooked, ½-inch pieces)
- ½ cup freshly grated Parmesan cheese, plus more for serving
- ¼ cup chopped fresh parsley
- ⅛ teaspoon black pepper

1. The day before you want to make the soup, rinse and pick over the dried beans. Drain, put in a large saucepan, and pour in 8 cups cold water. Let soak for 8 to 12 hours or overnight. (Alternatively, use the quick-soak method by bringing the water to a full boil and boiling for 1 minute; remove from the heat, cover, and let soak for 1 hour.) Place the pot of beans and water over moderate heat and bring to a boil. Skim off any foam that rises to the top. Add the bay leaves and garlic, cover, and simmer gently over low heat, stirring occasionally, until the beans are tender, 1 to 1½ hours. Remove from the heat and set aside. There will be about 6 cups cooked beans and 2 cups of cooking liquid. If using canned beans, drain, reserving 1 cup of the liquid.

2. Spoon the vegetable oil into a nonreactive heavy, medium pot and place over moderately high heat. Add the beef and brown well, 5 to 8 minutes. Pour in 1½ cups of the wine and add ½ cup water. (If using canned beans, add the bay leaves and garlic to the beef mixture at this point.) Cover partly and braise gently over low heat until tender, about 1 hour. If necessary, add a little more water. Set aside until needed.

3. Reserve 2 cups of the whole beans. Pour the remaining beans and cooking liquid (2 cups fresh or 1 cup canned) into a food processor and puree until smooth (there will be about 5 cups of soupy puree).

4. Spoon the olive oil into a large, heavy soup pot or Dutch oven (preferably nonstick because the starch in this soup has a tendency to stick) and place over moderate heat. Add the leeks and onion and sauté until softened and lightly browned, 5 to 7 minutes. Add the oregano, basil, thyme, and salt and cook for 2 minutes. Stir in the pureed beans and 6 cups of the chicken stock. Add the tomatoes and their juices, the cabbage, and carrots. Peel the potato and coarsely grate it directly into the pot. Add the celery, green beans, the reserved beef with its braising liquid, the reserved whole white beans, and the remaining ½ cup red wine. Bring to a boil, stirring frequently, over moderate heat. Reduce the heat to low and simmer,

VARIATIONS

Substitution: **When fresh basil is available, add it in place of the parsley.**

Vegetarian: **For a vegetarian version, omit the chicken and beef and replace the Chicken Stock with Vegetable Stock (page 72).**

Bigger flavor: **Extra garlic can be sautéed with the leeks and onion. Pesto can be served to garnish the soup.**

stirring occasionally to prevent sticking, until the vegetables are tender, about 30 minutes.

5. Add the spinach to the soup and simmer very gently while you cook the pasta.

6. Bring a medium pot of lightly salted water to a boil over high heat. Add the pasta and stir constantly until the water returns to a boil. Cook until the pasta is tender, 10 to 12 minutes. Drain well.

7. Add the pasta to the soup along with the chicken. If adding raw chicken, cook for about 5 minutes; if adding cooked chicken, a couple of minutes will do. Remove the minestrone from the heat; remove and discard the bay leaves. Stir in the grated Parmesan, the parsley, and pepper. If the soup is too thick, add the remaining 2 cups chicken broth. If making ahead, don't thin the soup until you reheat it. The soup can be frozen and reheated. Serve hot, sprinkled with additional Parmesan cheese.

Sherried Black Bean Soup

Dry sherry and lemon juice complement the flavor of black beans, and in this case good chicken broth and a smoked ham hock provide the background. This smooth pureed soup needs no adornment, but if you want to dress it up a bit, a dollop of sour cream, a sprinkling of scallions, and a wedge of lemon should do the trick.

MAKES ABOUT 8 CUPS

 1 **pound dried black beans**
 6 **cups Chicken Stock (page 73) or canned broth**
 1 **meaty smoked ham hock**
 2 **tablespoons olive oil**
 1 **large onion, chopped**
 2 **celery ribs, finely chopped**
 2 **carrots, peeled and finely chopped**
 2 **large garlic cloves, minced or crushed through a press**
 2 **bay leaves**
 1 **teaspoon dried thyme, crumbled**
 1 **cup dry sherry, plus more for reheating, if desired**
 3 **tablespoons fresh lemon juice**
 ½ **to 1 teaspoon salt**
 ¼ **teaspoon black pepper**
    **Sour cream (at room temperature), sliced scallions,
        and lemon wedges, for garnishing (optional)**

1. The day before you want to make the soup, rinse and pick over the black beans. Put them in a large soup pot and add 5 cups of cold water. Let soak for 12 hours or overnight (or give a quick soak; see page 16).

2. In a medium saucepan, combine the chicken stock and ham hock. Cover and simmer over low heat for 2 hours. If doing this a day ahead, chill and then degrease. Otherwise, simply degrease by skimming or blotting with a paper towel.

3. After the beans have soaked, place the soup pot over moderate heat and bring to a boil, stirring frequently. Reduce the heat to low and simmer, stirring occasionally, for 45 minutes.

4. Spoon the olive oil into a large, heavy skillet set over moderate heat. Add the onion, celery, and carrots and sauté until softened, about 5 minutes. Add the garlic, bay leaves, and thyme and sauté for 2 minutes. Turn the mixture into the pot of beans and add the broth, the ham hock, and ½ cup of the sherry. Bring to a boil, skimming off any foam that rises. Reduce the heat to low, partly cover, and simmer, stirring occasionally, until the beans are very tender, about 2 hours.

5. Stir in the remaining ½ cup sherry and the lemon juice. Simmer for 10 minutes. Remove the ham hock and bay leaves; let the soup cool slightly.

6. Working in batches, puree the soup in a food processor or blender. Pour into a medium sieve and force through. Discard any bits of skin that remain in the sieve.

7. Taste the soup. It will probably need at least ½ teaspoon of salt, depending on the saltiness of the broth and the ham hock. Stir in a little more if needed and add the pepper. Reheat over low heat, adding 1 or 2 tablespoons more sherry if desired. If the soup is too thick, stir in a little extra broth or water. Serve hot, with the garnishes.

Vegetable Stock

This vegetarian broth has rich, full flavor. Use it in place of chicken stock or meat stock for the recipes in this book, or whenever you want big vegetarian flavor.

MAKES ABOUT 2 QUARTS

- 3 leeks, roots trimmed, well washed, and coarsely chopped
- 5 large celery ribs, cut into 2-inch lengths
- 3 tomatoes, quartered
- 2 medium onions, sliced
- 2 carrots, sliced
- 8 ounces fresh mushrooms, coarsely chopped
- 2 small white turnips, sliced
- 4 large garlic cloves, sliced
- Stems from 1 bunch fresh parsley
- 2 bay leaves
- 2 teaspoons paprika
- ½ teaspoon dried oregano, crumbled
- ½ teaspoon dried thyme, crumbled
- ½ teaspoon dried tarragon, crumbled
- 8 whole cloves
- 8 black peppercorns
- 1½ teaspoons salt
- ¼ cup vinegar

1. Combine the leeks, celery, tomatoes, onions, carrots, mushrooms, turnips, garlic, parsley stems, bay leaves, paprika, oregano, thyme, tarragon, cloves, peppercorns, and salt in a nonreactive large stockpot or Dutch oven. Add 4 quarts of cold water and the vinegar and bring to a boil over high heat. Reduce the heat to moderate, partly cover, and simmer for 1 hour, mashing down on the vegetables once or twice as they cook. Uncover, increase the heat slightly, and boil gently for 1 hour longer.

2. Set a colander in a large bowl. Transfer the vegetables to the colander and let cool and drain. Press firmly with the bottom of a bowl or the back of a spoon to squeeze out as much vegetable juice as possible; discard the solids. Strain the broth through a fine sieve.

3. At this stage you will probably have 2½ to 3 quarts of stock. Return it to the pot and boil over moderately high heat until reduced to 2 quarts, 10 to 20 minutes. Taste for seasoning and add a pinch of salt, if needed. Use right away or let cool to room temperature. Chill. The stock will keep for several days in the refrigerator or can be frozen indefinitely.

Chicken Stock

This simple stock is the base for many dishes—from soups and sauces to casseroles. It's a flexible formula; you can use any chicken parts that are on sale (necks and backs are always a bargain) or you can use 1 or 2 whole chickens.

MAKES ABOUT 2 QUARTS

- 4 pounds chicken parts or split whole chickens
- 2 medium onions, sliced
- 2 celery ribs, sliced
- 2 carrots, sliced
- 2 large garlic cloves, sliced (optional)
- 5 large sprigs parsley, or a handful of parsley stems
- 2 bay leaves
- 1 teaspoon dried thyme, crumbled
- 1 teaspoon dried tarragon, crumbled (optional)
- 5 whole cloves
- 5 black peppercorns
- 1 cup dry white wine (optional)
- 1 teaspoon salt

1. Put the chicken in a large stockpot or Dutch oven, add about 4 quarts of cold water, and put in all the remaining ingredients. Cover partly and bring to a boil over moderate heat. Reduce the heat to low and simmer gently for 3 to 4 hours. If you are using whole chickens, take them out when the meat has cooked to the bone, 30 to 40 minutes after the water comes to a simmer. Let cool slightly, then take off the breast and thigh meat and reserve it for another use. Return the bones and trimmings to the pot and continue simmering.

2. Scoop out the large pieces with a slotted spoon and drain in a colander over a large bowl. Discard the solids. Strain the stock first through a colander and a second time through a fine sieve.

3. Let the stock cool to room temperature, then chill. The fat is easiest to remove when chilled but can be skimmed off sooner (see page 13). To make a stronger stock, reduce the liquid to the desired strength by boiling over high heat.

Doctoring Canned Broth

You can add a lovely smoky fragrance to canned chicken broth by simmering it, covered, with a thick slice of smoked ham or a ham hock over low heat for about an hour. Just be sure to start with an extra cup of broth.

For a simpler version, simmer canned stock with a sliced onion, carrot, celery stalk, and a sprig of parsley. You can add a bay leaf and a clove of garlic, if desired.

Rich Brown Beef Stock

Homemade beef stock is made from browned beef bones and is the base for many soups, sauces, and gravies.

MAKES 3 TO 4 QUARTS

 5 pounds beef bones, cut 1½ to 2 inches thick
 1 pound beef chuck roast, cut into 4 chunks
 1 large onion, cut into thick slices
 2 large carrots, quartered lengthwise
 2 cups full-bodied dry red wine
 3 celery ribs, cut up
 3 large garlic cloves, sliced
   Stems, cut from 1 bunch fresh parsley
 2 tablespoons tomato paste
 3 bay leaves
 2 teaspoons dried thyme, crumbled
12 peppercorns
 1 teaspoon salt

1. Adjust an oven shelf to the top third of the oven and preheat to 450° F. In a large, shallow roasting pan, combine the beef bones, chuck, onion, and carrots. Roast, turning the pieces, for 1 to 1½ hours, until dark brown on all sides. Take the pan from the oven and use tongs to transfer the bones and vegetables to a nonreactive large (8- to 12-quart) stockpot or Dutch oven.

2. Tilt the roasting pan and spoon off most of the fat. Place the pan over 1 or 2 burners turned to moderate heat. Pour in the wine and bring to a simmer, scraping up the brown bits to deglaze the pan. Pour the pan's contents into the stockpot and add the celery, garlic, parsley stems, tomato paste, bay leaves, thyme, peppercorns, and salt. Pour in 4 to 6 quarts of water, or enough to generously cover the bones; bring to a boil over moderate heat. Cover the pot, reduce the heat to low, and simmer gently, stirring occasionally, for 6 to 8 hours, or until rich and tasty—the longer, the better.

3. Place a colander in a very large bowl. With a slotted spoon, transfer the bones and vegetables to the colander and let drain for a few minutes. Discard. Pour the remaining contents of the stockpot into the colander and drain; discard the solids. Strain the stock through a medium sieve and finally, if desired, through a fine one or a sieve lined with damp cheesecloth. Let cool to room temperature. Chill, then degrease (see page 13). Refrigerate for up to 3 days or freeze for up to 6 months.

Quick Beef Stock

If you don't have time to make the Rich Brown Beef Stock, use this abbreviated substitution.

MAKES 6 CUPS

> 1 pound lean ground beef
> 1 cup dry white wine
> 1 carrot, chopped
> 1 large onion, chopped
> 1 celery rib, chopped
> 1 large garlic clove, minced or crushed through a press
> ½ teaspoon salt

1. Crumble the ground beef into a nonreactive large saucepan. Add 6 cups cold water and the wine and bring to a boil over moderate heat. Add the carrot, onion, celery, garlic, and salt and bring back to a boil. Reduce the heat to low, partly cover, and simmer for 1 hour.
2. Strain the mixture through a sieve, pressing to extract the liquid. Discard the solids. Skim off the fat (see page 13), then set the stock aside to cool to room temperature. Transfer to containers and refrigerate for up to 1 week or freeze for several months.

Clarifying Stock

Occasionally you might want crystal clear beef or chicken stock, say, for example, to make aspic or to serve as consommé. To clarify degreased stock, pour the stock into a saucepan and barely warm it. Stir in 1 egg white and 1 broken eggshell. Place over low heat and bring to a simmer. Keep at a bare bubble without disturbing for 5 minutes. Line a sieve with several layers of dampened cheesecloth, place over a bowl, and gently pour the stock through. The egg and shell will hold any particles that would make the stock cloudy.

Salads

Bonus Recipe

Mint Julep

Greek Salad

You can serve this vigorous salad by itself, with just hot toasted pita bread, or with a butterflied leg of lamb that's been marinated in garlic and olive oil and grilled over charcoal.

MAKES 2 MAIN-COURSE OR 4 SALAD-COURSE SERVINGS

4	cups torn-up, lightly packed romaine lettuce hearts
1	large cucumber, peeled, halved lengthwise, seeded, and sliced
1	large or 2 medium ripe tomatoes, cored, halved lengthwise, and thinly sliced
$\frac{1}{2}$	green bell pepper, thinly sliced
2	whole scallions, sliced
2	tablespoons drained capers, chopped if large
$\frac{1}{2}$	cup lightly packed fresh parsley leaves
$\frac{1}{3}$	cup extra-virgin olive oil
3	to 4 tablespoons fresh lemon juice
$1\frac{1}{2}$	tablespoons dried oregano, crumbled
1	teaspoon salt
$\frac{1}{4}$	teaspoon black pepper
6	ounces feta cheese, crumbled ($1\frac{1}{2}$ cups)
12	Kalamata olives

1. Arrange the lettuce over a large platter and alternate the cucumber and tomato slices, overlapping them around the edge. Toss the bell pepper, scallions, and capers and mound in the center.

FETA CHEESE

When I think of Greece, I think of slices of crumbly white feta cheese drizzled with green olive oil and sprinkled with oregano. This most famous, ancient Greek cheese is usually made from sheep's milk, but sometimes goat's milk is used. Domestic feta is often made from cow's milk. Feta cheese is relatively low in fat (6 grams per ounce compared to 9 grams per ounce for cheddar).

Feta cheese is sometimes called a "pickled cheese," because it is cured in brine. It should be eaten fresh because after two months in the brine it becomes overly salty. The best feta will be mildly salty and have a fresh, pure fragrance.

When shopping for feta, ask to taste a sliver. If several varieties are available, taste all of them, or ask to taste the newest.

If a wedge of feta is stored in brine at home, it will stay fresh longer than when just wrapped in plastic. You can ask for some of the brine when you buy the cheese, or you can combine half-milk, half-water, and a little salt—enough to reach the top of the wedge of feta.

2. In a food processor or blender, combine the parsley, olive oil, 3 tablespoons of the lemon juice, 1 tablespoon of the oregano, the salt, and pepper. Pulse to make a thick dressing. Taste and add 1 tablespoon more lemon juice, if desired.
3. Pour the dressing over the salad. Top with the crumbled cheese and the olives. Sprinkle with the remaining ½ tablespoon oregano.

Uncle Eddie's Coleslaw

This assertive salad is an integral part of my brother Eddie's Smoked Tongue Sandwich (page 193). You'll need to make the salad at least 6 hours ahead, or better yet, a day or two in advance, so the flavors and textures have time to develop. There's not as much mayonnaise in this recipe as in many coleslaws, and the bite of lemon juice and cider vinegar, paired with horseradish and two types of mustard, make it bold but delightful indeed.

MAKES ABOUT 6 CUPS

- ½ cup mayonnaise
- ½ cup sour cream
- 2 tablespoons brown mustard (Eddie uses Gulden's)
- 2 tablespoons cider vinegar
- 1 tablespoon fresh lemon juice
- 1 tablespoon sugar
- 2 teaspoons drained prepared horseradish
- ½ teaspoon dry mustard
- 2 teaspoons salt
- ¼ teaspoon celery seed
- ¼ teaspoon black pepper
- 10 cups (1½ pounds) shredded green cabbage

1. In a large bowl, stir together the mayonnaise, sour cream, brown mustard, vinegar, lemon juice, sugar, horseradish, dry mustard, salt, celery seed, and pepper. Add the cabbage and toss well to combine. The coleslaw will be dry at this point, but will moisten as the cabbage gives up its liquid.
2. Transfer the coleslaw to a bowl just large enough to hold it, cover, and refrigerate at least 6 hours. Toss occasionally. Serve cold.

OLIVE OIL

My favorite olive oil tastes fruity and fragrant—like good green olives. It is an extra-virgin olive oil from California that Zabar's in New York bottles with their private label. I use it for practically everything.

I am not fond of light oils with very little olive taste. Some varieties are nuttier and more pungent, others unctuous or understated. Some have floral aromas and nuances of lemon, orange, apple, or green grass. My best advice here is to experiment and find an olive oil you like. It should be labeled extra-virgin and it should taste of the olives that it was made from. Don't use a lesser grade for cooking and "the good stuff" for salads and dressings. Simply use your favorite for everything.

There are many sensational, luscious, seductive olive oils from (and I say this in alphabetical order because one is not necessarily better than any other) California, France, Greece, Italy, and Spain. Oils vary from year to year along with the olive crops and some manufacturers blend various combinations of olives in an attempt to make their oil consistent.

Store olive oil in a tightly sealed bottle in a cool dark place to maximize freshness. Olive oil is fragile and heat and light will quickly turn it rancid. It also has a low smoking point, so when frying foods like breaded chicken cutlets or shrimp, add a little plain vegetable oil to the pan.

Extra-Virgin. This is really the only kind of olive oil to buy. To make it, crushed olives are cold-pressed to extract the oil. It contains less than 1% oleic acid.

Superfine Virgin, Fine Virgin, and Virgin. These oils are also cold-pressed, but with more pressure. Each grade contains increased amounts of oleic acid (1½%, 3%, and 4%, respectively). After the fourth cold pressing, chemicals and solvents are added and heat is applied for maximum extraction of oil from the pulp and pits.

A Very Special Olive Oil. I recently discovered a very special Spanish olive oil, which rises to the top of the extra-virgin category. It is called Nuñez de Prado, "the flower of the oil." It is so special that each decanted bottle is assigned a serial number. Whereas 5 kilos of olives are needed to extract one liter of extra-virgin olive oil from the first pressing, 11 kilos are required to tease out a single liter of Nuñez de Prado.

The olives, plucked from the same family grove since 1795, are treated tenderly; on the day they are picked they are carefully washed. They are stone-milled to break them up, then gently squeezed so the oil drips down through a partial extraction. The oil is so pure that it contains less than .2% oleic acid. The unfiltered oil is then decanted to preserve the aromatic bouquet and flavor; that is why you will see a small sedimentation of olive particles in the bottom of each bottle.

Salade Niçoise

This classic French *salade composée* is a bright main-course salad. In Nice it is always made with canned tuna packed in olive oil, but I have had success with water-packed tuna if the dressing is flavorful enough. Be sure to have fresh basil or oregano or both, and you should make the vinaigrette ahead of time for the best, biggest flavor.

MAKES 4 SERVINGS

- 1 **pound tender green beans, topped, tailed, and halved lengthwise**
- 4 **small red-skinned potatoes (about 1 pound), boiled until tender**
  Anchovy Vinaigrette (page 97)
- 1 **large cucumber, or 2 medium Kirby cucumbers, peeled,**
  seeded, and sliced
- 3 **tomatoes, cored and cut into ¾-inch wedges**
- 2 **cans (6 to 7 ounces each) tuna packed in olive oil or water,**
  drained and separated into chunks
- 4 **hard-cooked eggs, peeled and quartered (see page 13)**
- ½ **cup Niçoise olives, or other black olives**
- 3 **tablespoons chopped fresh basil or oregano, or a combination of both**
- 2 **tablespoons drained small capers**
  Salt and pepper

1. Put the green beans in a steamer, cover, and steam over high heat until crisp-tender, 4 to 7 minutes. Alternatively, drop into 1 inch of lightly salted boiling water, cover, and boil, tossing occasionally, until tender. Drain, let cool thoroughly, and then chill.
2. Arrange the green beans, leaving a space across the center, on a large oval platter about 10 × 14 inches.
3. Peel the potatoes, cut lengthwise in half, and then cut crosswise into ¼-inch half rounds. Toss the potatoes with ¼ cup of the dressing and mound in the center of the platter. Arrange the cucumber slices around the edge. Top with the tomato wedges. Scatter the tuna over the top. Arrange the quartered eggs on top of the potatoes in a line across the center. Scatter the salad with the olives and sprinkle with the basil and capers. Spoon a little of the remaining dressing over the salad and serve the remainder on the side. Sprinkle very lightly with salt and pepper to taste. Serve cold, cool, or at room temperature.

CAPERS AND CAPER BERRIES

Capers are little olive-green buds with a big flavor. They always remind me of Nice, on the Mediterranean, where they grow on shrubs, and where they are sprinkled freely over Niçoise salads. To me, a bottle of them is like a bottle of the Riviera.

The tiniest unopened buds make the best capers. They have a mild peppery flavor with a fresh mossy accent and delicacy that could come only from a tender bud. These are called nonpareils and are the best and costliest. As the buds grow larger, their flavor and delicacy lessens and they lose value. Large capers, however, can still be used, but expect a more robust quality. Capers are usually packed in white wine or a brine made from wine vinegar and salt. Capers are also available packed in salt. These have the best caper flavor. To use them, place what you need in a sieve and rinse under cool water.

In recent years, caper berries—or the fruit of the vine—the size and color of green olives have become increasingly available. They are expensive but add a big burst of caper flavor. These are usually used as a garnish atop seafood or salad.

Caesar Salad

My first Caesar salad was at Caesar's Restaurant in Tijuana, Mexico, during the 1960s, long after Caesar Cardini invented it. My friend Julia Child assures me that the original salad, which she first sampled at Caesar's during the 1920s, contained no anchovies, and, indeed, when I was there forty years later, they were optional. But Caesar Cardini himself concocted her salad and who knows who made mine.

I'm not trying to be authentic with this recipe; there are plenty of those around. I'm simply presenting the salad the way I like to eat it, *with* anchovies *and* tomatoes. I also use a 3-minute egg in the dressing instead of the traditional 1-minute egg because I find that it does a better job of coating the greens.

This is a bold, addictive salad that you can really sink your teeth into. It is especially good with charcoal-grilled meat or poultry. It can also be a lunch all by itself. This recipe is simple to double or triple and should be tossed just before serving (that's why, at Caesar's, they make it at the table).

MAKES 4 SERVINGS

> Garlic Croutons (page 101)
> 1 large egg, at room temperature
> 1 large garlic clove, flattened and peeled
> 1 large head romaine lettuce, washed and dried
> ½ cup extra-virgin olive oil

6 **flat anchovy fillets, minced, or 1 tablespoon anchovy paste**
3 **tablespoons fresh lemon juice**
½ **teaspoon Worcestershire sauce**
¼ **cup freshly grated Parmigiano Reggiano cheese**
12 **cherry tomatoes, halved**
  Coarse freshly cracked pepper

1. Make the garlic croutons so they are fresh.
2. Bring a medium potful of water to a boil over high heat. Add the egg, reduce the heat to moderate, and cook for exactly 3 minutes. Cool the egg under running water.
3. Rub the interior of a large salad bowl with the flattened garlic; discard the garlic. Tear the lettuce into large bite-size pieces and add them to the bowl. Pour ¼ cup of the olive oil over the lettuce and toss to coat. Crack the egg into a small bowl and spoon out any of the white that clings to the shell. Stir to blend the white and yolk and pour over the salad. Add the minced anchovies (if using anchovy paste, dissolve it in the lemon juice before adding), the remaining ¼ cup olive oil, the lemon juice, and Worcestershire. Toss again. Sprinkle on the cheese and croutons and toss. Top with the cherry tomatoes and cracked pepper to taste (about ¼ teaspoon). No salt should be needed because of the saltiness of the anchovies, cheese, and Worcestershire sauce. Serve right away.

VARIATIONS

To make a meal: **For a hearty Caesar chef's salad, poach or charcoal grill a large whole chicken breast; cool, skin, bone, and shred, then toss with the salad. To embellish even further, crumble 4 slices of crisp well-drained bacon over the top. Peeled, seeded, sliced cucumber can also be added.**

Presentation: **To make a fancier salad, buy 4 large heads of romaine and use only the small inner leaves from the heart, leaving them whole.**

Panzanella

A bowl of this fragrant, ice-cold, Tuscan bread salad is all I need during the long hot summer days when tomatoes are ripe and juicy. Originally, this salad was concocted to make use of semolina bread when it became stale. But you can make it here at home from a sturdy loaf of any country-style, farmhouse, sourdough, or peasant bread.

MAKES 6 TO 8 SERVINGS

12 ounces sturdy, stale, country-style bread,
   torn into 1 × 2-inch pieces (6 to 8 cups)
3 large ripe tomatoes, cut into ¾-inch dice
1 large cucumber, peeled, seeded, and cut into ¼-inch slices
1 large red bell pepper, trimmed and cut into ¾-inch squares
1 large green bell pepper, trimmed and cut into ¾-inch squares
½ cup sliced whole scallions
½ cup finely chopped purple onion
½ cup chopped Italian flat-leaf parsley
½ cup chopped fresh basil leaves
½ cup sliced pitted black olives, brine-cured or oil-cured
2 tablespoons drained small capers (optional)
¼ cup plus 2 tablespoons extra-virgin olive oil
2 large garlic cloves, minced or crushed through a press
2 tablespoons red wine vinegar or fresh lemon juice
2 teaspoons salt
1 teaspoon dried oregano, crumbled
½ teaspoon black pepper

1. Put the pieces of bread in a large bowl and add cold water to barely cover. Let soak for about 1 minute to soften; drain. Picking up a small handful at a time, squeeze out the water; the bread should be damp, not wet. Put the pieces in a bowl, separating them to fluff them up a bit. Chill for at least 1 hour.

2. In a large salad bowl, combine the tomatoes, cucumber, and red and green bell peppers. Cover and chill for at least 1 hour.

3. Remove the salad bowl from the refrigerator and add the scallions, onion, parsley, basil, olives, and capers; toss and chill until ready to serve the salad.

VARIATION

To make a meal: **Toss in about 3 cups diced cooked chicken before adding the bread and dressing. Add an extra 1 to 2 tablespoons each of vinegar and oil.**

4. Combine 2 tablespoons of the olive oil and the garlic in a small skillet set over low heat. Let sizzle gently for about 1 minute without coloring. Pour the garlic oil into a jar. Add the remaining ¼ cup olive oil, the vinegar, salt, oregano, and pepper; shake well to make a dressing. (The dressing can be prepared up to a couple days ahead, and the other ingredients, up to about 3 hours in advance.)

5. Add the chilled bread to the salad bowl and toss. Pour on the dressing and toss again. Serve cold.

PARSLEY

I put parsley into practically everything. It is the workhorse of the herb garden, and I always keep a bagful in my refrigerator. Not only does it have a pleasant, fresh fragrance but it is inexpensive and remains fresh for a long time. I don't know why anyone would ever buy the dried version, which lacks parsley's best qualities (except the lasting power—dried parsley will have the same lack of fragrance and flavor when you buy it as five years later).

Parsley heads one of the two largest herb families (mint is the other). Dozens of vegetables, spices, and herbs have taken root from parsley—from carrots and celery to dill, cumin, anise, and caraway—and developed into entirely different plants with unique flavors and characteristics.

Fresh parsley has a simple, mild, herb flavor: peppery, bitter, and sweet, always dominated by that refreshing herbal aroma. Its unobtrusive qualities are why parsley works in harmony with just about every other flavor, except in confections and desserts. And since it is so attractive, it is often used to garnish and enhance other foods.

Curly leaf parsley is the most popular and commonly available variety. Although it has great fresh parsley fragrance and flavor, it is not quite as strong nor as deep in flavor as the flat-leaf variety. Flat-leaf, or Italian flat-leaf parsley, is the more flavorful and most closely resembles the original European parsley that seventeenth-century colonists brought with them to New England.

If parsley is wet when you buy it, let it dry at room temperature for a short time. If it is very wet, scatter over paper towels or place in front of a fan, to hasten the drying. Don't let it wilt. Store it in a plastic bag in the refrigerator.

Do not rinse parsley until just before using. Always pluck the leaves from the stems because the stems will add bitterness. Save stems for the stockpot, where the stronger flavor is desirable.

Uncle Bob's Antipasto Salad

My brother Bob doesn't cook very much, but he makes an outrageous antipasto salad. It is colorful and mouthwateringly tasty, festive, and fun. You can serve *Bruschetta* (page 27) or any good crusty bread as an accompaniment. Chicken-Basil Ravioli (page 140) is my favorite pasta to follow. But this salad is hearty enough to be supper all by itself. This recipe is easily expandable, so be sure to check out the variations to the recipe.

MAKES 4 TO 6 SERVINGS

> ½ cup Creamy Italian Dressing (page 100)
> 8 ounces asparagus or green beans, trimmed
> 2 large heads romaine lettuce, dark green outer leaves
>   discarded, remainder washed, dried, and chilled
> 1 large head radicchio, separated, washed, and dried
> 1 Belgian endive, trimmed and separated
> 4 carrots, peeled and cut lengthwise into thin slices
> 4 to 8 celery ribs, with leaves attached
> 4 ounces lean beef salami or ham, thinly sliced
> 4 ounces thinly sliced mild provolone cheese (4-inch diameter)
> 8 green Italian olives
> 8 black Italian olives
> 2 large red bell peppers, roasted and peeled (page 17);
>   or 1 jar (4 ounces) pimientos, drained and cut in ½-inch strips
> Salt and pepper, if needed

1. Prepare the dressing well ahead of time so the flavors have time to blossom.
2. Drop the asparagus or green beans into a large pot of salted boiling water and blanch until just tender, 1 to 3 minutes. Rinse under cold water and drain.
3. Tear the lettuce leaves into large bite-size pieces (the very smallest leaves from the heart can be left whole) and arrange on a large (at least 12 × 16-inch) platter. Tear the radicchio into large pieces and scatter over the lettuce. Arrange the endive spears, points up, around

VARIATIONS

Substitutions: **Add any of the following ingredients to your antipasto salad: marinated artichoke hearts, grilled zucchini, sliced raw fennel, radishes, scallions, tomato wedges (if there is no tomato to follow in the pasta course), large white beans, sliced purple onion, and arugula. Deviled eggs can be quartered and added in rows alongside the salami and cheese.**

the edge of the platter, interspersing them with the carrot slices and celery ribs.

4. Cut each salami or ham slice from the center out through the edge and overlap at the cut to shape into a cone. Arrange as a crosswise row toward one end of the platter. Cut the provolone slices in half and then shape them into cones as for the salami, arranging them at the other end of the platter. Put a green olive in each salami cone and a black olive in each cheese slice. Arrange the asparagus or green beans across the center and decorate with strips of red bell pepper. Shake the dressing thoroughly (or whisk) and pour all over the salad. Sprinkle with salt and pepper, if desired.

Smoked Salmon Pasta Salad

Wickedly expensive and addictively delicious, smoked salmon is one of my favorite treats. When combined with black olives, scallions, parsley, capers, and extra-virgin olive oil, a cool and refreshing pasta salad is the inevitable result.

MAKES ABOUT 8 CUPS

- 8 ounces medium shell pasta
- ¼ cup plus 1 tablespoon extra-virgin olive oil
- ½ cup sliced, pitted black olives in brine
- 1 cup sliced whole scallions
- ½ cup chopped fresh parsley, plus sprigs, for garnish
- 8 ounces smoked salmon, thinly sliced and cut into slivers
- 3 tablespoons drained capers
- 2 tablespoons fresh lemon juice
- 1 teaspoon anchovy paste
- 2 tablespoons red wine vinegar
- ¼ teaspoon black pepper

1. Bring a large pot of lightly salted water to a boil over high heat. Drop in the pasta and stir constantly until the water returns to a boil. Cook, stirring frequently, until tender but firm to the bite. Drain in a colander and rinse under cold running water. Drain well.
2. In a large bowl, toss the pasta with 1 tablespoon of the olive oil. Add the olives, scallions, and parsley and toss. Add the salmon and capers and toss again.
3. In a medium bowl, combine the lemon juice, anchovy paste, vinegar, and pepper. Gradually whisk in the remaining ¼ cup olive oil. Pour over the salad and toss to combine. Cover and chill for about 1 hour before serving. Serve cold, garnished with sprigs of parsley.

Octopus Seafood Salad

To my taste, tender octopus tastes something like lobster, and it's no wonder since its diet consists of crab, crab, and more crab! This fruit-of-the-sea salad is a delicious orchestration of flavors, textures, and fragrances—rich with octopus, shrimp, squid, and scallops, tomatoes, green olives, scallions, capers, parsley, and cilantro. Serve it ice-cold on a hot day, perhaps by the sea.

Octopus can be cooked very quickly to avoid toughening, or it can be simmered for a very long time (as in this recipe) to make it tender.

This recipe makes a big batch. Serve it to a crowd or eat the leftovers the next day. See the variations.

MAKES ABOUT 12 CUPS

> 2 octopus (about 3 pounds each)
> 1 cup dry white wine
> 1 medium onion, sliced
> 4 large parsley sprigs
> 2 large garlic cloves, sliced
> 12 black peppercorns
> 12 whole cloves
> 1 pound medium shrimp, shelled and deveined
> 2 tablespoons sea salt or coarse (kosher) salt
> 4 cups ice cubes
> 1 pound medium squid, cleaned, bodies cut into ¾-inch rings
>   and tentacle clusters halved
> 1 pound sea or bay scallops
> 2 cups diced ripe tomatoes
> 1 cup sliced pimiento-stuffed green olives
> ½ cup sliced whole scallions
> ½ cup chopped fresh cilantro (optional)
> ¼ cup finely chopped purple onion
> 2 tablespoons drained capers, chopped
> ½ cup chopped fresh parsley
> ⅓ cup fresh lemon or lime juice
> 1 teaspoon salt
> ¼ teaspoon black pepper
> ¾ cup extra-virgin olive oil

Note: Tradition calls for octopus to be treated roughly. For more tender octopus, slam it forcefully in the sink 15 to 20 times. Then proceed with the recipe.

1. Usually octopus in the fish market have already been cleaned. If not, ask the fishmonger to do it. Also, cut off 1 inch from the tip of each tentacle. Pour

hot water into a large kettle or Dutch oven to fill it at least three-quarters full. Place over high heat and bring to a boil. Hook the head of 1 octopus onto a long fork and slowly lower it, tentacles first, into the boiling water. As soon as its head is completely submerged, take it out. Cover the pot so the water returns to a boil as quickly as possible. Uncover, lower the octopus into the water as before, and remove. Repeat once more after the water again returns to a boil. This is a classic Spanish technique for ensuring tenderness. Reserve the octopus and repeat with the second one, again dipping 3 times.

2. Put the 2 octopus into a nonreactive large, heavy Dutch oven or casserole and ladle in 6 cups of the poaching liquid, or enough to almost cover. Add the wine, sliced onion, parsley sprigs, garlic, peppercorns, and cloves. Cover and bring to a simmer over moderate heat. Reduce the heat to low and simmer gently until very tender when pierced with a fork, 1½ to 2 hours. Take the octopus from the liquid and drain in a colander until cool enough to handle. Reserve the braising liquid.

3. If you wish, use a paring knife to peel off and discard the octopus skin.

4. Cut the tentacles and bodies into ½- to 1-inch pieces. Cover and chill.

5. Strain the braising broth and pour it into a nonreactive large saucepan. Place over high heat and bring to a boil. Reduce the heat, put the shrimp in a sieve, and lower into the water. Cook until opaque to the center, 1 to 2 minutes. Do not overcook. Remove and rinse under cold water. In a large bowl, toss the shrimp with the sea salt and ice cubes.

6. Place the squid in the sieve and lower into the water; cook just until done, 1 to 1½ minutes. Drain, rinse under cold water, and add to the ice. If using sea scallops,

SCALLIONS

I'm never without a bunch of scallions in the crisper drawer of my refrigerator. I almost always use the whole scallion from white base to dark green stems. Occasionally, though, I use just the white portion, for delicacy and purity of color.

In some parts of this country, scallions go by other names: green onions, spring onions, and shallots (which they are *not*) can be named for the same slender young green and white onions without fully developed bulbs at their bases.

Scallions have a light, very fresh, onion fragrance and flavor that tames and diminishes greatly upon cooking. Usually, in stir-fries, they are tossed in at the last moment so they heat slightly rather than cook completely.

If scallions are wet when you buy them, let them air-dry at room temperature for a few minutes, until dry but not wilted. Then, put them, untrimmed and unwashed, in a plastic bag and store in the vegetable drawer of your refrigerator. They will remain fresh for about 2 weeks (assuming they were in good condition when you bought them). Just before using, trim off the root ends and any wilted or ragged parts of the green stems. Pull off just the outermost layer and discard it, then rinse the scallion under cool water.

cut into quarters; if using bay scallops, leave whole. Put the scallops in the sieve and lower into the water. Poach just until cooked through to the center, 1½ to 2 minutes. Drain, rinse briefly under cold water, and add to the ice. Strain the broth for another use, such as a seafood soup or stew, or freeze it for future use.

7. When the seafood is well chilled, drain well and discard any ice cubes. In a large bowl, combine the seafood with the octopus. Add the tomatoes, olives, scallions, cilantro, purple onion, capers, and chopped parsley and toss to combine.

8. In a medium bowl, combine the lemon juice, salt, and pepper. Gradually whisk in the olive oil. Pour over the seafood, toss, cover, and chill for at least 2 hours or up to 1 day before serving. Serve chilled.

VARIATIONS

Substitution: **Omit the scallops, if desired. Or halve the recipe and omit the scallops and shrimp.**

Presentation: **For a sensational first-course serving, cut Haas avocados in half and remove the pits; serve stuffed with the salad, adding enough to spill over onto the plate (a full recipe is enough to serve in 24 avocado halves).**

Linguine and Grilled Beef Salad

Although charcoal-grilled beef adds considerable flavor and dimension, you can also use leftover roast beef or sliced roast beef from a delicatessen to make this tasty pasta salad. It is a fresh and colorful cilantro and parsley combination, best enhanced with sweet onions, such as Vidalias, Walla-Wallas, or Mauis.

MAKES 6 SERVINGS

- ¼ **cup rice vinegar**
- 2 **tablespoons mayonnaise**
- 2 **tablespoons extra-virgin olive oil**
- ½ **teaspoon dried oregano, crumbled**
- ½ **teaspoon ground cumin**
- 1 **teaspoon salt**
- ¼ **teaspoon black pepper**
- ¼ **teaspoon cayenne pepper**
- 8 **ounces linguine, broken in half**

8 ounces trimmed grilled steak or roast beef, thinly sliced

2 tomatoes, cut into ½-inch dice

1 medium sweet onion, peeled, halved lengthwise, thinly sliced,
and separated into half-rings

⅓ cup chopped fresh parsley, plus sprigs, for garnish

⅓ cup chopped fresh cilantro, plus sprigs, for garnish

2 cups shredded romaine or iceberg lettuce

1. In a large bowl, whisk together the rice vinegar, mayonnaise, and olive oil. Add the oregano, cumin, salt, black pepper, and cayenne and whisk to blend. Transfer to a jar with a tight-fitting lid and shake well before using.

2. Bring a large pot of lightly salted water to a boil over high heat. Drop in the linguine and stir constantly until the water returns to a boil. Cook, stirring frequently, until tender but firm to the bite. Drain and rinse under cold water. Shake thoroughly to drain well.

3. Transfer the pasta to a large bowl and toss with the salad dressing. Add the beef, tomatoes, onion, parsley, and cilantro and toss. Cover and chill thoroughly, 1 to 2 hours.

4. Just before serving, add the lettuce and toss. Serve cold, garnished with sprigs of parsley and cilantro.

VARIATIONS

Substitution: **Use grilled chicken breasts, torn into ½-inch shreds, instead of the beef.**

Substitutions: **Fresh basil can replace the cilantro, or you can use ⅔ cup mixed fresh herbs of your choice.**

Pasta Salad with Sugar-Snap Peas, Black Forest Ham, and Mushrooms

This is a fresh and colorful salad with flavors that range from sweet to meaty and textures from toothsome to velvet smooth.

MAKES 6 TO 8 SERVINGS (12 CUPS)

- 1 pound sugar-snap peas, stems tipped, topped, and strings removed
- 4 carrots, peeled and cut into ¼-inch julienne
- 8 ounces penne, penne rigati, or other macaroni
- ¼ cup plus 3 tablespoons olive oil
- 1 pound fresh portobello mushrooms or cremini mushrooms, sliced ¼ inch thick
- 2 to 3 large red bell peppers, roasted (page 17), peeled, seeded, and cut into ½-inch strips
- 8 ounces Black Forest ham or other good smoked ham, cut into ¼-inch julienne
- ¼ cup chopped fresh oregano, or 1 teaspoon crumbled dried oregano
- 2 tablespoons Dijon mustard
- 1½ teaspoons salt
- ½ teaspoon black pepper
- 3 to 4 tablespoons balsamic vinegar
- 3 cups lightly packed stemmed arugula, rinsed and dried

1. Bring a large pot with salted water to a boil over high heat. Add the sugar-snap peas and cook for 2 minutes from the time they hit the water. Scoop out with a slotted spoon and rinse in a colander under cold water. Add the

VARIATIONS

Substitution: Use smoked chicken or turkey in place of the ham or omit entirely.

Substitution: If sugar-snap peas are not available, use snow peas instead.

Substitution: Lemon juice or another vinegar may be used in place of the balsamic vinegar.

Substitution: White mushrooms may be used in place of the portobello.

carrots and cook for 2 minutes after the water returns to a boil. Scoop out with a slotted spoon and rinse under cold water.

2. When the water boils again, add the pasta and stir until the water returns to a boil. Cook, stirring frequently, until tender but firm to the bite. Drain in a colander and rinse to cool. Drain well. Transfer to a large bowl and toss with 1 tablespoon of the olive oil.

3. Place a large, heavy skillet over high heat. When very hot, spoon in 2 table-spoons of the olive oil and add the mushrooms. Cook, without stirring, until browned well, $1\frac{1}{2}$ to 2 minutes. Turn and cook for 1 to $1\frac{1}{2}$ minutes longer. Turn out over the pasta and add the roasted peppers, sugar-snap peas, carrots, ham, and oregano; toss to combine.

4. In a medium bowl, whisk together the mustard, salt, pepper, and 3 tablespoons of the vinegar. Gradually whisk in the remaining $\frac{1}{4}$ cup olive oil. Pour over the salad and toss to combine. Taste and add a little more vinegar, if desired. If making ahead, cover and chill. Add the arugula and toss well.

Tabbouleh

To me, this substantial salad is a showcase for juicy, ripe tomatoes, crunchy cool cucumbers, and crisp green bell peppers, flavored with lots of fragrant fresh mint.

MAKES ABOUT 10 CUPS

> 2 **cups medium bulgur wheat (about 12 ounces)**
> 3 **tomatoes, cored and cut into $\frac{1}{2}$-inch dice**
> 1 **large cucumber, peeled, seeded, and cut into $\frac{1}{2}$-inch dice**
> 1 **large green bell pepper, trimmed and cut into $\frac{1}{2}$-inch squares**
> 1 **cup thinly sliced whole scallions**
> $\frac{3}{4}$ **cup finely chopped fresh mint, plus mint sprigs, for serving**
> $\frac{3}{4}$ **cup finely chopped fresh parsley**
> 2 **teaspoons salt**
> $\frac{1}{2}$ **teaspoon black pepper**
> $\frac{1}{3}$ **cup extra-virgin olive oil**
> $\frac{1}{3}$ **cup fresh lemon juice**

1. Put the bulgur in a large bowl and add cold water to cover generously. Swish the grains to rinse and pour off the water. Repeat several times, until the water is no longer cloudy. Cover with fresh cold water and let soak for 1 hour.

2. Drain the bulgur in a medium sieve and return to the bowl. Line the sieve

with several layers of damp cheesecloth and pour in the wheat. Carefully pick up the bundle and squeeze out as much of the water as possible. Transfer the bulgur to a very large bowl.

3. Add the tomatoes, cucumber, bell pepper, scallions, chopped mint, parsley, salt, and pepper; toss well. Drizzle with the olive oil and lemon juice and toss again. Cover and chill thoroughly, at least 1 hour. Serve cold, with the mint sprigs.

MINT

Did you know that basil, oregano, rosemary, thyme, marjoram, and sage are all related to mint? It's true. Mint heads one of the two largest families of herbs (the other being parsley).

There are two basic types of mint: peppermint and spearmint. Both have a refreshing sweet aroma and cause a cooling sensation in the nose and mouth, leaving behind an icy tingling taste. Of the two, peppermint is generally the more pungent; spearmint is slightly milder. While peppermint is the main mint for flavoring candy, spearmint is used mostly for salads and for cooking or marinating.

One of my favorite recipes for showing off mint's dramatic refreshing flavor is the Middle Eastern Tabbouleh, which also includes big quantities of parsley.

When I lived in California, spearmint used to flourish in the backyard, by a dripping water faucet in the shade of the house. If you grow your own, consider experimenting with several varieties so you can sample a wide range of flavors, from lemon-orange mint to apple mint or chocolate mint.

Mint Julep

Consider doubling or tripling this recipe for a party. To make 1 cup of mint syrup, combine 1 cup sugar with $1/2$ cup water in a small saucepan and simmer over low heat for about 5 minutes. Remove from the heat and stir in $1/2$ cup chopped fresh mint. Let cool and then strain.

Mint juleps taste best when served in frozen silver julep cups, but 10-ounce tumblers work fine. Freeze the cups or glasses for 2 hours, then fill with crushed ice. Freeze at least 6 hours, or overnight. Remove from the freezer 10 to 20 minutes before serving, so a frost forms on the outside. Pour in $1/4$ to $1/2$ cup bourbon and 2 to 3 tablespoons of the mint syrup. Stick 3 or 4 large fresh mint sprigs into the top (this is important so you get lots of fragrance as you sip) and add 2 straws. Let them stand a few minutes before serving.

Calico Black Bean Salad

The festive colors and textures of sweet corn and peas contrast with rich black beans. A zesty lime dressing complements fragrant cilantro and juicy tomatoes. You can use canned black beans, frozen peas, and frozen corn kernels.

MAKES ABOUT 8 CUPS

- ½ cup olive oil
- 2 large garlic cloves, minced or crushed through a press
- 1 or 2 fresh jalapeño chilies, minced
  (partially seeded to remove heat, if desired)
- 2 teaspoons ground cumin
- 1 teaspoon dried oregano, crumbled
- 3 cups fresh or frozen corn kernels
- 1 teaspoon salt
- 1½ cups shelled fresh or frozen green peas
- 2 cans (16 ounces each) black beans, drained;
  or 3 cups cooked black beans
- 2 medium tomatoes, cut into ½-inch dice
- ½ cup sliced whole scallions or chopped purple onion
- ⅓ cup chopped fresh cilantro
- 1 tablespoon Dijon mustard
- ½ teaspoon black pepper
- ¼ cup fresh lime or lemon juice

1. Spoon 2 tablespoons of the olive oil into a large heavy skillet set over moderate heat. Add the garlic, jalapeños, cumin, and oregano and sauté until fragrant, about 30 seconds. Add the corn, toss, increase the heat to moderately high, and sauté for 2 minutes. Pour in ½ cup water, cover, and cook for 2 minutes. Turn the mixture into a large bowl and add the salt. Toss and set aside to cool to room temperature.

2. Drop the peas into a small pot of lightly salted boiling water and cook until tender, 3 to 5 minutes for fresh, 2 minutes for frozen. Rinse under cold water. Add the peas to the salad, along with the black beans, tomatoes, scallions, and cilantro.

3. Make a dressing by stirring together the mustard, pepper, and lime juice. Gradually whisk in the remaining ¼ cup plus 2 tablespoons olive oil. Pour over the salad and toss thoroughly. Cover and chill for at least 1 hour. Serve cold.

Shanghai Hot & Cold, Sweet & Sour Cabbage

Some version of this cold, stir-fried, saladlike dish is always part of the appetizer selection in Shanghai restaurants. But it is also at home alongside barbecued menus and on picnics. I like it so much and it's so inexpensive to make that I find myself putting it together quite frequently.

MAKES ABOUT 8 CUPS

- 3 tablespoons rice vinegar
- 2 tablespoons fresh lemon juice
- 2 tablespoons dry sherry or rice wine
- 2 tablespoons sugar
- 2 tablespoons Oriental sesame oil
- 1 teaspoon salt
- 3 tablespoons peanut oil or other vegetable oil
- 1 tablespoon minced fresh ginger
- 1 large garlic clove, minced or crushed through a press
- $\frac{1}{2}$ teaspoon dried red pepper flakes
- $\frac{1}{2}$ red bell pepper, trimmed and cut into julienne
- 1 carrot, peeled and cut into julienne
- 1 large head (2 pounds) napa cabbage,
    cut into $1\frac{1}{2}$- to 2-inch squares (12 to 14 lightly packed cups)

1. In a small bowl, stir together the rice vinegar, lemon juice, sherry, sugar, sesame oil, and salt. Set the sweet-and-sour mixture aside.
2. Place a large wok or Dutch oven over high heat until very hot. Add the peanut oil and swirl to coat the pan. Add the ginger, garlic, and hot pepper flakes and stir-fry for 5 to 10 seconds, until fragrant but not browned. Add the bell pepper and carrot julienne and stir-fry for 10 seconds. Add the cabbage and stir-fry for $1\frac{1}{2}$ to 2 minutes, or until slightly wilted but still crisp. Pour in the sweet-and-sour mixture and stir-fry for about 30 minutes, or until the cabbage is coated and seasoned. Turn out onto a large platter and let cool to room temperature. Transfer to a bowl, cover, and refrigerate until well chilled, tossing once or twice. Serve cold.

RICE VINEGAR

I always keep more than a dozen different varieties of vinegar in my kitchen cupboard, but I use more rice vinegar than any other kind. I love its light, tangy taste. It is fragrant, sweet, and refreshing, and since it is so light (both in color and character), you can use a little more than you would of any of the stronger vinegars. I often use rice vinegar for salads and marinades, and of course, for sweet-and-sour sauces and hot-and-sour soups.

ORIENTAL SESAME OIL

Adding a little of this big-flavored oil to dishes gives them an automatic Oriental authenticity. The deep amber-colored oil is pressed from roasted sesame seeds and has a pronounced nutty flavor. Don't buy the clear cold-pressed sesame oil and expect the same flavor—that one is made from untoasted seeds. Oriental sesame oil is used primarily as a seasoning rather than a cooking oil.

To appreciate its flavor to the fullest, add sesame oil at the end of cooking, just before serving. Many soups will benefit from a few drops. Sesame oil has a low smoking point and much of its flavor cooks out when heated. Kodoya is a consistently good brand to look for. Store it in the refrigerator for the longest shelf life.

Anchovy Vinaigrette

Use this bold salad dressing for the Niçoise Salad on page 81 or for any green salad you may toss together. It's wonderful alongside cold seafood salads.

MAKES ABOUT 1 CUP

    1 large garlic clove, minced or crushed through a press
    1 tablespoon anchovy paste
    1 tablespoon Dijon mustard
  $\frac{1}{4}$ teaspoon black pepper
  $\frac{1}{8}$ teaspoon cayenne pepper
    3 tablespoons fresh lemon juice
  $\frac{2}{3}$ cup extra-virgin olive oil
    2 tablespoons finely chopped fresh parsley

In a large bowl, mash the garlic into the anchovy paste and mustard. Stir in the black pepper, cayenne, and then the lemon juice. Gradually whisk in the olive oil until creamy. Stir in the parsley. Serve right away or cover and chill. If making ahead, whisk again before serving.

Sherry Vinaigrette

This tart and tangy salad dressing has a sharp sherry flavor mellowed by fruity green olive oil. I recall the early 1970s, when the first bottles of sherry vinegar were imported to New York from Spain. Now you can find them in practically any food shop.

MAKES ABOUT 1¼ CUPS

- **2 teaspoons Dijon mustard**
- **½ teaspoon dry mustard**
- **½ teaspoon dried oregano**
- **½ teaspoon dried basil**
- **¼ teaspoon dried thyme**
- **¼ teaspoon dried tarragon**
- **¼ teaspoon ground cumin**
- **½ teaspoon salt**
- **½ teaspoon black pepper**
- **¼ cup sherry vinegar**
- **2 tablespoons dry sherry**
- **½ cup extra-virgin olive oil**
- **⅓ cup flavorless vegetable oil**

Combine the Dijon and dry mustard in a deep medium bowl. Crumble in the oregano, basil, thyme, and tarragon. Add the cumin, salt, and pepper. Stir in the vinegar and the sherry. Gradually whisk in the olive oil and the vegetable oil. If making ahead, store in a tightly covered jar in the refrigerator and shake well before using.

VARIATIONS

Bigger flavor: Instead of using dried herbs, mince 2 to 3 tablespoons of fresh herbs—all one kind or any variety of those listed above.

Bigger flavor: For a spicier dressing, add ½ teaspoon cayenne pepper along with the salt and black pepper.

Russian Dressing

This delicious dressing is a requirement for the Reuben Sandwich on page 192, but is also superb with any salad. It has an affinity for California avocados and is also delicious with chopped chicken livers on rye bread.

MAKES ABOUT 1 CUP

- ½ **cup mayonnaise**
- ½ **cup homemade Chili Sauce (page 377) or Heinz bottled chili sauce**
- 1 **tablespoon drained prepared horseradish**
- 1 **teaspoon fresh lemon juice**
- 1 **teaspoon Worcestershire sauce**
- ¼ **teaspoon salt**
- ⅛ **teaspoon pepper**

In a medium bowl, stir the mayonnaise with a fork or a whisk until smooth. Add all of the remaining ingredients and stir to blend. Serve, or cover and chill.

Blue Cheese Dressing

This chunky-creamy dressing has a grand blue cheese flavor, mellowed with a splash of white wine. It is lighter than all those mayonnaise-based versions because it is made with sour cream and yogurt. It's an easy recipe to cut in half if you should happen to want less.

MAKES ABOUT 3 CUPS

- 1 **large garlic clove, halved crosswise**
- 8 **ounces crumbly blue cheese, crumbled (about 2 cups)**
- 1 **cup sour cream**
- 1 **cup low-fat plain yogurt**
- ¼ **cup mayonnaise**
- 1 **tablespoon dry white wine or vermouth**
- ½ **teaspoon salt**
- ¼ **teaspoon black pepper**

1. Score the cut side of each garlic half in a small crosshatch pattern with a sharp knife; rub the interior of a large bowl with the halves. Discard the garlic.
2. Place the crumbled cheese in the bowl and mash in the sour cream with a fork, leaving it slightly lumpy. Stir in the yogurt, mayonnaise, wine, salt, and pepper. Serve right away, or cover and refrigerate for several days.

Creamy Italian Dressing

This dressing has big, full flavor that's especially good on Uncle Bob's Antipasto Salad (page 86). It will taste best if made at least a day ahead. Use it as a dressing for simple salads or as a delicious marinade for grilled swordfish.

MAKES ABOUT 1½ CUPS

- 2 teaspoons dried oregano
- 2 teaspoons dried basil
- ½ teaspoon dried thyme
- ½ teaspoon dried rosemary
- 1 teaspoon salt
- ½ teaspoon coarsely ground black pepper
- ¼ cup red wine vinegar
- 1 tablespoon fresh lemon juice
- ¼ cup mayonnaise
- ¾ cup extra-virgin olive oil
- ⅓ cup freshly grated Parmesan cheese

Crumble the oregano, basil, thyme, and rosemary into a medium bowl. Stir in the salt, pepper, vinegar, and lemon juice. Whisk in the mayonnaise and then gradually whisk in the olive oil. Stir in the Parmesan cheese. Transfer to a jar with a tight-fitting lid and store in the refrigerator. Shake well before using.

Greek Feta Dressing

This zesty dressing is perfect over almost every salad; that is, except the Greek Salad on page 78—too much feta. Try it over romaine lettuce and other crunchy greens, with tomatoes and cucumbers, and with black olives. Make it a day ahead so the flavors of the feta and garlic have time to mingle.

MAKES ABOUT 1¼ CUPS

- 4 ounces Greek feta cheese, crumbled (about 1 cup)
- 1 large garlic clove, minced or crushed through a press
- ¼ cup fresh lemon juice
- 1½ teaspoons dried oregano, crumbled
- ½ teaspoon black pepper
- ½ cup extra-virgin olive oil

Crumble the feta cheese into a large bowl. Add the garlic and the lemon juice and mash the cheese into the lemon juice with a fork. Add the oregano and pepper and stir to combine. Gradually whisk in the olive oil. Whisk in 2 tablespoons cold water. Transfer to a jar with a tight-fitting lid and refrigerate for 24 hours. Shake well before using.

Garlic Croutons

Homemade croutons taste best. Start with good, firm white bread. These flavorful toasted cubes are a requirement for Gazpacho (page 52) or Caesar Salad (page 82), but can also be used for any other soup or salad.

MAKES ABOUT 2½ CUPS

> 3 **tablespoons olive oil**
> 2 **large garlic cloves, minced**
>   **Pinch of salt**
> 3 **cups fresh bread cubes (½ inch)**

1. Spoon the olive oil into a large, heavy skillet, but do not place it over the heat yet.
2. Combine the garlic with a pinch of salt and mash to a paste with the side of a chef's knife (or put it through a garlic press). Add it to the oil and place the pan over low heat. From the moment the garlic begins to sizzle, cook for 30 seconds. Add the bread cubes and toss to coat with the oil. Cook over low heat, tossing occasionally, until crisp, golden brown, and crunchy, about 20 to 30 minutes. Drain and cool on paper towels.

VARIATIONS

Substitution: **Use whole wheat bread instead of white.**

Substitution: **If desired, toast the cubes in butter instead of olive oil.**

Substitution: **To make herb croutons, add 1 teaspoon crumbled dried herbs in place of the garlic (half oregano and half rosemary is a good combination).**

Pastas, Noodles,

Spaghetti Western

Spaghetti alla Puttanesca

Linguine with White Clam Sauce

Linguine with Shrimp Sauce

Pasta Shells with Creamy Prosciutto Sauce

Bowties with Arugula and Smoked Ham

Peppered Pasta with Lemon

and Dumplings

Veal and Mushroom Cannelloni

Gorgonzola-Stuffed Shells

Creamy Baked Ziti with Beef and Mushrooms

Pesto Lasagne

Peter Piper's Macaroni and Cheese

Toasted Macaroni with Mushrooms

Malaysian Cellophane Noodles

Singapore Rice Noodles

Cool Sesame Noodles with Jade Cucumbers

Cold Chicken Wontons in Sesame Sauce

Cilantro Pasta Wontons

Homemade Egg Pasta

Basic Ravioli

Chicken-Basil Ravioli Filling

Salmon Ravioli Filling

Pesto Ravioli Filling

Mushroom-Porcini Ravioli Filling

Bonus Recipe

Eggroll Skins for Stuffed Pasta

Spaghetti Western

The great Mexican flavors of tomatoes, chilies, and cilantro marry well with Italian pasta. I like to use thin spaghetti or linguine for this dish. Good, juicy summer tomatoes make it extra-special.

MAKES 2 SERVINGS

> 1 tablespoon butter
> 1 tablespoon olive oil
> 1 fresh jalapeño chili, thinly sliced
> 1 large garlic clove, minced or crushed through a press
> 2 large ripe tomatoes, peeled (page 15), cut into ½-inch dice
> 8 ounces thin spaghetti or linguine
> ½ teaspoon salt
> ⅛ teaspoon black pepper
> ¼ cup finely chopped fresh cilantro
>   Freshly grated Parmesan cheese, for topping

1. Bring a large pot of lightly salted water to a boil over high heat.
2. In a nonreactive large, heavy skillet, melt the butter with the oil over moderate heat. Add the jalapeño and garlic and sauté for 30 seconds. Add the tomatoes and cook until fragrant, 3 minutes. Remove from the heat.
3. Drop the spaghetti into the boiling water and stir constantly until the water returns to a boil. Cook, stirring frequently, until the pasta is tender but firm to the bite. Drain in a colander. Toss with the sauce, adding the salt, pepper, and cilantro. Serve right away, topped with the cheese.

JALAPEÑO CHILI PEPPERS

Available fresh, dried (known as chipotles when smoked and dried), canned, or pickled, jalapeños are the best-known and most widely available chilies.

The thick, blunt-ended chilies are 1½ to 2 inches long and range in color from bright green to dark green, to green with blotches of orange, to bright red. They have a sharp, penetrating herbal fragrance and juicy-hot clean chili flavor. Their heat intensity can range from hot to very hot. For less heat, remove part or all of the seeds and ribs. To do this, quarter lengthwise and slice off the seeds and ribs.

Buy smooth, firm chilies and store them in a plastic bag in the refrigerator. When soft or wrinkled they begin to lose their flavor and potency.

Jalapeños are perfect for pickling and add great flavor to guacamole, sauces, stuffings, and casseroles.

PECORINO ROMANO

This sharp Italian grating cheese is practically as old as Rome itself. Made from sheep's milk and aged for three to nine months, it is stronger, zestier, and less "refined" than Parmesan.

Romano is aggressively pungent so it can hold its own when used with robust seasonings like chili peppers and anchovies. A little is usually added to punctuate the flavor of pesto.

This hard cheese can range in color from creamy-white to deep golden, has a fine crumbly dry texture, and is almost always grated. It is salty and contributes a bold, nippy quality to pasta.

Store Pecorino Romano as you would Parmesan (see page 107) and grate it just before using.

Spaghetti alla Puttanesca

This lively dish, named a long time ago for the Italian ladies of the night, is one of my favorite pastas. Its big flavor comes from a combination of anchovies and anchovy paste, oil-cured black olives, hot peppers, tomato, garlic, and Parmesan cheese with a good handful of parsley. If you chop and measure everything early in the day, the dish can be thrown together in the time it takes to cook the spaghetti.

MAKES 3 TO 4 SERVINGS

 3 tablespoons extra-virgin olive oil
 1 large garlic clove, minced or crushed through a press
 ¼ cup plus 2 tablespoons chopped fresh parsley
 1 large fresh or pickled jalapeño chili, finely chopped,
    or ½ teaspoon dried red pepper flakes
 ¼ cup packed finely chopped pitted oil-cured black olives
 1 can (2 ounces) flat anchovy fillets, drained and chopped
 2 teaspoons anchovy paste
 1 can (28 ounces) whole tomatoes, drained, seeded,
    and coarsely chopped
 12 ounces thin spaghetti
 4 tablespoons freshly grated Parmesan cheese

1. Bring a large pot of lightly salted water to a boil over high heat.
2. Meanwhile, spoon 2 tablespoons of the olive oil into a nonreactive medium skillet and set over low heat. Add the garlic and sizzle gently until softened, 1 to 2 minutes. Add ¼ cup of the parsley and the jalapeño, increase the

heat to moderate, and sauté for 1 to 2 minutes. Add the olives, anchovies, and anchovy paste and cook, stirring, for 2 minutes. Add the tomatoes and cook for 2 minutes. Remove from the heat and keep warm.

3. Drop the spaghetti into the boiling water and stir constantly until the water returns to a boil. Boil until tender but firm to the bite, 8 to 10 minutes. Drain.

4. Combine the pasta, sauce, and 2 tablespoons of the Parmesan in a very large bowl and toss. Serve on a shallow platter or in individual dishes, drizzled with the remaining 1 tablespoon olive oil and sprinkled with the remaining 2 tablespoons each of parsley and Parmesan.

Linguine with White Clam Sauce

Italian cookbook author and teacher Marcella Hazan taught me to add butter and Parmesan cheese to this famous clam sauce, a combination rarely used in other Italian clam dishes. The result is sensational.

MAKES 2 MAIN-COURSE OR 4 PASTA-COURSE SERVINGS

2 dozen small littleneck clams in their shells, scrubbed and rinsed well
3 tablespoons extra-virgin olive oil
⅓ cup finely chopped shallots or onion
2 large garlic cloves, minced or crushed through a press
½ teaspoon dried oregano, crumbled
¼ to ½ teaspoon dried red pepper flakes
½ cup dry white wine
8 ounces dried linguine
¼ cup finely chopped Italian flat-leaf parsley, plus more, for serving
¼ cup coarsely grated Parmesan cheese, plus more, for serving
1½ tablespoons butter

1. Put the clams in a large, heavy pot, cover, and place over high heat. Cook until the clams open, 3 to 5 minutes. As they open, remove the clams to a colander set over a bowl to catch any juice. Let stand until cool enough to handle. Working over the bowl of clam juice, pry open the clams and scoop out the clam meat with a spoon. Place the clams in the juice as you remove them. Discard any clams that cannot be easily pried open.

2. One at a time, swish around the clams in the juice to rinse off any sand and reserve. Pour the clam juice through a fine sieve into a measuring cup; you

will need ¾ cup strained clam juice. Chop the clams; cover with plastic wrap and set aside.

3. Bring a large pot of lightly salted water to a boil over high heat.

4. Meanwhile, in a nonreactive heavy saucepan, combine 2 tablespoons of the olive oil and the shallots or onion. Place over moderate heat and sauté, stirring frequently, until the shallots or onion pieces are translucent, about 5 minutes. Stir in the garlic, oregano, and ¼ teaspoon of the red pepper flakes and sauté for 2 minutes. Pour in the wine and bring to a boil over moderate heat. Cook until reduced by half, 3 to 5 minutes. Add the ¾ cup clam juice and boil over moderate heat until reduced by about one-third, 3 to 5 minutes. Taste and add ¼ teaspoon more red pepper flakes, if you like. Remove from the heat.

5. When the pot of water comes to a full, rolling boil, drop in the linguine and stir constantly until the water returns to a boil. Cook, stirring frequently, until tender but firm to the bite, 8 to 10 minutes. Drain. Transfer the pasta to a large bowl and toss with the remaining 1 tablespoon olive oil.

6. Meanwhile, place the sauce over moderate heat and bring to a boil. Reduce the heat to low, stir in the clams, and cook for 2 minutes. Remove the sauce from the heat and stir in ¼ cup of the parsley and ¼ cup of the grated Parmesan. Stir in the butter until it melts. Transfer the pasta to a platter, pour on the sauce, and toss. Sprinkle with the additional parsley and Parmesan and serve right away.

PARMESAN CHEESE

I'm surprised that you can still buy those round cardboard containers of pregrated, so-called Parmesan cheese in the supermarket. But since you can, I think it's worth noting just how much is missing from such products.

Cheese begins losing flavor shortly after it has been grated, so it's not a good idea to buy any cheese that has been grated in advance. But even more troublesome is that you don't know what they are grating when they label it "Parmesan." Some good Italian markets grate Parmesan on a daily basis, and I find this to be quite acceptable, though you lose that first burst of aroma that comes with grating by hand.

Authentic Parmesan cheese is labeled *Parmigiano Reggiano* and must be made in or near Parma, Italy. It is best purchased in a wedge that contains part of the rind, which will always be branded with the words *Parmigiano Reggiano.*

True Parmigiano Reggiano will be pale golden in color, not white, and will have a tangy-pungent, well-aged aroma with a background fragrance of a grassy meadow on a rainy day. The cheese has been aged for at least eighteen months and should have a deep, penetrating salty flavor and complex buttery dimension. It should leave no bitter aftertaste.

To store Parmigiano Reggiano, wrap the wedge in several layers of damp cheesecloth or paper towels and then put it into a plastic bag and keep it in the refrigerator, unwrapping, grating, and rewrapping as you use it.

Linguine with Shrimp Sauce

This dish was born one day when linguine with red clam sauce was on my mind. The idea of using ground shrimp instead of clams occurred to me and I headed straight for the fish market to buy a pound of shrimp. As soon as I got home, I concocted this saucy seafood and pasta dish.

MAKES 4 MAIN-COURSE OR 8 PASTA-COURSE SERVINGS

- 3 tablespoons extra-virgin olive oil
- 1 cup chopped shallots or onion
- 2 large garlic cloves, minced or crushed through a press
- 2 bay leaves
- 1 teaspoon dried oregano, crumbled
- 1 teaspoon dried basil, crumbled
- ½ teaspoon dried red pepper flakes
- ¼ teaspoon dried rosemary, crushed
- 1 tablespoon all-purpose flour
- 1 bottle (8 ounces) clam juice
- ½ cup plus 2 tablespoons dry white wine
- 1 can (28 ounces) peeled whole tomatoes, chopped with their juices
- 2 tablespoons tomato paste
- 1 tablespoon sugar
- 2 teaspoons salt
- ¼ teaspoon black pepper
- 1 pound linguine or thin spaghetti
- 1 pound medium shrimp, shelled and deveined
- ½ cup chopped fresh parsley
- 1 tablespoon butter
- 1 tablespoon fresh lemon juice
- Freshly grated Parmesan cheese (optional)

1. Spoon the olive oil into a nonreactive large saucepan set over moderate heat. Add the shallots, garlic, bay leaves, oregano, basil, red pepper flakes, and rosemary and sauté until softened, about 5 minutes. Stir in the flour and cook for 1 minute. Pour in the clam juice and ½ cup of the white wine; stirring constantly, bring to a boil. Cook until thickened slightly, about 5 minutes.

2. Stir in the tomatoes and their juices, the tomato paste, sugar, salt, and pepper. Bring to a boil over moderate heat. Reduce the heat to low and simmer gently, stirring frequently, for about 30 minutes to blend the flavors and thicken slightly.

3. Meanwhile, bring a large pot of lightly salted water to a boil. When the sauce is almost done, add the linguine and cook until tender but firm to the bite. Drain.

4. While the pasta cooks, cut the shrimp in half and pulse in a food processor until coarsely ground. Add the shrimp and the remaining 2 tablespoons wine to the sauce and cook just until the shrimp turn opaque, about 1 minute. Remove from the heat and stir in $\frac{1}{4}$ cup of the parsley, the butter, and the lemon juice. In a large bowl, combine the pasta and sauce and toss well. To serve, top each portion with a little of the remaining chopped parsley and pass the Parmesan.

Pasta Shells
with Creamy Prosciutto Sauce

This is a simple throw-together pasta dish given a wallop of big flavor by prosciutto. If there is time, make the sauce an hour or two ahead and then reheat it for the biggest flavor of all. The ricotta adds richness and creaminess, and the shells scoop up bits of the prosciutto and cheese. If this is a pasta course, serve it with a lighter meat dish, such as chicken, turkey, veal, or seafood.

MAKES 4 TO 8 SERVINGS

>   2 tablespoons olive oil
>   2 large garlic cloves, minced or crushed through a press
>   1 teaspoon dried oregano, crumbled
> $1\frac{1}{2}$ pounds whole-milk ricotta cheese
> $\frac{1}{2}$ cup dry white wine
> $\frac{1}{2}$ teaspoon salt
> $\frac{1}{4}$ teaspoon grated nutmeg
> $\frac{1}{4}$ teaspoon black pepper
>   8 ounces thinly sliced (not paper-thin) prosciutto,
>   cut into $\frac{1}{2}$-inch squares
> $\frac{1}{2}$ cup thinly sliced whole scallions
> $\frac{1}{2}$ cup chopped fresh parsley
>   1 pound medium pasta shells
> $\frac{1}{2}$ cup freshly grated Parmesan cheese

1. If you are not making the sauce in advance, bring a large pot of lightly salted water to a boil.

2. Spoon the olive oil into a nonreactive large, heavy skillet and add the garlic

and oregano. Place over low heat and sizzle gently until soft but not browned, about 2 minutes. Stir in the ricotta and heat gently until the cheese melts and begins to simmer. Stir in the wine, salt, nutmeg, and pepper and cook until the sauce returns to a simmer. Stir in the prosciutto, scallions, and all but 2 tablespoons of the parsley and cook for 1 to 2 minutes. Remove from the heat. (If making ahead, reheat gently before adding the Parmesan and pasta.)

3. Drop the pasta shells into the boiling salted water and stir constantly until the water returns to a boil. Cook, stirring frequently, until the pasta is tender but firm to the bite, 12 to 14 minutes. Drain, shaking well in a colander.

4. Toss the shells until coated with the hot sauce. Add the Parmesan, toss, and serve right away, sprinkled with the reserved 2 tablespoons parsley. If the sauce should become dry, add a little milk or wine. A bit more salt may be needed too, depending on the saltiness of the Parmesan and prosciutto.

Bowties with Arugula and Smoked Ham

In this recipe, the peppery arugula, smoked ham, and sweet leeks mingle with the tomato to punctuate the pasta. The dish is best served right after assembling.

MAKES 6 TO 8 SERVINGS

   3 tablespoons extra-virgin olive oil
   8 ounces smoked ham, sliced ¼ inch thick and cut into 1-inch triangles
   2 large leeks, trimmed, well-washed, halved, and cut into ¼-inch slices
   ⅓ cup chopped shallots or onion
   2 large garlic cloves, minced or crushed through a press
   1 cup dry white wine

1 **teaspoon salt**
¼ **teaspoon pepper**
1 **can (16 ounces) peeled tomatoes, drained and coarsely chopped**
3 **large bunches arugula (about 12 ounces total), washed, dried, stemmed, and coarsely chopped**
¼ **cup chopped fresh basil**
1 **pound bowtie pasta (farfalle)**
Freshly grated Parmesan cheese, for serving

1. Warm 1 tablespoon of the olive oil in a nonreactive large skillet over moderate heat. Add the ham and sauté until lightly browned, 2 to 3 minutes. Scoop out with a slotted spoon and reserve.
2. Add the remaining 2 tablespoons oil to the skillet. Add the leeks, shallots or onion, and garlic and sauté until lightly browned and softened, about 5 minutes. Return the ham to the skillet and add the wine, salt, and pepper. Bring to a boil and cook for 2 minutes. Add the tomatoes and arugula, reduce the heat to low, and simmer for 5 minutes. Remove the pan from the heat and stir in the basil. (The recipe can be made to this point several hours ahead of time.)
3. Bring a large pot of lightly salted water to a boil over high heat. Add the pasta and stir constantly until the water returns to a boil. Cook until tender but firm to the bite, 9 to 11 minutes. Drain well, toss with the warm sauce, and turn out onto a large platter. Top with cheese and serve right away.

ARUGULA AND OTHER BITTER GREENS

Arugula, a luscious bitter salad green, has a hot, peppery flavor with nuances of mustard and radish. It adds flavor, texture, and punctuation to salads, but also retains its robust character when cooked.

Arugula wilts easily and can become waterlogged, so be sure to buy perky, fresh leaves and use them as soon as possible. If it is in good condition, arugula will keep in the refrigerator for a day or two.

Four other favorite bitter greens that give a good kick to the taste buds whether raw or cooked are Belgian endive, chicory (or curly endive), radicchio, and escarole.

Peppered Pasta with Lemon

This light and fragrant side-dish pasta is so simple that you'll find yourself turning to it time and time again. It goes especially well with seafood, chicken, pork, vegetables, veal—just about anything you can imagine. You can use homemade Chicken Stock, which I highly recommend, or canned broth. I like to use double-strength homemade chicken stock, so I reduce 2 cups to the 1 cup called for here. This lemon-pepper sauce is especially appealing with angel hair pasta, vermicelli, thin spaghetti, or thin linguine.

MAKES 4 SIDE-DISH SERVINGS

> 1 tablespoon olive oil
>
> 1½ teaspoons butter
>
> 1 tablespoon all-purpose flour
>
> 1 cup double-strength Chicken Stock (page 73) or canned broth
>
> 3 tablespoons fresh lemon juice
>
> 2 teaspoons minced lemon zest
>
> 8 ounces thin pasta, such as angel hair (capellini), vermicelli, thin spaghetti, or thin linguine
>
> ¼ cup chopped fresh parsley
>
> 1 teaspoon coarse or cracked black pepper
>
> ½ teaspoon salt

1. Bring a large pot of lightly salted water to a boil over high heat.
2. Meanwhile, in a nonreactive heavy saucepan, warm the olive oil and butter over moderate heat. When the butter melts, stir in the flour and cook, stirring constantly, until the flour is toasted golden brown, 2 to 3 minutes. Pour in the chicken stock and continue stirring until it comes to a boil. Reduce the heat and simmer for 1 minute. Stir in the lemon juice and simmer for 1 minute. Remove from the heat and stir in the lemon zest. Keep the sauce warm.
3. Drop the pasta into the boiling water and stir until the water returns to a boil. Cook, stirring frequently, until tender but firm to the bite. Drain the pasta in a colander and turn out onto a large platter. Pour the lemon sauce on top, then sprinkle with the parsley, black pepper, and salt. Toss and serve right away.

LEMONS

Growing up in Southern California in the early 1950s, I had as my playground a fragrant lemon grove with a crisp backdrop of snowcapped mountains. It was there that I played hide-and-seek, learned to make lemonade that had pucker-power, and later, kissed my first girlfriend. Back then, wooden crates with brightly colored packing labels could be seen neatly stacked at the loading dock of the nearby railway station in downtown Covina, in the San Gabriel Valley. In those days, shortly before tract homes and freeways replaced the stunningly beautiful lemon groves, Covina was one of the biggest citrus-growing centers in this country.

A patchwork of lemon trees embroidered its way up to the mountain foothills, and nearby Foothill Boulevard (better known to outsiders as Route 66) was strictly off-limits. Nevertheless, my little friends and I frequently could be seen sitting at our rickety roadside stand selling lemons and lemonade to thirsty passersby. The sunny climate was almost ideal—for kids and for lemons.

Although some of us tend to idealize childhood memories, the tree-ripened fruit I squeezed for juice back then really did taste better. Today's lemons sold in the market are picked while still green and then cured and ripened further in climate-controlled warehouses. And although the flavor from tree-ripened fruit is superior, these man-managed ripening procedures result in better-looking lemons that last longer.

The bright yellow outer layer, called the zest, contains essential oils that add lemon flavor and fragrance without the tartness that comes with lemon juice. Tart and tangy lemon juice goes far beyond Old-Fashioned Lemonade (page 197). It is a vigorous appetite stimulant, and its versatility ranges from squeezing a zesty wedge over simple seafood or vegetables for heightening flavor to becoming the star in such luscious dishes as Peppered Pasta with Lemon. Paired with limes, it makes a light and refreshing old-fashioned dessert, the Lemon-Lime Meringue Pie on page 336. Because of their high acid and pectin content, lemons are useful in making jam, jelly, and marmalade as well.

While those fragrant lemon groves from my childhood are gone from my life, they are still a part of my dreams and the citrus-perfumed lemon with its zesty flavor remains.

Veal and Mushroom Cannelloni

Here is an especially delicious dish, one that's perfect for entertaining. It is rich and filling and full of flavor and texture. The tender veal in the filling is enhanced best with dried porcini and fresh mushrooms. The filling seems to bounce against the homemade pasta, and the cannelloni are bathed with mellow cream sauce and robust Red-Hot Bolognese Sauce. Make the Bolognese sauce a day, or even a week, ahead. You can store it in the freezer. Make the pasta a day ahead, if desired.

MAKES 8 SERVINGS

Homemade Egg Pasta dough (about 1 pound; page 137), made with 3 eggs

3 **cups Red-Hot Bolognese Sauce (page 357)**

Veal Filling (Makes about 5 cups)

½ **ounce dried porcini or cèpes**

2 **tablespoons olive oil**

1 **large onion, finely chopped**

2 **large garlic cloves, minced or crushed through a press**

½ **teaspoon dried thyme or oregano, crumbled**

¼ **teaspoon grated nutmeg**

½ **teaspoon salt**

¼ **teaspoon black pepper**

1½ **pounds ground veal**

½ **cup minced smoked ham**

8 **ounces fresh mushrooms, finely chopped**

½ **cup chopped fresh parsley**

2 **tablespoons all-purpose flour**

½ **cup dry white wine**

2 **tablespoons tomato paste**

1½ **cups whole-milk ricotta cheese**

¾ **cup freshly grated Parmesan cheese**

1 **large egg**

Cream Sauce

4 **tablespoons (½ stick) butter**

⅓ **cup all-purpose flour**

2½ **cups milk**

½ **cup dry white wine**

½ **teaspoon grated nutmeg**

1 **teaspoon salt**

Assembly

½ **cup freshly grated Parmesan cheese**

1. If you have made the pasta dough ahead of time and stored it in the refrigerator, let it come to room temperature before rolling it out. The pasta should be rolled after the filling and sauces are made. If you have made the Red-Hot Bolognese Sauce ahead of time, heat it gently before using. Lightly oil two 13 × 9-inch baking pans.

2. To make the veal filling, put the porcini in a small bowl and add ½ cup of boiling water. Set aside to soak for 30 to 60 minutes, until softened. Drain, reserving the liquid. Finely chop the porcini. Strain the soaking liquid through a fine-mesh sieve.

3. Spoon the olive oil into a large, heavy skillet set over moderate heat. Add the onion and sauté until softened and lightly colored, about 5 minutes. Add the garlic and thyme and sauté for 2 minutes. Sprinkle on the nutmeg, salt, and pepper. Crumble in the veal and sauté, breaking up the meat with a spoon, until lightly browned, about 5 minutes. Add the ham and fresh mushrooms and sauté for 3 to 4 minutes. Stir in the parsley and porcini and cook for 3 minutes. Sprinkle on the flour and stir to moisten. Pour in the wine, the strained porcini liquid, and the tomato paste and cook, stirring, until thick, 1 to 2 minutes. Turn the filling into a large bowl and set aside to cool to room temperature. When cool, stir in the ricotta, Parmesan, and egg.

4. To make the cream sauce, melt the butter in a heavy, medium saucepan over moderate heat. Add the flour and cook, stirring, for 2 to 3 minutes; the mixture will be dry. Pour in the milk and cook, stirring constantly, until thickened and the mixture comes to a simmer. Stir in the wine, nutmeg, and salt. Reduce the heat to low and simmer, stirring frequently, until the sauce is very thick, 3 to 4 minutes. Spread ¼ cup of the sauce into each of the 2 prepared pans.

5. Preheat the oven to 400° F. Put a very large pot of lightly salted water on to boil over high heat. Roll out the pasta according to the instructions on page 138 and cut into 36 to 40 rectangles, each 3 × 4 inches.

6. Each piece of pasta should cook for only about 10 seconds. Cook the pasta, 4 to 6 at a time, counting the 10 seconds. Scoop out and immediately plunge the pasta into a large bowl of cold water. Remove and drain in a single layer on sheets of paper towels. As the water in the bowl becomes warm, replenish with cold water. Continue cooking the pasta in batches until all is cooked.

7. In assembling the cannelloni, work on a plate or small board with one at a time. Spread each pasta rectangle with about 2 tablespoons of the filling, leaving a ½-inch border all around. Starting with one short end, loosely roll up. As they are done, arrange the cannelloni in 2 lengthwise rows of 10, a total of 20 in each pan.

8. Spoon 1½ cups of the heated Red-Hot Bolognese Sauce over the cannelloni in each pan. Then sprinkle ¼ cup of the Parmesan over the cannelloni in each pan. Bake on separate shelves until bubbly and golden brown, 15 to 20 minutes, reversing the pans, if necessary, to brown evenly. Let stand for 10 minutes before serving. Serve hot.

VARIATIONS

Substitution: Use ground chicken or beef in place of the veal.

Simpler: If they're available, buy prerolled pasta sheets. You can also use commercial Bolognese sauce; just spice it up with a bit of hot pepper flakes.

Gorgonzola-Stuffed Shells

The gentle flavor of the traditional ricotta filling gets a big lift from Gorgonzola. This is a flexible dish because you can make it a couple days ahead. Serve as a hearty vegetarian entrée or pasta course, and you'll like it as a good midnight snack, too.

MAKES 6 TO 8 SERVINGS

      4 cups Simple Fragrant Tomato Sauce (page 355,
            or any of the tomato sauces on pages 356–359)
    1½ pounds whole-milk ricotta cheese (3 cups)
      8 ounces Gorgonzola cheese, crumbled (about 2 cups)
      4 ounces whole-milk mozzarella, grated (1 cup)
      ¾ cup freshly grated Parmesan cheese
      ½ cup chopped fresh parsley
      1 large egg
      ¼ teaspoon grated nutmeg
      ½ teaspoon salt
      ¼ teaspoon black pepper
      1 box (12 ounces) jumbo pasta shells (36 to 40)
      2 tablespoons olive oil

1. Pour the tomato sauce into a nonreactive saucepan and bring to a simmer over moderate heat. Turn off the heat and reserve.

2. Preheat the oven to 350° F. Lightly oil two 13 × 9 × 2-inch baking pans. Spread ½ cup of the sauce in each pan. Put a large pot of lightly salted water over high heat and bring to a boil. If the water boils before you are ready to cook the shells, cover the pot and reduce the heat to low.

3. In a large bowl, combine the ricotta, Gorgonzola, mozzarella, ½ cup of the Parmesan, the parsley, egg, nutmeg, salt, and pepper. Stir until well blended.

4. Drop the shells into the boiling water and stir frequently with a slotted spoon (a fork would pierce the shells) until the water returns to a boil. Boil, stirring frequently to prevent sticking, until tender but firm to the bite, 9 to 10 minutes. Drain and rinse briefly under cool water.

5. Stuff each shell with about 2 scant tablespoonfuls of the filling, squeezing gently and reshaping if necessary so the pasta resembles a shell again. Arrange 18 to 20 stuffed shells in each pan. Spoon half of the remaining tomato sauce over the shells, using 1½ cups for each pan. Divide the remaining ¼ cup grated Parmesan between the pans. Drizzle 1 tablespoon of the olive oil over the shells in each pan.

6. Bake the shells, uncovered, for about 30 minutes, or until hot and bubbly; or cover and refrigerate. (Bake the cold stuffed shells at 350° F. for 40 to 45 minutes.)

GORGONZOLA

This sharp and creamy blue cheese is named for the small town north of Milan where it originated. The very best Gorgonzola is aged in the grottos and caves of the Valsassina.

Gorgonzola is made in layers. Although it is called a blue cheese, the flecks of color are actually more green. The cheese is sharp and creamy and milder than blue cheeses like Roquefort. The categories of Gorgonzola range from *dolce* (sweet) to *piccante* (sharp). The mild, younger dolce Gorgonzola is aged just 90 to 150 days. There is a third category, called White Gorgonzola (Pannarone), that is lighter and sweeter and aged just 60 days. Gorgonzola is often served as a dessert cheese.

VARIATIONS

Lower calorie: To lower the fat and cholesterol content, use part-skim ricotta and mozzarella and omit the olive oil that is drizzled over the top.

Substitutions: Chopped basil can be used in place of the parsley and any crumbly blue cheese can be used in place of the Gorgonzola.

Creamy Baked Ziti with Beef and Mushrooms

This is a big, hearty pasta casserole bubbling over with creamy cheese sauce (made from four cheeses). The beefy mushroom filling is flavored with tomato, in good contrast to the creamy sauce.

MAKES 8 SERVINGS

- 1½ tablespoons olive oil
- 1 large onion, coarsely chopped
- 2 large garlic cloves, minced or crushed through a press
- 2 teaspoons dried basil, crumbled
- 1 teaspoon dried oregano, crumbled
- 1 pound lean ground beef, such as sirloin or round
- 1 pound fresh mushrooms, sliced
- 1½ cups dry white wine
- 1 can (6 ounces) tomato paste
- 1½ teaspoons salt
- ½ teaspoon black pepper

Creamy Cheese Sauce

- ¼ cup olive oil
- 4 tablespoons (½ stick) butter
- 1 large garlic clove, minced or crushed through a press
- 1 cup all-purpose flour
- 5½ cups milk
- ½ teaspoon grated nutmeg
- ½ cup dry white wine
- 1 cup grated sharp cheddar cheese (4 ounces)
- 1 cup grated Swiss cheese, such as Emmentaler (4 ounces)
- 1 cup grated Monterey Jack or Muenster cheese (4 ounces)
- ¾ cup freshly grated Parmesan cheese (about 4 ounces)
- 1½ teaspoons salt
- ¼ teaspoon black pepper
- 1 pound ziti or ziti rigati

1. Spoon the olive oil into a nonreactive large Dutch oven or casserole and place over moderate heat. Add the onion and sauté until softened, about 5 minutes. If it seems dry, add 1 to 2 tablespoons water and let it boil away. Add the garlic, basil, and oregano and cook for 1 minute. Push the ingredients to one side of the pan. Crumble in the beef and brown well, about 5 minutes. Add the mushrooms and cook for 2 minutes. Stir in the wine, tomato paste, salt, and pepper. Reduce the heat and simmer, stirring occasionally,

for about 20 minutes, to make a thick filling. (This filling may be made a day ahead and stored in the refrigerator.)

2. Preheat the oven to 350° F. Lightly oil a lasagne dish or other large, shallow, 4-quart casserole. Bring a large pot of lightly salted water to a boil over high heat.

3. In a large, heavy Dutch oven or casserole, combine the olive oil, butter, and garlic. Place over moderate heat and stir until the butter melts. Add the flour and cook, stirring constantly, for 2 minutes. Pour in about half the milk and whisk until blended. Pour in the remaining milk and add the nutmeg. Whisk over moderate heat until the sauce comes to a boil. Add the wine, reduce the heat to low, and simmer, stirring or whisking constantly, until thickened, 3 to 4 minutes. Remove from the heat and stir in the cheddar, Swiss, and Monterey Jack cheeses and ½ cup of the Parmesan until melted. Add the salt and pepper. Set aside 1½ cups of the sauce for the top of the casserole.

4. Meanwhile, add the ziti to the boiling water and stir constantly until the water returns to a boil. Cook until tender but firm to the bite, 12 to 14 minutes. Drain in a colander, shaking well. Add the ziti to the cheese sauce and stir so the hollow tubes fill with the sauce.

5. Turn half of the pasta and cheese sauce into the prepared casserole. Spoon on half of the beef and mushroom filling. Spread the remaining pasta mixture over and spoon on the rest of the beef filling. Spoon the reserved cheese over all and sprinkle with the remaining ¼ cup Parmesan. Place on a baking sheet or large sheet of aluminum foil. Bake for 30 to 35 minutes, until bubbly and browned. Serve hot. (If making ahead, reheat the cold casserole at 350° F. for 45 to 60 minutes.)

VARIATION

Lower calorie: **For a lighter version, replace the beef with ground chicken and use low-fat milk in place of the whole milk; you can also use half the amount of cheese called for to make it even lighter. The butter can be replaced with olive oil to cut cholesterol.**

Pesto Lasagne

The sweet bouquet of fresh basil is a perfect partner with a creamy ricotta filling in this lovely layered lasagne. The meat sauce can be prepared several days ahead and refrigerated, or frozen for 6 months.

MAKES 8 SERVINGS

Meat Sauce (Makes 6 cups)

- 2 tablespoons olive oil
- 2 medium onions, finely chopped
- 1 celery rib, finely chopped
- 1 carrot, finely chopped
- 3 large garlic cloves, minced or crushed through a press
- 2 teaspoons dried oregano, crumbled
- ½ teaspoon dried thyme, crumbled
- 2 bay leaves
- 1 pound lean ground beef
- 1 can (28 ounces) crushed tomatoes
- 2 cups full-bodied dry red wine
- 1½ teaspoons salt
- ½ teaspoon black pepper

Cheese Filling

- 2 pounds whole-milk ricotta (about 4 cups)
- 1¼ cups freshly grated Parmesan cheese
- ½ cup chopped fresh parsley
- 1 large egg
- ¼ teaspoon grated nutmeg
- ½ teaspoon salt
- ½ teaspoon black pepper

Pesto

- ¼ cup extra-virgin olive oil
- 2 large garlic cloves, minced or crushed through a press
- 1½ cups lightly packed fresh basil leaves, rinsed
- ¼ cup chopped walnuts
- ¼ cup freshly grated Parmesan cheese
- ¼ teaspoon black pepper

Assembly

- 16 curly-edged lasagne noodles (12 to 14 ounces)
- 1 pound whole-milk mozzarella cheese, coarsely grated (4 cups)

1. To make the meat sauce, spoon the olive oil into a nonreactive large, heavy saucepan set over moderate heat. Add the onions, celery, and carrot and

sauté until softened, 5 to 7 minutes. Add the garlic, oregano, thyme, and bay leaves and cook for 1 to 2 minutes. Crumble in the ground beef, increase the heat to moderately high, and cook until lightly browned. Stir in the tomatoes, wine, salt, and pepper and bring to a boil. Reduce the heat to low and simmer, stirring occasionally, until thickened slightly and reduced to 6 cups, 45 to 60 minutes.

2. To make the cheese filling, reserve $\frac{1}{4}$ cup of the ricotta cheese for the pesto. Turn the remaining ricotta into a large bowl and stir in 1 cup of the Parmesan, the parsley, egg, nutmeg, salt, and pepper until well combined.

3. To make the pesto, pour the olive oil into a small, heavy skillet and set over low heat. Add the garlic and sizzle gently until fragrant but not browned, 1 to 2 minutes. Let cool slightly. In a food processor or blender, combine the basil, garlic oil, walnuts, Parmesan, pepper, and the reserved $\frac{1}{4}$ cup ricotta. Process to a puree.

4. Put a large, wide pot of lightly salted water on to boil over high heat. Preheat the oven to 375° F. Lightly coat a 13 × 9 × 2-inch baking pan with olive oil.

5. When the pot of water comes to a boil, drop in the lasagne noodles one at a time. (You may want to cook a full pound of noodles and later choose the

BASIL

I love fresh basil because I can add it to almost anything and create a bigger flavor. Not only is it delicious and versatile, but a bouquet of it in the kitchen is the best air freshener I know. Its sweet aroma starts the mouth watering with anticipation before the basil even touches the taste buds. Although basil has a dazzling flavor all its own, there are discernible undertones of mint, pepper, licorice, and clove.

Keep basil on hand so you can snip off a few leaves and add instant flavor to any salad, sauce, or pasta concoction. And, of course, it is the star of the pungent green paste called pesto. Fresh basil has more flavor than dried, but the dried version is an important condiment to keep on hand. It is especially wonderful in combination with oregano and thyme.

For flavoring Italian dishes, this aromatic herb's only rival is oregano. A member of the mint family, native to India, Africa, and Asia, basil is a sweet and intense herb that grows profusely in the sun. Both its aroma and its flavor intensify as it matures so the herb will have a stronger flavor in summer than in spring.

The fresher and perkier the basil is when you buy it, the longer it will stay so. I used to keep fresh basil in a plastic bag in the refrigerator, until I discovered that it prefers to be treated like a bouquet of fresh flowers. Now I snip off an inch of the stems and quickly put them in a vase containing about 2 inches of tepid water. Then I enclose the bouquet loosely in a plastic bag to act as a greenhouse (and keep the leaves from drying). I change the water each day and snip off a little more from the stems. Handled this way, the basil stays fresh and perky for about a week.

best 12 to 14 because sometimes they break during cooking.) Boil until tender but still firm, 8 to 10 minutes (the lasagne will bake for 45 minutes or longer and the noodles will finish cooking). Drain the lasagne and rinse in a large bowl of cold water. Drain flat on paper towels.

6. Spread 1 cup of the meat sauce in the prepared pan. Arrange 4 of the lasagne noodles in the pan, slightly overlapping and trim to fit, if necessary. Spoon one-third of the ricotta cheese mixture over the noodles and dab it with one-third of the pesto. Sprinkle one-fourth of the mozzarella on top and spoon on 1 cup of the remaining meat sauce. Repeat the layering 2 more times and top with the last 4 noodles. Spread on 1 cup more sauce, the remaining mozzarella, dab on 1 cup more sauce, and sprinkle the remaining $\frac{1}{4}$ cup Parmesan on top. The pan will be full. Place the pan of lasagne on a large sheet of foil to catch any overflow.

7. Bake in the center of the oven until well browned and bubbly, about 45 minutes. Let stand for at least 20 minutes before cutting. Cut into squares and serve hot.

Peter Piper's Macaroni and Cheese

Pickled peppers add a spark to this old-fashioned casserole. I like it best served right after baking, but it also reheats quite well. I don't use American cheese very often, but a little added to macaroni and cheese makes it creamy.

MAKES 6 SIDE-DISH SERVINGS

- 8 ounces elbow macaroni
- 5 tablespoons butter
- $\frac{1}{2}$ cup all-purpose flour
- 3 cups milk
- $\frac{1}{4}$ teaspoon grated nutmeg
- 1 teaspoon salt
- $\frac{1}{4}$ teaspoon black pepper
- 2 cups (8 ounces) coarsely grated sharp cheddar cheese
- 1 cup (4 ounces) chopped American cheese
- 2 to 3 tablespoons finely chopped homemade Pickled Jalapeños (page 384) or store-bought
- 8 soda crackers, crushed

1. Place a large pot of lightly salted water over high heat and bring to a boil. Meanwhile, preheat the oven to 375° F. Butter a 9-inch square baking pan.
2. When the water boils, add the macaroni and stir constantly until the water returns to a boil. Boil, stirring frequently, until tender, 10 to 14 minutes. (Macaroni and cheese is made with macaroni that is more tender than al dente.) Drain the macaroni in a colander and rinse with cold water.
3. Melt 4 tablespoons of the butter in a large, heavy saucepan over moderate heat. Stir in the flour and cook, stirring, for 1 or 2 minutes. The mixture will be thick. Pour in 1 cup of the milk and stir with a fork to dissolve the flour. Add the remaining 2 cups milk, the nutmeg, salt, and pepper and stir constantly over moderate heat until the sauce thickens and boils. Reduce the heat to low and simmer, stirring frequently, for 2 to 3 minutes. Add the cheddar and American cheeses and stir until melted. Remove from the heat and stir in 2 tablespoons of the jalapeños. Add the macaroni and stir until the sauce fills the pasta. Taste for spiciness and add a tablespoon more chopped jalapeños, if desired. Turn the mixture into the buttered pan.
4. Melt the remaining 1 tablespoon butter in a small saucepan. Add the crushed crackers and toss to coat. Sprinkle the mixture over the macaroni and cheese. Bake until bubbly and golden brown, 25 to 30 minutes. Let stand for 5 minutes and serve hot. (Leftover macaroni and cheese can be reheated in a 350° F. oven for 20 to 30 minutes.)

VARIATIONS

Substitution: **For a smoky version of macaroni and cheese, substitute 2 cups (8 ounces) grated smoked Gouda cheese for the cheddar.**

Substitution: **1 whole or partially seeded fresh jalapeño, minced, can replace the pickled jalapeños.**

Addition: **1 to 1½ cups julienned smoked ham may be added to create a ham and cheese version.**

Toasted Macaroni with Mushrooms

This unorthodox treatment of browning uncooked macaroni in olive oil contributes a wonderful new flavor to the pasta. It is not boiled in the traditional sense; rather, chicken stock is added to plump up the pasta as it makes a sauce.

MAKES 2 TO 4 SERVINGS

> 4   tablespoons extra-virgin olive oil
> 8   ounces fresh mushrooms, thinly sliced
> ¼   cup chopped fresh parsley, plus more, for serving
> 1   large garlic clove, minced or crushed through a press
> 1   teaspoon dried oregano, crumbled
> 1   teaspoon dried basil, crumbled
> ½   cup dry white wine
> 8   ounces elbow macaroni
> 2   cups Chicken Stock (page 73) or canned broth
> ¼   cup light cream
> ⅓   cup freshly grated Parmesan cheese, plus more, for serving
> ¼   teaspoon black pepper
>   Pinch of salt, if needed

1. Spoon 2 tablespoons of the olive oil into a large, heavy skillet set over high heat. Add the mushrooms and sauté until browned, 3 to 4 minutes. Reduce the heat; add the parsley, garlic, oregano, and basil and cook for 2 minutes. Pour in the wine and simmer for 3 to 5 minutes to allow the mushrooms to absorb some of the wine. Remove from the heat and reserve.
2. Place a large saucepan over moderately high heat. Spoon in the remaining 2 tablespoons olive oil and add the macaroni. Toss and stir constantly until the pasta is toasted deep golden brown, 3 to 5 minutes. Pour in the chicken

VARIATIONS

Vegetarian: **For a totally vegetarian version, use vegetable broth in place of the chicken stock.**

Bigger flavor: **If exotic mushrooms such as porcini, cremini, or shiitake are available, by all means use them in place of the domestic white mushrooms.**

To make a meal: **Three-quarters of a cup diced cooked meat, such as beef, chicken, or pork, can be added with the cream.**

stock and bring to a boil, stirring occasionally, over high heat. Reduce the heat and simmer, uncovered, until the pasta is almost tender and the stock is almost absorbed, about 12 minutes.

3. Stir in the mushroom mixture and the cream and cook for 3 to 4 minutes to blend the flavors. Remove from the heat and stir in ⅓ cup of the Parmesan and the pepper. If necessary, add a little salt to taste (the saltiness of the cheese and broth will determine this). Serve hot, sprinkled with additional Parmesan and parsley.

OREGANO

I use more dried Greek or Italian oregano than any other herb in my kitchen. It's amazing to me that this wonderful herb wasn't even popular in this country before 1940. Only after servicemen, who became enamored of oregano in Europe during World War II, asked for it here did oregano become widely available. During the 1950s, "the pizza herb" became the rage.

There are two types of oregano: European (belonging to the mint family) and Mexican (belonging to the verbena family). In general, the oregano you buy, unless it is from a Mexican grocer, will be the European variety.

EUROPEAN OREGANO

This is the most popular oregano of all, whether it is from Italy, Greece, Turkey, or home soil. When you taste this oregano there's no confusing it with other herbs. It has a very simple but assertive flavor that "screams" oregano—probably why it is so appealing and popular. It has a strong, familiar scent when sniffed and a flavor that suggests pine with a bitter citrus undertone. When taken "straight," it causes a hot peppery sensation on the tongue.

MEXICAN OREGANO

The warm, acrid aroma of Mexican oregano suggests complexity. It has a more complex fragrance that suggests a combination of flavors. Mexican oregano contributes pine and citrus undertones with the flavor nuance of a toasted straw.

Mexican cooks almost never use oregano in a starring role; most often it appears in small amounts to enhance other ingredients, such as strongly flavored chilies and highly seasoned sauces.

MARJORAM

This delicate oreganolike herb is often confused with oregano, even though marjoram, which belongs to the mint family, is milder. Marjoram has a sweet aroma and flavor and the qualities of oregano with an undertone of citrus zest. It can be used freely in soups and salads and in many pasta dishes. One of my favorite spaghetti dishes consists of tossing the hot pasta with olive oil, fresh marjoram, and Parmesan cheese. It is a good, simple way to appreciate the fresh herb.

Malaysian Cellophane Noodles

No one could be bored while eating this colorful, clear noodle creation. That it's healthy and sensible won't even enter your mind because you'll be too busy enjoying the subtleties and complexities. It is critical to have all of the ingredients prepared before you start to cook.

MAKES 4 SERVINGS

- 1 tablespoon dried tiny shrimp
- 12 large dried Chinese black or shiitake mushrooms
- 7 to 8 ounces cellophane noodles (bean threads or glass noodles)
- 3 tablespoons Thai or Vietnamese fish sauce (*nuoc mam* or *nam pla*)
- 3 tablespoons soy sauce
- 1 tablespoon rice vinegar
- 1 teaspoon sugar
- 2 large eggs
- 2 teaspoons Oriental sesame oil
- 4 tablespoons peanut or other vegetable oil
- 1 medium to large onion, cut lengthwise into ¼-inch-wide slivers
- 1 small red bell pepper, cut into ¼-inch julienne
- 1 small green bell pepper, cut into ¼-inch julienne
- ½ cup shredded green cabbage
- 1 carrot, peeled and cut into fine julienne
- 8 ounces medium shrimp, shelled and deveined, if necessary
- 2 teaspoons minced fresh ginger
- 1 large garlic clove, minced or crushed through a press
- 1 fresh hot chili pepper, such as jalapeño, slivered
- 8 ounces lean ground pork
- 8 whole scallions, cut diagonally into 2-inch lengths
- 2 tablespoons chopped fresh cilantro

1. Put the dried shrimp in a small bowl or cup and add ½ cup of boiling water. Set aside to soften for 30 minutes; drain and finely chop. Reserve.
2. Meanwhile, put the dried mushrooms in a bowl and add 1 cup of boiling water. Set aside to soak until softened, about 30 minutes. Drain, reserving ¼ cup of the soaking liquid. Cut off and discard the stems and cut the mushroom caps into fine julienne. Strain the soaking liquid through a fine-mesh sieve. Reserve until needed.
3. Put the cellophane noodles in a large bowl and pour in enough hot water to cover generously. Set aside to soak until softened, about 30 minutes. Drain well. Use kitchen shears to cut the mass of noodles in half. Reserve in a strainer until needed.

DRIED SHRIMP

Dried shrimp add an air of authentic flavor to Malaysian, Vietnamese, and Chinese dishes. You can choose the itsy-bitsy ¼-inch ones (which are usually left whole) to those that are a full inch in length. Usually, the smaller the shrimp, the smaller the price.

Dried shrimp are cured in brine and dried to preserve them, so they should be soaked in water before adding to a recipe. Since dried shrimp have such a pungent, concentrated, sea flavor, just a few are needed. I have a preference for the smallest ones because their flavor is not quite as bold as the bigger ones, yet still robust enough for adding plenty of flavor. I might add that the flavor of dried shrimp is probably an acquired taste, but one that you should start acquiring right away.

These are best stored in the refrigerator in a tightly sealed jar.

4. In a small bowl, stir together the ¼ cup strained mushroom liquid with the fish sauce, soy sauce, rice vinegar, and sugar. Reserve until needed.

5. In a small bowl, stir together the eggs and sesame oil. Place a small, heavy skillet over moderately high heat and spoon in ½ tablespoon of the peanut or vegetable oil. When very hot, pour in the egg mixture and immediately reduce the heat to low. Scramble gently until just set; turn out onto a plate and reserve.

6. Place a large, heavy wok or skillet over high heat. When very hot, spoon in 1½ tablespoons of the peanut oil. Tilt the pan to coat the interior with oil. Add the onion, bell peppers, cabbage, and carrot and stir-fry until lightly browned, about 1 minute. Add 2 tablespoons water and stir-fry until it boils away. Turn out onto a platter and reserve.

7. Return the wok to high heat and spoon in 1 tablespoon of the peanut oil. Add the fresh shrimp and stir-fry until almost cooked to the center, 1 to 1½ minutes. Transfer to a plate and reserve.

8. Wipe out the wok with a paper towel and return it to high heat. Spoon in the remaining 1 tablespoon oil and add the ginger, garlic, hot pepper, minced dried shrimp, and mushrooms. Stir-fry until fragrant, 10 to 15 seconds. Crumble in the pork and stir-fry until no longer pink, 1 to 1½ minutes. Add the scallions and stir-fry for 30 seconds.

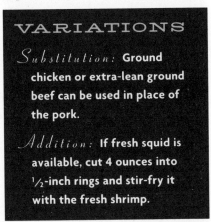

VARIATIONS

Substitution: Ground chicken or extra-lean ground beef can be used in place of the pork.

Addition: If fresh squid is available, cut 4 ounces into ½-inch rings and stir-fry it with the fresh shrimp.

9. Return all of the ingredients and sauces to the wok and toss for 1 minute, until well combined and heated thoroughly. Remove from the heat and toss in the cilantro. Turn out onto a large platter and serve hot.

Singapore Rice Noodles

The word *Singapore* tagged onto a recipe usually indicates the presence of curry, as in this popular rice noodle dish. The recipe moved up the Malay peninsula to China and became an important part of Chinese cuisine. The rice noodles (also called rice sticks) can be soaked well ahead of time, but be sure to serve this dish as soon as it is stir-fried to show off its great variety of textures, colors, and flavors. Prepare all of the ingredients before you start to cook.

MAKES 4 SERVINGS

7 to 8 ounces fine dried rice noodles (rice sticks)
3 large eggs
1½ tablespoons homemade Curry Powder (page 385) or store-bought
2 teaspoons Oriental sesame oil
5 tablespoons peanut or other vegetable oil
8 ounces small to medium shrimp, shelled and deveined, if necessary
4 ounces lean raw pork, trimmed and cut into ¼-inch julienne
4 ounces skinless and boneless chicken breast, cut into ¼-inch julienne
1 tablespoon minced fresh ginger
1 large garlic clove, minced or crushed through a press
1 or 2 fresh hot chili peppers, such as jalapeños,
    partly seeded and slivered
3 ounces Chinese barbecued pork or smoked ham,
    cut into ¼-inch julienne (½ cup)
½ red bell pepper, cut into ¼-inch julienne
½ green bell pepper, cut into julienne
12 whole scallions, cut diagonally into 1½-inch lengths
1½ cups fresh bean sprouts or shredded napa cabbage
½ cup Chicken Stock (page 73) or canned broth
3 tablespoons soy sauce
2 tablespoons dry sherry
    Pinch of salt
2 tablespoons chopped fresh cilantro (optional)

1. Bring a large pot of water to a boil. Drop in the rice noodles and boil until tender but firm to the bite, 1 to 2 minutes. Drain and rinse under cold water. Let the noodles air-dry and firm up in a colander for at least 30 minutes or as long as 2 to 3 hours; toss occasionally.

2. When you are ready to prepare the dish, whisk together the eggs, ½ teaspoon of the curry powder, and all of the sesame oil until blended. Spoon ½ tablespoon of the peanut or vegetable oil into a heavy skillet or wok set over moderately high heat. Pour in the egg mixture and immediately reduce the heat to low. Scramble the eggs until just set; turn out onto a plate and reserve.

3. Return the skillet to moderately high heat and spoon in ½ tablespoon of the oil. Add the shrimp and stir-fry until just barely cooked, about 1 minute (they will cook more later). Remove the shrimp and reserve in a small bowl.

4. Return the skillet to moderately high heat and spoon in 1 tablespoon of the oil. Add the pork and chicken and stir-fry until just cooked, about 1 minute. Remove and reserve in a small bowl.

5. Place a large, heavy wok over high heat. When very hot, spoon in 2 tablespoons of the oil. Add the ginger, garlic, chilies, and the remaining 1 tablespoon plus 1 teaspoon curry powder. Stir-fry until fragrant, about 30 seconds. Add the Chinese pork or ham and red and green bell peppers and stir-fry for 30 seconds. Sprinkle on 1 to 2 tablespoons of water and cook until it boils away. Push the ingredients to the sides of the wok and add the remaining 1 tablespoon oil. Add the scallions, bean sprouts, and noodles and toss over high heat until very hot, about 30 seconds. Pour in the chicken stock and bring to a boil. Return the shrimp, pork, and chicken to the wok and add the soy sauce and sherry. Toss well and add the salt and the reserved scrambled eggs. Sprinkle on the cilantro and turn out onto a large platter. Serve hot.

Cool Sesame Noodles with Jade Cucumbers

I use tahini (Middle Eastern sesame paste) in my favorite version of this classic Chinese cold noodle concoction because I love its rich, clear flavor contribution. The sauce needs a toasted sesame flavor nuance, so a dose of Oriental sesame oil is added. The peanut butter is an important ingredient for flavor and consistency. You don't actually chill this dish, but the sauce can be made up to a day or two ahead and stored in the refrigerator. You then rinse the freshly cooked noodles under cold running water to cool them, toss with the sauce, and serve.

MAKES 4 SERVINGS

- 1 tablespoon peanut or other vegetable oil
- 1½ tablespoons minced fresh ginger
- 1 large garlic clove, minced or crushed through a press
- ¼ cup tahini (Middle Eastern sesame paste)
- ¼ cup smooth peanut butter
- 2 tablespoons soy sauce
- 2 tablespoons rice wine or dry sherry
- 1 tablespoon Oriental sesame oil
- 1 to 2 tablespoons rice vinegar
- 1 tablespoon sugar
- ¼ teaspoon cayenne pepper
  Salt
- 8 ounces thin linguine or thin spaghetti
- 1 large cucumber, peeled, seeded, and cut into ¼ × ½-inch julienne
- ¼ cup chopped fresh cilantro or sliced whole scallions
- ¼ cup chopped roasted peanuts

1. Spoon the peanut or vegetable oil into a small skillet set over moderately low heat. Add the ginger and garlic and sizzle until fragrant but not browned, 1 to 2 minutes. Set aside to cool.

TAHINI

This Middle Eastern sesame paste is made by grinding untoasted sesame seeds into a thick, rich, nutlike butter. It has a big, full flavor but without the toasted dimension of Oriental sesame pastes.

Tahini settles into a mass in its jar or can and should be stirred until homogenized before measuring. Once it regains its creamy consistency, it's a good idea to keep it that way. If you buy it in a can, transfer it to a jar with a tight-fitting lid and store it in the refrigerator, where it will remain fresh for a year or longer.

SHAO-HSING RICE WINE

This rich, fermented Chinese rice wine, sometimes called yellow wine, has a deep complex flavor and fragrance reminiscent of a good dry sherry. The two are interchangeable, though I usually use slightly less Shao-Hsing in place of sherry because of its intensity.

The wine, which comes from mainland China or Taiwan, has a deep golden-brown color and sweet nutty fragrance. The best quality Shao-Hsing is labeled Hua Tiao Chiew (Pagoda blue label is excellent), but there is a basic Shao-Hsing from Taiwan that is quite good and more reasonably priced. I buy it most frequently from a liquor store in Chinatown, but it is also available in Chinese markets.

Rice wine will keep on your pantry shelf with vinegars and the like at room temperature for a couple years.

2. In a large bowl, stir together the tahini, peanut butter, soy sauce, rice wine, sesame oil, and 1 tablespoon of the rice vinegar. Add the sugar, cayenne, and 1 tablespoon of cold water. Taste the sesame sauce and if a sharper sauce is desired, add 1 tablespoon rice vinegar. Add a pinch of salt, if needed. Cover and chill the sauce until ready to serve.

3. Bring a large pot of lightly salted water to a boil over high heat. Drop in the pasta and stir constantly until the water returns to a boil. Cook, stirring frequently, until tender but firm to the bite, 8 to 10 minutes. Drain in a colander and rinse with cold water. Drain again, shaking out the water. In a large bowl, toss the pasta with the sesame sauce.

4. Ring a large platter with the julienned cucumber, mound the noodles in the center, and sprinkle with the cilantro and peanuts.

VARIATIONS

To make a meal: Top the noodles with 8 ounces of shredded poached chicken breast or julienne of roast pork or beef before garnishing with the cilantro and peanuts.

Substitution: This dish is greatly complemented by crunchy vegetables; you can substitute steamed, chilled broccoli florets for the cucumber.

Cold Chicken Wontons in Sesame Sauce

Inspiration for this dish came from Chinese cold sesame noodles, but I use wonton skins filled with ground chicken breast. And since I wanted big flavor and texture, I experimented with different shapes that would increase the folds that would entrap the rich, creamy sauce.

MAKES 5 TO 6 DOZEN (6 MAIN-COURSE OR 12 APPETIZER SERVINGS)

. Sesame Sauce

- 1 tablespoon peanut or other vegetable oil
- 1 tablespoon minced fresh ginger
- 1 large garlic clove, minced or crushed through a press
- ⅓ cup tahini (Middle Eastern sesame paste)
- ⅓ cup smooth peanut butter
- 1½ tablespoons Oriental sesame oil
- 1 tablespoon sugar
- ½ teaspoon cayenne pepper
- 2 tablespoons dry sherry
- 2 tablespoons rice vinegar
- 2 tablespoons soy sauce
- ⅓ cup Chicken Stock (page 73) or canned broth

Wontons

- 2½ tablespoons peanut or other vegetable oil
- 1 tablespoon minced fresh ginger
- 1 garlic clove, minced or crushed through a press
- 1 leek, trimmed, well-washed, quartered lengthwise, and minced;
  or ⅔ cup finely chopped onion
- 1 pound skinless and boneless chicken breasts, cubed
- 1 cup finely chopped fresh or canned water chestnuts
- 2 whole scallions, minced
- 1 tablespoon dry sherry
- 1 tablespoon Oriental sesame oil
- 1 tablespoon soy sauce
- ½ teaspoon salt
- ¼ teaspoon black pepper
  Cornstarch
  60 to 72 thick or medium square wonton skins
  (1 pound will yield 80 to 90 skins)

Garnish

- 1 large cucumber, washed and thinly sliced

1. To make the sesame sauce, spoon the peanut or vegetable oil into a small skil-

SOY SAUCE

This essential flavoring for Oriental and Asian cooking is made from fermented soybeans and grain plus salt and water. Soy sauce has a complex bouquet of aromas and flavor nuances that enhance other ingredients in cooking.

Although there are hundreds of different varieties of soy sauce, the two broad and basic categories are Chinese and Japanese. In general, Chinese soy sauces are saltier than Japanese ones. They range from intensely salty to sweet and mellow.

Light and Thin: This is your basic all-purpose soy sauce. The description refers to consistency, not sodium content. Thin soys are from the top of the vat while darker, thicker ones are from the bottom. Good Chinese labels to look for include: Koon Chun and Pearl River. Kikkoman Shoyu is an excellent Japanese soy sauce.

Dark or Black: This category is sweeter and less salty than the thin. Dark soy sauces contribute a darker color to foods. They range in color from rich amber to mahogany to extremely black. Good Chinese labels to look for are Koon Chun Double Black and Pearl River Bridge Golden Label Superior. Good Japanese labels include San-J Tamari and Kikkoman.

Lite or Reduced Sodium: This a relatively new category of soy sauces. Some have excellent flavor. Look for Kikkoman Lite and Eden Double-Brewed Low Sodium Shoyu.

let set over moderately low heat. Add the ginger and garlic and sizzle until fragrant but not browned, about 1 minute. Scrape the mixture into a medium bowl and let cool. Using the same pan, combine the tahini, peanut butter, sesame oil, sugar, and cayenne. Stir in the sherry, rice vinegar, soy sauce, and chicken stock to make a smooth, creamy sauce. Cover and chill until needed. (The sauce can be prepared a day or two ahead of time.)

2. To make the filling, spoon 1 tablespoon of the peanut or vegetable oil into a medium skillet set over moderate heat. Add the ginger and garlic and sizzle until fragrant, about 1 minute. Add the leek or onion, increase the heat to moderately high, and sauté until softened, about 3 minutes. (If the pan seems dry, add 1 tablespoon of water during the last minute and continue cooking.) Transfer to a plate and let cool.

3. Using a food processor or meat grinder, grind the chicken breasts moderately fine. Turn into a large bowl and add the cooled leek mixture. Stir in the water chestnuts, scallions, and remaining 1½ tablespoons peanut oil. Stir in the sherry, sesame oil, soy sauce, salt, and pepper and mix well. You will have about 3 cups of filling.

4. To shape the wontons, lightly dust a sheet of waxed paper with cornstarch. Have ready a small bowl of water. Place 1 square of dough in front of you and rotate it 45° so that it is a diamond shape in front of you. Spoon about 2 teaspoons of the filling into the center. Dip your finger into the water and moisten the 2 top edges. Fold up the bottom point, enclosing the filling and making a triangle, but fold it so that the 2 top points are slightly askew. Pinch to enclose the filling, squeezing out any air as you pinch around the edges. Dab a little water on the right side point and bring the left and right side points together, overlapping them by about ½ inch. Pinch together; at this point the wonton will resemble a nurse's cap. Repeat, shaping all of the wontons and placing them on the waxed paper.

5. To cook the wontons, bring a large, heavy pot of lightly salted water to a boil over high heat. One at a time, quickly drop in half the wontons. When the water returns to a boil, usually about 3 minutes later, pour in 1 cup of cold water. Quickly return the water to a boil. Lift out 1 wonton and cut into the corner to test for tenderness; usually about 3 minutes will do it. Scoop out the wontons with a large skimmer or strainer and cool in a bowl of cold water for 10 to 15 seconds. Drain again, shaking off the water. Transfer the wontons to a large bowl, add the cold sesame sauce, and toss. Repeat the cooking and draining procedure with the remaining wontons, and add them to the sauce. Chill the wontons and sauce for 30 to 60 minutes before serving.

6. To serve, ring a large platter with thin slices of cucumber and mound the cold wontons and sesame sauce in the center. You might want to garnish the top with scallions. Serve cold.

VARIATION

Presentation: **Cut the florets from a large head of broccoli and blanch them in a large pot of lightly salted water until tender-firm, about 3 minutes. Drain, rinse under cold water, interspersed with sticks of red bell pepper if desired, and arrange around the edge of a large serving platter; mound cold wontons in the center and sprinkle with sliced scallions and/or chopped peanuts.**

Cilantro Pasta Wontons

Adding chopped cilantro to fresh pasta adds freckles, fragrance, and flavor. The moist filling is a marriage of shrimp and pork with oyster sauce and more cilantro. You can shape the wontons several hours ahead, but be sure to cook them shortly before serving. You will need a pasta machine.

MAKES ABOUT 64

  Cilantro Pasta dough (page 138)
  1 tablespoon vegetable oil
  2 teaspoons grated fresh ginger
  1½ cups finely chopped napa cabbage
  8 ounces ground pork
  10 to 12 ounces shrimp, shelled, deveined, and minced
  1 large egg
  2 tablespoons Chinese oyster sauce
  1 tablespoon dry sherry or rice wine
  1 tablespoon cornstarch
  ½ teaspoon sugar
  ½ teaspoon salt
  ¼ cup chopped fresh cilantro
  1 whole scallion, minced
  2 teaspoons Oriental sesame oil

1. Prepare the Cilantro Pasta dough at least 1 hour ahead of time.
2. Place a large skillet or wok over moderately high heat. Add the vegetable oil and swirl or tilt the pan to coat with the oil. Add the ginger and stir-fry for 10 seconds. Add the cabbage, increase the heat to high, and stir-fry until lightly browned, 2 to 3 minutes. Turn out into a large bowl and let cool to room temperature.
3. Crumble the pork over the seasoned cabbage and stir in the shrimp, egg, oyster sauce, sherry, cornstarch, sugar, and salt. Add the cilantro, scallion, and sesame oil and mix thoroughly. (If making ahead, cover and chill in the refrigerator for up to 8 hours.)
4. Divide the pasta dough into 4 pieces. Dust each with flour and roll through a pasta machine, reducing the width between the rollers each time you pass it through, until the pasta is as thin as possible. Halfway through you should cut the strips crosswise in half and continue rolling out until you have 8 strips, each about 4 inches wide and 24 inches long. Cut each strip into 3-inch squares, lightly dust them with flour, and stack them. Keep covered to prevent drying out as you work.
5. Lightly dust a sheet of waxed paper with cornstarch. Have ready a small bowl

or cup of water. Place 1 square of pasta in front of you and rotate it so it has a diamond shape. Spoon about 2 teaspoons of the filling onto the center. Dip your finger into the water and moisten the 2 top edges. Fold up the bottom point, enclosing the filling and making a triangle, but fold it so the 2 top points are slightly askew. Pinch to enclose the filling, squeezing out any air as you seal it all around. Dab a little water on the right side point and bring the left and right points together, overlapping them by about ½ inch. Pinch together (the wonton will resemble a nurse's cap). Repeat, shaping all of the wontons, and placing them on the waxed paper. (If making ahead, cover loosely with plastic and refrigerate for several hours.)

6. Bring a large pot of lightly salted water to a boil over high heat. Drop in half the wontons and stir gently. Partly cover the pot and return the water quickly to a boil. Reduce the heat and gently boil the wontons until tender but firm to the bite, 6 to 10 minutes. (The timing depends on the thickness of the pasta. Whereas commercially rolled wontons will cook in just 2 to 3 minutes, wontons made from homemade pasta take considerably longer, depending on their size and thickness. To test for doneness, remove a wonton from the water, cut off 1 corner, and bite into it.) When done, remove the wontons with a skimmer or strainer and cook the remaining wontons. Drain well.

7. Serve the wontons hot, with the Soochow Black Vinegar Dipping Sauce (page 370) or the Vietnamese Dipping Sauce (page 369), or make into a soup as described below. Chili sauce can be served alongside.

VARIATION

Serving: To make a wonderful wonton soup, you'll need about 6 cups of chicken stock. Add a few slices of fresh ginger and simmer it for a few minutes, then ladle it over the wontons. Sprinkle with sliced scallions and chopped parsley and serve hot. (This type of dumpling soup is not usually served with much broth.)

Homemade Egg Pasta

If you don't have a pasta machine for kneading and rolling out the dough, make the dough a bit on the soft side so you can roll it with a rolling pin.

To sample the flavor and texture of the pasta at its purest and simplest, toss freshly cooked and drained pasta with olive oil, butter, or a combination of the two. Then sprinkle with freshly grated Parmesan cheese.

MAKES 1 TO 1¼ POUNDS, ENOUGH FOR 4 TO 6 SERVINGS

> 3 to 3¼ cups all-purpose flour
> 4 large eggs

1. Place 3 cups of the flour in a large, shallow bowl and make a well in the center. Pour the eggs and 1 tablespoon cold water into the well.
2. Using a fork, stir the eggs and water together with a circular motion. As you stir, gradually incorporate the flour into the egg. Continue stirring with the circular motion until the dough becomes too thick to stir. Then, with floured fingers, incorporate enough of the remaining flour to make a stiff but not dry dough. Remove the dough and knead it, adding some of the remaining flour, if necessary, to make a satin-smooth dough that is neither sticky nor dry. It will be better if the dough is on the soft side rather than dry. The kneading, which can be done on a lightly floured surface or with both hands while pinching and folding, should take 10 minutes. Cover and let rest for 1 hour. If making ahead, wrap and chill in the refrigerator for up to 2 days.
3. To roll out with a pasta machine, shape the pasta into a neat rectangle that measures about 8 × 4 inches. Cut it into 6 equal pieces. On a lightly floured surface, pat out each piece to about 3 × 5 inches. Knead the dough further by passing each piece through the widest setting of a pasta machine. Fold the dough into thirds, turn 180°, and then roll through the machine again. Repeat this procedure again.
4. Continue passing the pasta through the machine, reducing the setting each time up to the second to last setting, or until the dough is about ¹⁄₁₆ inch thick. The pasta will be 4 to 4½ inches wide. As the pieces become thin and too long to handle, cut them crosswise in half to make them more manageable. Dust the sheets lightly with flour and drape them over a dowel or a rod. Lacking one, lay them out flat without stacking. Let dry for 10 to 20 minutes to firm up slightly before cutting. If drying flat, turn them over and let them dry a little longer. They should not be too moist or too dry before cutting.
5. Choose the pasta cutting blade desired (such as linguine or fettuccine widths).

Pass each sheet of pasta through with one hand while the other catches the cut pasta. Swirl the strands into a loose coil on a lightly floured sheet of waxed paper and continue, making a new bundle from each sheet of dough.

The pasta can be boiled right away or left to dry completely and stored in plastic or a jar. Dried pasta will take longer to cook than fresh. And, of course, thicker pasta will take longer to cook than thin. The only true test for doneness is to bite into it. Although the best pasta is cooked until tender but firm to the bite (al dente, as the Italians say), this is a matter of personal taste. Pastas flavored with herbs lose fragrance and flavor potency as the pasta dries.

Note: To cut pasta by hand, let the sheets of pasta dry just enough to keep them from sticking together when stacked (as above). Lightly flour the top sheet and roll up loosely around a rolling pin. Pull out the rolling pin. Dip a sharp knife blade into flour and slice through crosswise to make the widths you want (say, $1/4$ to $1/3$ inch for fettuccine or an inch or more for pappardelle). Loosely coil the strands in bundles on floured waxed paper.

VARIATIONS

Lemon Pasta: **Add 2 tablespoons grated lemon zest to the flour and 1 tablespoon lemon juice with the eggs.**

Basil Pasta: **Combine 1 cup fresh basil with the eggs and 1 tablespoon olive oil in the food processor or blender and puree, then add to the well in the flour.**

Cilantro Pasta: **Combine 1 cup fresh cilantro leaves with the eggs in the food processor or blender and puree, then add to the well in the flour.**

Basic Ravioli

Here is the technique for making and cooking ravioli. The pasta and the filling can be prepared a day or two ahead, but the ravioli must be shaped and cooked on the day you plan to serve them. You need a pasta machine to do this. But see the hint on page 143 about using eggroll skins.

MAKES 96 TWO-INCH RAVIOLI, ENOUGH FOR 8 SERVINGS

> **Homemade Egg Pasta dough (page 137)**
> 3 **cups ravioli filling (any of the fillings on pages 141–142)**
> **Olive oil or melted butter**

1. Shape the pasta into a neat even rectangle about 4×8 inches. Cut into thick pieces. Dust each lightly with flour. Working with 1 piece of dough at a time, pat each into a 3×5-inch rectangle. Knead the dough further by passing it through the widest setting of a pasta machine 3 times.
2. Continue passing the pasta through the machine, reducing the space between the rollers each time, until the pasta is as thin as possible, $\frac{1}{16}$ inch or less. The pasta will be 4 to $4\frac{1}{2}$ inches wide.
3. Cut each length of pasta lengthwise into 2 even pieces. Place 1 piece on a work surface. Spoon or pipe the filling of your choice, using about $1\frac{1}{2}$ teaspoons for each, onto the dough, placing it about $\frac{1}{2}$ inch in from the edges, and spaced about 1 inch apart. Make a double row the length of the strip of pasta. Dip a pastry brush in water and paint lengthwise down the center, then along the edges, and finally crosswise between the mounds. Drape the second sheet of dough over the filling starting at one end and using a finger to push down lengthwise between the mounds so it adheres along the center and the air is pushed out. Lightly press the 2 long outer edges together and cut the ravioli into 2-inch squares with a sharp knife or a fluted pastry wheel. Pick them up one at a time and seal the edges, pressing together. Place the ravioli on a floured baking sheet or paper. Repeat with the remaining filling and pasta.
4. Fill 1 or 2 large pots with lightly salted water and bring to a boil over high heat. Quickly drop the ravioli in, one at a time, putting about 4 dozen into each pot. Stir once or twice and let the water return to a boil. Lower the heat so that they boil gently and cook until tender but firm to the bite, 3 to 6 minutes depending on the thickness of the pasta. The only way to test is to take one out, cut off a corner, and bite into it. Drain the ravioli and toss with a little olive oil or melted butter to keep them from sticking.
   Note: The ravioli can be served in chicken stock or with sauce, depending on your taste. They can also be simply tossed with the butter and oil and sprinkled with fresh herbs and/or Parmesan cheese.

Chicken-Basil Ravioli Filling

Use this fragrant, light chicken filling to stuff pasta and then serve them with any of the tomato sauces on page 356 to 359, let them cool and toss them into a salad, or serve them in chicken broth, about 6 to a cup, for a good first-course pasta soup. Use the plain egg pasta for making the ravioli.

MAKES ABOUT 3 CUPS (ENOUGH TO FILL 96 TWO-INCH RAVIOLI)

> 3 tablespoons olive oil
> 1 large garlic clove, minced or crushed through a press
> ½ teaspoon dried oregano, crumbled
> ¼ teaspoon grated nutmeg
> 2 cups lightly packed cooked and diced chicken breast
> 1½ cups whole-milk ricotta cheese
> 1½ cups coarsely chopped fresh basil leaves
> ½ cup freshly grated Parmesan cheese
> ¾ teaspoon salt

1. Spoon the olive oil into a small, heavy skillet and place over low heat. Add the garlic, oregano, and nutmeg and sauté without browning for 1 to 2 minutes. Remove from the heat and let cool.
2. In a food processor, combine the chicken with the seasoned olive oil. Pulse on and off until coarsely ground. Alternatively, put the chicken through a meat grinder.
3. In a large bowl, combine the ground chicken, ricotta, basil, Parmesan, and salt. Mix thoroughly. Cover and chill until needed, for up to 2 days.

Salmon Ravioli Filling

This pretty pink salmon filling is especially delicious shaped into ravioli made from the Lemon Pasta on page 138. The ravioli are also fine just tossed with butter, grated Parmesan cheese, and chopped parsley, or make them into a seafood pasta salad.

MAKES ABOUT 2½ CUPS (ENOUGH TO FILL 96 TWO-INCH RAVIOLI)

> 1½ pounds salmon steaks, skinned and boned to yield
> 1 pound of 1-inch cubes
> 1 large egg
> ¼ cup minced whole scallions
> 2 tablespoons fresh lemon juice
> 1 teaspoon salt

¼ teaspoon dried tarragon, crumbled
¼ teaspoon grated nutmeg
⅛ teaspoon cayenne pepper
⅛ teaspoon black pepper
½ cup heavy cream

1. Partly freeze the salmon cubes to firm them, about 15 minutes.
2. Put the salmon in a food processor and pulse 3 to 4 times. Add the egg, scallions, lemon juice, salt, tarragon, nutmeg, cayenne, and black pepper. With the motor running, add the cream in a steady stream, mixing only until blended. Transfer the filling to a bowl, cover, and refrigerate until needed.

Pesto Ravioli Filling

MAKES ABOUT 2½ CUPS (ENOUGH TO FILL 96 TWO-INCH RAVIOLI)

1 tablespoon olive oil
1 tablespoon butter
1 large garlic clove, minced or crushed through a press
2 cups lightly packed fresh basil leaves
2 large eggs
½ cup freshly grated Parmigiano Reggiano cheese
¼ cup grated Pecorino-Romano cheese
¼ cup chopped walnuts
¼ teaspoon grated nutmeg
1 cup whole-milk ricotta cheese
½ cup plain, dry bread crumbs
2 tablespoons heavy cream
¼ teaspoon salt
    Pinch of black pepper

1. In a small skillet, combine the olive oil, butter, and garlic over low heat. Sizzle gently until fragrant but not browned, about 1 minute. Set aside to cool.
2. In a food processor, combine the basil, eggs, Parmigiano Reggiano, Pecorino, walnuts, and nutmeg. Process to a puree. Turn into a large bowl and stir in the garlic mixture, the ricotta, bread crumbs, cream, salt, and pepper. Mix well. Cover and chill for at least 1 hour or for up to a day.

Mushroom-Porcini Ravioli Filling

Use this earthy mushroom filling to make robust ravioli, especially suitable for fall dining. I used to make these for my good friend James Beard, and he loved them.

MAKES ABOUT 3 CUPS (ENOUGH TO FILL 96 TWO-INCH RAVIOLI)

- ½ ounce dried porcini
- 3 tablespoons olive oil
- 1 large onion, finely chopped
- 1 large garlic clove, minced or crushed through a press
- 1½ pounds fresh mushrooms, finely chopped (this can be done in a food processor)
- ¼ cup dry white wine
- 1 teaspoon dried basil, crumbled
- 1 teaspoon salt
- 1 tablespoon all-purpose flour
- ¼ cup plain, dry bread crumbs
- 3 tablespoons milk
- 1 large egg

1. Soak the porcini in ⅓ cup of boiling water until softened, 30 to 60 minutes. Drain the porcini, reserving the soaking liquid. Chop the porcini; strain the soaking liquid through a fine-mesh sieve.

2. Spoon 2 tablespoons of the olive oil into a large, heavy skillet set over moderate heat. Add the onion and sauté until softened, 3 to 5 minutes. Add the garlic and sauté for 1 minute. Add the remaining 1 tablespoon olive oil and the chopped fresh mushrooms; increase the heat to high and cook until lightly browned, 2 to 3 minutes. Add the porcini, the strained soaking liquid, wine, basil, and salt. Boil over high heat until the liquids evaporate and the mixture becomes dry, about 5 minutes. Stir in the flour and cook, stirring, for 2 minutes longer. Remove from the heat and set aside to cool to room temperature.

3. In a small bowl, stir together the bread crumbs and milk. Stir in the egg. Let stand until softened, 2 to 3 minutes. Stir into the mushroom mixture. Cover and refrigerate until needed.

Eggroll Skins for Stuffed Pasta

Though commercial wonton skins make a popular shortcut for ravioli making, I've discovered that eggroll skins are thicker, sturdier, and altogether a better choice for homemade ravioli, agnolotti, and other stuffed pastas.

A 2-pound package contains about twenty 6-inch squares, and I cut them into eighty 3-inch squares. Be sure to keep them covered to prevent drying out.

1. Make a "glue" by mixing 1 egg yolk with 1 tablespoon of water in a cup. If you want to make triangular ravioli or crescent agnolotti, each one will require a 3-inch square or round of dough. Round or square ravioli will require 2 pieces for each.

2. To make triangular ravioli, spoon about 1½ teaspoons of filling diagonally across the center of a 3-inch square. Brush 2 edges with the egg and fold over, pinching out any air and sealing. Place on a tray dusted with flour or corn-starch and repeat.

To make square ravioli, spoon 2 teaspoons of filling in the center of one 3-inch square; pat the filling into a 1½-inch round. Brush all 4 edges with the egg. Top with a second square and pinch together, squeezing out the air. Trim with scissors or a knife to a 2½-inch square; place on a sheet dusted with flour.

To make round ravioli, cut the 3-inch squares with a 3-inch round cutter. Spoon or pipe 2 teaspoons of filling in the center of one round and pat to a 1½-inch round. Paint the edges with the egg and top with a second round. Pick up and pinch together, squeezing out the air and sealing well. Place on a floured tray.

To make agnolotti, cut the 3-inch squares with a 3-inch round cutter. Spoon or pipe a line of about 1½ teaspoons of the filling in the center. Paint half the edge with the egg and fold the dough over to make a half round. Place the crescents on a floured tray.

3. To cook agnolotti or ravioli, bring a large pot of lightly salted water to a boil over high heat. Drop in 12 to 18 stuffed pastas (or enough to cook without crowding the pot), cover, and bring back to a boil. Reduce the heat to moderate and boil gently, uncovered, until tender but firm to the bite, 4 to 5 minutes. Scoop out with a skimmer or strainer and toss with butter or olive oil. Serve with a pasta sauce or in chicken broth.

Vegetables in Starring

Hot and Cold Asparagus

Barbecued Three-Bean Bake

Big Flavor Boston Baked Beans

Green Beans with Spicy Beef Sauce

Bacon-Browned Cabbage

Chilies Rellenos

and Supporting Roles

Corn and Red Pepper Pancakes

Smoky Eggplant Parmesan

Cucumber-Radish Raita

Hickory Gingered Eggplant

Browned and Braised Belgian Endive with Lime Butter

Sake-Soaked Mushrooms

Russian Radishes in Sour Cream

Sautéed Radishes

Deep-Dish Spinach Pie

Cajun Succotash

Grilled Vegetable Terrine with Goat Cheese

Parmesan-Fried Green Tomatoes

Hot and Cold Asparagus

Sweet, hot, sour, cold, and *crunchy* are words that will come to mind upon your first bite into this salad version of a Chinese stir-fry. It will need about an hour to chill, and if marinated longer, will lose color but gain flavor.

MAKES 6 SIDE-DISH SERVINGS

2 pounds fresh medium asparagus
3 tablespoons vegetable oil
1 tablespoon minced fresh ginger
1 garlic clove, minced
1 teaspoon dried red pepper flakes, or more to taste
¼ cup rice vinegar
3 tablespoons sugar
2 tablespoons Oriental sesame oil
1 teaspoon salt
½ teaspoon black pepper
1 red bell pepper, trimmed and cut into ¼ × 2-inch sticks

1. Using a swivel-bladed peeler, peel the lowest third of each asparagus spear and trim off ½ inch from the ends. Cut on a sharp diagonal into 2-inch lengths.
2. Bring a large pot of lightly salted water to a boil over high heat. Drop in the asparagus and blanch for 2 minutes from the time they hit the water. Drain and rinse under cold water.
3. Spoon the vegetable oil into a small, heavy skillet and add the ginger, garlic, and red pepper flakes; place over moderately low heat and sizzle until fragrant but not colored, about 1 minute. Remove to a large bowl and let cool slightly.
4. Add the vinegar, sugar, sesame oil, salt, and black pepper to the bowl. Add the asparagus and bell pepper, toss, cover, and chill. Serve cold.

VARIATIONS

Lower calorie: **To cut some of the calories, reduce the vegetable oil to 1 tablespoon and the sesame oil to 1 teaspoon.**

Presentation: **For a festive touch, use half yellow and half red bell pepper.**

Addition: **Sliced scallions can be added.**

Barbecued Three-Bean Bake

This smoky casserole of beans and barbecue sauce was always an important part of the backyard barbecues when I was a boy. Sometimes my mother made this with just pink beans, sometimes she added kidney beans, and sometimes she left out the lima beans entirely, depending on her mood or on what was available. The smokier the bacon, the better the beans.

MAKES ABOUT TWELVE 1-CUP SERVINGS

8 ounces dried large lima beans, rinsed and picked over
8 ounces dried pink beans, rinsed and picked over
8 ounces dried black beans, rinsed and picked over
1 pound sliced hickory-smoked bacon, cut into ¾-inch pieces
2 large onions, chopped
4 large garlic cloves, minced or crushed through a press
1 cup canned tomato puree
⅓ cup light corn syrup
¼ cup unsulphured molasses
¼ cup soy sauce
⅔ cup cider vinegar
1 teaspoon ground cumin

1. Place the lima beans, pink beans, and black beans in separate bowls. Add enough cold water to each bowl to cover generously. Set aside to soak overnight.
2. Drain each batch of soaked beans and place each in a separate medium saucepan. Add 6 cups of cold water to each. Place over moderate heat and bring the water to a boil. Reduce the heat to low, partially cover, and simmer until each type of bean is just tender: 10 to 15 minutes for the lima beans, 45 to 60 minutes for the pink beans, and 1 to 1½ hours for the black beans. (Cook the beans only until just tender to the bite, not mushy.) Drain the beans, reserving 1½ cups of the cooking liquid from the pink beans; discard the rest.
3. Preheat the oven to 325° F. Put the bacon in a large, heavy skillet over moderate heat. Cook, stirring frequently, until crisp and golden brown, 5 to 7 minutes. Remove the bacon with a slotted spoon and drain. Pour off and discard all but 2 tablespoons of the bacon fat.
4. Add the onions to the skillet and sauté over moderate heat until soft and translucent, about 5 minutes. Add the garlic and sauté for 1 minute more. Remove from the heat.
5. In a large bowl, stir together the tomato puree, corn syrup, molasses, and soy sauce. Stir in the vinegar, cumin, and the reserved 1½ cups of cooking liq-

uid from the pink beans. Add all of the beans, along with the onions and bacon. Mix well.

6. Turn the beans into a 3½- to 4-quart casserole or bean pot. Bake, uncovered, for 2 to 2½ hours, stirring once after an hour, until the beans are slightly soupy and tender. (If the beans dry out too much during baking, add a little water.) Serve hot or at room temperature. The beans will taste best if the casserole can rest for an hour before serving.

Note: Leftovers reheat well. Just add a little water (¼ to ½ cup) and bake in a preheated 350° F. oven for 20 to 30 minutes.

APPLE CIDER VINEGAR

While the standard table vinegar used in France is made from grapes and the most popular vinegar in the United Kingdom is derived from malt, the preferred table vinegar in the United States comes from apple.

Apple cider vinegar has a big, full, sour flavor and a sweet, fruity fragrance. The vinegar is produced from the fermentation of natural unprocessed apple juice; the natural sugar converts to alcohol and then into acetic acid.

Any substance that contains sufficient sugar for fermentation into alcohol can be turned into vinegar. Apple juice is ideal because it has such a pleasant flavor and high sugar content.

I find myself reaching for it more than any other vinegar because I like the complex flavor contributes to food. I also grew up with it on my table. Heinz is the brand I use.

Big Flavor Boston Baked Beans

I have experimented with many versions of Boston baked beans over the years—adding a little of this and a little of that—but this is the formula that I love best and I follow it to a T when I make them. These beans are what I crave when I begin thinking about picnics and barbecues. They are designed to taste great alongside Smashed Potato Salad (page 170).

The beans must soak for 8 hours and bake for 7 hours, so plan your time accordingly. If they are for dinner, soak the beans overnight and then put them in the oven in the morning. If they are for a picnic, soak the beans during the day and bake them overnight. This is easily doubled for a crowd.

MAKES ABOUT EIGHT 1-CUP SERVINGS

1 **pound dried small white beans, such as California, Michigan, navy, pea, or great northern, rinsed and picked over**

    3   tablespoons firmly packed brown sugar
    2   teaspoons dry mustard
 1½   teaspoons salt
   ½   teaspoon dried thyme, crumbled
    3   tablespoons light unsulphured molasses
   ¼   cup ketchup
    3   tablespoons cider vinegar
    1   large garlic clove, minced or crushed through a press
    1   chunk (8 to 12 ounces) lean hickory-smoked slab bacon
         with rind, cut into 2 pieces
    1   medium onion, peeled

1. Place the beans in a large bowl and add cold water to cover generously. Soak them for 8 hours or overnight. Alternatively, you can use the quick soak method (see page 16).
2. Drain the beans and put them in a large pot. Add 6 cups of cold water. Partially cover the pot and slowly bring the water to a boil over moderate heat, about 30 minutes. Reduce the heat to low and simmer for about 15 minutes; the beans will not be tender, but they are ready when you remove

MOLASSES

This thick, dark syrup—the favorite flavoring for baked beans—is the by-product of the cane sugar refining process. It is also the flavor of brown sugar.

Molasses ranges from light and unsulphured to dark and blackstrap. They are classified as first, second, and third boil, with the flavor varying from the lightest and sweetest (for table use) to the thickest blackstrap, which is the least sweet and most bitter.

The flavor and quality of molasses is determined by the maturity of the cane, by the amount of sugar extracted, and by the refining process used. In general, the finest is unsulphured molasses imported from the West Indies. It is light and delicate with a good, transparent dark color. New Orleans molasses, made from Louisiana sugarcane, has a shorter ripening time and often contains sulphur dioxide to aid in the clarification process.

Molasses is the only sweetener that contains significant vitamins and minerals (potassium, iron, calcium, phosphorous, and traces of riboflavin, thiamin, and niacin).

I remember that my mother frequently used the saying "as slow as molasses in January" when someone wasn't moving as swiftly as she wanted. Indeed, molasses thickens considerably when chilled.

Although I simply measure molasses in a measuring cup and then scoop it out with my finger, some recommend oiling the cup for easy removal.

a few in a slotted spoon, blow on them, and the skin bursts. Drain the beans, reserving 2 cups of the cooking liquid.

3. Preheat the oven to 250° F. In a medium bowl, stir together the brown sugar, mustard, salt, thyme, molasses, ketch-up, vinegar, and garlic. Stir in the reserved 2 cups cooking liquid.

4. Using a sharp paring knife, score each piece of bacon in a 1-inch grid, cutting almost through to the rind. Place 1 piece in a 2½-quart bean pot or casserole along with the onion. Add all of the drained beans. Pour in enough of the seasoned liquid to barely cover the beans. Top with the remaining slab of bacon, rind side up; cover with a lid or aluminum foil. Bake for 5 hours, checking from time to time and adding a little water if the beans become dry (the liquid should always reach halfway up the top layer of beans).

5. Uncover the pot and bake for 2 hours longer. Let the beans stand for at least 1 hour before serving. If making ahead of time, add ½ cup water and reheat at 350° F. for about 30 minutes.

Green Beans with Spicy Beef Sauce

I like to make these well ahead of time and reheat them to get the fullest flavor. More often than not, I serve them with a roast chicken and mashed potatoes instead of a Chinese menu. These beans make a robust and spicy side dish.

MAKES 6 SIDE-DISH SERVINGS

- 8 ounces lean ground beef
- 3 tablespoons dry sherry
- ½ teaspoon cornstarch
- 2 tablespoons Chinese hot bean sauce
- 1 tablespoon dark soy sauce
- 1 tablespoon black Chinkiang vinegar or balsamic vinegar
- 2 teaspoons sugar
- 1 teaspoon Oriental sesame oil
- ½ cup Chicken Stock (page 73) or canned broth
- 3½ tablespoons peanut or vegetable oil
- 2 pounds tender young green beans, topped, tailed, strings pulled, and halved on a severe angle
- 1½ tablespoons minced fresh ginger
- 1 large garlic clove, minced or crushed through a press
- ¼ cup minced whole scallions

1. Crumble the ground beef into a medium bowl and stir in 1 tablespoon of the sherry. Cover and marinate in the refrigerator until needed.
2. In a small bowl, combine the remaining 2 tablespoons sherry with the cornstarch and stir to dissolve. Stir in the bean sauce, soy sauce, vinegar, sugar, and sesame oil. Stir in the stock or broth; set the sauce aside until needed.
3. Place a large wok over high heat and spoon in 2 tablespoons of the oil. When the oil is hot, add the green beans and stir-fry over high heat until well browned, 3 to 5 minutes. Pour in $\frac{1}{4}$ cup water, cover the wok, and cook until the beans are crisp-tender, about 1 minute. Transfer to a platter.
4. Dry the wok with a paper towel. Return it to high heat and spoon in the remaining $1\frac{1}{2}$ tablespoons oil. When the oil is hot, add the ginger and garlic and stir-fry until fragrant, 10 to 15 seconds. Crumble in the beef and stir-fry to brown well, about 1 minute. Add the scallions and stir-fry for 30 seconds. Stir the sauce and add it to the wok. Bring to a boil and cook, tossing, until slightly thickened. Add the beans and toss until heated thoroughly, about 3 minutes. Turn out onto a platter and serve hot or warm.

CHINESE BEAN PASTES AND SAUCES

This is one huge family of sauces and pastes—the terms are loosely interchangeable—made from fermented yellow or brown soybeans. There are dozens of different kinds, ranging from sweet and salty to mellow or dragon's-breath hot. They come in consistencies from soupy-chunky to smooth and spoonable; some are pourable like ketchup, others more like relish.

Bean sauce, brown bean sauce, and yellow bean sauce all fit into the category of "mother sauces." They can be used interchangeably to add color and a distinct fermented soybean flavor and to thicken sauces. Personally, I think that the versions containing whole beans have more flavor, but of course you will want the smooth ones for certain dishes. Hoisin is a sweet and piquant brown bean sauce that has complex flavor additions of garlic and spice. It is always creamy smooth. Chinese barbecue sauce is also a brown bean sauce.

When chilies and spices are added to mother sauces, hot bean sauces and Sichuan bean sauces result. This category has a particularly deep and complex fermented flavor beneath its fiery quality. Just a spoonful added to a dish or a sauce adds tremendous depth of flavor.

Red bean paste is a thick puree of fermented red beans and sugar. It is used in making dim sum desserts and pastries.

Koon Chun is a good reliable label to look for when you buy bean sauces and pastes. They often come in cans, so after opening transfer them to jars with lids and store in the refrigerator, where they will keep fresh for a year or two. Hot bean sauces, however, will begin to lose some of their heat intensity after six months.

Bacon-Browned Cabbage

The simple, earthy flavor of cabbage is greatly enhanced by a thorough browning and then by adding sweet-and-sour flavor. The dish makes a good accompaniment to any roast meat or even a charcoal-grilled burger with raw onions and tomato.

MAKES 6 TO 8 SIDE-DISH SERVINGS

> 8 slices hickory-smoked bacon, cut into ½-inch squares
> 1 small head (1½ pounds) green cabbage, quartered,
>   cored, and chopped into ½- to 1-inch pieces
> 1 large onion, chopped
> 1½ tablespoons sugar
> 3 tablespoons cider vinegar
> 1 teaspoon salt
> ¼ teaspoon black pepper

1. Place a large, heavy skillet over moderate heat and add the bacon. Cook until crisp and golden brown, 5 to 8 minutes. Tilt the pan and spoon off all but 2 to 3 tablespoons of the fat.
2. Add the cabbage and onion to the pan and sauté until deep golden brown, 15 to 20 minutes. Add 2 tablespoons of water any time the pan seems dry or the vegetables begin to stick; the water will evaporate and encourage the cooking and browning.
3. When the cabbage becomes deep, golden brown, stir in the sugar, vinegar, salt, and pepper and cook for 3 minutes. Taste for seasoning and adjust, if desired, by adding a pinch more sugar, a splash more vinegar, or a bit more salt. Serve hot or warm.

Chilies Rellenos

I have an insatiable appetite and passion for fresh poblano chilies. Living in New York, I have to pay a pretty price for them, not the bargain they are in the Southwest, where they are abundant. Sometimes I buy an entire ten-pound box of them just to get the wholesale price. In this recipe they are roasted and carefully peeled and seeded so their stems remain intact, then stuffed with cheese and passed through a light, fluffy batter before cooking. This is one of the world's great classics and one that I have been cooking for more than twenty-five years. You can roast and peel the chilies a day ahead.

MAKES 8 (4 TO 8 SERVINGS, DEPENDING ON THE MENU)

Tomato Sauce

> 1 **tablespoon vegetable oil**
> 1 **onion, finely chopped**
> 1 **large garlic clove, minced or crushed through a press**
> ½ **teaspoon dried oregano, crumbled**
> ½ **teaspoon ground cumin**
> 1 **bay leaf**
> 1 **cup Chicken Stock (page 73) or canned broth**
> 1 **can (28 ounces) seeded and chopped whole tomatoes with their juices**
> ¼ **cup chopped fresh cilantro**
> ½ **teaspoon salt**

Chilies Rellenos

> 8 **large fresh poblano chili peppers (1½ to 2 pounds)**
> 6 **ounces Monterey Jack cheese**
> 6 **ounces cheddar cheese**
> 4 **large eggs, separated**
> ¼ **teaspoon salt**
> ¼ **cup all-purpose flour**
>   **Vegetable oil**
>   **Cilantro sprigs, for garnish**

1. Make the sauce. In a nonreactive saucepan, heat the vegetable oil over moderate heat. Add the onion and sauté until soft but not browned, 3 to 5 minutes. Stir in the garlic, oregano, cumin, and bay leaf and cook for 1 minute. Pour in the stock or broth and bring to a simmer. Add the crushed tomatoes and their juices and simmer for about 5 minutes. You should have about 4 cups of thin sauce. Remove from the heat; stir in the cilantro and salt. Set aside and keep warm or reheat for serving.

2. To prepare the chilies, place the whole chilies directly in the flames of a gas burner turned to high or about 3 inches from the heat of a broiler. Turn frequently as the chilies roast until black and blistered all over. Let cool for a couple of minutes; seal in a plastic bag and let cool to room temperature.

3. Rub off the charred skin (this may be done in a colander under gently running water, but you will lose some of the juices). Using a knife, make a slit from the stem end almost to the point of each pepper. Working carefully to avoid tearing, cut through and remove the seed core at the stem end. Remove any other seeds and cut off any loose ribs. Drain on paper towels.

4. Cut both cheeses into long, narrow, pointed sticks (elongated triangles) about ½ inch wide and 2 to 3 inches long.

5. Place a chili pepper in front of you and put in enough pieces of the cheese to

fill it without overstuffing. As they are assembled, put the chilies on a tray or platter.

6. Set a large, heavy skillet over moderate heat and preheat for 3 to 5 minutes. Reduce the heat to low and keep the pan hot.

7. Put the 4 egg whites in a large bowl and add the salt. Beat until soft peaks form and the whites are almost stiff. Add the egg yolks and flour and beat just to blend.

8. Pour ⅛ inch of vegetable oil into the hot skillet. (As you cook the chilies it might be necessary to adjust the heat between moderate and low; you don't want the chilies to brown too quickly or the cheese inside will not melt.) Pick up 1 stuffed chili pepper and gently and carefully lower it into the batter with your hands (this is messy but the best way); use the same hand to scoop some of the batter over the chili. Transfer the chili pepper to the hot oil. Repeat until 4 chilies are in the pan at once. Cook for 3 to 4 minutes per side, turning only once. Drain briefly on paper towels. Repeat with the remaining 4 chilies.

9. If using a platter, pour half of the sauce over the platter and top with the Chilies Rellenos. Spoon the remaining sauce over the tops. If using individual plates, spoon ¼ cup of the sauce on each plate, add a chili pepper, and top with ¼ cup more sauce. Garnish with sprigs of cilantro.

VARIATION

To make a meal: **Soften a large flour tortilla and spread it with about ⅓ cup hot refried or pureed beans. Place 1 hot Chili Relleno (they can be made a day ahead, chilled, and reheated in the microwave for a minute) across the bottom third of the tortilla, add about ¼ cup sauce, and roll up, tucking in the ends halfway. Place seam side down and serve.**

Corn and Red Pepper Pancakes

These delicate little pancakes showcase summer corn and red peppers. Browning the kernels in butter brings out the natural sweetness and intensifies the flavor. Bell pepper, scallions, cilantro, cumin, and lemon juice perform the rest of the magic. They are lovely around a roast chicken.

MAKES 24 TO 30 PANCAKES

  3 tablespoons butter
  2 cups fresh or thawed frozen corn kernels, cut from 4 to 5 medium ears
  ½ cup finely chopped red bell pepper
  ½ cup sliced whole scallions
  ¼ cup chopped fresh cilantro
  ½ cup all-purpose flour
  ¼ teaspoon baking powder
  ½ cup heavy cream
1½ tablespoons fresh lemon juice
  ½ teaspoon dried oregano, crumbled
  ½ teaspoon ground cumin
  ⅛ teaspoon cayenne pepper
  1 teaspoon salt
  1 teaspoon sugar
  3 large eggs, separated
  Vegetable oil

1. Melt 2 tablespoons of the butter in a large, heavy skillet over moderate heat. Add the corn and bell pepper, increase the heat to moderately high, and sauté until lightly browned, about 5 minutes. Pour in ¼ cup water and deglaze the pan, stirring up any browned bits that cling to the pan. Cook until the liquid boils away. Turn the mixture into a large bowl and let cool to room temperature.

2. Add the scallions, cilantro, flour, and baking powder to the bowl and toss to combine. Stir in the cream. Add the lemon juice, oregano, cumin, cayenne, salt, and sugar. Stir in the egg yolks.

3. Place 1 or 2 large, heavy skillets or griddles over moderate heat and preheat until very hot. Reduce the heat to low.

4. Meanwhile, in a deep bowl, beat the egg whites until almost stiff. Stir a large spoonful of the whites into the corn mixture; fold in the remaining beaten whites. Coat the skillets or griddles with a scant ¹⁄₁₆ inch of vegetable oil and heat the oil. When very hot, add ½ teaspoon of the remaining butter to each. Spoon in 3 tablespoons of batter for each pancake and spread it into a 3-inch round. Regulate the heat as necessary

VARIATIONS

Substitution: **Use fresh basil in place of the cilantro and omit the cumin.**

Bigger flavor: **Roast and peel the bell pepper before chopping.**

Lower cholesterol: **Use olive oil in place of the butter and light cream in place of the heavy cream.**

between low and moderate and cook the pancakes until golden brown on the bottom, about 3 minutes. Turn and cook for about 2 minutes longer. The pancakes will be fragile; carefully transfer them to a baking sheet lined with paper towels. Keep warm in a 300° F. oven or serve right away. Repeat, adding oil and butter to the pans as needed, until all of the batter is cooked.

Smoky Eggplant Parmesan

This version of the classic Italian treatment of eggplant is different from others because it has a fragrant smoky aroma, contributed by smoked mozzarella cheese. It's a good idea to fry the eggplant slices several hours before you assemble this dish. And since it relies on juicy ripe tomatoes, get the most flavorful ones you can find.

MAKES 8 MAIN-DISH SERVINGS

- 3 or 4 large eggplants (4½ pounds total weight)
- 1 tablespoon salt
- 1 cup all-purpose flour
  Peanut oil
  Olive oil
- 12 ounces smoked mozzarella cheese, coarsely grated (3 cups)
- 2½ to 3 pounds ripe tomatoes, cored and cut into ¼-inch-thick slices
- ½ cup chopped fresh Italian flat-leaf parsley
- 1 cup freshly grated Parmesan cheese

1. Slice off the ends of the eggplants and use a swivel-bladed vegetable peeler to remove the skin. Cut crosswise into ¼-inch-thick slices. Arrange the slices on racks over the sink and sprinkle lightly with 1½ teaspoons of the salt. Let stand for 15 minutes. Turn the slices and sprinkle them with the remaining 1½ teaspoons salt; let stand until beads of liquid appear all over the surface, 30 to 45 minutes longer. Wipe off the salt and moisture with paper towels, blotting them thoroughly.
2. Put the flour in a shallow dish. Place a large, heavy skillet over moderately high heat. The eggplant should be fried in about ¼ inch of oil that is made up of three-quarters peanut oil and one-quarter olive oil. Pour in the oils and heat to about 375° F. (just below the smoking point). You'll have to regulate the heat between high and moderately high as you cook. Dredge a few slices of eggplant in the flour and put them into the hot oil. Add

enough to fill the skillet in a single layer. Fry until deep golden brown, about 3 minutes. Turn and brown the other side for about 2 minutes longer. Drain on paper towels. Continue until all of the eggplant is browned, adding more oil as needed. Once browned, the slices can be stacked between layers of paper towels and drained for several hours.

3. Preheat the oven to 400° F. Lightly oil a 13 × 9-inch baking dish.

4. Arrange one-third of the eggplant slices, overlapping, to cover the bottom of the pan. Scatter one-third of the mozzarella over the eggplant. Arrange one-third of the tomatoes over the cheese; sprinkle with half of the parsley and ⅓ cup of the Parmesan. Repeat the layering twice more, omitting the parsley from the top layer.

5. Bake in the center of the oven for 35 to 40 minutes, or until very hot and bubbly. Let cool for at least 20 minutes before serving. (This casserole is great when made well ahead of time and reheated at 350° F. for 30 to 40 minutes. You can also heat individual portions in a microwave oven on full power for 2 to 3 minutes.) Serve hot or warm.

Cucumber-Radish Raita

This cool and refreshing vegetable side dish is in good contrast to the heat of tandoori-roasted meat dishes. It's a great recipe for spring, using fresh radishes and mint, to accompany a spring lamb.

MAKES 6 TO 8 SIDE-DISH SERVINGS

     3 large cucumbers
     2 teaspoons salt
  1½ teaspoons ground cumin
  1½ cups low-fat plain yogurt
   ¾ cup sour cream
   ½ cup finely chopped fresh mint
   ¼ teaspoon black pepper
    10 to 12 red radishes, trimmed and thinly sliced

1. Peel the cucumbers. Cut them lengthwise in half and spoon out the seeds. Cut the cucumber halves crosswise into ⅛-inch slices. Toss in a colander with 1½ teaspoons of the salt and let drain for 30 minutes in the sink.

2. In a small, dry skillet, toast the ground cumin over moderate heat, shaking the pan until fragrant, about 1 minute. Turn into a bowl and stir in the yogurt, sour cream, mint, pepper, and the remaining ½ teaspoon salt.

Squeeze a handful of cucumbers at a time to remove the excess liquid. Add the cucumbers and toss well. Cover and refrigerate for about 1 hour.

3. Just before serving, stir in the radishes.

Hickory Gingered Eggplant

If you like really big flavors as I do, you're going to love this concoction. It's somewhere between a dip, a relish, and a spread. First, you'll need a hardwood charcoal fire outdoors for the smoke; hickory or mesquite work well. (You can use a few charcoal briquettes on the bottom to get the fire going, then put the chunks of hardwood on top. For the smoke, hardwood shavings and chips soaked in water will do the trick.) If you're making this dish for a party, double the recipe—it disappears a lot faster than you think. Serve it with sesame pita crisps or spoon it onto a salad plate.

MAKES ABOUT 2½ CUPS

> 2 medium eggplants (each about 1¼ pounds)
> 3 tablespoons fresh ginger juice (page 14)
> 2 tablespoons soy sauce
> 1½ tablespoons Oriental sesame oil
> 1 tablespoon sugar
> ¼ teaspoon salt (optional)

1. Put a layer of charcoal briquettes in a barbecue or hibachi and top with big chunks of hardwood. Ignite and let burn until glowing charcoal embers remain. Meanwhile, put about 3 cups of hardwood chips in a bowl of warm water and soak until needed. Using a long fork, prick each eggplant about 15 times.

2. When the charcoal is glowing, sprinkle on about 2 cups of the soaked wood chips. Place the eggplants on the grill about 5 inches above the coals. Cover loosely with a tent or dome of aluminum foil and smoke, turning occasionally with tongs and adding the remaining wood chips when the others cease smoking, until the eggplants are very soft and well charred, about 45 minutes. If flames break out during the smoking, spritz with water to squelch. Slide the eggplants onto a plat-

VARIATIONS

Addition: **To dress this up a bit and add yet another flavor dimension, you can sprinkle the top with chopped cilantro before serving.**

Presentation: **For a party, consider doubling the recipe and then serving in a large hollowed-out raw eggplant.**

ter and let cool completely. They can be held at room temperature all day or covered and refrigerated if grilling a day ahead.

3. Tilt the platter and discard any juices that have accumulated (they will be bitter). Cut the eggplants lengthwise in half and place, cut sides down, on a cutting board. Using a paring knife, peel off and discard the charred skin; if any flesh comes off with the skin, scrape it off and reserve it. Chop the flesh into ½-inch pieces and put in a bowl.

4. Stir in the ginger juice, soy sauce, sesame oil, and sugar. Taste for seasoning and add the salt, if needed. Cover and chill. Serve cool. If making a day ahead, cover and refrigerate.

Browned and Braised Belgian Endive with Lime Butter

The little whitish green heads of the bitter green called Belgian endive have a big flavor all their own, but when you brown them in butter and braise them, then squeeze them with lime juice and melt butter over the top, the flavor becomes even bigger and better. These are especially good with steaks, pork chops, lamb chops, and roast chicken, but I confess to sometimes making a meal of them all by themselves. This is easily doubled.

MAKES 2 TO 4 SIDE-DISH SERVINGS

> 4 **firm Belgian endive**
> 2 **tablespoons butter**
> 1 **tablespoon fresh lime juice**
> **Salt and pepper**

1. Trim about ⅛ inch from the stem end of each endive. Pull off any outer wilted leaves. Cut the heads lengthwise in half.

2. Place a nonreactive large skillet over moderately high heat and add 1 tablespoon of the butter. Arrange the endive halves, cut sides down, in the pan and sauté until deep golden brown, about 4 minutes. Turn them, pour in ½ cup hot water, cover, and braise just until tender, 2 to 3 minutes. Remove with a slotted spoon and arrange on a small platter.

3. Spread the remaining 1 tablespoon butter over the tops and spoon the lime juice over the tops. Sprinkle lightly with salt and pepper. Serve hot.

Sake-Soaked Mushrooms

The sake permeates the mushrooms as they braise. Serve this as you would a relish or condiment. It tastes great with the Gingered Scrod Fillets (page 278) or with grilled seafood, roast chicken, and barbecued pork or beef steaks. And it is a delightful addition to a picnic.

MAKES 4 TO 6 SIDE-DISH SERVINGS

    1 **cup sake**
  1½ **tablespoons soy sauce**
    1 **tablespoon rice vinegar**
    1 **tablespoon sugar**
    5 **large thin slices fresh ginger**
    1 **large garlic clove, minced or crushed through a press**
    1 **pound large fresh mushrooms, rinsed, drained, stemmed, and caps thinly sliced**
    1 **teaspoon Oriental sesame oil**

1. In a nonreactive medium saucepan, combine the sake, soy sauce, rice vinegar, sugar, ginger, and garlic. Bring to a boil over moderate heat. Add the mushrooms, reduce the heat to moderately low, and simmer, uncovered, tossing occasionally, until the liquid is almost completely evaporated, 25 to 30 minutes. Remove from the heat.

2. Remove and discard the ginger slices. Stir in the sesame oil. Set aside to cool to room temperature. Cover and refrigerate. Serve cold. (This recipe can be prepared a day or two ahead.)

SAKE

The so-called rice wine of Japan, sake is actually produced from fermented rice using a technique similar to beer making. The final product, however, more closely resembles a wine than a beer. It is fragrant and colorless. It has a fermented flavor and subtle sweet nuance. Heating sake releases its full aroma, and it is generally served warm as a beverage.

By the way, sake does not age well. It is best used within the year that it is made. Heat and light can destroy it, so store your sake in a cool, dark place.

Because of the amino acids in sake, it has a slight tenderizing effect on meats and seafood. The flavor cuts the saltiness of soy sauce and balances fishy aromas.

Russian Radishes
in Sour Cream

I love to go to Coney Island in Brooklyn. Usually it is just an excuse to end up in my favorite Russian neighborhood, nearby Brighton Beach. This is a colorful community with lots of little shops selling exotic Russian ingredients, big delicatessens selling homemade Russian food, fanciful bakeries, and charming restaurants. The highlight of the day always is lunch. Recently at lunch with my good friend, Robert Ramsey, I enjoyed an appetizer of sliced radishes with rich clotted sour cream. I'm not sure how they make it, but at home you can come mighty close by mixing large-curd cottage cheese with sour cream. Dressed with dill and a squeeze of lemon, the cool, rich creaminess is in perfect contrast to slices of crisp, juicy radish. Although you can make the dressing a day ahead, don't add the radishes until serving time. Serve with sandwiches or with a selection of cold appetizers that include Hickory Gingered Eggplant (page 158) and Grilled Vegetable Terrine with Goat Cheese (page 165) and, of course, that Russian flatbread called *lavash*. Chicken or lamb shish kebabs grilled over charcoal would make a seductive main course.

MAKES 4 TO 6 SIDE-DISH SERVINGS

- 1 **cup sour cream**
- ¾ **cup large-curd cottage cheese**
- 2 **tablespoons snipped fresh dill, plus 1 sprig, for garnish**
- 1½ **teaspoons lemon juice**
- ½ **teaspoon salt**
- ⅛ **teaspoon pepper**
- 3 **cups chilled sliced radishes (30 medium)**

1. In a medium bowl, stir together the sour cream, cottage cheese, and dill. Stir in the lemon juice, salt, and pepper. If making ahead, cover and refrigerate.
2. Put the radishes in a large bowl and toss with half the dressing. Mound on a small platter and spoon the remaining dressing over the top. Garnish with the sprig of dill and serve cold.

VARIATIONS

Lower fat: **For a less rich dressing, use yogurt in place of the sour cream.**

Substitution: **For those who do not care for dill, simply omit and the dish will be delicious. Most often this appetizer is served plain, without the dill.**

Sautéed Radishes

This recipe is fun to serve because most people cannot identify the vegetable. Radishes already have a big flavor, but once they're sliced and browned, they change totally in texture and flavor. I have kept the seasonings very simple so you can enjoy them as they are. Serve with any vegetarian menu or with roasted or grilled meats and poultry. This is easily doubled.

MAKES 2 TO 4 SIDE-DISH SERVINGS

> 1 tablespoon vegetable oil
> 3 cups thinly sliced large red radishes
> 2 tablespoons chopped fresh parsley
> ½ teaspoon salt
> Pinch of black pepper

1. Set a large, heavy skillet over moderate heat and preheat until very hot, 4 to 5 minutes.
2. Spoon in the oil and increase the heat to high. Add the radishes and toss to coat with the oil. Sauté until translucent and well browned, about 5 minutes. Remove from the heat and toss with the parsley, salt, and pepper. Serve hot.

Deep-Dish Spinach Pie

This makes a great luncheon main course or super hors d'oeuvre when cut into small squares. Serve hot, warm, or cold. The big flavors of feta, lemon, and tarragon star here.

MAKES 6 TO 8 MAIN-DISH SERVINGS

> Flaky Pastry (page 337)
> 1 egg yolk, beaten
> 2 pounds fresh spinach, stemmed and washed
> ½ teaspoon dried tarragon, crumbled
> ¼ cup fresh lemon juice
> 1 cup crumbled feta cheese (about 4 ounces)
> 4 large eggs, at room temperature
> 1 cup heavy cream
> 1 cup light cream
> ½ teaspoon salt
> ¼ teaspoon grated nutmeg

1. Preheat the oven to 400° F. On a lightly floured surface, roll out the pastry to a 13-inch square. Loosely drape it into an 8-inch square baking pan; press the dough to conform to the pan. Roll up the overhanging pastry to make a raised edge and crimp decoratively. Place a sheet of aluminum foil slightly larger than the pan over the dough and press it to conform to the pastry. Fill with pie weights, dried rice, or dried beans.

2. Bake the pastry shell until the crimped edge is set, about 10 minutes. Carefully remove the pie weights and foil, return the shell to the oven, and bake, poking the bottom with a fork if the pastry bubbles up, for about 8 minutes, or until the bottom is dry and firm.

3. Generously paint enough of the beaten egg yolk over the bottom of the pastry shell to coat well. Return the shell to the oven and bake until set, about 2 minutes. Let cool on a rack. Reduce the oven temperature to 350° F.

4. Meanwhile, place the wet spinach leaves in a nonreactive large pot. Cover and cook over moderately high heat, stirring once or twice, until wilted and greatly reduced in bulk, about 3 minutes. Drain the spinach in a colander; press with the back of a spoon to extract the excess liquid. Coarsely chop the spinach; there will be 1½ to 2 cups.

5. In a large bowl, combine the spinach, tarragon, lemon juice, and feta cheese. Toss well.

6. In another bowl, whisk together the eggs, heavy cream, light cream, salt, and nutmeg.

7. Arrange the spinach mixture in the partially baked shell and pour the egg mixture over it. Place the baking pan on a baking sheet and bake for about 50 minutes, or until puffed all over and lightly speckled golden brown. Cool on a rack for 1 hour before cutting. Cut into squares or refrigerate until serving time.

NUTMEG

Although it is agreed that nutmeg should be used sparingly, to enhance and become a background flavor, not really to be tasted, I find that often a little more than just a grating is needed to lend dishes a bold rather than bland flavor—just enough to catch up with the other flavorings but still remain in the background.

Preground nutmeg loses its flavor quickly. Always buy whole nutmeg—which will keep well for a couple of years—and an inexpensive nutmeg grater, and grate as needed.

Cajun Succotash

Okra doesn't become gelatinous when cooked this way; each of the vegetables remains distinct, retaining its individual characteristics. The colors are pretty— yellow, red, and green, with tasty charred edges. This dish is great with grilled meats, roast chicken, and meat loaf.

MAKES ABOUT 6 SIDE-DISH SERVINGS

> 6 slices hickory-smoked bacon, cut into small squares
> 1 pound small fresh okra, trimmed and cut into ½-inch slices
> 2½ tablespoons olive oil
> 2 cups fresh corn kernels
> 1 medium onion, finely chopped
> 1 red bell pepper, cut into ½-inch squares
> 1 large garlic clove, minced or crushed through a press
> ½ teaspoon dried thyme, crumbled
> ½ teaspoon ground cumin
> 1 teaspoon sugar
> 1 teaspoon salt
> ¼ teaspoon black pepper
> ⅛ to ¼ teaspoon cayenne pepper

1. Place a large, heavy skillet over moderate heat. Add the bacon and cook, stirring frequently, until crisp and golden brown, 5 to 8 minutes. Remove with a slotted spoon; drain on paper towels. Spoon off all but about 1½ tablespoons of the fat.
2. Add the okra to the skillet and increase the heat to moderately high. Tossing occasionally, cook the okra until well browned, almost charred, 12 to 15 minutes. Remove from the heat and reserve.
3. Spoon 1½ tablespoons of the olive oil into the skillet and add the corn. Brown well, tossing, for about 5 minutes over moderately high heat. Remove and add to the okra.
4. Spoon the remaining 1 tablespoon olive oil into the skillet and reduce the heat to moderate. Add the onion and bell pepper and sauté until softened and lightly browned, 3 to 5 minutes.
5. Add the garlic, thyme, cumin, sugar, salt, black pepper, and ⅛ teaspoon of the cayenne; cook for 2 minutes. Pour in ¼ cup water and bring it to a boil. Return the bacon, okra, and

VARIATIONS

Lower cholesterol: **Discard all of the bacon fat and replace with olive oil. If using a nonstick skillet, the quantity of olive oil can be cut by half.**

Addition: **One-quarter of a cup chopped fresh parsley can be added before serving.**

corn to the skillet. Cook, tossing, until hot. Taste and add $\frac{1}{8}$ teaspoon more cayenne, if desired. Serve hot.

Grilled Vegetable Terrine with Goat Cheese

Many of my favorite flavors are here: smoky grilled vegetables, goat cheese, black olives, olive oil, and fresh basil. At first the quantity of vegetables seems enormous, but after trimming and grilling them, their bulk is reduced considerably. Make the terrine a day ahead and serve cold slices with leaves of radicchio and arugula. The vegetables will taste best if you add some hardwood chips to the charcoal fire.

MAKES 8 TO 10 SIDE-DISH SERVINGS

- 2 **pounds red bell peppers (4 to 6 large)**
  Hardwood chips, for grilling (optional)
- 3 **eggplants (1 pound each), ends trimmed**
- 2 **pounds zucchini (4 large), ends trimmed**
- $\frac{1}{2}$ **cup olive oil**
- $\frac{1}{2}$ **cup finely chopped fresh basil**
- $\frac{1}{2}$ **teaspoon salt**
- 10 **to 12 ounces mild fresh goat cheese, such as Montrachet, at room temperature**
- 8 **ounces Italian or Greek black olives, pitted and halved**
  Radicchio leaves, arugula, and vinaigrette or olive oil, for serving

1. Roast the bell peppers according to the technique on page 17. If you want to roast them over charcoal, the technique is the same, but the peppers will take slightly longer to roast. When cool, rub off the skins and cut out the stems; pull out the seeds and ribs.
2. Build a charcoal fire in an outdoor barbecue. Meanwhile, soak 2 to 3 cups of hardwood chips in warm water until needed.
3. Cut the eggplants and zucchini lengthwise into slices $\frac{1}{4}$ to $\frac{1}{3}$ inch thick. Lightly brush one side of enough slices to fit on the grill at one time. When the charcoals are ash-covered, drain the hardwood chips and scatter a handful over the coals. Place the grill in position and preheat. Add a layer of vegetables, oiled side down. Lightly brush the tops with olive oil. Grill, turning once, until softened and charred, 3 to 4 minutes per side. Remove the vegetables as done and stack on a platter. Repeat with the remaining

wood chips, vegetables, and olive oil. Let the vegetables cool completely before assembling the terrine.

4. Lightly oil a 9 × 5-inch loaf pan. Line it with plastic wrap so the ends extend beyond the top edge. Oil the plastic wrap. The terrine will be assembled with 4 layers of vegetables separated by 3 layers of cheese and olives. Cut the pieces of bell pepper to fit as needed. Layer the best-looking pieces of roasted pepper in the prepared pan, using about one-fourth. As each vegetable layer is formed, sprinkle very lightly with about 2 teaspoons of the chopped basil and a pinch of the salt. (Be judicious because the cheese and olives are salty.) Layer in the following order: one-fourth each of the roasted peppers, zucchini, and eggplant (add basil and salt to each), then one-third of the cheese, dotted about or spread slightly, and last one-third of the olives. Repeat the layering 3 times. For the final layer, arrange the eggplant, then the roasted pepper, and end with the zucchini. Pat to make compact. The pan will be very full. Fold the plastic wrap over the top and cover with more plastic wrap.

5. Place the pan on a tray and lightly weigh down with cans or bricks. Refrigerate overnight.

6. To serve, remove the top sheet of plastic wrap. Invert a serving platter over the loaf pan. Invert and remove the loaf pan. Peel off the plastic wrap. The zucchini will release a good amount of liquid, but this is natural and should simply be drained off or blotted up. Serve the terrine cold, cut into 1-inch slices, garnished with the radicchio and arugula and drizzled with vinaigrette or olive oil.

Parmesan-Fried Green Tomatoes

Once a year, every year, I get a craving for fried green tomatoes. Maybe it's genetic—my mother made them once a year, too. Most people fry them plain, with just a cornmeal coating and often in bacon fat, but I like to spice them up and fry them crunchier, with grated cheese mixed with the cornmeal. Remember, not all green tomatoes are the same; the ones almost ready to turn pink will be the juiciest.

MAKES 6 SIDE-DISH SERVINGS

4 medium green tomatoes (1½ pounds)
⅔ cup all-purpose flour
2 large eggs

⅔ **cup coarse yellow cornmeal**

⅔ **cup freshly grated Parmesan cheese**

2 **teaspoons dried oregano, crumbled**

1 **teaspoon salt**

¼ **teaspoon black pepper**

2½ **tablespoons olive oil**

2 **tablespoons butter**

1. Cut out the woody stem end of each tomato; slice the tomatoes about ¼ inch thick. You will get about 6 good slices from each, plus the end pieces.

2. Choose 3 shallow dishes for the coating ingredients. Put the flour in one; whisk the eggs with 1 tablespoon water in the second; and stir together the cornmeal, Parmesan, oregano, salt, and pepper in the third. Do not coat the tomato slices until you are ready to cook them, and then coat only as many as will fit into the pan at one time (6 or 7).

3. Place a large, heavy skillet over moderately high heat. Add 1 tablespoon of the olive oil and ½ tablespoon of the butter. Dip 1 tomato slice in the flour, turning it to coat both sides lightly. Dip into the egg, turning once to coat both sides, and then put it into the cornmeal mixture; tap it several times and turn to coat evenly. Put the coated tomato slice into the hot skillet. Continue coating and adding slices until the pan is full (in a single layer). Fry until deep golden brown, turning once, 2 to 3 minutes per side. (It may be necessary to regulate the heat between moderate and moderately high as you cook.) Drain on paper towels. Repeat, adding ½ tablespoon each of olive oil and butter to the pan for each new batch. Sprinkle lightly with salt and serve hot or warm.

VARIATIONS

Lower cholesterol: **To cut cholesterol, fry in a 50-50 mixture of olive oil and vegetable oil (omitting the butter).**

Substitutions: **For a smoky flavor, fry in bacon fat. Use finely grated Swiss or cheddar cheese for a flavor change. Tarragon can be substituted for the oregano.**

One Potato, Two More . . .

Potato, Three Potato,

Smashed Potato Salad

Herb Garden Potato Salad

Uncle Jim's Old-Fashioned Potato Salad

Home-Fried Potatoes with Arugula and Mushrooms

Cajun Fries

Curry Mashed Potatoes

Scalloped Potatoes with Ham and Cheese

Potatoes and Chorizo

Orange Candied Sweet Potatoes

Squashed Potatoes

Bonus Recipes

Cilantro Hash Browns   Flavor-Whipped Potatoes

Smashed Potato Salad

You've got to try this. It is a great Southern-style potato salad that is the perfect punctuation to any barbecue, spicy fried chicken, or the Harlem Meat Loaf on page 226. You start with russet baking potatoes because they smash better than most others. Very little mayonnaise is used because the salad should be slightly dry. If it seems dry at first, don't worry, it will moisten up upon chilling.

MAKES 6 TO 8 SERVINGS

- 3 pounds Idaho russet potatoes
  Salt
- 3 large eggs, hard-cooked (page 13)
- ½ cup mayonnaise
- 2 tablespoons spicy brown mustard
- 1 tablespoon sugar
- 1 tablespoon cider vinegar
- ½ teaspoon black pepper
- ½ teaspoon paprika
- ⅓ cup finely chopped mixed sweet pickles (see Note)
- ⅓ cup minced whole scallions
- ⅓ cup finely chopped fresh parsley, plus sprigs, for garnish
- 2 tablespoons chopped canned roasted red
    bell pepper or pimiento (optional)

Note: This variety is usually labeled "Mixed Sweet Pickles" and contains pickles, cauliflower, pearl onions, and red peppers.

1. Put the potatoes in a large pot and add enough cold water to cover generously. Add a big pinch of salt. Place over high heat, partly cover, and bring to a boil. Lower the heat slightly to prevent boiling over and boil vigorously until tender when pierced with a fork, 35 to 40 minutes for medium potatoes or 45 to 55 minutes for large ones. Drain and let cool to room temperature.

2. Peel and finely chop the eggs into a bowl. Mash slightly with a fork. Stir in the mayonnaise, mustard, sugar, vinegar, pepper, paprika, sweet pickles, scallions, chopped parsley, bell pepper, and 2 teaspoons salt. Cover and chill until needed.

3. Peel the potatoes. Cut into chunks and put them in a large bowl. Smash with a fork or potato masher to a texture somewhere between mashed and chunky. Pour the dressing over the potatoes and stir until evenly blended. Cover and chill for several hours or overnight.

4. To serve, turn out onto a platter or serving bowl. Sprinkle lightly with additional paprika and garnish with the parsley sprigs. Serve cold.

Herb Garden Potato Salad

The salad is beautifully green and white and has a big, fresh, tangy herbal flavor. This is a perfect showcase for chervil. You'll need about a cup and a half of fresh herbs, in any combination, but radish roses would make a striking garnish.

MAKES 6 TO 8 SERVINGS

  3 pounds small to medium red-skinned potatoes
     Salt
  3 tablespoons dry white wine
  ½ cup chopped fresh parsley
  ½ cup chopped fresh chervil or cilantro
  ½ cup chopped fresh chives or sliced whole scallions
  3 tablespoons chopped fresh tarragon, or ½ teaspoon dried
  1 tablespoon chopped fresh oregano
  1 tablespoon Dijon mustard
  ½ teaspoon black pepper
  3 tablespoons herb-flavored vinegar
  ¼ cup extra-virgin olive oil

1. Put the unpeeled potatoes in a large pot and add cold water to cover by 1 inch. Add a little salt, cover, and bring to a boil over high heat. Reduce the heat to moderately high, partly cover, and cook until tender when pierced with a long fork, about 20 to 25 minutes for small or 25 to 30 minutes for medium. Drain and set aside until just cool enough to handle.
2. It is important that the potatoes are still warm for this step. If the potato skins are in good shape, you can leave them unpeeled, or peel if desired. Cut 2 or 3 potatoes in half lengthwise, then cut crosswise into ¼-inch slices. Put

CHERVIL

I think of this delicate herb as the darling of the herb garden. It is worthless when dried, but if fresh is available, add as much as you want to salads, sauces, and dressings.

Chervil is light, bright green, and has lacy fernlike leaves. It is closely related to parsley and has a similar appearance, though it is much softer, more delicate, and fragile. Its fresh, aromatic flavor is reminiscent of anise and pepper, sweeter and more aromatic than parsley. It is always best added at the last moment, just before serving. Cooked, it will lose its delicacy and become bitter.

Chervil blends well with most other herbs. It does not interfere with their flavors but enhances them. It is an important element in French *fines herbes* (along with parsley, chive, sage, savory, and basil).

the slices in a large bowl and drizzle with a little of the wine so drops fall on each slice. As they cool the wine soaks in. Continue slicing and layering until all of the potatoes and wine are used. Let cool to room temperature.

3. Add all of the fresh herbs to the potatoes and toss gently with a rubber spatula so potatoes do not break.
4. In a medium bowl, stir together the mustard, pepper, and 2 teaspoons salt. Stir in the vinegar and then gradually whisk in the olive oil. Pour over the potatoes and toss gently with a rubber spatula so all of the slices are coated. Cover and chill for about 2 hours.
5. Toss gently. Mound on a platter and garnish with radish roses, if desired.

VARIATIONS

To make a meal: Peel and seed a large cucumber, cut into ¼-inch slices, and chill. Just before serving, stir in. You can also fold in 1 cup sliced radishes just before serving and/or finely diced red and green bell pepper. Fresh poached salmon and tuna, separated into large flakes, can be tossed with the salad, in which case you might want to add some fresh chopped dill and garnish with sliced, hard-cooked eggs.

Uncle Jim's Old-Fashioned Potato Salad

One of my favorite meals in the whole wide world is this delicious potato salad with a Charcoal-Grilled Hamburger on a kaiser roll (page 185), Big-Flavor Boston Baked Beans (page 148), and corn-on-the-cob. Don't make this salad a day ahead. It is at its absolute best after chilling for just 1 to 3 hours. The dressing may taste too salty at first, but it will balance as the potatoes chill.

MAKES 6 TO 8 SERVINGS

> 3 **pounds red-skinned potatoes**
> **Salt**
> 4 **hard-cooked eggs (page 13)**
> ¾ **cup mayonnaise**
> 2 **tablespoons brown mustard**
> 2 **tablespoons cider vinegar**
> ½ **teaspoon black pepper**
> ½ **cup thinly sliced whole scallions**
> ¼ **cup finely chopped fresh parsley, plus sprigs, for garnish**
> **Paprika**

1. Put the unpeeled potatoes in a large, heavy pot and add cold water to cover by 1 inch. Sprinkle lightly with salt, partly cover, and bring to a boil over high heat. Boil the potatoes until tender when pierced with a fork, 30 to 40 minutes (if you have used small potatoes, they will take 25 to 30 minutes, while large ones will take 40 to 50 minutes). Pour off the water and let the potatoes cool to room temperature.

2. Peel the eggs and rinse them; reserve 1 for garnish. Coarsely grate the remaining 3 eggs into a large bowl. Using a fork, mash the grated eggs against the side of the bowl. Stir in the mayonnaise, mustard, vinegar, pepper, and 2 teaspoons salt.

3. Peel the potatoes and cut roughly into 1-inch chunks; the salad will be most appealing if the chunks are uneven rather than in perfect cubes. Add the scallions and chopped parsley and toss. Cover and chill for 1 to 3 hours.

4. To serve, toss gently and mound onto a platter or in a bowl. Slice the remaining egg and arrange the slices in an overlapping row across the center. Sprinkle lightly with paprika and garnish with 3 or 4 small parsley sprigs. Chill for 1 to 3 hours. Serve cold.

VARIATIONS

Additions: **For a deliciously fragrant salad, add about ¼ cup mixed chopped fresh herbs, such as oregano, basil, chervil, thyme, and/or tarragon. Black olives can be added to the salad and used to garnish the top.**

Home-Fried Potatoes with Arugula and Mushrooms

No herbs are needed here—you can rely on the big, earthy flavor of arugula and well-browned potatoes to make this hearty breakfast or brunch dish. Although the mushrooms are optional, they add a wonderful dimension.

MAKES 6 SERVINGS

- 2 **pounds red-skinned boiling potatoes (6 medium)**
- **Salt**
- 2½ **tablespoons olive oil**
- 1 **pound arugula, well washed, tough stems removed, and leaves dried**
- 2 **tablespoons butter**
- 1 **onion, finely chopped**
- 1 **teaspoon sweet paprika**
- **Pinch of black pepper**
- 8 **ounces fresh mushrooms, cut into ½-inch dice (optional)**

1. Several hours or even a day ahead, put the potatoes in a large pot and add cold water to cover generously. Add a big pinch of salt and place over high heat; partly cover and bring to a boil. Boil over moderately high heat until tender when pierced with a fork, 35 to 45 minutes. Drain the potatoes and let cool to room temperature. Peel the potatoes and cut them into irregular 1-inch chunks.

2. Place a large well-seasoned or nonstick skillet over moderate heat for 3 to 4 minutes. Increase the heat to high, spoon in 1 tablespoon of the olive oil and then all of the arugula. Sauté for 1 to 2 minutes, tossing until wilted. Transfer to a sieve and let drain, but do not press.

3. Wipe the skillet clean with a paper towel; set over moderate heat. Add the remaining 1½ tablespoons olive oil and 1½ tablespoons of the butter. Add the potatoes and onion; sprinkle with the paprika, 1¼ teaspoons salt, and the pepper. Fry, without stirring, until lightly browned, 5 to 7 minutes. Toss the mixture and cook, tossing frequently, until browned, 5 to 7 minutes longer.

4. Push the potatoes to one side of the pan. Add the mushrooms, if using, and the remaining ½ tablespoon butter. Increase the heat to high and sauté until browned, 1 to 2 minutes. Add the drained arugula and toss to combine. Mound on a platter and serve hot.

Cilantro Hash Browns

Although I wasn't sure if hash browns flavored with cilantro qualified as a big enough flavor to be a full-fledged recipe on their own, they are so full of flavor they are worth
telling you about. Both the cilantro and the deeply browned potatoes contribute tremendous flavor—just great with bacon, eggs, and salsa or sliced tomatoes.

TO SERVE 4:

One day ahead of time, boil 1½ pounds (6 medium) red-skinned or waxy boiling potatoes
until tender, 30 to 35 minutes. Drain, cool to room temperature, and chill. Peel the potatoes and shred them through the coarse side of a grater into a large bowl. Toss with
about ⅓ cup chopped cilantro and ½ teaspoon salt.

Place a large griddle or 2 skillets over moderate heat. When very hot, lightly coat with
vegetable oil. Using a scant cupful of the potato mixture for each, scoop out 4 mounds
and place directly on the griddle or skillets. Press lightly and shape into 4 × 6-inch ovals.
Reduce the heat and add bits of butter (¼ teaspoon for each) around the edges. Cook,
pressing occasionally to compact them, until crisp and deep golden brown, 8 to 10 minutes. Add a few drops of oil if the potatoes seem dry. Flip with a spatula and brown for 4
to 5 minutes longer. Serve hot.

Cajun Fries

When long, slender sticks of potato are partially cooked and then dipped into
a spicy light batter, they become crunchy and addictively delicious upon deep-
frying. They are great with burgers or with the Crunchy Louisiana Catfish (page
281) and lemonade or iced tea. Serve with Hot and Spicy Ketchup (page 376),
Quick Chili Sauce (page 377), or Blue Cheese Dressing (page 99).

MAKES 6 SERVINGS

Batter

    1 cup all-purpose flour
    1 tablespoon cayenne pepper
    2 teaspoons ground cumin
  1½ teaspoons dried oregano, crumbled
  1½ teaspoons dried thyme, crumbled
    1 teaspoon salt
    ½ teaspoon black pepper

Potatoes

    5 large, long russet baking potatoes (5 ounces each)
      Vegetable oil, for deep-frying
      Salt

1. Make the batter. In a large bowl, stir together the flour, cayenne, cumin, oregano, thyme, salt, and black pepper. Whisking constantly, pour in 1½ cups cold water and blend until smooth. Cover and chill for at least 1 hour or as long as 1 day.
2. Peel the potatoes and cut lengthwise into sticks about ⅓ inch thick. Drop them into a large bowl of cold water as they are cut.
3. Pour about 1½ inches of vegetable oil into a large, heavy, deep kettle or electric deep-fryer. Heat the oil to 325° F. for the initial frying.
4. Drain the potatoes and dry them thoroughly by rolling them up in a clean cotton towel. Make sure that they are completely dry or they will cause the hot oil to spatter. Working in batches without crowding, fry the potatoes at 325° F. for 5 minutes. Drain. (The potatoes can be cooked to this stage several hours ahead.)
5. Heat the oil to 375° F. Stir the cold batter and add one batch of potatoes. One at a time, drop the potato sticks into the hot oil and deep-fry until crisp and deep golden brown, 3 to 4 minutes. Drain. Sprinkle lightly with salt and serve hot.

Curry Mashed Potatoes

If you like curry, you've got to try this. There's nothing meek about this treatment—these potatoes are at the same time big and bold, hot and spicy, tart and tangy, *and* creamy and comforting, as only mashed potatoes can be. They are perfectly at home with a simple roast chicken with gravy and green peas.

MAKES 6 SERVINGS

3 **pounds russet baking potatoes**
Salt
3 **tablespoons butter**
1 **large onion, finely chopped**
1 **tablespoon minced fresh ginger**
1 **large garlic clove, minced or crushed through a press**
2 **tablespoons Curry Powder (page 385) or store-bought**
½ **cup sour cream**
½ **cup plain low-fat yogurt**
¼ **teaspoon black pepper**

1. Peel the potatoes and cut them into 1-inch chunks, dropping them into a large pot of cold water as they are cut. Add a big pinch of salt, cover, and

bring to a boil over high heat. Boil until tender when pierced with a fork, 15 to 20 minutes. Drain and return to the hot pan.

2. Meanwhile, melt 2 tablespoons of the butter in a large heavy skillet over moderate heat. Add the onion and sauté until softened, about 5 minutes. Add the ginger and garlic and cook for 3 minutes. Add 2 tablespoons water and stir constantly over high heat until the onion browns, about 3 minutes. Stir in the curry powder and cook for 3 minutes. Stir in 2 tablespoons water and remove from the heat.

3. Add the spice mixture to the potatoes along with the remaining 1 tablespoon butter, the sour cream, yogurt, 1¼ teaspoons salt, and pepper. Beat with a small electric mixer or mash with a potato masher until fluffy. Serve hot.

Flavor-Whipped Potatoes

Potatoes show off other flavors in a wonderful way. They seem to soak them up and balance them while adding a creamy consistency that helps release optimum flavor.

To make about 6 cups of whipped potatoes, peel 3 pounds of russet baking potatoes; cut them into 1-inch chunks and drop them into a large pot of cold water as they are cut. Add a big pinch of salt, partly cover, and place over moderately high heat. Boil until tender when pierced with a fork, 15 to 20 minutes. Drain and return to the hot pot. Shake over moderate heat for a minute to dry; turn off the heat.

Add ½ cup milk (or light cream or half-and-half), 3 to 4 tablespoons butter, 1 teaspoon salt, ¼ teaspoon black pepper, and ¼ teaspoon grated nutmeg. Beat with a handheld electric mixer until fluffy. If too thick, add about 2 tablespoons extra milk. Taste and add ¼ teaspoon more salt, if needed.

VARIATIONS

Basil-whipped potatoes: **Reduce the butter to 2 tablespoons and add 2 tablespoons extra-virgin olive oil. Beat in ½ cup finely chopped fresh basil. To serve, scoop onto plates and make a well; add a dab of butter, and if desired, a light sprinkling of grated Parmesan.**

Cilantro-whipped potatoes: **Follow the basic recipe above, adding ⅓ cup chopped cilantro leaves, 1½ teaspoons fresh lemon juice, and ½ teaspoon ground cumin before whipping.**

Sesame-whipped potatoes: **Follow the basic recipe, reducing the butter to 1½ tablespoons and adding 1½ tablespoons Oriental sesame oil. When serving, make a well and top with a dab of butter and a sprinkling of lightly toasted sesame seeds.**

Scalloped Potatoes with Ham and Cheese

Scalloped potatoes are always my favorite dish at potluck suppers. They are creamy, homey, and wonderful, and this hearty version is full of flavor. It's just what to make for dinner when you have leftover ham. It can be served with beef, chicken, or lamb and is substantial enough to accompany a vegetarian entrée.

MAKES 8 SERVINGS

- 1½ cups grated sharp cheddar cheese (6 ounces)
- ⅓ cup all-purpose flour
- 2½ teaspoons sweet paprika
- 1½ teaspoons salt
- ¼ teaspoon grated nutmeg
- ¼ teaspoon cayenne pepper
- ¼ teaspoon black pepper
- 3 pounds (8 to 10 medium) red-skinned potatoes
- 8 ounces lean smoked ham, sliced ⅛ to ¼ inch thick and cut into 1-inch pieces
- 4 whole scallions, minced
- 3 tablespoons butter, cut into bits
- 3 cups milk

1. Preheat the oven to 375° F. Lightly oil a 13 × 9-inch baking pan.
2. In a medium bowl, toss together the grated cheese, flour, 2 teaspoons of the paprika, the salt, nutmeg, cayenne, and black pepper until evenly distributed.
3. Peel the potatoes, dropping them into a large bowl of cold water as they are peeled. Removing one at a time as you work, thinly slice (⅛ to ¼ inch) a potato and arrange the slices, slightly overlapped, in the baking pan; repeat until you have used one-third of the potatoes. Scatter on half the ham pieces and sprinkle with half the scallions. Distribute half the cheese mixture over and dot with 1 tablespoon of the butter. Repeat twice more, using only potatoes, cheese, and butter on the top layer. Pour in the milk and sprinkle with the remaining ½ teaspoon paprika. Cover the pan with foil.

VARIATIONS

Substitutions: **Leave out the' ham and layer with freshly roasted and peeled poblano chili peppers (page 17) or with canned green chilies, and use 4 ounces each of Monterey Jack and cheddar cheese. For a richer dish, use 1 cup light or heavy cream in place of some of the milk.**

4. If desired, cover the oven shelf with a sheet of foil to catch any spills if the milk should bubble over. Bake, covered, for 45 minutes.

5. Remove the foil and spoon some of the milk from around the edges up over the potatoes. Bake, uncovered, for 25 to 30 minutes longer, or until browned and bubbly and the potatoes are tender when pierced with a fork. Remove from the oven and let stand for at least 15 minutes before serving. Use a slotted spatula to serve.

Potatoes and Chorizo

This classic Mexican combination is big on flavor. It makes a hearty side dish with an omelet or a delicious filling for burritos and tacos.

MAKES ABOUT 5 CUPS

> 6 medium (1 to 1½ pounds) red-skinned boiling potatoes
> 12 ounces (1½ cups) Mexican Chorizo (page 256), or store-bought
> 1½ tablespoons vegetable oil
> 1 medium onion, finely chopped
> ½ teaspoon salt

1. Put the potatoes in a large, heavy saucepan and cover generously with cold water. Place over high heat and bring to a boil. Partly cover and boil over moderately high heat until tender, 20 to 30 minutes. Drain and let cool. They can be cooked a day ahead. Peel and cut into ¾-inch cubes.

2. Place a large, heavy nonstick skillet over moderately high heat. Slit the casings of the chorizo and crumble the meat into the hot pan. Sauté, stirring occasionally. At first, liquid will release; it will boil away. Continue cooking until the meat begins to sizzle and is nicely browned. Remove the chorizo with a slotted spoon and reserve in a bowl. Tilt the pan and spoon off and discard the fat.

3. Spoon the vegetable oil into the skillet and add the potatoes, along with the chopped onion and salt. Cook over moderate heat, tossing and stirring occasionally, until deep golden brown and crusty, 12 to 15 minutes. Return the chorizo to the pan and toss to heat briefly, about 2 minutes. Serve hot.

Orange Candied Sweet Potatoes

Here is a fresh sweet potato side dish for holiday entertaining or family dinners at any time of year. The sweet potatoes are tasty with orange, caramel, butter, and vanilla—all topped with toasted pecans.

MAKES 8 TO 12 SERVINGS

> 3 **pounds (6 medium) sweet potatoes**
> 1 **tablespoon grated orange zest**
> ¾ **cup fresh orange juice**
> 4 **tablespoons (½ stick) butter**
> ⅓ **cup packed dark brown sugar**
> ¼ **teaspoon grated nutmeg**
> ¼ **teaspoon salt**
> 1 **teaspoon vanilla extract**

Garnish (optional)

> 1 **tablespoon butter**
> ½ **cup finely chopped pecans**

1. Preheat the oven to 400° F. Put the unpeeled sweet potatoes in a large, shallow baking dish. Bake in the top third of the oven for 45 to 55 minutes, or just until tender when pierced with a fork. Remove and let cool to room temperature. (The sweet potatoes can be baked a day ahead of time.) Peel the sweet potatoes and cut them into ¾-inch-thick slices.
2. In a small bowl, stir together the orange zest and orange juice.
3. Melt the butter in a large, heavy skillet set over moderately high heat. Stir in the brown sugar and let sizzle until foamy, 1 to 2 minutes. Pour in the orange juice mixture and add the nutmeg and salt. Boil until fragrant, 1 or 2 minutes.
4. Add the sweet potatoes to the skillet and toss gently over high heat until coated with the liquid. Reduce the heat to moderately low and cook gently so the potatoes do not fall apart, just until they absorb some of the liquid and become glazed, 2 to 3 minutes. Remove from the heat, stir in the vanilla, and toss gently.
5. If preparing the garnish, melt the butter in a small skillet over moderate heat. Add the pecans and toss until toasted, 2 to 3 minutes. To serve, turn the sweet potatoes out onto a large platter and sprinkle the toasted pecans over the top. Serve hot. (The potatoes can be made well in advance and then reheated in a microwave or 325° F. oven. Just be sure to add the toasted pecans after reheating.)

Squashed Potatoes

Light, fluffy, and colorful, these "squashed" potatoes combine roasted butternut squash with boiled russet potatoes, a fall seasoning of nutmeg and mace, and sage. The tang comes from sour cream, boosted with a bit of vinegar, to enhance the sweetness of the squash. This is especially delicious with the Pork Roast Tamarindo (page 251), or any pork or roasted poultry dish.

MAKES ABOUT 6 CUPS (6 SERVINGS)

- 1 medium (2-pound) butternut squash, halved and seeded
- 2 pounds russet baking potatoes (4 to 6 medium)
- ½ cup sour cream
- 2 tablespoons butter
- 1½ teaspoons cider vinegar
  About 1½ teaspoons salt
- ½ teaspoon dried sage, crumbled
- ¼ teaspoon grated nutmeg
- ¼ teaspoon mace
- ¼ teaspoon black pepper

1. Preheat the oven to 400° F. Place the squash, cut sides down, on a sheet of aluminum foil or in a shallow baking pan. Roast in the top third of the oven for about 1 hour, or until very soft and deep golden brown.
2. About 20 minutes before the squash is tender, peel the potatoes and cut into 1-inch cubes. Drop into a medium pot of lightly salted cold water; partly cover and place over high heat. When the water boils, reduce the heat to moderately high and boil until tender, about 15 minutes.
3. Drain the potatoes and return them to the pot. Shake over high heat for a minute to dry them; remove from the heat. Add the sour cream, butter, vinegar, salt, sage, nutmeg, mace, and pepper. Mash with a potato masher or beat with a handheld electric mixer on low speed until fluffy.
4. Spoon out the squash flesh from the skin (or pare, whichever you find easiest) and add it to the potatoes. Beat briefly until fluffy. Taste for salt and add a pinch more, if needed. Serve hot. If making ahead of time, reheat over low heat.

Sandwiches

Carpetbagger Burgers

Rich-Boy Po' Boys

Cuban Sandwich

T.N.T.B.L.T.

Bacon and Egg Salad Sandwiches

Reuben Sandwich

Tortas Milanesa

Grilled Turkey Sandwich with Pesto and Provolone

Turkey and Mortadella Muffuletta

Falafel Salad Sandwiches with Taratoor Sauce

Cold-Press Chicken and Vegetable Sandwich

Bonus Recipes

Building a Burger Platter   The Best Hamburger-Indoors or Out

Soft-Shell Crabs   Two Tender Long-Braised Meats

Smoked Tongue Sandwich   Pork Sandwich

Old-Fashioned Lemonade

Carpetbagger Burgers

The flavor combination of beefsteak with oysters is a favorite of mine, a taste of the land and the sea. Carpetbag steak is a classic preparation in which you cut a pocket into a thick steak and stuff it with oysters. Here I have marinated oysters in Worcestershire sauce and Tabasco and sandwiched them between burger patties. Although you can broil them, I usually grill them over charcoal. These are *big* burgers for hearty appetites.

MAKES 2 LARGE SANDWICHES

> 6 medium oysters, shucked
> 1 teaspoon Worcestershire sauce
> 1 teaspoon Tabasco sauce
> 1 pound extra-lean ground beef round or sirloin
> 2 teaspoons olive oil
> 2 kaiser rolls, split
> Mayonnaise
> Tomato slices
> Sweet onion slices, such as Vidalia, Maui, or Walla-Walla

1. Combine the raw oysters, Worcestershire, and Tabasco in a small bowl. Set aside to marinate for 30 to 60 minutes.

Building a Burger Platter

One of my favorite dinners is a hamburger platter with all the trimmings. I just grew up eating them in California, and they're what I crave most in New York during the summer when tomatoes are juicy and corn is ripe for the picking.

Flavor and texture are important to the hamburger platter. You want contrast between bites. There's that smoky aroma and flavor and those juices dripping down your chin. Alongside might be corn-on-the-cob and Big Flavor Baked Beans, Cajun Fries or Smashed Potato Salad plus a few potato chips for crunch. Perhaps add some refrigerator dill pickles (all these recipes are in the book).

Get some large kaiser rolls with poppy seeds or sesame seeds, split them, and toast them in a skillet, a toaster oven, or over charcoal. (I like them slightly charred.)

Spread the rolls, top and bottom, with just a tiny bit of mayonnaise or a good spoonful of Russian Dressing (page 99). Add a smear of brown mustard and a couple thin slices of dill pickle and a thick slice of sweet onion. Add the burger and top with 1 to 3 slices of ripe juicy tomato (depending on the diameter and on how much you love tomatoes). Sprinkle with salt and pepper and add a crunchy lettuce leaf. Press the top of the roll into place.

Ideal beverages are iced tea with lemon, lemonade, beer, or root beer.

The Best Hamburger—
Indoors or Out

My very favorite hamburger is cooked outdoors over hardwood charcoal, but you can cook a real good burger in a cast-iron skillet on top of your stove.

I don't like fatty beef so I always choose the leanest I can find (juice and fat are two different things). Lean sirloin, chuck, or round all make good hamburgers, but the key is having it freshly ground. I usually have my butcher grind sirloin to order, but sometimes I grind it at home. You need 1 pound of lean trimmed beef for 3 hamburgers.

To use a food processor: Cut the beef into 1-inch cubes and partially freeze until firm. Put them in a food processor fitted with a metal blade. Press the pulse buttons several times to grind the meat to a coarse texture. Do not overprocess or the texture will be too smooth.

To use a meat grinder: Fit a meat grinder (such as one that fits onto a KitchenAid mixer) with the fine ($\frac{1}{8}$-inch) disk. Put the meat through once and do not pack it together as it comes out.

The key to a tender burger is very little handling of the meat. Gather the beef into one clump, pressing lightly just so it holds together. Divide it into thirds and gently shape each into a $3\frac{1}{2}$-inch patty, $\frac{3}{4}$ to 1 inch thick.

To cook over charcoal: Build a charcoal fire (preferably before you grind the beef) and soak some hardwood chips in water. Put the grill over the glowing charcoal and let heat for 5 minutes. When you are ready to cook, remove the grill, add the drained chips, and return to the grill. Let the chips smolder for a couple minutes, then add the burgers. Grill to taste, about 3 to 4 minutes per side for medium rare. If you want cheeseburgers, add sliced or grated cheese as soon as you turn the burgers and loosely tent them with foil.

To cook in a skillet: Place a large, heavy cast-iron skillet over high heat. Sprinkle it with about 1 teaspoon of coarse (kosher) salt and let heat 3 to 5 minutes. Plop in the burgers, leaving about 1 inch between them. Press the tops gently with a spatula and let cook without moving over high heat for about 2 minutes; lower the heat to moderate and cook about 2 minutes longer, until good and crusty. Turn with the spatula, scraping the pan bottom so the brown crust is not left behind in the pan. Sprinkle with salt and pepper and cook to taste, about 2 minutes longer for medium. Add cheese as above.

2. Meanwhile, light a charcoal fire in a hibachi or outdoor grill or preheat the broiler.
3. Divide the ground beef into 4 equal portions; pat each into a 5-inch round on a sheet of waxed paper. Remove the oysters with a slotted spoon and place 3 in the center of each of 2 patties. Invert the other 2 patties over them and peel off the waxed paper. Using a fork, crimp the edge of the patties together all around to seal well. Reshape the edge as needed. Lightly rub

the exterior of each burger with 1 teaspoon of the olive oil.

4. Grill or broil the burgers to taste, turning every 3 or 4 minutes. They will be cooked to medium in 8 to 10 minutes; cook longer for well done. Lightly toast the rolls during the last couple of minutes of cooking.

5. Spread the toasted rolls lightly with mayonnaise and add the burgers. Top with the tomato and onion. Serve right away.

VARIATIONS

Substitutions: **Instead of using raw oysters, try this sandwich with canned smoked oysters. Simply drain them and use 5 to 7 small ones in place of the raw oysters.**

Substitutions: **Herb butter or Russian dressing can be used instead of mayonnaise.**

SWEET ONIONS

After learning as much as I could about the onion (a member of the lily family), the most fascinating fact I unearthed was that onions grown in one geographic location are totally different when transplanted to another. In other words, Vidalia, Maui, and Walla-Walla onions are not the same when grown in Las Vegas or Kansas. Their size, color, sweetness, hotness, juiciness, and shape have been cultivated through careful breeding to suit specific climates and locations, and they become stubborn and fussy when moved.

Vidalia, Maui, and Walla-Walla onions are sweet and juicy, and sure to be controversial, depending on where you live; each location claims to grow the sweetest and juiciest. Me, I love them all because I can add big, thick slices to my charcoal-grilled hamburgers without the teary hotness of some other raw onions.

Rich-Boy Po' Boys

In New Orleans, po' boys are stuffed French rolls overflowing with a variety of ingredients—sliced potatoes to fried oysters and everything in between. Soft-shell crabs, available during the spring, can be quite costly since the little critters have to be caught just after molting but before growing a new shell. After cleaning they are entirely edible. Here, the edges become crispy with browned Parmesan coating. Prepare the Creole Rémoulade in advance. This is an easy recipe to cut in half.

MAKES 4 SANDWICHES

- **4** soft-shell crabs, cleaned
- **¾** cup Creole Rémoulade (page 368)
- **¼** cup freshly grated Parmesan cheese
- **2** tablespoons all-purpose flour
- **½** teaspoon dried oregano, crumbled
- **½** teaspoon dried basil, crumbled
- **½** teaspoon ground cumin
- **½** teaspoon salt
- **¼** teaspoon black pepper
- **¼** cup vegetable oil
- **4** French or Italian rolls (each about 5 inches long), split
- **1** lemon, quartered

1. Have the soft-shell crabs freshly cleaned and rinsed, and have the Creole Rémoulade prepared and chilled.
2. Preheat the oven to 350° F. In a shallow dish, combine the Parmesan, flour, oregano, basil, cumin, salt, and pepper. Mix to combine. If the crabs have dried, rinse them again to moisten so the coating will adhere.
3. Place a large, heavy skillet over moderately high heat and heat the vegetable oil to just below the smoking point. Dredge 2 crabs in the coating mixture to lightly coat on both sides. Shake off any excess coating. Place them, smooth side down, in the hot oil. Dredge the remaining 2 crabs and add to the pan (if you are using a skillet that will hold only 2 crabs, cook in 2 batches). Brown on one side very well, until deep golden brown and crisp, 2 to 3 minutes. Turn, reduce the heat to moderately low, and cook until cooked through, 3 to 5 minutes longer.
4. Meanwhile, split the rolls and put them, cut sides up, directly on the oven shelf until hot and toasted, about 5 minutes.
5. To assemble 1 sandwich, spread each half of the roll with 1½ tablespoons of the rémoulade. Add a crab and squeeze 1 piece of the lemon

Soft-shell Crabs

Soft-shell crabs should be alive when you buy them and kept alive until you are ready to cook them. Your fishmonger will usually clean the crabs for you, but here's how to do it yourself: use kitchen shears to cut off the "face" of the body just behind the eyes, removing about ½ inch. Reach into the opening and pull out the sand pouch or stomach. Turn the crab over and use your fingers to pry up the apron or narrow flap (on females this will be triangular; on males, T-shaped). Fold it down and pull off gently so the intestinal vein comes with it. Turn the crab right side up and lift up one pointed side of the top shell; fold it back so you can see the gills. With a paring knife, scrape off and discard the gills from both points. Fold the points back in place. Rinse the crabs. They are now completely edible.

over it. Add the top of the roll. With a long serrated knife, cut on a severe diagonal. Repeat, assembling the other sandwiches. Serve hot or warm.

> ## VARIATION
>
> *To make a meal:* **The soft-shell crabs make a marvelous main course without the rolls. Serve 2 per person with lemon juice and/or Creole Rémoulade. For an even bigger sandwich, instead of spreading rémoulade over the rolls, add a mound of Uncle Eddie's Coleslaw (page 79).**

Cuban Sandwich

This famous sandwich features roasted fresh pork and smoked ham. It's a magical combination enhanced with melted cheese, mayonnaise, and dill pickles. The sandwiches are prepared on crusty rolls and toasted on a griddle with a hinged top, so that the roll grills from the bottom and the top at the same time. The weight of the top griddle compresses the sandwich slightly as it toasts.

MAKES 1 SANDWICH

- 1 hero roll (about 8 inches long), split
- 1 to 2 tablespoons mayonnaise
- 4 to 6 thin slices dill pickle (optional)
- 2 ounces thinly sliced baked ham
- 2 ounces thinly sliced roast pork
- 1 ounce sliced Muenster cheese
- 1 tablespoon butter, softened

1. Assuming you do not have a double-hinged griddle like they have in restaurants, preheat a large, heavy griddle or skillet over moderate heat.
2. Meanwhile, open the hero roll and spread each side with half of the mayonnaise. Add the dill pickle slices. Put the baked ham on one side of the roll and the roast pork on the other. Top with the cheese and close the roll to assemble the sandwich.
3. Add half the butter to the hot griddle and let melt. Add the sandwich and top with a heavy weight, such as a heavy pot or cast-iron skillet. Cook until deep golden brown on the bottom, 3 to 5 minutes. Spread the remaining

butter over the top, turn, weight down again, and grill until toasted, 3 to 4 minutes. Cut the sandwich on a severe diagonal. Serve hot.

T.N.T.B.L.T.

Inspiration for this version of an American classic sandwich came from the club sandwiches I love to order in Mexico. The heat of the jalapeño mayonnaise can be adjusted to your taste.

MAKES 1 SANDWICH

- 2 tablespoons Jalapeño Mayonnaise (page 366)
- 2 slices good white or whole wheat bread, toasted
- 4 crisp slices fried lean bacon
- 2 or 3 thin slices ripe tomato
  Salt
- 2 crisp lettuce leaves, torn to fit the bread

Spread 1 tablespoon of the mayonnaise over each slice of toast. Arrange the bacon on one slice and top with the tomato. Sprinkle lightly with salt and add the lettuce. Invert the other slice of toast over the top to make a sandwich. Cut in half diagonally and serve with potato chips, if desired.

Bacon and Egg Salad Sandwiches

If you make this salad 8 hours before serving, the smoky bacon flavor will permeate in a wonderful way. Serve the sandwiches with salted radishes and sweet pickles.

MAKES 4 SANDWICHES

- 8 large eggs, hard-cooked (page 13)
- 6 slices hickory-smoked bacon, fried until crisp
- ⅓ cup plus 1 tablespoon mayonnaise
- 1½ tablespoons brown or yellow mustard
- ¼ to ½ teaspoon salt
- 8 slices white or whole wheat bread, toasted; or 4 toasted kaiser rolls
  Lettuce leaves, for serving

1. Peel the eggs and finely chop into a bowl, or put through an egg slicer in 2 directions.
2. Crumble in the bacon. Stir in the mayonnaise, mustard, and ¼ teaspoon of the salt. Cover and chill for at least 2 hours.
3. Taste the egg salad and add a little more salt, if needed. Pile the salad onto toast or the bottom portion of the rolls. Add lettuce leaves and the remaining toast or roll tops. Serve cold.

VARIATIONS

Serving: Instead of serving as sandwiches, serve on lettuce leaves as a salad.

Additions: Three tablespoons minced scallion or onion can be added, or try ¼ cup chopped fresh parsley.

MUSTARD

The four varieties of mustard seed are white, yellow, brown, and black. The white and yellow seeds are indigenous to southern Europe, the brown and black seeds, to the Himalayas. The tender young leaves can be eaten as a vegetable, like spinach or turnip greens.

Mustard is second only to pepper as the most popular spice consumed in the United States. This is due to the popularity of yellow hot dog mustard.

Unlike most other aromatic spices, mustard has no aroma when dry. It must be moistened and left for at least ten minutes to develop its sharp, hot, tangy flavor through enzymatic action. After an hour it begins to lose its hotness unless an acid such as vinegar or lemon juice has been added and the mustard refrigerated. The darker the color of the seed, the more pungent the flavor of the mustard.

The three forms of mustard seeds are:

Dry mustard, sometimes called powdered, "mustard flour," or "ground mustard," is made by hulling the seeds before grinding. Usually a blend of white and brown are combined. Pungency is increased by adding extra brown mustard flour. English Colman's is tops.

Prepared mustard is a paste of mustard, usually with added salt and vinegar and frequently other flavorings (see separate listing of types). Although they have a long life in the refrigerator, the flavor diminishes as they age.

Whole seeds are used to flavor pickles and Indian dishes and often are ground into curry powders and seasoning pastes.

The prepared mustards are:

• *American yellow hot dog or ball park mustard.* This bright yellow, mild mustard is colored and flavored with turmeric. It is just slightly sharp with vinegar and not hot. It is best on hot dogs and cold cuts. French's is a good brand. It is interesting to note that France is the biggest importer of French's yellow mustard (for those who require a milder mustard, and for hot dogs).

• *American brown mustard.* Similarly mild as yellow mustard, but with a deeper, more rounded, less harsh flavor, this type is a good choice for hot dogs, deviled eggs, and potato salads. Gulden's is a good brand.

• *Chinese mustard.* Usually made at home from dry mustard, hot water, and rice vinegar, this mustard makes a hot and tangy dip for seafood, dumplings, and egg rolls. It is best made ten minutes to an hour before serving, so the enzymes can work to develop the flavor. Colman's is a good choice.

• *Creole mustard.* This grainy mustard from Louisiana is made from yellow and brown mustard seeds marinated in vinegar. It is sharp, hot, and spicy with full, well-balanced flavor. Zatarain's is a popular brand that I find delicious.

• *Dijon mustard.* Although invented in Dijon (Burgundy's capital), this mustard is now made throughout France. It is usually made with white Burgundy wine and brown or black mustard seeds. The texture and flavor vary tremendously from brand to brand, from watered down to salty and sour. Somewhere in between is the best. Dijon mustard should be bright and smooth with a mild, pleasant bite and full, well-rounded flavor. Maille and Dessaux are excellent French brands. Grey Poupon is the best of the domestic Dijon-style mustards.

• *Prepared English mustard.* These are fire-hot and sharp with vinegar and can enrage the mouth in a wonderfully exciting way. They range from smooth to grainy.

• *Grainy German mustard.* The best German mustards come from Dusseldorf and usually are grainy. They can range from hot and salty to sweet and dark, and some have horseradish added for hotness. All brands are different.

• *Swedish mustard.* With an affinity for herring and cold seafood and sausages, these mustards range from smooth and sweet to hot and grainy.

Store mustards in the refrigerator, where they will keep for a year or two.

Reuben Sandwich

There are too many stories, really, for anyone to know the true origin of the reuben sandwich. I'm just glad that *someone* invented it. Here's my favorite way of making the hefty sandwich with its great big flavor. Instructions for cooking corned beef are on page 193, but you can also make this from deli-sliced corned beef.

MAKES 1 LARGE SANDWICH

    2 slices rye bread with caraway seeds
    2 tablespoons Russian Dressing (page 99)
    2 teaspoons brown mustard
    1 slice Swiss cheese (1 ounce)
    4 ounces thinly sliced corned beef
    ½ cup sauerkraut, drained well on paper towels
    1 tablespoon butter, softened

1. Preheat a large, heavy griddle or skillet over moderately low heat.
2. Meanwhile, spread 1 side of 1 slice of bread with 1 tablespoon of the dressing. Spread the other slice of bread with the mustard. Put the cheese on the slice with the dressing, trimming it to fit the bread and layering the trimmings on top. Arrange the corned beef over the mustard side and spread the remaining 1 tablespoon dressing on the corned beef. Top with the sauerkraut. Invert the cheese-topped bread over the corned beef to make a sandwich.
3. Spread half of the butter over the top slice of bread and invert onto the hot griddle. Spread the remaining butter over the other slice of bread. Cook until toasted and golden; the cheese should melt, but you don't really want the sandwich hot throughout, 3 to 4 minutes per side. Transfer to a plate with a spatula, cut on a severe diagonal, and serve.

VARIATIONS

Substitutions: Use pumpernickel bread instead of rye. If desired, eliminate the mustard and spread both sides of the bread with Russian dressing, or use thinly sliced baked Virginia ham in place of the corned beef.

Two Tender Long-Braised Meats

I didn't want to include an entire chapter of sandwiches without telling you how to cook corned beef and smoked tongue. Here's how:

Corned Beef. You lose about half the weight of a corned beef after cooking and trimming. If it weighs 4 pounds when you buy it, you will have about 2 pounds of good lean meat.

Place a 3- to 4-pound lean, trimmed, thin cut of corned beef in a large pot or Dutch oven and add enough cold water to cover generously. Sprinkle on 20 whole cloves. Partially cover the pot and bring the water to a simmer over moderately low heat. Reduce the heat to low and simmer gently until very tender when pierced with a fork, 3 to 4 hours. Let the corned beef cool in the liquid. Serve hot, warm, or cold, thinly sliced across the grain.

Smoked Tongue. Beef tongue used to be a great bargain, but now it fetches a high price. After all, there's only one to a cow. Tongue can be purchased fresh, smoked, or corned. It must simmer for a long time to become tender, but the reward is great texture and flavor.

Place a whole 3½- to 4½-pound smoked beef tongue in a large casserole or Dutch oven. Add cold water to cover generously; sprinkle on 25 whole cloves. Partially cover and bring to a boil over moderate heat. Reduce the heat to low and simmer until very tender when pierced with a long fork, 2½ to 3 hours. Let cool completely in the liquid. Chill.

Drain the tongue, discarding the liquid. Pull off the skin with a paring knife. Using a sharp slicing knife, cut the tongue crosswise into thin slices. The slices from the tip will be the neatest and leanest. Use for sandwiches or cold cut platters, and serve with an assortment of mustards.

Smoked Tongue Sandwich

The bold tangy flavor of Uncle Eddie's Coleslaw (page 79) makes a great complement to smoky, clove-tingled tongue. Here is how to make my favorite tongue sandwich: Toast 2 slices of rye bread and arrange about ⅓ cup of the coleslaw over 1 slice in an even layer. Arrange 3 to 4 ounces of thinly sliced smoked tongue (deli-bought makes a good substitution) and 1½ ounces of thinly sliced Swiss cheese on top. Set the remaining slice of bread in place, cut on a severe diagonal, and serve with pickles and potato chips.

Tortas Milanesa

Tortas are the popular Mexican hero sandwiches sold on just about any corner in every town in Mexico. They are almost always made from *bolillos,* which are similar to soft French rolls with pointed ends (the ends are usually cut off before making the sandwich). Although they can be filled with any ingredient—from chicken or beef to cheese and potatoes—one of my favorites is a breaded pork cutlet. In Mexico, any breaded cutlet is called *Milanesa.* The rolls are smeared with a dab of refried beans and topped with avocado, tomato, lettuce, pickled jalapeño, and sometimes cream or sour cream.

MAKES 4 SANDWICHES

> 4 center-cut pork chops (each about ½ inch thick,
> about 1 pound total weight), or 4 slices boneless pork loin, trimmed
> 3 tablespoons all-purpose flour
> 2 large eggs
> ¾ cup plain, dry bread crumbs
> 4 tablespoons vegetable oil
> Salt
> 4 *bolillos* or French rolls
> 1 cup refried beans, heated
> 4 teaspoons fresh lime juice
> 16 thin slices ripe tomato
> 1 perfectly ripe California avocado, such as Haas
> 6 tablespoons sour cream
> 2 to 4 pickled jalapeño chilies, sliced
> 1 cup shredded crisp lettuce, such as romaine or iceberg

1. If starting with pork chops, cut out the bone from each chop and trim away any excess fat. Place the pork cutlets between separate sheets of waxed paper or plastic wrap and pound with a mallet or cleaver, working from the center outward, until they are about ⅛ inch thick.
2. Place the flour in a shallow dish. Put the eggs in a separate shallow dish and stir with a fork. Put the bread crumbs in a third shallow dish.
3. Preheat a large, heavy skillet over moderately high heat. Add 3 tablespoons of the vegetable oil and heat until almost smoking; adjust the heat as necessary.
4. Dredge both sides of 1 pork cutlet in the flour and tap off the excess. Dip into the eggs to lightly coat and then place in the crumbs, turning and tapping until coated evenly and the crumbs adhere. Gently shake off any loose crumbs over the dish. Place the cutlet into the hot oil and coat a second cutlet. Add to the pan and fry, 2 at a time, until deep golden brown, 2 to 3

minutes on the first side. Turn and fry until the pork is cooked to the center, 1 to 2 minutes. Drain the cutlets on paper towels. Lightly sprinkle with salt. Repeat, coating and cooking the remaining 2 cutlets.

5. Preheat the oven to 350° F. (Alternatively, the rolls may be warmed in a toaster oven.) With your fingers, pull out about half of the soft bread centers from each side of the rolls to make room for the filling. Heat or toast the rolls until hot, 3 to 5 minutes. Spread each cut side of bread with 2 tablespoons of the refried beans. Add a cutlet to each bottom portion and spoon 1 teaspoon of the lime juice over each cutlet. Top each with 4 tomato slices and a pinch of salt.

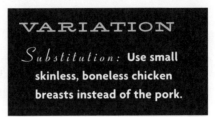

VARIATION

Substitution: **Use small skinless, boneless chicken breasts instead of the pork.**

6. Peel and pit the avocado; cut into 12 slices. Arrange 3 avocado slices over the tomatoes on each sandwich and spoon on 1½ tablespoons of the sour cream. Add 1 or 2 jalapeño slices to each and top with some of the shredded lettuce. Set the top portions in place and slice on a severe diagonal. Serve with ice-cold Mexican beer.

Pork Sandwich

My favorite way to use leftover Pork Roast Tamarindo (page 251) is in a special sandwich. You will need the tamarind sauce from the roast and Curried Mayonnaise (page 364).

To make 2 sandwiches, heat 2 split kaiser rolls or French rolls in a 350° F. oven for about 5 minutes. Spoon about ¼ cup of the tamarind sauce into a nonreactive small saucepan and add 6 to 8 ounces of thinly sliced roast pork. Place over moderate heat until hot, turning the meat once or twice.

Spread 1 tablespoon of the mayonnaise over each side of the toasted rolls, and add the sliced pork. Top with thin tomato slices, lettuce leaves, and salt and pepper to taste. Add the roll tops, slice in half on a severe diagonal, and serve right away.

Grilled Turkey Sandwich with Pesto and Provolone

The pesto melts into the bread as this flavorful sandwich toasts on the griddle. The ingredients are layered on a poppy seed kaiser roll and weighted down as you would when making a Cuban sandwich. Serve with a cold marinated salad, antipasto, or hot soup.

MAKES 1 SANDWICH

> 1 poppy seed kaiser roll
> 2 tablespoons Pesto (page 361)
> 3 or 4 thin slices turkey breast (3 to 4 ounces)
> 1 slice (1 ounce) mild provolone cheese
> 2 teaspoons butter, softened

1. Preheat a griddle or heavy skillet over moderately low heat.
2. Meanwhile, using a long serrated knife, split the roll horizontally. Spread each side with half the pesto. Arrange the turkey slices on the bottom half and top with the cheese. Add the top portion of the roll. Spread the top of the roll with 1 teaspoon of the butter.
3. Invert the sandwich onto the hot griddle. Cover with a square of aluminum foil and weight down with a heavy pot or small cast-iron skillet. Reduce the heat to low and grill until lightly toasted, 4 to 5 minutes. Spread the remaining 1 teaspoon butter over the roll, turn, weight down as before, and grill until toasted and the cheese is melted. Cut into quarters and serve hot.

VARIATIONS

Substitutions: Use any other good melting cheese such as Monterey Jack, Muenster, or mozzarella in place of the provolone. Chicken can replace the turkey and thin slices of dill pickle can be added. If you want to make this sandwich with thin slices of roast beef, add slices of ripe summer tomato, too.

Turkey and Mortadella Muffuletta

A muffuletta is a big, round, New Orleans hero sandwich. The sandwich is great for picnics because you can make it well ahead of time and it travels well. This muffuletta tastes especially good with the Calico Black Bean Salad on page 95 or potato salad. It is a relative of the Cold-Press Chicken and Vegetable Sandwich on page 200, but here a relish is made from artichoke hearts and black olives with anchovies and capers.

MAKES 6 TO 8 SERVINGS

¼ cup olive oil
1 large garlic clove, minced or crushed through a press
1 jar (6 ounces) marinated artichoke hearts, drained
1 can (6 ounces) pitted large black olives
½ cup pimiento-stuffed green olives
1 can (2 ounces) flat anchovy fillets, drained
2 tablespoons fresh lemon juice
1 tablespoon capers, drained
1 teaspoon dried oregano, crumbled
¼ to ½ teaspoon cayenne pepper
½ teaspoon black pepper
1 large round loaf of firm or sturdy unsliced bread (9 to 10 inches in diameter)
8 ounces thinly sliced cooked turkey breast
8 ounces thinly sliced mild provolone cheese
8 ounces thinly sliced mortadella

1. Combine the olive oil and garlic in a small, heavy skillet set over low heat. Let sizzle until softened but not colored, about 2 minutes. Set aside to cool.

2. In a food processor, combine the artichoke hearts, black olives, green olives, anchovies, lemon juice, capers, oregano, cayenne, black pepper, and garlic-oil mixture. Pulse to make a coarse relish. If making ahead, cover and chill.

3. Split the loaf of bread horizontally in half. Using your fingers, pull out some of the soft bread center from each half to make it slightly concave, about ½ inch deep. Discard the soft center or reserve for another use. Spread half of the relish over the bot-

Old-Fashioned Lemonade

I don't use a recipe when I make lemonade. I just throw the ingredients together until the mixture tastes good. To get you started, here's my favorite basic formula.

Makes about 5 cups

In a glass pitcher or big bowl, combine 1 cup freshly squeezed lemon juice with ¾ cup sugar (superfine if you have it) and stir until the sugar dissolves. Stir in 4 cups of cold water. Taste for tartness and add a little more sugar if desired. Thinly slice 1 lemon and add. Refrigerate if making ahead. Serve over ice cubes in tall glasses, garnishing each with one of the lemon slices.

tom portion of bread. Layer on half of the turkey, half of the provolone, and half of the mortadella. Repeat the layering, spreading the remaining relish over the top portion. Press together, wrap tightly in plastic, and then in aluminum foil. Set in the refrigerator and weight down with a heavy pot or cans of food. Chill for at least several hours or overnight. Serve cold, cut into wedges.

VARIATIONS

Addition: **You can add thinly sliced tomatoes to the center just before serving, if desired. Be sure to use good, juicy summer tomatoes.**

Serving: **You may also make this sandwich on a long loaf of Italian bread. Add sliced tomatoes and fresh basil leaves just before serving.**

Substitutions: **Use cold cuts or roast chicken in place of the turkey and mortadella and your favorite cheese in place of the provolone.**

Falafel Salad Sandwiches with Taratoor Sauce

These full-flavored, crunchy Middle Eastern morsels made from bulgur wheat and garbanzo beans are usually deep-fried. But one day, I discovered how good they could be when browned in just a little oil in a nonstick skillet. This is tasty vegetarian fare—hearty, fragrant, and full of fine flavor and texture.

MAKES 8 SANDWICHES

Taratoor Sauce (page 371)
1/3 cup medium-grain bulgur wheat
1 tablespoon olive oil
1 large garlic clove, minced or crushed through a press
1 1/2 teaspoons ground cumin
1 can (16 to 19 ounces) garbanzo beans (chickpeas), rinsed and drained
1/2 cup chopped fresh cilantro, plus additional, for serving
1/2 cup chopped fresh parsley

¼ **cup fresh lemon juice**

1 **teaspoon salt**

½ **teaspoon cayenne pepper**

½ **cup fresh pita bread crumbs (about ½ pita, ground in a food processor)**

Vegetable oil

8 **pita breads (6-inch size)**

4 **cups chopped crisp lettuce, such as romaine or iceberg**

1½ **cups diced ripe tomatoes**

1½ **cups diced peeled and seeded cucumber**

1. Make the Taratoor Sauce and chill it. (This can be done a day or two in advance. If the sauce thickens too much, stir in a little cold water to make a creamy consistency.)

2. Put the bulgur in a bowl and pour in 2 cups of cold water. Let soak until softened, about 30 minutes. Line a sieve with a triple layer of damp cheesecloth and drain the bulgur. Squeeze out the excess water. (This can also be done in small handfuls, lacking cheesecloth.)

3. Spoon the olive oil into a small skillet. Add the garlic and cumin and place over low heat. Sizzle gently until fragrant but not browned, 1 to 2 minutes. Let cool.

4. In a food processor, combine the drained garbanzo beans, cilantro, parsley, lemon juice, salt, cayenne, the garlic-cumin oil, and 1 tablespoon cold water. Process to a coarse puree. Turn out into a bowl and stir in the bulgur and pita bread crumbs. Cover and refrigerate for at least 1 hour.

5. If you like your pita bread hot, preheat the oven to 350° F.

6. Using a scant ⅓ cup of the falafel for each, shape the mixture into eight 2½ × 4-inch ovals and place on a sheet of waxed paper. Place a large nonstick skillet over moderate heat. When very hot, pour in ¹⁄₁₆ inch of vegetable oil. Fry the falafel, regulating the heat as necessary, until crisp and deep golden brown, 3 to 4 minutes per side. Drain on paper towels. Alternatively, shape the falafel into 1- or 1½-inch balls and deep-fry at 365° F. for 3 to 4 minutes.

7. Warm the pita bread in the oven for 3 to 5 minutes. Slice off about 1 inch from one edge and insert a falafel into each. Add about ½ cup of the lettuce, 3 tablespoons of the tomatoes, 3 tablespoons of the cucumbers, and 2 tablespoons of the Taratoor Sauce. Sprinkle with about 1 tablespoon of additional chopped cilantro, if using, and serve right away.

Cold-Press Chicken and Vegetable Sandwich

This big-flavored chicken version of the French classic *pain bagna* is an entire cold meal encased in a loaf of bread. It is perfect for hot weather entertaining and for picnics. The layers are drizzled with olive oil, and since the sandwich is pressed and chilled overnight, the juices from the cucumber blend with the olive oil and saturate the bread. You'll find yourself making this over and over again during the hot summer season. Choose a firm, squat, round loaf of bread, such as sourdough, farmer, or peasant bread. You can start with a deli-cooked chicken or simply roast one yourself at home.

MAKES 6 SERVINGS

- ½ cup minced oil-cured pitted black olives (about 24)
- 2 tablespoons Dijon mustard
- 2 tablespoons fresh lemon juice
- 1 tablespoon anchovy paste
- 4 tablespoons extra-virgin olive oil
- 1 round loaf of firm white bread, such as sourdough, farmer, or peasant (9 to 10 inches in diameter)
- 1 large cucumber, peeled
- 4 medium tomatoes (about 1 pound), thinly sliced
- ¾ teaspoon salt
- ¾ teaspoon black pepper
- 2 large red bell peppers, roasted (page 17), peeled, seeded, and quartered
- 6 to 8 thin slices sweet white onion, separated into rings
- 8 ounces thinly sliced cooked chicken breast

1. In a bowl, using a fork, mash together the minced olives, mustard, lemon juice, anchovy paste, and 2 tablespoons of the olive oil. Set the dressing aside.
2. Split the loaf horizontally in half. Score the inside of both the top and bottom portions all around, cutting ½-inch-deep gashes about 1 inch apart. Spread half of the dressing over the cut surface of each bread half.
3. Using a swivel-bladed vegetable peeler, shave the cucumber as though you were peeling it, making long, narrow, paper-thin slices. Continue until you reach the seeds on all sides; discard the core of seeds. Arrange half of the paper-thin slices over the bottom portion of the bread. Arrange 2 of the sliced tomatoes over the cucumber and sprinkle with ¼ teaspoon of the salt and ¼ teaspoon of the pepper. Add 4 pieces of the bell peppers and half of the onion rings. Drizzle 1 tablespoon olive oil over the onion rings. Add the sliced chicken in an even layer. Sprinkle with ¼ teaspoon each of the salt

and pepper. Reverse the order and continue layering, ending with the remaining 1 tablespoon olive oil and the remaining sliced cucumber. Set the top of the bread over the sandwich and press to flatten slightly. Wrap in several layers of plastic wrap and then 2 layers of aluminum foil to seal tight.

4. Place the sandwich upside down on a dinner plate and top with a platter weighted down with cans or anything else that will help to press the sandwich and make the juices soak into the bread as it chills. Refrigerate for at least 12 hours, turning right side up and replacing the weights after 5 to 6 hours.

5. To serve, unwrap the sandwich, cut in half, and then cut into wedges. Serve cold.

VARIATIONS

Vegetarian: **To make a delicious version of this sandwich, omit the anchovy paste and chicken breast.**

Substitutions: **Instead of using chicken breast, use cold cuts such as smoked ham, salami, or roast beef. Also, green olives can be substituted for the black olives, if desired.**

Little Birds and

Big Birds

Bonus Recipes

Indian Summer Chicken

I concocted this simple dinner dish for times when you want exotic big flavors in minutes. The flavorings are Asian Indian, but the colors are like an American Indian summer. Serve with mango chutney and perhaps sliced fresh mango, basmati rice, iced tea, or cold beer. Let the sour cream warm to room temperature while you work.

MAKES 4 SERVINGS

4 tablespoons vegetable oil
4 skinless and boneless chicken breast halves,
   thinly sliced across the grain
¼ cup all-purpose flour
1¼ to 1½ cups Chicken Stock (page 73) or canned broth
⅓ cup slivered almonds
¼ cup golden raisins
2 teaspoons homemade Curry Powder (page 385) or store-bought
½ teaspoon ground cumin
¼ teaspoon ground cinnamon
¼ teaspoon cayenne pepper
⅛ teaspoon ground cloves
½ teaspoon salt
1 tablespoon minced fresh ginger
1 large garlic clove, minced or crushed through a press
½ cup sour cream, at room temperature

1. Place a large, heavy skillet over high heat. When very hot, spoon in 1 tablespoon of the oil. Combine half of the chicken with 2 tablespoons of the flour in a sturdy plastic or paper bag; twist or seal the top and shake vigorously to coat the chicken with flour. Add the floured chicken to the skillet and sauté on one side until deep golden brown, about 2 minutes. Turn the pieces and cook for 1 minute. Transfer to a plate. Repeat, using the remaining chicken, flour, and 1 tablespoon of the oil.
2. Pour ½ cup of the stock or broth into the skillet and bring to a boil over high heat. Boil until the liquid is reduced by half, 2 to 3 minutes. Pour the glaze over the chicken pieces; clean the skillet.
3. Spoon 1 tablespoon of the oil into the pan; add the almonds and toast over moderately low heat, tossing, for 1 to 2 minutes. Remove and reserve. Add the raisins and toss for 15 to 20 seconds, or until lightly browned. Add to the chicken.
4. In a cup, stir together the curry powder, cumin, cinnamon, cayenne, cloves, and salt.

5. Spoon the remaining 1 tablespoon oil into the skillet and set over moderate heat. Add the ginger and garlic and sizzle, mashing with a fork, for 10 to 15 seconds. Stir in the spice mixture and cook for 10 seconds. Pour in ¾ cup of the stock and bring to a full boil, stirring. Add the chicken and raisins and heat for 1 minute. Stir in the sour cream and heat to a simmer. If too thick, add about ¼ cup more stock. Turn out onto a serving platter and top with the slivered almonds.

Petit Coq au Vin

These little birds take on great big wine flavor if you prepare them several hours ahead. Tiny hens, baby carrots, little mushrooms, and pearl onions add up to one big dish. Serve in large, deep soup plates with parsleyed new potatoes.

MAKES 4 SERVINGS

> 1 bottle (750 ml) hearty dry red wine, such as Burgundy
> 2 cups Chicken Stock (page 73) or canned broth
> 1 large garlic clove, minced or crushed through a press
> 1 large bay leaf
> ½ teaspoon dried tarragon, crumbled
> ½ teaspoon dried thyme, crumbled
> 8 to 12 ounces baby carrots, peeled
> 8 ounces pearl onions (¾ inch diameter)
> 6 slices smoked bacon, finely chopped
> 2 plump Cornish game hens (1½ to 2 pounds each)
> 3 tablespoons vegetable oil
> 3 teaspoons sugar
> 6 tablespoons all-purpose flour
> ¼ cup brandy or Cognac
> 2 tablespoons tomato paste
> 8 ounces small whole fresh mushrooms
> 1 tablespoon butter
> ½ teaspoon salt
> ¼ teaspoon black pepper
> 2 tablespoons chopped fresh parsley

1. In a nonreactive large saucepan, combine the wine, stock or broth, garlic, bay leaf, tarragon, and thyme. Bring to a boil over moderately high heat and boil until reduced to 3 cups, 15 to 20 minutes. Remove from the heat and reserve.

2. Bring a large pot of lightly salted water to a boil and drop in the carrots and unpeeled pearl onions. When the water returns to a boil, cook for 2 minutes. Drain and rinse under cold water; peel the onions.

3. Put the bacon in a small, heavy skillet and cook over moderate heat, stirring frequently, until crisp and golden brown. Remove with a slotted spoon and drain. Discard the fat.

4. Using kitchen shears or a sharp knife, cut out the backbone of each hen and discard it. Cut each bird into serving pieces: 2 thighs, 2 drumsticks, 2 breasts, 2 wings.

5. Place a large, heavy skillet over moderately high heat. Spoon in 1 tablespoon of the vegetable oil, add the carrots and onions, and sprinkle with 1 teaspoon of the sugar. Brown, tossing, until the vegetables are speckled, 2 to 3 minutes. Sprinkle on 1 teaspoon more sugar and continue browning until speckled and deep caramel brown, 5 to 7 minutes. Remove with a slotted spoon and reserve.

6. Spoon 1½ tablespoons of the oil into the skillet and place over moderately high heat. Put 3 tablespoons of the flour in a brown paper bag with half of the chicken pieces. Shake to coat thoroughly and put the pieces into the hot oil. If you have a spatter screen, use it; otherwise, brown, uncovered and without turning, until deep golden brown, 4 to 5 minutes. Turn and brown for 2 to 3 minutes longer. Take the pieces out and put them in a large, heavy casserole. Repeat with the remaining 3 tablespoons flour, coating the remaining pieces of poultry. Add the remaining ½ tablespoon oil to the skillet and brown the pieces as before.

7. After removing all the pieces, avert your face and tilt the pan away from you. Carefully pour in the brandy or Cognac, which will ignite immediately. (If it doesn't, use a match.) Shake the pan until the flames subside. Stir in the reduced wine, the tomato paste, and the remaining 1 teaspoon sugar. Bring to a boil over moderate heat.

8. Pour the wine sauce over the Cornish hens in the casserole. Add the onions, carrots, and bacon and bring to a boil over moderate heat. Reduce the heat to low, cover, and simmer until tender and cooked to the bone, 20 to 30 minutes.

9. Meanwhile, trim off the bottom half of the mushroom stems. Melt the butter in a large skillet over moderately high heat. Add the mushrooms and brown, adding about 2 tablespoons of water if the pan seems dry, for 2 to 3 minutes. Add the mushrooms to the casserole, along with the salt and pepper. Cook for 3 to 5 minutes to blend the flavors. The casserole will be best if left to rest for at least an hour or two and reheated gently over low heat. Serve hot, sprinkled with parsley.

TARRAGON

This sweet-smelling herb has such a unique and strong, dominant personality that it can overshadow and even fight with other herbs and flavorings. Craig Claiborne called it "seductive and satisfying," and I agree.

Tarragon contributes an aniselike flavor with a hint of clover and pepper. It also gives a lingering, slightly numbing sensation to the tongue. It is especially popular in Europe and is an integral component of French *fines herbes.*

Two types of tarragon are available: French, or "true," tarragon and the less flavorful Russian tarragon. French tarragon is the one most commonly used in cooking; it has glossy elongated leaves and is darker in color and more aromatic than the Russian variety.

Tarragon is especially suited to complement chicken, seafood, eggs, tomatoes, rich creamy sauces, and flavored butters.

Slash-and-Burn Chicken

Although slash-and-burn farming techniques may have been responsible for the downfall of the Mayan civilization, when the method is applied to chicken, the result is a moist, tender bird with smoky charcoal flavor. And there is heat from red and black peppers and from the fire itself. Slashing and marinating the chicken helps the marinade permeate the flesh. The orange juice in the marinade gently tenderizes, while the dark Mexican beer adds a yeasty mellow background flavor. Add tortillas, beans, rice, grilled vegetables, and a salad for a fiesta. If you double the marinade, there will be enough for 3 chickens. Note that this must marinate overnight.

MAKES 4 SERVINGS

> 1 whole or halved 3-pound chicken
> ¾ cup dark Mexican beer, such as Negro Modelo
> ⅓ cup fresh orange juice
> 1 tablespoon dried red pepper flakes
> 1 large garlic clove, minced or crushed through a press
> 1 teaspoon dried oregano or thyme, crumbled
> 1 teaspoon black pepper
> 1½ cups hardwood chips, for barbecuing
> 1 tablespoon vegetable oil

1. If starting with a whole chicken, use poultry shears or a large, heavy knife to cut along both sides of the backbone; remove and discard. Chop off the

wing tips and open the 2 halves to butterfly the bird. Cut 2 deep slashes into each side of the breast, 2 into each thigh, and 1 into each drumstick. (If using halves, simply slash.)

2. In a large bowl, stir together the beer, orange juice, pepper flakes, garlic, oregano, and black pepper. Add the chicken; cover and marinate in the refrigerator for 12 to 24 hours.

3. Light a hardwood charcoal fire. While the coals and grill are heating, remove the chicken from the marinade and let drain at room temperature. Meanwhile, soak the wood chips in a large bowl of warm water.

4. When the coals are glowing and lightly covered with ash, arrange the chicken, skin side up, on the grill and lightly brush the flesh with the vegetable oil. Cook for 15 minutes. Turn and cook for 10 minutes longer.

5. Carefully remove the grill and chicken, scatter the drained wood chips over the charcoals, and set the grill and chicken back in place. Cook until the meat is tender to the bone, turning every 5 to 10 minutes, for 35 to 45 minutes. If the fire flares up, spritz with a little water to extinguish the flames. Serve hot or warm.

Crunchy-Spicy Fried Chicken

The yogurt and lemon juice in this marinade contribute an old-fashioned buttermilk tang, while Tabasco and cayenne add spice. If they were in the coating instead of the marinade, they would brown too quickly. This fried chicken is spicy enough, but not overly so and is delicious served cold.

MAKES 6 TO 8 SERVINGS

    4 pounds chicken parts, or 2 medium chickens,
        cut into serving pieces, breasts quartered
    1 cup low-fat plain yogurt
    ¼ cup fresh lemon juice
    2 tablespoons Tabasco sauce
    2 teaspoons cayenne pepper
    1 teaspoon celery salt
      Vegetable oil, for frying
    1½ cups all-purpose flour
    1 tablespoon ground cumin
    1 tablespoon dried oregano, crumbled
    1½ teaspoons salt
    1 teaspoon black pepper

1. Pull the skin off the chicken pieces (except the wings) and discard it; cut off the wing tips. Also, if frying wings, cut out the *V*-shaped flap of skin at the elbow.
2. Prepare the marinade. In a large bowl, stir together the yogurt, lemon juice, Tabasco, cayenne, and celery salt. Add the chicken pieces, cover, and refrigerate for 2 hours.
3. Pour enough vegetable oil into a deep fry pan, Dutch oven, or electric deep-fryer to reach a depth of about 1½ inches. Set over moderately high heat and heat until the oil reaches 360° F. on a deep-fat thermometer. Reduce the heat, if necessary, to maintain a steady temperature. (If you are using an electric deep-fryer, it will automatically maintain the temperature, and I do recommend this appliance.)
4. In a large, sturdy brown paper bag, combine the flour, cumin, oregano, salt, and pepper. Remove about one-third of the chicken pieces from the marinade, put them in the bag, and shake to coat. One at a time, lower the chicken into the hot oil and fry until crispy and deep golden brown; the time will vary, depending upon the size and cut, 12 to 15 minutes. It will take some practice to judge, and you will be wise to cut into the thickest part of a piece occasionally to check to see if it is cooked to the bone. When the chicken pieces are done, remove and drain on paper towels. Continue coating and frying the chicken until all of it is cooked. Drain well. Serve hot, warm, or cold.

TABASCO SAUCE

America's favorite hot pepper sauce has been a staple condiment since the Civil War. And it's still made the same way today, in Louisiana, from the same secret McIlhenny family formula.

Tabasco is a fiery hot sauce with a bright red-orange color and piercing fermented chili and vinegar aroma. Crab cakes wouldn't be the same without it, and neither would a shrimp cocktail or jambalaya, red beans and rice, or gumbo. Some splash it freely over fried catfish or use it to douse scrambled eggs.

The taste of Tabasco sauce sneaks up on you. The heat of the chili peppers bursts at the back of your tongue, waking up taste buds you never knew you had, and then travels through your throat. The sharpness of the vinegar and salt point up the pleasant fermented chili flavor, lingering and intensifying on the tongue. The more you use, the more you want. In short, I find it addictive.

To make it, red-hot peppers (*Capsicum frutescens*) are ground to a mash and combined with Avery Island salt, then aged in white oak barrels for three years. The only other ingredient is vinegar. The peppery liquid is drained from the vats and bottled. It is this lengthy fermentation that contributes the deep, complex flavor.

For the longest shelf life at home, store Tabasco sauce in the refrigerator. When exposed to light, it tends to lose its bright color.

Enchiladas Verde

Great color, flavor, and texture combine with the fragrant aroma of cilantro to make this one of my favorite Mexican dishes. The tomatillos add a welcome tangy taste on the tongue, there's a little heat from the jalapeños, and the crumbled *queso cotija* gives depth. This is a practical and economical recipe because you start with a whole chicken and you can cook it and make the sauce early in the day. Then, shortly before dinner, all you need to do is soften the corn tortillas and assemble and bake the enchiladas.

MAKES 12 (4 SERVINGS)

Chicken Filling
- 1 chicken (3 pounds), quartered, or 2 whole chicken breasts
- 2 large garlic cloves, sliced
- 1 bay leaf
- 1 teaspoon dried oregano, crumbled
- 5 whole cloves
- ¼ cup sour cream
- ¼ cup finely chopped white onion, Vidalia onion, or whole scallions
- ¼ cup chopped fresh cilantro
- ½ teaspoon ground cumin
- ½ teaspoon salt
- ⅛ teaspoon pepper

Salsa Verde
- 1 pound fresh tomatillos (15 to 20 medium),
    or 2 cans (each 13 ounces) *tomatillos*
- 1 or 2 fresh jalapeño chilies, thinly sliced
- ½ teaspoon salt
- 1 tablespoon olive oil

Enchiladas
- ⅓ cup vegetable oil
- 12 corn tortillas
- ½ cup crumbled *queso cotija* or salted farmer cheese
    Sour cream, sliced radishes, chopped onion,
      and cilantro leaves, for garnishing (optional)

1. To make the chicken filling, place the chicken in a large, heavy pot and pour in 3 to 4 cups cold water. Add the garlic, bay leaf, oregano, and cloves. Partially cover and bring to a boil over moderate heat. Reduce the heat to low and simmer gently until the chicken is cooked to the bone, 25 to 30 minutes. Remove the chicken with tongs; set aside on a platter to cool.

2. Boil the cooking liquid over high heat until reduced to about 2 cups, 5 to 10 minutes. Pour the broth into a bowl and degrease by skimming or blotting with paper towels. You will need 1¾ cups of broth.

3. When the chicken is cool enough to handle, pull off and discard the skin and bones. Tear the meat into ½-inch-wide shreds and put them in a medium bowl. Add ¼ cup of the broth to moisten the meat and stir in the sour cream, onion, cilantro, cumin, salt, and pepper. (The filling can be prepared a day ahead; cover and refrigerate.)

4. To make the salsa verde, pull the papery husks from the tomatillos. Rinse and quarter them and place in a nonreactive medium saucepan. Pour in the remaining 1½ cups chicken broth. (If using canned tomatillos, simply drain and add.) Add the jalapeños and salt and bring to a boil over moderate heat. Reduce the heat to low and simmer until the tomatillos are falling apart, 12 to 15 minutes. Allow to cool slightly; puree in a blender or food processor.

5. Spoon the olive oil into a large, heavy skillet or Dutch oven (which will minimize spattering) and place over high heat. Pour in the pureed sauce. "Fry" the sauce (this is an authentic Mexican technique for bringing out the flavor in sauces) until reduced to 2½ cups, 3 to 5 minutes. (The sauce can be made a day ahead; cover and store in the refrigerator. Reheat before using.)

6. To make the enchiladas, preheat the oven to 400° F. Place a medium skillet (just slightly larger than a corn tortilla) over moderately high heat. Pour in the vegetable oil. When very hot, use tongs to lower 1 tortilla into the oil. Swish it back and forth and turn it quickly several times to soften, 10 to 15 seconds. The tortilla should soften and then barely begin to stiffen; drain on paper towels. Repeat, stacking them between paper towels and blotting up the excess oil from the top each time.

7. Assemble the enchiladas directly in the 13 × 9-inch baking pan they will bake in. Reheat the salsa in a medium skillet until fairly warm but not boiling hot. Dip 1 tortilla into the sauce to lightly coat and place it in the pan. Dip a second tortilla in the sauce to coat so you are assembling 2 enchiladas at a time. Spoon 2½ to 3 tablespoons of the filling

QUESO COTIJA

This aged, dry, crumbly Mexican cheese, with its creamy white color and salty, slightly acidic flavor, gives Mexican foods an air of authenticity when freshly grated over the top. It is most frequently used to garnish tacos, tostadas, refried beans, enchiladas, soups, and stews. *Queso cotija* has a pungent aroma. Readily available in Mexican food markets, it keeps for a long time wrapped in plastic and stored in the refrigerator (six months or longer). If you cannot find *queso cotija*, substitute Romano.

in a line across the lower quarter of each tortilla and roll up tightly. Place seam side down in the pan and begin to make 2 crosswise rows of enchiladas. Repeat with the remaining ingredients, evenly spacing the enchiladas. Spoon any remaining sauce over the tops of the enchiladas.

8. Bake the enchiladas until heated through, about 10 minutes. Scatter the cheese over the tops and serve, garnished, if desired, with dollops of sour cream and a sprinkling of onion and cilantro. Serve radish slices on the side.

VARIATIONS

Lower calorie: **To cut some calories and fat, very lightly brush each side of the corn tortillas with oil (2 tablespoons will be enough to coat all of them) and heat in an ungreased nonstick skillet to soften. Omit the sour cream.**

FLAVORED CHEESES

Although cheesemakers have been adding flavor to cheeses for a long time, there has been a huge trend in this area in recent years, especially by creative cheesemakers in Wisconsin.

I chose jalapeño Jack cheese for the Chicken Jalapeño Gratinada (opposite) because it has a big cheese and chili flavor and a good creamy consistency. The cheese is also available in dill and pesto flavors. There are some new Havarti cheeses, flavored with dill or pepper, that are rich, buttery, and full of flavor. And now you can even find feta cheese flavored with basil, tomatoes, or peppercorns.

Smoked cheeses are more popular than ever, too, and some of the fine new ones available include gouda, Swiss, mozzarella, Monterey Jack, provolone, and fontina. There are also many fine cheese spreads with highly flavored ingredients like salami, pepperoni, and sun-dried tomatoes.

One of my favorites is a Sicilian cheese called Pepato; a good domestic version is made by Casaro in Wisconsin. It is a hard Romano cheese, richly studded with whole black peppercorns. I find it sensational grated over hot buttered corn or sliced into wafers to fill omelets, burgers, and meat loaf. It also makes the most fabulous ravioli you'll ever taste. But perhaps the best thing about it is that it needs no adornment at all.

Chicken Jalapeño Gratinada

If you keep some pounded chicken cutlets on hand in the freezer, stacked between sheets of waxed paper, you can put this dish together in a matter of minutes. You'll need jalapeño Jack cheese, because that's where most of the flavor comes from. Consider Caesar salad and pinto beans with bacon and zucchini as accompaniments.

MAKES 4 SERVINGS

- ¼ **cup all-purpose flour**
- 2 **tablespoons olive oil**
- 4 **fresh or frozen skinless and boneless chicken breast halves (5 to 6 ounces each), pounded until thin**
- 1 **teaspoon butter**
- 1 **fresh or pickled jalapeño chili, minced**
- 1 **large garlic clove, minced or crushed through a press**
- ½ **teaspoon dried oregano, crumbled**
- ½ **teaspoon ground cumin**
- 1 **cup fresh or canned peeled, seeded, and chopped tomatoes**
- ¼ **cup dry white wine or Mexican beer**
- ½ **teaspoon salt**
- ⅛ **teaspoon black pepper**
- 4 **whole scallions, thinly sliced**
- 4 **ounces jalapeño Jack cheese, coarsely shredded (1 cup)**

1. Preheat a large, heavy skillet over moderately high heat. Put the flour in a shallow dish. When the skillet is hot, spoon in 1½ tablespoons of the oil and reduce the heat to moderate, if necessary, to prevent smoking. One at a time, dredge 2 of the chicken cutlets in the flour. Transfer to the hot oil and brown on one side until golden, about 3 minutes. Turn and cook for 1 minute. (Do not overcook; the chicken will cook again as the cheese melts.) Transfer the cutlets to a platter, add the remaining ½ tablespoon oil, dredge the 2 remaining cutlets in the same manner, and brown as before. Transfer to the platter.

2. Add the butter to the skillet along with the jalapeño, garlic, oregano, and cumin. Sauté for 1 minute over moderate heat. Add the tomatoes, wine or beer, salt, and pepper and bring to a boil. Cook for 2 minutes. Spoon half of the sauce into a small bowl.

3. Return the cutlets to the skillet in a single layer; top with the scallions and cheese. Spoon the reserved sauce over the cheese, cover, and cook over low heat until the cheese melts, about 3 minutes. Serve hot.

Malaysian Curried
Hen Hot Pot

Here is a comforting one-dish supper with wonderful exotic flavors. It takes a long time to cook a stewing hen (fowl), but the result is a good quantity of deep-flavored gravy. You will also need some special ingredients, such as coconut milk, lemongrass, cellophane noodles, and fish sauce—all readily available at most Oriental grocery stores. I like to make my own curry powder for its fine full-flavored contribution. Green beans and potatoes soak up the flavors and add heartiness. It's a good idea to cook the hen a day ahead.

MAKES 8 SERVINGS

Stewed Hen

    3 tablespoons vegetable oil
    2 medium onions, thinly sliced
    ¼ cup minced fresh ginger
    3 large garlic cloves, minced or crushed through a press
    3 tablespoons Curry Powder (page 385)
    1 large stewing hen or roasting chicken (5 to 6 pounds), quartered
    2 cans (12 to 14 ounces each) unsweetened coconut milk or
          3 cups homemade coconut milk (page 215)
    2 stalks fresh lemongrass
    1 cinnamon stick, 3 inches long

Hot Pot

    2 tablespoons vegetable oil
    1 tablespoon minced fresh ginger
    1 large garlic clove, minced or crushed through a press
    1 teaspoon Curry Powder
    1 stalk fresh lemongrass
    4 ounces dried cellophane noodles (bean threads)
    1½ pounds small red-skinned or all-purpose potatoes,
          peeled and cut into 1-inch chunks
    1 pound thin green beans, trimmed
    ¼ cup fresh lemon juice
    2 to 3 tablespoons Thai or Vietnamese fish sauce (*nam pla* or *nuoc mam*)
    1 large onion, cut lengthwise into ½-inch-wide strips

Toppings (optional)

    ½ cup sliced whole scallions
    ½ cup chopped fresh cilantro
       Vietnamese chili-garlic sauce

1. Make the hen. Spoon the vegetable oil into a large Dutch oven or casserole and place over moderate heat. Add the onions, ginger, and garlic and sauté

Making Coconut Milk

Pierce the 3 "eyes" of a fresh coconut with hammer and nail. Drain upside down over a cup. If the liquid is fresh tasting, drink it or make the Ceviche on page 275; if fermented tasting, discard it.

Bake the coconut in a roasting pan at 375° F. for 15 minutes. Wrap it in a towel and, with a hammer, crack the shell. Separate the flesh from the shell, prying when necessary. Rinse the pieces of flesh and peel off any dark skin with a vegetable peeler. Coarsely grate the coconut. You will have about 4 cups.

Bring 1 quart of water to a simmer over low heat (watch carefully so that it does not boil). Add the coconut and let cool to room temperature.

Line a sieve with about 6 layers of cheesecloth. Place over a bowl and pour in the coconut milk mixture. Let drain, then pick up the bundle and squeeze out as much milk as possible. Discard the solids. You should have about 3 cups.

---

until softened, about 5 minutes. Add 2 tablespoons water and let it boil away. Add the curry powder and cook, stirring, for 2 minutes longer. Place the pieces of hen on top and pour in the coconut milk and about 4 cups water, or enough to come about two-thirds of the way up the hen. Pound the stalks of lemongrass several times with a hammer to release the flavor. Add the lemongrass and cinnamon stick and bring to a boil. Reduce the heat to low, cover, and simmer gently until the hen is very tender, 3½ to 4½ hours. (The roasting chicken will take only about 1½ hours.)

2. Take out the pieces of hen and drain in a colander set over a large bowl. Fish out the lemongrass and cinnamon stick and discard. Pour the broth into a large bowl and let cool to room temperature. If making a day ahead, chill and degrease by removing the solidified fat on top. Otherwise, skim off the fat and blot up the last traces with paper towels.

3. Make the hot pot. Spoon 1 tablespoon of the oil into a large, heavy casserole (such as a well-seasoned Chinese sand pot) or a 4-quart Dutch oven and place over moderate heat. Add the ginger, garlic, and curry powder and cook until fragrant, about 1 minute. Pound the

LEMONGRASS

This aromatic tropical grass is a cousin to citronella. Looking somewhat like a tough, tall, grassy scallion, the plant has a bulb at the base of its stalk that is used for flavoring. The stem can be used, too; just be sure to pound it to help release the flavor, and then remove it after it has done its job.

Lemongrass imparts a lovely exotic lemon-balm flavor, giving character and authenticity to Southeast Asian recipes, such as ones from Vietnam, Thailand, Malaysia, and Singapore.

The bulbs freeze well, so consider buying a good supply when available fresh, and freezing the bulbs for future use.

stalk of lemongrass several times with a hammer and add it to the pot. Pour in all of the reserved broth and about 2 cups of water. Bring to a boil over moderate heat.

4. Meanwhile, pull the skin and bones from the hen and tear the meat into $\frac{1}{2} \times$ 2-inch pieces. Place the cellophane noodles in a bowl and cover generously with hot water; let soak until softened, about 30 minutes.

5. Add the potatoes to the broth and simmer for 10 minutes. Add the green beans and cook for 10 minutes longer. Stir the pieces of hen, the lemon juice, and 2 tablespoons of the fish sauce and cook until the potatoes and green beans are tender, 5 to 10 minutes. If the liquid is not abundant, add a little more water. Taste and add the remaining 1 tablespoon fish sauce, if desired.

6. Spoon the remaining 1 tablespoon oil into a large, heavy skillet and place over moderately high heat. Add the onion and stir-fry until slightly softened but still crunchy, just 1½ minutes. Add the onion to the hot pot. Serve hot, with the toppings if using.

VARIATIONS

Lower calorie: **For a less rich dish, halve the quantity of coconut milk.**

Substitution: **If lemongrass is unavailable, add 1 teaspoon grated lime or lemon zest along with the lemon juice.**

Summer Savory Chicken

Chop a generous tablespoon of summer savory and push it beneath the skin (between the skin and meat) of a whole 1-pound chicken breast. Rub the skin with a little olive oil or soft butter and put it in a shallow roasting pan. Roast in the top third of a 450° F. oven for 15 minutes. Reduce the temperature to 300° F. and roast until the meat is just cooked to the bone, 15 to 20 minutes longer. Let stand for 10 minutes before carving or serving. Sprinkle lightly with salt and pepper.

Note: *You can also mix the chopped savory with a little soft butter before stuffing it under the skin.*

Barbecued Chicken

Here's my favorite way to make the greatest mouthwatering, lip smacking, big-flavored barbecued chicken. You'll need about 1½ cups of Rus's Own Barbecue Sauce (page 363), 8 skinless chicken thighs or 1 whole broiler-fryer cut into serving parts, and a hardwood charcoal fire outdoors. I also recommend soaking 2 to 3 cups of hardwood chips in water for 30 minutes to an hour before cooking, if you want extra hardwood smoke flavor.

Build a charcoal fire. When the coals are hot and glowing and covered with gray ash, preheat the grill rack. Then remove the rack, drain the chips, and scatter half of them over the coals. Return the rack and let it smolder for a few minutes. Set the chicken pieces (without any sauce) on the grill and cook for 12 to 15 minutes, turning several times. Remove the chicken and grill, add the remaining drained wood chips, and set the grill and chicken back in place. Brush generously with the sauce and turn every 5 minutes, cooking and basting until the meat is cooked to the bone, 20 to 30 minutes longer. (However, this can vary tremendously depending on the intensity of the heat and the weather. Also, the breast pieces will be done sooner than the others.)

You should use about 1 cup of the sauce for basting and heat ½ cup for serving alongside. Sprinkle salt and pepper over the hot chicken and serve with the remaining sauce.

BARBECUE SAUCE

Although the Chinese originated barbecue sauce, theirs is quite different from ours. The Chinese is a version of hoisin sauce or bean sauce, while we took the idea and made it into a smoky, sharp, zesty sauce that usually is based on tomatoes. Sometimes it is made with ketchup, which, it is fun to note, was also invented by the Chinese.

Most American barbecue sauces contain tomato, mustard, vinegar, onion, garlic, chili peppers, and Worcestershire sauce, and sometimes Liquid Smoke.

SAVORY

Too often overlooked, this herb with its big, fragrant bouquet tastes like a combination of oregano, thyme, sage, and pepper blended together in one herb. It has a pleasant, bitter quality that complements legumes, so it is often included with peas, beans, and lentils.

Summer savory is slightly more delicate than winter savory, which has a piney, evergreen quality. Both are sharp in flavor. Of the two, summer savory is the more common. Its flavor blends well with other herbs and it makes chicken especially succulent. It also adds depth and excitement to beef stews and vegetable soups.

Honey-Broiled Duck Breasts with Pomegranate and Tangerine Sauce

This is an elegant main-course dish, best for special occasions and fancy entertaining. Most butchers will remove duck breasts for you, and some shops sell skinless and boneless duck breasts. You can brown all the duck bones and trimmings and use them to make stock, or add them browned to chicken stock and simmer for 45 minutes. This recipe makes enough sauce for 6 duck breasts, but since they are expensive, I give you the option of serving fewer. Serve with potatoes or pilaf and pan-fried spinach or watercress and baby carrots. Homemade stock is important here.

MAKES 4 TO 6 SERVINGS

- 6 cups Chicken Stock (page 73)
- 3 large pomegranates
- ¼ cup Cognac or brandy
- 6 to 8 tangerines
- 1 large garlic clove, sliced
- 3 whole cloves
- 1 bay leaf
- ¼ teaspoon dried thyme, crumbled
- ½ cup heavy cream
- 1 tablespoon butter
  Pinch of salt
- 4 to 6 skinless and boneless duck breast halves (about 4 ounces each)
- 4 to 6 teaspoons honey
  Pepper

1. Pour the stock into a nonreactive large saucepan and boil over moderately high heat until reduced to 1½ cups, 30 to 45 minutes. Watch carefully during the final 15 minutes.
2. Meanwhile, break open the pomegranates and pull off most of the rind and white pith. Reserve about ¼ cup of the pomegranate seeds for garnish. Puree the remaining seeds in a food processor. Strain through a sieve, pressing with a spoon to extract as much juice as possible. You will need 1½ cups of pomegranate juice for this recipe.
3. As soon as the stock is reduced to 1½ cups, pour in the 1½ cups of pomegranate juice and the Cognac or brandy. Cut off two 3 × 1-inch strips of tangerine rind and add them to the saucepan along with the garlic, cloves, bay leaf, and thyme. Bring to a boil and boil until reduced by half, about 15 minutes.
4. Cut off 5 strips of tangerine rind, each about ¾ inch wide and 2 inches long,

and reserve for garnish. Squeeze the tangerines and strain the juice; you will need ½ cup.

5. When the sauce has reduced, add the cream and tangerine juice. Boil over moderate heat until reduced to about 1½ cups, 5 to 7 minutes. Strain the sauce and transfer to the top of a double boiler set over simmering water. Whisk in the butter and add salt to taste. Keep hot.

6. Preheat the broiler. Meanwhile, place the strips of tangerine rind, smooth side down, on a board and slice away any pith. Cut the strips into fine julienne. Blanch in a small pan of boiling water for 1 minute; drain.

7. Line a broiler pan with aluminum foil. Arrange the duck breasts on the foil and brush each with 1 teaspoon of the honey. Sprinkle lightly with pepper. Broil until well browned and cooked until slightly pink in the center, about 5 minutes. Remove from the broiler and let rest for 5 minutes before slicing.

8. Spoon 3 to 4 tablespoons of the sauce onto each heated dinner plate. Cut each breast half across the grain in thin slices and fan over the sauce. Sprinkle with a few of the reserved pomegranate seeds and some of the tangerine julienne. Serve hot.

VARIATION

Serving: **Two whole roasted ducklings can be served with this sauce.**

Mexican Corn Tortilla Stuffing

This fragrant corn stuffing is rich with texture and flavor. The excitement comes from the combination of corn kernels, toasted corn tortillas, chopped cilantro, scallions, roasted poblanos, and a little Mexican beer. Serve with zucchini and corn with lime butter and a salsa on the side. It's enough for a 16-pound turkey, but the recipe can be halved easily.

MAKES ABOUT 9 CUPS

- 8 ounces sliced hickory-smoked bacon, finely chopped
- 2 medium onions, finely chopped
- 1 large garlic clove, minced or crushed through a press
- 2 tablespoons vegetable oil or bacon fat
- 8 corn tortillas, cut into 1/2-inch squares
- 1 pound ground lean pork
- 2 cups fresh or frozen corn kernels
- 1 pound fresh poblano chilies, roasted (page 17), peeled, and coarsely chopped, or 2 cans (4 ounces each) peeled mild green chilies
- 1 can (6 ounces) pitted, medium black olives, drained
- 1 cup sliced whole scallions
- 1 cup coarsely chopped canned tomatoes, well drained
- 4 large eggs
- 1/2 cup Mexican beer, such as Dos Equis, or chicken broth
- 1/4 cup cider vinegar
- 2 tablespoons chili powder
- 1 tablespoon ground cumin
- 2 teaspoons dried oregano, crumbled
- 1/4 teaspoon ground cinnamon
- 1 tablespoon salt
- 1/2 teaspoon black pepper
- 1 1/4 cups plain, dry bread crumbs

Stuffing and Roasting a Turkey

Stuffing cooked in a casserole never tastes quite as good as that cooked inside a bird (or a chop, a steak, or a fish). I've cooked up many experimental stuffings over the course of my cooking career, and each time I create a new one, I test the recipe in several ways. For turkey, I always stuff the main cavity, put some under the neck skin and the remainder in a casserole. The same stuffing baked under the neck skin has a totally different texture from that baked in the main cavity. And the stuffing baked in a casserole is different still.

If you bake your stuffing in a casserole, it will come out best if you spoon some meat or poultry drippings over the top during baking and cover the casserole tightly. Or, better yet, top with chicken parts, turkey parts, or pork chops.

My personal favorite is the stuffing that has baked under the neck skin of a turkey or a chicken. So, when I roast a bird, I greatly expand that area by carefully sliding my fingers between the skin and the meat, around the wing joint and partly over the breast, and stuff it to monstrous proportions, pushing the stuffing around the wing joint and over the breast.

Of course, any of these stuffings can be used to stuff large roasting chickens, but since they have been designed with turkeys in mind, you might want to have the recipes. There will still be too much for just one bird, so you will have to bake some in a casserole.

Preheat the oven to 425°F. while you prepare the bird. For great-tasting pan juices, chop 3 medium onions and place them in your roasting pan.

Rinse the turkey inside and out and pat dry with paper towels. Expand the neck cavity if desired. Rub both cavities with half a lemon or a tablespoon of vinegar. Almost fill the main cavity, leaving just a little room at the top for expansion. Turn the bird upside down (I do all this in the kitchen sink for easy handling, then replace any stuffing that may fall out during handling) and fill the neck cavity. Secure the neck skin to the back of the turkey with skewers or toothpicks. Turn breast side up, tuck wing tips inward underneath, and place on the bed of onions (if you have a turkey sling, place it in pan first). Rub the bird lightly with olive oil or soft butter.

Slide the pan, uncovered, into the oven drumsticks first and roast according to the chart (below). When the turkey becomes golden brown, loosely cover with an aluminum foil tent. Baste the bird every 30 or 40 minutes. It is done when the thigh meat registers 175°F. to 180°F. on a meat thermometer, or when the juices run clear (not pink) when the thigh is pierced with a long fork. Remove from the oven and let stand 20 to 30 minutes before carving.

Turkey Size	Approx. amt. of stuffing to fill main cavity	Approx. amt. of stuffing to fill neck cavity	Initial 425° F. roasting	Additional roasting at 325° F.
12 lb.	3 cups	2 to 3 cups	30 min.	2½ to 3 hours
14 lb.	4½ to 5 cups	3 to 4 cups	30 min.	3½ to 4 hours
16 lb.	5 to 6 cups	4 to 4½ cups	30 to 40 min.	4 to 4½ hours
18 lb.	6 to 7 cups	4½ to 5 cups	45 min.	4½ to 5 hours

1. Warm a large, heavy skillet over moderate heat. Add the bacon and cook, stirring frequently, until crisp and golden brown, about 10 minutes. Spoon off all but 2 tablespoons of the fat. Add the onions and sauté until softened and lightly colored, about 5 minutes. Add the garlic and cook until softened, about 2 minutes. Turn out into a large bowl and let cool to room temperature.

2. Spoon the vegetable oil into a large, heavy skillet set over high heat. When very hot, add the cut-up tortillas and toss constantly over moderately high heat for 30 seconds. Continue cooking, without stirring, until browned well, 3 to 5 minutes. The tortillas will crisp as they cool.

3. Crumble the ground pork into the onion-bacon mixture. Add the corn, poblanos, olives, scallions, tomatoes, eggs, beer, vinegar, chili powder, cumin, oregano, cinnamon, salt, and pepper. Add the tortilla pieces and toss to combine. Add the bread crumbs and toss lightly.

Italian Sausage and Mushroom Stuffing

If you can't find fresh fennel bulbs, use celery instead, adding a few extra fennel seeds to boost the flavor. The best stuffings are always baked in the bird, both in the main cavity and under the expanded neck cavity. Read the instructions on page 220. This is plenty for a 16-pound turkey.

MAKES ABOUT 8 CUPS

1 loaf (12 ounces) stale Italian bread, cut into ½-inch cubes (about 8 cups)

½ ounce dried porcini or cèpes

1½ teaspoons olive oil

1 large fresh fennel bulb (1 to 1½ pounds), preferably with some of the leafy green tops attached; or 1 cup finely diced celery

1 cup finely chopped onion

2 garlic cloves, minced or crushed through a press

12 ounces lean sweet Italian sausage with fennel (about 4 links, or see recipe, page 258)

8 ounces fresh mushrooms, coarsely chopped in a food processor or finely chopped by hand

½ cup freshly grated Parmesan cheese

¼ cup chopped parsley, preferably Italian flat-leaf

¼ cup chopped fresh fennel leaves, if available

    1½ teaspoons dried basil, crumbled
    ½ teaspoon dried oregano, crumbled
    ¼ teaspoon ground fennel seeds
    4 large eggs
    ½ teaspoon salt
    ¼ teaspoon black pepper
    ¼ cup dry white wine
    1 tablespoon fresh lemon juice
    About ½ cup Chicken Stock (page 73) or canned broth

1. Preheat the oven to 350° F. Put the bread cubes in a large roasting pan and toast, tossing every 10 to 15 minutes, until deep golden brown, about 45 minutes. You should have about 6 cups of toasted croutons.
2. Put the dried porcini in a small bowl and add ¼ cup of boiling water. Let soak until softened, about 30 minutes.
3. Spoon the olive oil into a heavy skillet and place over moderately high heat. Add the fennel and onion. Sauté until softened and lightly browned, 5 to 8 minutes, adding 1 or 2 tablespoons water as needed if the pan becomes dry. Add the garlic and sauté for about 2 minutes. Turn into a very large bowl.
4. Slit the casings of the Italian sausage and crumble the meat into a large, heavy skillet set over moderate heat. Brown well, stirring occasionally. Remove the sausage with a slotted spoon and transfer to the bowl of sautéed ingredients. Tilt the pan and discard all but 1 tablespoon of the fat. Add the mushrooms to the skillet, increase the heat to high, and sauté until lightly browned, 2 to 3 minutes. Spoon over the sausage; stir in the Parmesan, parsley, fennel leaves, basil, oregano, and ground fennel.
5. Drain the porcini; strain the soaking liquid through a fine sieve. Finely chop the porcini and add them to the stuffing mixture. Add the eggs, salt, and pepper and stir to combine; add the toasted croutons and toss. Pour in the porcini liquid, wine, and lemon juice and toss. Drizzle on ¼ cup of the stock or broth and toss to moisten. The croutons should be neither wet nor dry. Drizzle with the remaining ¼ cup stock or broth, if needed.

Meat: Beef, Veal,

Harlem Meat Loaf

I went to several popular Harlem restaurants to sample meat loaves before creating this bold version. All of those that I tasted were spicy and full of flavor. One contained fried cabbage and green peppers; another, roasted red peppers and jalapeños. I have combined all their best qualities into one big-flavored loaf. Although I like to use lean ground beef, the pork should be moderately fatty.

MAKES 6 TO 8 SERVINGS

> 2 tablespoons olive oil
> 2 cups finely chopped green cabbage
> 1 medium onion, chopped
> 1 teaspoon salt
> 2 large garlic cloves, minced or crushed through a press
> 2 fresh or pickled jalapeño chilies, finely chopped, with the seeds
> 2 teaspoons dried basil, crumbled
> ½ teaspoon dried oregano, crumbled
> ½ teaspoon dried thyme, crumbled
> 1 teaspoon celery salt
> ½ teaspoon black pepper
> 3 tablespoons cider vinegar
> 1 large red bell pepper, roasted (page 17), peeled, seeded, and finely chopped
> 1 large green bell pepper, roasted, peeled, seeded, and finely chopped
> 1 cup drained canned tomatoes, chopped
> ½ cup chopped celery leaves from the heart (optional)
> ½ cup chopped fresh parsley
> ⅔ cup Quick Chili Sauce (page 377), Heinz chili sauce, or Hot and Spicy Ketchup (page 376)
> ¼ cup dry white wine
> 1 tablespoon Worcestershire sauce
> 2 large eggs
> 1 pound lean ground beef
> 1 pound ground pork
> 1 cup finely crushed soda cracker crumbs

1. Spoon the olive oil into a large, heavy skillet set over moderately high heat. Add the cabbage, onion, and ½ teaspoon of the salt and sauté until soft and deep golden brown, 10 to 12 minutes. Add 1 to 2 tablespoons of water any time the vegetables seem dry. The water will boil away and encourage the

cooking. If necessary, increase the heat slightly during the last minute to achieve deep browning.

2. Stir in the garlic, jalapeños, basil, oregano, thyme, celery salt, and pepper. Sauté over moderate heat for 2 minutes. Add the vinegar and cook until it boils away. Turn the mixture into a very large bowl and set aside to cool to room temperature. (The recipe can be prepared to this point a day ahead.)

3. Preheat the oven to 350° F. Lightly oil a 13 × 9-inch baking dish.

4. When the sautéed mixture has cooled, add the roasted bell peppers, tomatoes, celery leaves if using, parsley, ⅓ cup of the chili sauce, the wine, Worcestershire, eggs, and the remaining ½ teaspoon salt. Crumble in the ground beef and pork and mix thoroughly with your hands. Add the cracker crumbs and mix just to blend. Shape the mixture into a 12 × 5-inch loaf and transfer to the prepared pan. Spread the remaining ⅓ cup chili sauce over the top.

5. Bake the meat loaf for 1¼ to 1½ hours, or until the internal temperature in the center reaches 155° to 160° F. on a meat thermometer. If the drippings begin to brown too much during baking, pour ¼ cup of water or white wine into the pan. Let stand for about 15 minutes before cutting into thick slices. If you want to make gravy and there are sufficient pan drippings, tilt the pan and see the recipe on page 229.

VARIATIONS

Substitution: **If you don't want to roast and peel bell peppers, substitute a 4-ounce jar of pimientos and sauté a finely chopped fresh green bell pepper along with the cabbage and onion.**

Bigger flavor: **Consider arranging 6 half slices of bacon over the chili sauce just before you bake the meat loaf.**

Italian Meat Loaf

Italian sausage, Parmesan cheese, and fennel contribute their big flavors to this "mamma mia" loaf. Your mouth will water long before you pull the loaf from the oven. Whole mushrooms are layered within, so the slices are beautiful. If you can't find fresh fennel, diced celery can replace it, and you'll still get plenty of fennel flavor from the seeds and the sausage. Serve with pasta or potatoes.

MAKES 6 TO 8 SERVINGS

2 tablespoons olive oil

2 cups diced fennel or celery

1 large onion, finely chopped

2 large garlic cloves, minced or crushed through a press

2 teaspoons dried basil, crumbled

1 teaspoon dried oregano, crumbled

¼ teaspoon crushed fennel seeds

1½ pounds lean ground beef round or sirloin

8 ounces Italian sweet sausages with fennel, casings removed
    (for a homemade version, see page 258)

1 can (28 ounces) crushed tomatoes

1 cup freshly grated Parmesan cheese

1 large egg

¼ cup chopped fennel greens or celery leaves

⅓ cup dry white wine

2 tablespoons red wine vinegar or fresh lemon juice

1 teaspoon salt

½ teaspoon black pepper

1 cup fresh bread crumbs made from firm white bread

20 whole medium mushrooms (10 to 12 ounces)

1. Spoon the olive oil into a large, heavy skillet set over moderate heat. Add the fennel or celery and the onion and sauté until softened, 5 to 8 minutes. Add the garlic, basil, oregano, and fennel seeds and cook for 2 minutes. If the mixture seems dry, add 1 to 2 tablespoons water and let it boil away. Set aside to cool to room temperature.

2. Preheat the oven to 350° F. Lightly oil a shallow 13 × 9-inch baking pan.

3. Crumble the beef and sausage into a large bowl. Add the sautéed vegetables and 1 cup of the crushed tomatoes. Reserve 2 tablespoons of the Parmesan

VARIATIONS

Substitutions: **To make a lighter meat loaf, use 1 pound ground chicken and ½ pound ground beef instead of 1½ pounds beef. To lighten further, sauté the crumbled sausage and drain off the fat before adding.**

Additions: **During the summer, add 1 cup chopped fresh basil for a big, fresh, Italian flavor.**

and add the remainder to the bowl. Add the egg, fennel or celery greens, wine, vinegar, salt, and pepper. Mix thoroughly with your hands. Add the bread crumbs and mix until combined.

4. To begin layering the loaf with mushrooms, remove one-third of the mixture and shape it, into a shallow rectangle about 4 × 9 inches long, in the baking pan; top with 10 of the whole mushrooms, arranged in 2 rows, pushing the stem ends down into the meat. Top with half of the remaining meat, building up the layer by first placing some of the meat between the mushrooms. Add the remaining mushrooms in 2 rows as before and top with the remaining meat. If any mushrooms are poking through, push them in until just covered with meat. Pat the loaf gently into shape.

5. Pour the remaining crushed tomatoes over the loaf and sprinkle with the reserved 2 tablespoons Parmesan. Bake for about 1½ hours, or until the internal temperature reaches 155° to 160° F. Let the loaf rest for 15 minutes before serving. Tilt the pan and degrease the drippings. Cut the loaf into 1-inch slices and spoon some of the tomato sauce over each.

Meat Loaf Pan Gravy

You can make a simple gravy from the pan drippings left after baking any of the meat loaves. Tilt the pan (with meat loaf still in place) and use a metal spatula to scrape the pan drippings to one end. Spoon out into a cup. Spoon off or blot off most of the fat. Combine with enough stock or canned broth to make 1½ cups.

Melt 1½ tablespoons of butter or olive oil in a small saucepan over moderate heat. Stir in 2 tablespoons of all-purpose flour and cook, stirring, for 1 minute. Pour in the broth mixture and ¼ cup dry white wine or vermouth. Stir until the mixture boils. Simmer for 2 minutes. Taste for seasoning and add salt, if needed. Serve hot.

Mexican Meat Loaf

Flavored with Mexican chorizo and dotted with black olives, this fiesta loaf is fragrant and spicy. It is good with Chunky Guacamole (page 38), corn tortillas, and roasted or mashed potatoes. Be sure to use the soft Mexican chorizo, *not* the dried Spanish ones used for paella.

MAKES 6 TO 8 SERVINGS

1½ tablespoons vegetable oil

2 medium onions, chopped

1 large garlic clove, minced or crushed through a press

1 teaspoon dried oregano, crumbled

1 teaspoon ground cumin

12 ounces lean ground beef

12 ounces ground pork

8 ounces homemade or store-bought soft Mexican Chorizo (page 256), casings removed and meat crumbled

1 cup coarsely chopped drained canned tomatoes

1 large egg

½ cup chopped fresh cilantro, plus more, for topping

½ cup sliced whole scallions

¼ cup cider vinegar

1 tablespoon sweet paprika

1½ teaspoons salt

½ teaspoon black pepper

1 can (6 ounces) pitted large black olives, drained

¾ cup fresh bread crumbs made from firm white bread

½ cup canned tomato sauce

1. Spoon the oil into a large, heavy skillet set over moderate heat. Add the onions and sauté until softened, 3 to 5 minutes. Add the garlic, oregano, and cumin and cook for 2 minutes. Set aside to cool to room temperature.

VARIATIONS

Substitutions: **For a lighter version, use 1 pound ground chicken and ¼ pound each of ground beef and pork. Sauté the chorizo in a small skillet and drain off the fat before adding.**

Lower calorie: **Replace the whole olives with 1 cup fresh or frozen corn kernels.**

2. Preheat the oven to 350° F. Lightly oil a shallow 13 × 9-inch pan.

3. Crumble the beef, pork, and chorizo into a large bowl. Add the tomatoes, egg, ½ cup cilantro, scallions, vinegar, paprika, salt, and pepper. Scrape the onion mixture over the ingredients and mix thoroughly with your hands. Add the olives and bread crumbs and mix until evenly distributed. Shape the mixture into a 12 × 5-inch loaf in the pan.

4. Spread the tomato sauce over the top of the loaf. Bake for 1¼ to 1½ hours, or until the internal temperature reaches 155° to 160° F. Sprinkle the top with additional chopped cilantro and let stand for 15 minutes. Cut into 1-inch slices.

Big Boy Chili and Beans

Here is the big casserole of old-fashioned, ranch-style chili and beans that my friends most often request. It is a beautiful terra-cotta color and has a deep, delicious flavor achieved by braising *and* baking. The chili is superb with no adornment at all, or can be served with accompaniments—say, sour cream, grated cheese, black olives, and sliced scallions; it is also perfect for making chili dogs. The chili will be best if you start cooking a day before you plan to serve it. After it simmers for 3 hours it must cool to room temperature before baking for 2 hours. This technique produces a remarkable texture and flavor.

MAKES ABOUT 20 CUPS (12 GENEROUS SERVINGS)

- 2 tablespoons vegetable oil or bacon fat
- 1½ pounds onions, coarsely chopped
- 3 large garlic cloves, minced or crushed through a press
- 2 pounds lean ground beef, sirloin, or chuck
- 2 pounds lean ground pork
- ¾ cup chili powder, preferably a mix of half ancho and half pasilla, but any will do
- 3 tablespoons unsweetened cocoa powder
- 2 to 3 tablespoons sugar
- 1 tablespoon plus 1 teaspoon ground cumin
- 1 tablespoon plus 1 teaspoon dried oregano, crumbled
- 2 teaspoons fennel seeds (optional)
- 2 teaspoons salt
- ½ teaspoon cayenne pepper (optional)
- 3 bay leaves
- 1 can (28 ounces) whole tomatoes, undrained and roughly chopped
- 1 can (8 ounces) tomato sauce
- 3 bottles (12 ounces each) dark or medium beer, such as Mexican Dos Equis, Heineken, or Beck's

Beans
- 6 slices hickory-smoked bacon, finely chopped
- 1 pound dried small pink beans, soaked (page 16) and still in their soaking liquid
- 1 large garlic clove, minced or crushed through a press
- 2 teaspoons salt

1. Spoon the oil into a large, heavy casserole or Dutch oven set over moderate heat. Add the onions and sauté until softened and lightly colored, about 10 minutes. Add the garlic and sauté for 2 minutes. Reserve.
2. Return the pot to moderate heat and crumble in the beef and pork. Increase

the heat to high and brown well, without stirring, for 5 minutes. Reduce the heat to moderately high and brown, stirring occasionally, for 15 minutes longer.

3. Return the onions to the pot and stir in ½ cup of the chili powder, 2 tablespoons of the cocoa, 2 tablespoons of the sugar, 1 tablespoon of the cumin, 1 tablespoon of the oregano, fennel seeds, salt, cayenne, and bay leaves. Add the tomatoes and their juices, the tomato sauce, 2 bottles of the beer, and 4 cups of water. Bring the mixture to a boil over moderate heat. Reduce the heat to low and simmer, uncovered, for 3 hours. Stir gently every 30 minutes, but do not stir during the last 15 to 20 minutes so all of the fat will rise to the top.

4. Meanwhile, prepare the beans. Put the bacon in a large, heavy saucepan set over moderate heat. Cook, stirring frequently, until crisp and deep golden brown. Spoon off all but 1 tablespoon of the fat.

5. Drain the beans (no matter which soaking technique you have used) and measure the liquid. Add water to make 6 cups. Add the beans and liquid to the bacon in the pan and bring to a boil, stirring frequently, over moderate heat. Reduce the heat to low, partially cover, and simmer for 1 hour. Add the garlic and salt, partially cover, and simmer until the beans are tender, about 1 hour longer. Remove from the heat and set aside.

VARIATIONS

Substitutions: **Use all beef or use 2 pounds of ground turkey and 1 pound each of beef and pork.**

Quicker: **To save time, you can substitute four 1-pound cans of small pink beans or black beans, drained and rinsed, for the dried beans (and omit the bacon, garlic, and salt called for with the beans). Skip steps 4 and 5 and add them in step 6.**

6. When the chili has cooked for 3 hours, degrease it, skimming off most of the fat. Place a paper towel flat on the surface to soak up any remaining fat; repeat, if necessary. Stir in the remaining ¼ cup chili powder, 1 tablespoon cocoa, 1 teaspoon cumin, and 1 teaspoon oregano. Taste for balance of acidity to sweetness and stir in the remaining 1 tablespoon sugar, if needed. Add the beans and their cooking liquid. Set the chili aside to cool to room temperature. If making ahead, cover and refrigerate overnight.

7. Preheat the oven to 300° F. Stir the remaining 1 bottle of beer into the chili. Bake, uncovered, for 2 hours, stirring once in a while. Serve hot.

Peter Prestcott's Big Batch Bigos

When I first began working at *Food & Wine* magazine many years ago, I was Peter Prestcott's assistant. What I love most about Peter's vigorous cooking style is that everything he cooks has *big flavor!* I learned much from Peter over the years and want to share one of his recipes. Bigos is a Polish hunter's stew and can be made a million ways. Peter's hearty version is enough for a party and tastes best when made a day ahead. This recipe is easily halved.

MAKES 18 SERVINGS

- 1½ ounces dried wild mushrooms, such as cèpes or porcini
- 4 pounds sauerkraut, preferably bulk or in refrigerated pouches
- 8 ounces meaty salt pork, cut into ½-inch cubes
- 1 bottle (750 ml) dry red wine
- 2 cans (6 ounces each) tomato paste
- 5 large garlic cloves, minced or crushed through a press
- 3 bay leaves
- 3 pounds smoked kielbasa sausage, cut into ½-inch slices
- 1 cup vodka, preferably Polish
- 2 tablespoons butter
- 2 tablespoons olive oil
- 3 pounds lean trimmed beef chuck, cut into 1-inch cubes
- 2 tablespoons caraway seeds
- 2 cups coarsely chopped kosher dill pickles
- 2 pints sour cream, at room temperature, for serving (optional)

1. Put the dried mushrooms in a bowl and add 1 cup of hot water. Let soak until softened, about 30 minutes. Drain the mushrooms, reserving the liquid. Finely chop the mushrooms; strain the soaking liquid through a fine sieve.
2. Meanwhile, put the sauerkraut into a colander and rinse well under cold run-

CARAWAY SEEDS

Caraway is the remarkably potent flavoring often found in rye bread. I am practically addicted to the morning comfort of caraway rye toast dripping with melted butter.

But caraway seeds are much more than that. Caraway is the choice flavoring for dishes like sauerkraut and sausages, Hungarian goulash, Polish bigos, and many breads and rolls. The seeds contribute a unique flavor that is warm and sweet, then pleasantly bitter with a slight clovelike numbing on the tongue, along with an unexpected nuttiness and undertone of dill.

Caraway and cumin are similar in appearance. Both are members of the parsley family, but their flavors are so different that we associate caraway with German cooking and cumin with Mexican and Asian Indian.

ning water. Drain and squeeze out as much moisture as possible with your hands.

3. Pour about 4 cups of water into a medium saucepan and bring to a boil over high heat. Add the salt pork and blanch for 5 minutes. Drain in a strainer, discarding the liquid.

4. In a nonreactive large Dutch oven or stockpot, combine the mushrooms, their soaking liquid, the sauerkraut, salt pork, wine, tomato paste, garlic, and bay leaves. Bring to a boil over moderate heat. Reduce the heat to low, cover, and simmer for 2 hours.

5. Add the kielbasa to the sauerkraut mixture, cover, and cook for 15 minutes. Increase the heat to moderate. Averting your face, pour in the vodka. Ignite it and shake the pan until the flames subside. Reduce the heat to low and simmer, uncovered, for 15 minutes. Set aside.

6. In a large, heavy skillet, combine 1 tablespoon of the butter and 1 tablespoon of the olive oil over high heat. Add half of the beef cubes and half of the caraway seeds and cook, tossing occasionally, until the beef is well browned on all sides, 5 to 6 minutes. Transfer the meat to the bigos. Add the remaining 1 tablespoon butter and 1 tablespoon olive oil to the pan and brown the remaining beef with the remaining caraway seeds as before. Add to the bigos. Cover the pot and cook over low heat, stirring occasionally and adding a little water if the liquid reduces too much, until the beef is tender, 1½ to 2 hours. (If making a day ahead, let cool to room temperature, cover, and refrigerate. Reheat over low heat.)

7. Just before serving, stir in the pickles. Put the sour cream in a serving dish and let guests spoon a dollop onto each serving, if desired.

SAUERKRAUT

Many of our favorite pickled and preserved foods came to us, in a roundabout way, from China, and sauerkraut is one of them. Chinese cooks pickled cabbage to preserve it for winter, when food was scarce. The Tartars brought the formula to Europe, and the Germans and Austrians developed the concept into sauerkraut.

Sauerkraut is shredded green cabbage layered with salt and left to ferment until sharp and sour. Depending on one's taste preference from mild to sharp, sauerkraut can be rinsed, drained, or left unrinsed. It is best bought in bulk, in vacuum-sealed pouches, or in fresh-packed jars at delicatessens.

One good cooking method is to simmer the drained sauerkraut in a mixture of chicken broth and white wine, with some caraway seeds and juniper berries thrown in.

Store sauerkraut in the refrigerator in a jar with a tight-fitting lid.

Yangchow Meaty Fried Rice

Here is the ultimate fried rice with the biggest flavor. It's a specialty of a town near Shanghai and is a tumble of ingredients: chicken and barbecued pork to shrimp and peas, all flavored with Chinese oyster sauce, ginger, sesame oil, sherry, and garlic. Fried rice must be made from cold cooked rice; consider buying a quart from a Chinese restaurant or making the rice the day before you want to prepare this dish. You do need a wok to make this properly.

MAKES 6 SERVINGS

- 8 ounces medium shrimp, peeled and deveined
- 1 tablespoon bottled oyster sauce
- 1 tablespoon plus 1 teaspoon grated fresh ginger
- ½ teaspoon sugar
- 3½ teaspoons Oriental sesame oil
- 4 large eggs
- ½ teaspoon salt
- 4 tablespoons peanut or vegetable oil
- 8 ounces skinless and boneless chicken breast, thinly sliced across the grain
- 1 large garlic clove, minced or crushed through a press
- 1 onion, slivered lengthwise
- ¾ cup thinly sliced Chinese barbecued pork or smoked ham
- 1 quart (4 cups) cooked white rice, well chilled
- 1 cup frozen peas, thawed
- 2 tablespoons Chinese rice wine or dry sherry
- 2 tablespoons soy sauce
- 1½ cups shredded iceberg lettuce
- ½ cup thinly sliced whole scallions

1. Put the shrimp in a medium bowl and add the oyster sauce, 1 teaspoon of the grated ginger, the sugar, and ½ teaspoon of the sesame oil. Set aside to marinate at room temperature for 30 minutes.
2. In a large bowl, whisk the eggs with 2 teaspoons of the sesame oil and ¼ teaspoon of the salt. Place a nonstick medium skillet over moderately high heat. Spoon in 1 tablespoon of the oil and swirl to coat the pan. Pour in the eggs, reduce the heat slightly, and when the eggs begin to set, stir and lightly scramble. Turn out into a bowl and reserve.
3. Spoon ½ tablespoon of the peanut oil into the same skillet and place over high heat. Add the shrimp and its marinade and stir-fry until almost cooked, about 30 seconds. Turn out into a bowl and reserve.

4. Pour ½ tablespoon of the oil into the skillet and stir-fry the chicken over high heat just until cooked, about 1 minute. Turn out and reserve.

5. Place a large wok over high heat. When very hot, spoon in the remaining 2 tablespoons oil and tilt the wok around to coat with the oil. Add the remaining tablespoon ginger and the garlic and stir-fry for 10 seconds. Add the onion and pork and stir-fry until lightly browned, about 1 minute. Crumble in the rice and cook, tossing occasionally, until heated through, about 3 minutes. Add the peas and cook for 1 minute. Add the reserved eggs, shrimp, and chicken; spoon in the rice wine or sherry, soy sauce, and the remaining ¼ teaspoon salt. Stir-fry for about 30 seconds. Add the lettuce and scallions and toss briefly. Turn out onto a large serving platter; serve hot.

VARIATIONS

Substitutions: **Omit the chicken entirely or replace it with sliced pork loin or slivers of beef sirloin. Omit the peas and add julienned fresh snow peas.**

Beefsteak Ranchero with Fresh Tomato Salsa

These tasty, tender, charcoal-grilled steaks, which marinate overnight, are delicious with corn tortillas, fresh tomato salsa, a pot of pinto beans, corn-on-the-cob, and grilled scallions.

MAKES 2 TO 3 SERVINGS

Marinated Steaks

- 1 **small onion, thinly sliced**
- 1 **large garlic clove, thinly sliced**
- ½ **cup chopped fresh cilantro**
- 1 **fresh or pickled jalapeño chili, thinly sliced**
- 1 **ripe tomato, thinly sliced**
- 2 **large shell steaks, cut about 1 inch thick, trimmed**

Fresh Tomato Salsa

- 2 **large ripe juice tomatoes, cut into ½-inch dice**
- ¼ **cup chopped fresh cilantro**
- ¼ **cup minced white onion or whole scallions**
- 2 **tablespoons extra-virgin olive oil**

1 small fresh or pickled jalapeño chili, minced (seed or partially seed the fresh pepper if you do not want a hot salsa)

½ teaspoon salt

¼ teaspoon black pepper

1. Marinate the steaks. In a shallow dish just large enough to hold the steaks, layer half of the onion, garlic, cilantro, jalapeño, and sliced tomato. Place the steaks on top of these ingredients and cover with the remaining onion, garlic, cilantro, jalapeño, and tomato. Cover and refrigerate for at least 12 hours or overnight.
2. Meanwhile, prepare the fresh tomato salsa. In a medium bowl, combine the tomatoes, cilantro, minced onion, olive oil, jalapeño, salt, and pepper. Set aside at room temperature for up to 2 hours, or cover and refrigerate. Let return to room temperature before serving.
3. Prepare a barbecue grill and preheat, if necessary. Place the grill rack about 5 inches above the heat source and preheat it for 5 minutes. Remove the steaks from the dish, brushing off any marinade that clings. Put the steaks on the grill and cook, turning with tongs every 3 minutes, to the desired degree of doneness; if the meat is chilled, the steaks will take 10 to 12 minutes for medium-rare. Serve hot, with room-temperature salsa.

VARIATION

Presentation: **You can cut the grilled beefsteak into strips and make fajitas with flour tortillas. Serve with guacamole.**

Gloria's Enchiladas Grande

Gloria Ontiveros, my best friend Timothy's mother, made these enchiladas for every party she threw in the 1960s. But she usually had a second tray of them stashed somewhere. Though they are not very Mexican, I think of them as L.A.–style cooking—*before* all the fussy culinary nonsense began. No one understood the addition of hard-cooked eggs back then and maybe they still don't. But Gloria always put them in and I always liked the addition so have kept them that way. The enchiladas are mild, not hot, and can be made hours ahead and reheated. Be sure to have all the ingredients ready before you make the sauce. Serve with a pot of beans, a Caesar salad, and lots of cold Mexican beer.

MAKES 18 (6 TO 9 SERVINGS)

Enchiladas

- ½ cup plus 1 tablespoon vegetable oil
- 2 medium onions, finely chopped
- 1½ pounds lean ground beef, round or sirloin
- 1 or 2 fresh jalapeño chilies, minced
- 1 large garlic clove, minced or crushed through a press
- 1 teaspoon dried oregano, crumbled
- 1 teaspoon ground cumin
- 1 teaspoon salt
- ¼ teaspoon black pepper
- 18 corn tortillas
- 5 large eggs, hard-cooked (page 13), peeled, and coarsely chopped
- 1¼ cups thinly sliced whole scallions
- 1 cup chopped cilantro leaves
- 1 pound medium-sharp cheddar cheese, coarsely grated (4 cups)
- 1 can (6 ounces) pitted large black olives, drained

Sauce

- 2 tablespoons vegetable oil
- 1 large garlic clove, minced or crushed through a press
- ¼ cup all-purpose flour
- ¼ cup chili powder
- 1 teaspoon dried oregano, crumbled
- 1 teaspoon ground cumin
- ¼ teaspoon ground cinnamon
- 3 cups Chicken Stock (page 73) or canned broth
- 1 can (8 ounces) tomato sauce
- ½ teaspoon salt

For Serving (optional)

- 1 pint sour cream, at room temperature
- 18 medium radishes, trimmed and sliced
- Cilantro sprigs

1. Make the enchiladas. Spoon 1 tablespoon of the vegetable oil into a large, heavy skillet set over moderate heat. Add the onions and sauté until softened, 3 to 5 minutes. Push the onions to one side of the pan and crumble in the ground beef. Increase the heat slightly and add the jalapeño, garlic, oregano, cumin, salt, and pepper. Cook, stirring frequently, until the beef is browned. Remove from the heat and turn the filling into a medium bowl.

2. Place a heavy, medium skillet (just slightly larger than a corn tortilla) over moderately high heat. Pour in the remaining ½ cup vegetable oil and heat

until the surface shimmers. Meanwhile, stack 5 paper towels and cut them crosswise and lengthwise into quarters. With tongs, lower 1 tortilla into the oil; it should sizzle instantly. If necessary, regulate the heat between high and moderately high. Turn several times until the tortilla softens and then barely begins to stiffen, 10 to 15 seconds. Place on a square of paper towel on a plate. Repeat, stacking the tortillas between squares of paper towel.

3. Put the chopped eggs, scallions, cilantro, cheese, and olives into separate bowls.

4. Preheat the oven to 425° F. Lightly oil a 15 × 10-inch jelly-roll pan.

5. Make the sauce. Choose a wide, medium skillet or sauté pan that will hold about 4 cups of sauce (a saucepan is too deep for dipping the tortillas into the sauce). Pour the oil into the pan and set over moderate heat. Add the garlic and sauté until softened but not browned, about 1 minute. Stir in the flour and cook, stirring, for 1 minute. Add the chili powder, oregano, cumin, and cinnamon and stir-fry for 1 minute; the mixture will be dry, but do not add any extra oil. Pour in the stock or broth and tomato sauce and bring to a boil, stirring or whisking constantly. Reduce the heat to low and simmer until smooth and creamy, about 2 minutes. Stir in the salt. The sauce should be the consistency of creamy soup. If necessary at any time, stir in 1 to 2 tablespoons of water. Keep the sauce warm.

6. Assemble. Peel the paper towels off the tortillas. Have the bowls of ingredients nearby so you can work assembly-line fashion near the hot sauce. With tongs, lower a tortilla into the sauce and remove it right away so it is lightly coated. Put it on the prepared pan and dip a second tortilla. As you work, make 2 lengthwise rows of 9 enchiladas each. Across the lower third of each coated tortilla, layer about 3 tablespoons of the meat filling, 1½ to 2 tablespoons of the chopped egg, 1 tablespoon of the scallions, 1 scant tablespoon of cilantro leaves, 2 to 3 tablespoons of the cheese, and 2 whole olives evenly spaced. Spoon 1 tablespoon of the sauce over the ingredients and carefully roll up the ingredients in the tortilla. Place seam side down at one end of the pan. Continue assembling the enchiladas until the pan is full. Spread any remaining sauce over the tops, taking care to coat the outer ends of the enchiladas. Sprinkle the remaining cheese over the top.

7. Bake the enchiladas until hot and bubbly, 15 to 20 minutes. Serve hot or warm, adding a dollop of sour cream and a few radishes alongside each, if desired. Garnish with sprigs of cilantro.

Lemony Veal-Stuffed Cabbage

Lemon and veal work beautifully to enhance a creamy filling that's flavored with bits of ham and ground pork. This is a light and refreshing version of an Old World cabbage dish. The rolls are great served simply in the broth, if you would prefer to skip the creamy sauce at the end of the recipe. Look for large, solid heads of whitish-green cabbage to obtain the best leaves for stuffing.

MAKES 24 (8 SERVINGS)

- ½ cup long-grain white rice
- 2 teaspoons grated lemon zest
- ½ teaspoon black pepper
- 2 large (3-pound) heads green cabbage
- 2 pounds ground veal
- 8 ounces lean ground pork
- 1 cup finely chopped smoked ham (about 6 ounces)
- 1 cup light cream
- 3 large eggs
- 1 medium onion, coarsely grated
- ¼ cup chopped fresh dill, plus 6 dill sprigs for the pot
- ¼ cup fresh lemon juice
- 2 teaspoons salt
- 6 thin lemon slices
- 4 cups Chicken Stock (page 73) or canned broth
- ¼ cup all-purpose flour
- 1 large package (8 ounces) cream cheese, cut into bits and at room temperature
  Lemon wedges, for serving

1. Pour 3 cups of water into a medium saucepan and bring to a boil over high heat. Slowly add the rice, so the boiling does not stop, and then boil for 5 minutes, until just partially cooked. Drain the rice in a strainer; turn into a large bowl. Add the lemon zest and pepper, toss, and set aside to cool.

2. Pour about 2 inches of water into a large Dutch oven or kettle. Bring to a boil over high heat. Using a sharp knife, cut out the cone-shaped core from each head of cabbage. Place 1 head, cored end down, into the boiling water; cover and boil over moderately high heat for 5 minutes. Turn the cabbage and loosen any outer leaves. Continue cooking until the outer leaves are tender and translucent, 10 to 16 minutes. Remove the tender leaves and continue cooking until you have the 12 best and biggest leaves from each head. (The smaller center heart of the cabbage will be chopped and used to line the pan.) Repeat with the second head of cabbage.

3. When the leaves are cool, use a paring knife to slice off just the raised portion of each vein. (Some cooks prefer to cut out the entire vein, and if this is easier for you, do so. It is quite a simple matter, though, if you place a leaf flat in your hand with the raised portion of the vein upward and slice parallel to the leaf, just removing the raised portion.)

4. Reserve the 24 best leaves and coarsely chop the remaining cabbage leaves and heart. You will have 4 to 5 cups of chopped cabbage, plus the 24 leaves.

5. Crumble the ground veal and pork over the rice. Add the chopped ham, cream, eggs, onion, chopped dill, lemon juice, and salt; mix with your hands until well blended.

6. Place 1 cabbage leaf, deveined side down, in front of you. Shape about ⅓ cup of the filling into a log along the lower third of the leaf. Fold the bottom of the leaf over the filling; fold in the sides and roll up tightly. Set aside, seam side down. Assemble the remaining cabbage rolls in the same manner.

7. Scatter the chopped cabbage over the bottom of a nonreactive large Dutch oven or kettle. Arrange half of the stuffed cabbage rolls, seam sides down, in a compact layer on top. Prick each roll twice with a long fork. Add 3 of the dill sprigs and 3 of the lemon slices. Pour in 2 cups of the stock or broth. Add the remaining cabbage rolls; prick each twice with a fork. Top with the remaining dill sprigs, lemon slices, and the remaining 2 cups stock or broth. If necessary, add enough water to almost cover the cabbage rolls. Cover the pot and bring to a boil over moderately high heat. Reduce the heat to moderately low and simmer until tender, about 1½ hours. Although the cabbage rolls will be delicious at this point, the flavors will blossom if left to stand at least 1 hour.

8. If you want to make the cream sauce, carefully transfer the cabbage rolls to a platter. Discard the lemon slices and dill sprigs. Place the flour in a sieve and hold it over the broth and chopped cabbage that remain in the pot. Tap the sieve once, so just a film of flour sifts onto the surface, and stir in the flour to blend. Continue tapping and stirring so the flour does not lump. Place over moderately high heat and stir constantly until the mixture boils. Add the cream cheese and stir until smooth, 2 to 3 minutes. Return the cabbage rolls and any accumulated liquid to the pot. To serve, arrange 2 cabbage rolls on a plate and spoon some of the sauce and chopped cabbage on top. Garnish with lemon wedges and dill sprigs and serve hot.

Thai Satay with Cucumbers and Peanut Sauce

Satay are skewered meats cooked over charcoal. They are most frequently served as an appetizer, but they also make a great main course, served with rice and vegetables, and perhaps a Zombie or iced tea.

MAKES 24 SKEWERS (6 TO 8 SERVINGS)

- 1½ pounds trimmed pork loin, beef sirloin, or beef rib steaks
- 1 tablespoon homemade Curry Powder (page 385) or store-bought
- ½ cup canned or homemade unsweetened coconut milk
- 2 tablespoons fresh lime juice
- 1 tablespoon sugar
- ½ teaspoon salt
- ¼ to ½ teaspoon cayenne pepper
- 24 medium (8-inch) bamboo skewers
- 2 tablespoons vegetable oil

Peanut Sauce

- 1 cup unsweetened coconut milk
- ⅓ cup chunky peanut butter
- 2 tablespoons fresh lime juice
- 1 tablespoon Thai fish sauce (*nam pla*)
- 2 tablespoons Oriental sesame oil
- 1 teaspoon sugar
- ⅛ teaspoon cayenne pepper

Cucumbers

- 4 medium Kirby cucumbers, or 2 large regular cucumbers
- 2 cups ice cubes
- 2 teaspoons salt
- 3 tablespoons rice vinegar
- 2 tablespoons fresh lime juice
- 2 teaspoons sugar
- 1 fresh hot chili pepper, such as a jalapeño, seeded and minced
- ¼ cup chopped fresh cilantro
- 4 whole scallions, thinly sliced

1. Cut the pork or beef into strips about 3 inches long, ½ inch wide, and ¼ inch thick.
2. In a bowl, stir together the curry powder, coconut milk, lime juice, sugar, salt, and cayenne to taste. Add the meat, toss to coat well, cover, and refrigerate for 1½ hours. Meanwhile, soak the bamboo skewers in warm water.
3. To make the peanut sauce, pour the coconut milk into a nonreactive small saucepan and simmer over moderate heat until reduced slightly, about 5

minutes. Remove from the heat and stir in the peanut butter, lime juice, fish sauce, sesame oil, sugar, and cayenne. Stir until silky smooth; transfer to a small bowl and let cool to room temperature.

4. To prepare the cucumbers, trim the ends from the cucumbers and peel. If using Kirby cucumbers, cut into ⅛-inch slices; if using regular cucumbers, halve lengthwise and seed, then cut crosswise into thin slices. In a large bowl, toss the cucumbers with the ice cubes, salt, and ½ cup of cold water. Let stand for 30 minutes.

5. Drain the cucumbers, reserving ¼ cup of the liquid. In a bowl, combine the rice vinegar, lime juice, sugar, chili pepper, and reserved ¼ cup liquid. Add the cucumbers, cilantro, and scallions. Toss; cover and chill for about 1 hour.

6. To cook the satay, prepare a barbecue grill and preheat, if necessary, or preheat the broiler. Take the meat from the marinade and thread each piece, folding it back and forth in an *S* shape, onto a soaked skewer. After assembling all of them, brush lightly with the vegetable oil.

7. When ready to cook, set the grill rack in place and preheat it. Grill the skewers, turning frequently, until just cooked through, about 10 minutes on a grill or 6 to 8 minutes under the broiler. Serve the satay hot, on a bed of the marinated cucumbers, with the peanut dipping sauce on the side.

VARIATION

Substitution: **Use skinless and boneless chicken breasts or thighs in place of the pork or beef, but marinate them for just 30 to 40 minutes (prepare the cucumbers, peanut sauce, and grill ahead of time).**

Zombie

My dictionary states that, "In voodoo, a zombie is the body of a dead person given the semblance of life." It's also the name of one of my favorite cocktails.

Here's how to make a 3½-cup batch: In a small pitcher combine 1 cup each of fresh orange juice and pineapple juice with ½ cup apricot nectar and 3 to 4 tablespoons of fresh lime or lemon juice. Stir in ¼ cup each of light rum, red rum, and dark rum. Add a few ice cubes and 1 to 2 tablespoons grenadine syrup or liqueur. Pour over tall glasses of ice. Float about 2 teaspoons of 151 proof rum on top and garnish with an orange slice, maraschino cherry, and a sprig of mint if desired. Add a tall straw and serve.

Burgundy Beef Stew

The big flavor here is achieved by thoroughly browning the cubes of beef chuck and braising them in Burgundy with beef broth. The flavors are boosted further with herbs and vegetables.

MAKES 8 SERVINGS

   3 pounds lean, trimmed beef chuck, cut into pieces roughly 1 inch thick and 2 inches square
2½ tablespoons olive oil
   ¼ cup all-purpose flour
   4 cups Rich or Quick Beef Stock (pages 74, 75), Chicken Stock (page 73), or canned broth
   3 cups full-bodied red Burgundy wine
   ¼ cup tomato paste
   4 large garlic cloves, minced or crushed through a press
   4 bay leaves
   1 teaspoon dried thyme, crumbled
   2 teaspoons salt
   3 pounds small new potatoes (18 to 24), peeled
   1 pound small carrots, peeled and cut into 1½-inch lengths
  12 ounces small white onions or pearl onions (1- to 1½-inch diameter), peeled
   8 ounces whole medium mushrooms
   2 tablespoons cornstarch
   ¼ cup chopped fresh parsley

1. Pat the beef dry on paper towels. Spoon 1½ tablespoons of the olive oil into a large, heavy casserole or Dutch oven set over moderately high heat. When very hot, add one-third of the beef in a single layer without crowding and brown very well on one side, 4 to 5 minutes. Turn the pieces and brown the other side for about 2 minutes, regulating the heat as necessary between moderately high and high to ensure thorough browning. Transfer the browned beef to a platter. Brown the remaining beef in 2 batches, adding ½ tablespoon of the remaining oil each time. Reserve all of the beef on the platter as it is browned.

2. Spoon the flour into the casserole, stir to moisten, and cook over moderate heat for 1 minute; the mixture will be dry. Pour in the stock and wine and bring to a boil, stirring constantly, over moderate heat. Stir in the tomato paste and bring to a boil. Reduce the heat to low; stir in the garlic, bay leaves, thyme, and salt. Return the meat to the pot, cover tightly, and braise gently over low heat until tender but not falling apart, 2 to 2½ hours.

3. Uncover the pot and add the potatoes, carrots, and onions. Cover the pot and simmer until the vegetables are tender and the meat is very tender, 45 to 60 minutes.

4. Add the mushrooms and cook for 10 minutes. Remove the bay leaves.

5. In a cup, dissolve the cornstarch in 2 tablespoons cold water. Stir the mixture into the stew and simmer for 1 to 2 minutes, or until thickened slightly. Stir in the parsley and taste for seasoning; add a pinch more salt, if needed. Serve hot or let cool to room temperature and then reheat gently.

Big-Taste Grilled Ribs

These ribs are sweet and sour, hot and crunchy, tender and juicy, and plenty messy. They are also good and smoky. Start the recipe early in the day so the ribs can marinate for 8 to 12 hours.

MAKES 2 TO 4 SERVINGS

> 4 pounds lean, meaty pork spareribs, cut into 2- to 3-rib portions
> 1/3 cup minced fresh ginger
> 1 medium onion, finely chopped
> 2 large garlic cloves, minced or crushed through a press
> 1/3 cup light soy sauce
> 1/3 cup dry sherry
> 1/3 cup rice vinegar
> 1/4 cup sugar
> 1/2 teaspoon black pepper
> 1/2 cup apricot preserves
> 2 tablespoons brown mustard
> 1 tablespoon Oriental sesame oil
> 1/2 teaspoon cayenne pepper
> 2 to 3 cups mesquite or hardwood chips

1. Using the tip of a paring knife, cut slits between the ribs so the marinade can penetrate. In a large bowl, combine the ginger, onion, garlic, soy sauce, sherry, vinegar, sugar, and black pepper. Stir to combine and add the pieces of ribs. Cover and marinate in the refrigerator for 8 to 12 hours.

2. Preheat the oven to 300° F. Lightly oil a large roasting pan. Take the ribs from the marinade and put them, bone side up, in the pan. Strain the

marinade and reserve it. Bake the ribs for 1½ to 2 hours, turning with tongs every 30 minutes, or until cooked to the bone. (Can be prepared to this point a day ahead.)

3. In a nonreactive small saucepan, combine the apricot preserves, mustard, sesame oil, cayenne, and ¼ cup of the marinade. Bring to a boil. Reduce the heat to low and simmer until slightly thickened, 2 to 3 minutes. Set the glaze aside.

4. Meanwhile, soak the wood chips in a bowl of warm water for 30 minutes to 1 hour. Prepare a barbecue grill and preheat, if necessary. Drain the mesquite chips. Position the grill rack over the heat source and preheat it. Remove the grill rack and sprinkle the chips over the heat source. Set the rack back in place. Grill the ribs, turning frequently, for about 10 minutes. Brush the ribs with some of the glaze and turn frequently until glazed and good and brown, 10 to 15 minutes. Serve hot or warm.

Pork Tenderloin with Poblano and Ancho Chilies

In this recipe, two big flavors come from two forms of a single chili pepper. Ancho chili is the mature, dried version of the fresh green poblano, but their individual flavors are totally different. Be sure to choose dried anchos that are pliable—not brittle—for the best results.

MAKES 6 SERVINGS

> 1¾ to 2 pounds pork tenderloins (2 to 3 medium)
> 3 ounces dried ancho chili peppers (6 large)
> ½ cup diced tomato
> 1 cup chopped onion
> 2 large garlic cloves, minced or crushed through a press
> 2 tablespoons cider vinegar
> 1 teaspoon dried oregano, crumbled
> 1 teaspoon ground cumin
> ¼ teaspoon black pepper
> 2½ tablespoons vegetable oil
> 2½ to 3 cups Chicken Stock (page 73) or canned broth
> ½ teaspoon salt
> 1 tablespoon all-purpose flour
> 1 pound fresh poblano chili peppers
> (4 to 6 large), roasted (page 17), peeled, and cut into 1-inch pieces

1. Using the tip of a sharp knife, prick the pork tenderloins all over, about 20 times each, making cuts about ½ inch deep.
2. Place a large, heavy, dry skillet or griddle over moderate heat. Pull the stems from the ancho chilies and tear the chilies in half. Shake out the seeds and pull out any loose ribs. Place the chili pieces in the hot skillet and press down with a spatula to flatten. Heat, turning once after 30 seconds, just until soft and fragrant, about 45 seconds but no longer than 1 minute. Transfer the chilies to a bowl. Add 3 cups of boiling water and set aside to soak for 15 minutes. Remove about one-third of the chili pieces for the marinade. Reserve the rest in the water until needed.
3. In a food processor or small grinder, combine the drained chili pieces with the tomato, ½ cup of the onion, half of the garlic, the vinegar, ½ teaspoon of the oregano, ½ teaspoon of the cumin, and the pepper. Process to a puree; you will have about 1 cup of marinade.
4. Put the tenderloins in a zip-lock bag or shallow dish and pour the marinade over. Marinate in the refrigerator for 1½ hours.
5. Preheat the oven to 300° F. Remove the tenderloins from the refrigerator and marinate at room temperature for 30 minutes longer, while the oven pre-heats. Lightly oil a shallow 12 × 9-inch baking dish or casserole.
6. Place a large, heavy skillet over moderately high heat and spoon in 1½ table-spoons of the vegetable oil. Remove the tenderloins from the marinade, brushing off any excess. Reserve all of the marinade (you will have about ¾ cup). Put the tenderloins in the hot skillet and brown thoroughly, turn-ing several times to brown all over, until deep brown, 10 to 12 minutes. Transfer the tenderloins to the oiled baking dish. To deglaze the skillet, pour in 1 cup of the stock or broth and all of the reserved marinade. Turn the heat to high and boil the mixture, scraping any browned bits that cling to the pan. Pour the sauce over the tenderloins.
7. Bake the tenderloins for 45 to 60 minutes, or until just cooked and no longer pink in the center (the best way to tell is to cut through the thickest part of one of the tenderloins). Remove the tenderloins from the sauce and cover with aluminum foil; reserve the sauce.
8. Spoon the remaining 1 tablespoon vegetable oil into a large, heavy skillet set over moderate heat. Add the remaining ½ cup onion and sauté until soft-ened, 3 to 5 minutes. Add the remaining garlic, ½ teaspoon oregano, ½ teaspoon cumin, and the salt. Sauté for 2 minutes. Sprinkle on the flour and cook, stirring, for 1 minute. Add 1½ cups of the remaining stock and all of the reserved sauce. Bring to a boil, stirring, over moderate heat. Simmer for 3 minutes. Add the poblanos and reduce the heat to very low.
9. Drain the remaining soaked ancho chilies. Working with 1 piece at a time,

place it, skin side down, on a flat surface. Using a knife with a thin blade, slide the blade between the flesh and the skin to remove. (If this is difficult for you, simply scrape the flesh from the skin.) Discard the skin. Coarsely chop the ancho and add to the sauce. Simmer gently for 5 minutes.

10. Slice the tenderloins ¼ to ½ inch thick. Add the slices to the sauce and heat very gently. Taste for salt and add more, if needed.

11. To serve, spoon three-fourths of the sauce onto a large platter and overlap the pork slices in 2 or 3 rows down the center. Spoon the remaining sauce in a line across the slices. Serve hot or warm.

DRIED CHILIES

You can throw a whole dried chili pepper into just about any pasta sauce or stew and make a bigger flavor. The seeds will remain inside and the chili can be removed before the sauce is done. For more heat and intensity, split the chili and let the seeds remain.

But chili peppers are not just for adding hotness. No two varieties of chili pepper are the same—and there are hundreds of them. Each has a different flavor and heat intensity. They are amazingly complex and contribute unique distinctions, undertones, and nuances.

The flavor of a chili becomes concentrated when dried, and it becomes hotter as the moisture evaporates. However, dried chilies should not be brittle-hard for maximum flavor; rather, leather-hard, slightly flexible is best.

To use dried chilies for most sauces and recipes, tear the chilies open and shake out the seeds. Lightly toast the chilies to bring out their flavor. This process can contribute bitterness, however, if the heat is too high; 1 minute on a moderately hot griddle is all that should be needed.

Toasting can be skipped entirely and the chilies will have gorgeous flavor anyway. To reconstitute dried toasted or untoasted chilies, pour boiling water over them in a bowl and let soften until plump and meaty, 15 to 20 minutes. (Alternatively, simmer the dried chilies in water for 5 minutes and then drain.) Usually the liquid is discarded, but a little can be added when pureeing (adding too much will contribute bitterness).

DRIED RED PEPPER FLAKES

Several varieties of hot chili peppers are combined to balance the heat intensity and flavor of this versatile, reliable condiment. It is an excellent product to keep on hand. Add a pinch to any pasta sauce or stew for a spark of interest. Buy the brightest red ones; the darker ones can be bitter.

CHILI POWDER

Mexican aficionados scoff at chili powder. Although surely the Aztecs made it, today it is considered an American condiment. Authorities generally agree that it is best to use whole chilies and spices separately, but I like chili powder and use it frequently. The very best ones are unseasoned. If you can find them, buy powdered ancho and pasilla chilies, or mix them together half and half. The powders range from mild to hot, depending on the blend. To maintain maximum freshness and flavor, store chili powders in jars in the refrigerator.

CHIPOTLE CHILIES—SMOKY DELIGHTS

When ripe, red, fresh jalapeño chili peppers are dried and then smoked over fragrant hardwood, they turn into wrinkled, shriveled, dark reddish-brown chipotle chilies. They contribute a seductive smoky aroma and flavor to foods cooked with them. Chipotles are extremely hot and have a strong, full flavor. Only a few are needed in cooking.

Buy chipotles dried or packed in vinegar or adobo (a light chili-vinegar sauce). My favorite, very convenient, bottled taco sauce is Bufalo brand Salsa Chipotle.

ANCHO CHILIES

When fresh poblano chilies ripen on the vine, they turn bright red. When dried, they become ancho chilies. The ancho chili has a sharp, rich, fruity flavor with a slight sweetness and light bitter undertone. The chilies are 3 to 4 inches long and 2 to 3 inches wide. They should be slightly flexible, not brittle, with wrinkled skin, and dark reddish brown in color. If they are not available, substitute mulato chilies.

MULATO CHILIES

Slightly larger (4 to 6 inches long and 2 to 3 inches wide) and more expensive than all of the other dried chilies, the mulato chili is smooth skinned and blackish brown in color.

This chili has a rich, full flavor with a subtle nuance of chocolate and a wide range of heat intensity from mild to moderately hot. Often confused with ancho chilies, mulatos have a similar appearance. But if you hold one up to the light or slit it open and inspect it closely, the mulato will be dark brown inside while the ancho will appear brighter red. Sauces made with mulato chilies are brownish black.

GUAJILLO CHILIES

This burgundy-colored dried chili with its smooth, tough skin has a sharp, simple flavor and a tangy rather than sweet quality. Its heat intensity ranges from moderately hot to very hot.

The chilies are 4 to 5 inches long, rather tapered, and 1 to 1½ inches wide. Guajillo chilies give a bright red color to sauces and often are used for enchiladas and stews. Because the skin is so tough, the sauce is usually strained.

PASILLA CHILIES

When fresh chilaca chilies are dried, they become pasilla chilies. They have a complex flavor that is rich and sharp and gives great depth to sauces. Their heat intensity ranges from moderately hot to very hot. The chilies have wrinkled, reddish-brown skin and are about 5 inches long and 1 to 1½ inches wide.

Uncle John's Chile Verde

I could live on poblano chili peppers. So could my brother John. You'll need 3 pounds of them for this recipe. In a pinch cans of roasted and peeled green chilies will do, though you'll be missing the big flavor that roasting and peeling the poblanos contribute.

Serve this dish with a pot of pinto beans and some flour tortillas. The flavor will be best if made ahead, allowed to cool to room temperature, and then reheated.

MAKES 8 SERVINGS

- 3 pounds trimmed, lean pork leg, butt, or shoulder, cut into 1-inch cubes
- 6 tablespoons all-purpose flour
- 6 tablespoons vegetable oil
- 4 medium onions, halved lengthwise and cut into thin half rounds
- 3 large garlic cloves, minced or crushed through a press
- 2 bay leaves
- 1 tablespoon plus ½ teaspoon dried oregano, crumbled
- 2½ teaspoons ground cumin
- 1 can (16 ounces) tomatoes with their juices, cut up
- 4 cups Chicken Stock (page 73), canned broth, or water
- ¼ cup cider vinegar
- 1 tablespoon salt
- ½ teaspoon black pepper
- 3 pounds fresh, firm poblano chili peppers (12 to 18 large), roasted (page 17), peeled, and torn into ½-inch-wide strips

1. Pat the pork cubes dry on paper towels. Put 2 tablespoons of the flour in a bag and add one-third of the meat cubes. Shake to coat. Spoon 1½ tablespoons of the oil into a nonreactive large skillet over moderately high heat. Add the floured cubes to the hot oil and cook until deep golden brown on one side, 4 to 5 minutes. Use tongs to turn the pieces and brown all over, 2 to 3 minutes longer, turning as they brown. The initial browning on the first side is the most important. Remove the cubes with a slotted spoon and reserve. Repeat the flouring and frying twice more, until all of the pork is browned.

2. Spoon the remaining 1½ tablespoons of oil into the skillet and set over moderate heat. Add the onions and sauté until softened and lightly browned, about 10 minutes. Add the garlic, bay leaves, 1 tablespoon of the oregano, and 2 teaspoons of the cumin. Sauté for 2 minutes. Pour in the tomatoes and their juices and bring to a boil, scraping the pan to deglaze.

3. Transfer the mixture to a large casserole or a Dutch oven. Add the pork cubes, stock or broth, vinegar, salt, and pepper and bring to a boil over moderate heat. Reduce the heat to low, partially cover, and simmer, stirring occasionally, until the meat is almost tender, 1 to 1½ hours. If the sauce becomes too thick, add a little water.

4. Add the roasted chilies, the remaining ½ teaspoon oregano, and the remaining ½ teaspoon cumin. Partially cover and simmer until the meat is very tender but not falling apart, 45 to 60 minutes longer. Remove the bay leaves. Serve hot or, preferably, let cool to room temperature and reheat gently over low heat. Serve with hot tortillas.

Pork Roast Tamarindo

The sweet-tart flavor of tamarind pulp brings out the full flavor and sweetness of pork—in this case, a pork shoulder roast.

MAKES 6 SERVINGS

> Tamarind Sauce (page 373; see step 1)
> 2 tablespoons unsulphured molasses
> 1 pork shoulder roast (5 to 6 pounds)
> Salt and pepper

1. Make a double batch of the Tamarind Sauce, omitting the salt and adding no extra water after the 2 cups of boiling water. Stir in the molasses.

2. Using a long fork or a knife tip, jab the pork roast all over, 30 times or more, making slits ½ inch deep. Put the pork in a large zip-lock bag or bowl and pour the Tamarind Sauce over. Cover and refrigerate. Marinate for

TAMARIND

These big, brown, leathery pods that grow on a tall tropical tree are full of sticky brown paste and seeds. You can buy the pods whole and peel and seed them, scraping out the pulp, or buy it in paste form with or without the seeds. Look for it in Chinese, Asian, Indian, and Latin American markets; you might also find it strained and concentrated. Usually the pulp is soaked in hot water before straining.

Tamarind is agreeably acidic and contributes a sour tang and slightly bitter flavor to foods in a very pleasant, refreshing way. It gives a subtle hint of molasses flavor and an extra sharp dose of concentrated lemon.

24 hours, turning several times.

3. Preheat the oven to 300° F. Take the pork roast from the marinade and reserve the marinade. Put the roast, fatty side down, in a Dutch oven just large enough to hold it. Spoon half of the marinade over the top. Cover and roast for 1½ hours.

4. Uncover the roast, turn over, and pour the rest of the marinade over the top. Cover and roast for 1 hour longer.

5. Increase the oven temperature to 375° F. Uncover the roast, turn it, and roast, spooning the marinade over the top every so often, for about 30 minutes, or until the meat is cooked to the bone and a meat thermometer registers 165° F. when inserted into the thickest part of the meat, without touching the bone.

6. Transfer the roast to a platter; sprinkle lightly with salt and pepper. Let rest for at least 15 minutes before carving.

7. Meanwhile, pour all of the pan drippings into a tall heatproof measuring cup and spoon off the fat from the top. (If making ahead, cool the drippings to room temperature so the fat will solidify and can be removed easily.) You will have about 1½ cups of pan drippings.

8. Serve the roast hot or warm, cut into slices. Spoon a little of the sauce over each serving. Serve with hot tortillas.

Mexican Licuado de Tamarindo

Here is the coolest, most refreshing, thirst-quenching drink imaginable. To make about 2½ quarts, put an 8-ounce block of tamarind pulp in a large bowl. Pour in 4 cups of boiling water and ¼ cup sugar. Mash the pulp with a fork and set aside to cool to room temperature.

Force the mixture through a sieve and discard any seeds or tough fibers. Add 5 to 6 cups of cold water and taste for sweet-sour balance. Add more water or sugar to taste. Chill and serve in tall glasses over ice cubes.

Pork Chops with Sage and Porcini

Dried porcini have such a big flavor that one ounce is plenty to flavor a casserole that serves six. (It's a good thing because they have a big price tag, too.) This is hearty robust fare best suited for fall and winter. Serve with roasted or mashed potatoes (or noodles) and carrots, a green vegetable, and hot bread. This is a wonderful way to use fresh sage leaves.

MAKES 6 SERVINGS

- 1 ounce dried porcini
- 2 tablespoons vegetable oil
- 6 large, well-trimmed, center-cut pork chops (10 to 12 ounces each, cut $1\frac{1}{4}$ inches thick)
- 1 pound fresh white or brown mushrooms, sliced
- $\frac{1}{4}$ cup chopped fresh sage, plus 18 whole sage leaves
- 2 large garlic cloves, minced or crushed through a press
- 3 tablespoons all-purpose flour
- 1 to $1\frac{1}{4}$ cups dry white wine
- 1 cup light cream
- $\frac{1}{2}$ cup Chicken Stock (page 73) or canned broth
- 1 teaspoon salt
- $\frac{1}{4}$ teaspoon black pepper
- 1 tablespoon cornstarch (optional)

1. Put the porcini in a small bowl and pour in 1 cup of boiling water. Set aside to soften for 30 to 60 minutes. Drain, reserving the liquid (it is full of flavor). Finely chop the porcini; strain the soaking liquid through a fine sieve.
2. Preheat the oven to 325° F. Spoon the oil into a nonreactive large skillet over

SAGE

Sage was once the most popular herb in America, before we "discovered" oregano after World War II. It is still a favorite flavoring for pork, sausages, and turkey stuffings.

Sage is a hardy evergreen that belongs to the mint family and is native to the Mediterranean region.

The strong, pungent aroma of sage intensifies when rubbed or crushed, and its pleasant camphor quality is balanced with an undertone of citrus flavor. I like to top pork chops with whole fresh sage leaves, which are considerably milder than dried sage, and bake them until the flavor permeates.

Buy the most fragrant sage (pinch or rub a leaf and sniff your fingers). You should be sparing with dried sage; half a teaspoon will go a long way.

moderately high heat. Put 3 of the pork chops in the pan and brown one side very well, moving occasionally so they don't stick, 4 to 5 minutes. Turn and brown the remaining sides, about 3 minutes. Remove and reserve; no more fat should be needed. Brown the remaining 3 chops in the same manner. Arrange all 6 chops in a 13 × 9-inch baking pan or other large shallow pan just large enough to hold them in a single layer.

3. Add the sliced mushrooms to the drippings in the skillet and brown over moderately high heat for 3 to 4 minutes. Add the chopped sage and garlic and cook for 2 minutes. Sprinkle on the flour and stir to moisten. Pour in 1 cup of the wine and all of the porcini liquid. Bring to a boil, stirring constantly, over moderate heat. Stir in the cream, stock or broth, chopped porcini, salt, and pepper. Bring the sauce to a boil.

4. Arrange 3 whole sage leaves on top of each pork chop; spoon the porcini sauce over them. Cover with a triple layer of aluminum foil, crimping the edges securely all around. Bake for 2 hours, or until the pork chops are very tender. If desired, you can keep the covered chops warm in a 200° F. oven for up to 1 hour.

5. The sauce will be delicious as it is, but you can thicken it, like a gravy, if desired. Carefully take the chops from the pan with a spatula, leaving the mushrooms and whole sage leaves on top of them, and arrange on a platter. Turn the contents of the pan into a nonreactive medium saucepan. In a cup, dissolve the cornstarch in the remaining ¼ cup wine. Stir into the sauce and bring to a boil, stirring, over moderate heat. Simmer for 1 minute. Serve on the side.

VARIATIONS

Substitutions: **Use cèpes or other dried European mushrooms in place of the porcini. Omit the sage and use 1½ teaspoons dried oregano, rosemary, or thyme in the sauce. Although you could use 1-inch pork chops, I don't recommend using any that are thinner.**

Curried Pork

Always great for a dinner party or buffet, this long-simmered stew has a deep, complex flavor. I encourage you to make your own curry powder for the biggest flavor of all, but commercially blended curry powder will also produce excellent results. Have fun with the condiments by presenting them on a large tray with fresh fruit garnishes; include cubes of fresh mango, bottled mango chutney, peanuts, and grated coconut.

MAKES 8 SERVINGS

- 6 tablespoons vegetable oil
- 3 pounds pork leg or shoulder, cut into 1-inch cubes
- 4 large onions (2 pounds), coarsely chopped
- ¼ cup minced fresh ginger
- 4 large garlic cloves, minced or crushed through a press
- ¼ cup plus 2 teaspoons homemade Curry Powder (page 385) or store-bought
- 1¼ cups canned or homemade unsweetened coconut milk
- ½ cup canned tomato sauce
- 1 large tart green apple, peeled, cored, and grated
- 2 teaspoons salt
- 2 tablespoons fresh lemon juice
  Basmati rice, for serving
  Assorted condiments, for serving

1. Spoon 1½ tablespoons of the oil into a large, heavy skillet set over moderately high heat. Pat the cubes of meat dry with paper towels. Add half of the cubes to the hot oil and cook, without turning, until very well browned on one side, 4 to 5 minutes. Turn the pieces and brown the remaining sides for 2 to 3 minutes longer. Turn into a nonreactive large casserole or Dutch oven. Spoon 1½ tablespoons more oil into the skillet and brown the remaining meat cubes in the same manner. Turn into the casserole; do not clean the skillet.

2. Spoon 2 tablespoons of the remaining oil into the skillet you used for browning the meat and place over moderate heat. Add the onions and sauté, stirring frequently and adding 1 to 2 tablespoons water each time the pan seems dry, until medium caramel brown, 15 to 20 minutes. Stir constantly during the last few minutes and increase the heat, if necessary, to achieve the dark color.

3. Add the remaining 1 tablespoon oil to the skillet along with the ginger, garlic, and ¼ cup of the curry powder. (If you are using a commercial blend, depending on its potency, you might want to add 1 teaspoon each of

ground cumin and coriander and a pinch of cayenne to boost the flavor.) Stir over moderate heat for 2 minutes to cook the spices. Pour in 1 cup of the coconut milk and the tomato sauce; the mixture will be thick and pasty. Cook, stirring, for 2 minutes. Scrape the mixture into the casserole of browned pork.

4. Place the casserole over moderate heat and pour in 3 cups of hot water. Add the grated apple and the salt. Bring the curry to a simmer. Reduce the heat to low, cover, and simmer very gently, stirring occasionally, until the pork is tender, about 2 hours.

5. Stir in the lemon juice and the remaining 2 teaspoons curry powder. If the sauce is too thick, add a little water. Cover and continue simmering until the pork is very tender but not falling apart, 30 to 60 minutes.

6. Stir in the remaining ¼ cup coconut milk. Serve hot with rice and assorted condiments. (This curry can be made a day or two ahead and just tastes better as the flavors blossom. Reheat gently over low heat, adding a little water if the sauce is thick.)

VARIATIONS

Substitutions: **Prepare this curry with beef or lamb, substituting pound for pound. One cup of applesauce can be substituted for the grated apple.**

Lower fat: **The coconut milk can be replaced with chicken broth to reduce the fat content.**

Mexican Chorizo

Here's a big flavor Mexican ingredient that I like very much. It is used most often to flavor other foods. I've used it in the Mexican Meat Loaf (page 229) and to make the Potatoes and Chorizo (page 179). Traditionally, it is served with scrambled eggs, sometimes in a flour tortilla as a burrito. You can also add sautéed chorizo to pinto beans for a very simple and well-seasoned pot of chili and beans.

There are many different kinds of Mexican chorizo. In general, Mexican chorizo sausages are fresh and soft, compared to Spanish and Portuguese chorizos, which are often air-dried and firm. I have not asked you to go to the trouble of stuffing casings. Instead, just stir the ingredients in a bowl. This version is bright red because so much sweet paprika is added for color and flavor. I hope that my friend Diana Kennedy doesn't mind my taking license to use chili powders instead of whole dried chilies, but I am trying to make this as easy as possible.

MAKES ABOUT 2½ POUNDS

2	pounds coarsely ground pork butt
½	cup lard, softened
½	cup cider vinegar
⅓	cup chili powder, preferably a 50-50 mix of ancho and pasilla, but commercial will do
¼	cup sweet paprika
1	tablespoon salt
1½	teaspoons sugar
2	large garlic cloves, minced or crushed through a press
2	teaspoons dried oregano, crumbled
2	teaspoons ground cumin
½	teaspoon dried thyme, crumbled
½	teaspoon cayenne pepper
½	teaspoon black pepper
¼	teaspoon ground cinnamon
¼	teaspoon ground cloves

1. Crumble the ground pork into a very large mixing bowl. Add the lard along with the vinegar, chili powder, paprika, salt, sugar, garlic, oregano, cumin, thyme, cayenne, black pepper, cinnamon, and cloves. Mix thoroughly with your hands.
2. Transfer the mixture to a container just large enough to hold it, cover, and refrigerate for at least 24 hours before using. The chorizo will stay fresh in the refrigerator for up to 1 week; if keeping longer, freeze.

PAPRIKA

When I was growing up, paprika was always used in our house for color rather than for flavor. I wasn't sure why, because I knew that I could taste it, but that's what everybody said.

Well, of course, paprika is full of fine sweet flavor. It has a deep, distinctive, sweet red pepper flavor with a range from mild to medium to hot.

The best paprikas are imported from Hungary and Spain. Once you get it home, store it in the refrigerator (as with all chili powders, because chilling preserves the moisture content).

Italian Sausages with Fennel, Parmesan, and Parsley

No ordinary Italian sausages, these are the best ever! And they're lower in fat than usual. The fennel seeds are plumped in white wine to bring out maximum flavor, and there is enough Parmesan in the sausages to start mouths watering every time you cook some. You won't need the sausage casings and stuffing equipment if you shape the mixture into patties.

MAKES ABOUT 4 POUNDS (24 TO 30 PATTIES OR LINKS)

- ½ cup dry white wine
- 2 tablespoons fennel seeds
- 1 tablespoon dried oregano, crumbled
- 1 tablespoon dried basil, crumbled
- 3¼ pounds lean coarsely ground pork, such as shoulder, butt, or leg
- 12 ounces ground pork fat
- 2 cups freshly grated Parmesan cheese
- 1 cup chopped fresh parsley
- 1½ tablespoons coarse (kosher) salt, or 2 teaspoons fine table salt
- 1 tablespoon coarsely ground black pepper
- 2 teaspoons dry mustard
- 1 teaspoon ground or rubbed sage
- 4 lengths of narrow sausage casings, each 3 to 4 feet long (optional)
- 24 to 30 pieces of cotton string, each 5 inches long (optional)

1. In a nonreactive small saucepan, combine the wine with ½ cup water and bring to a boil over high heat. Remove from the heat and stir in the fennel seeds, oregano, and basil; set aside to cool to room temperature.

2. In a very large bowl, combine the ground pork, pork fat, Parmesan, parsley, salt, pepper, mustard, and sage. Add the cooled wine mixture. Mix thoroughly with your hands until all of the ingredients are blended evenly. (If you want to taste it for seasoning, shape a small patty and cook it in a small skillet.)

3. If you are making patties, use about ⅓ cup of the mixture for each; place each on a small square of paper and arrange in a single layer on a baking sheet. Freeze until solid; stack and seal in a plastic bag and freeze.

To make links, rinse the sausage casings in a bowl of cold water to remove the salt. Place one end of one length over the water faucet and let cold water run slowly through it. Repeat with all the casings; set aside in a small bowl. Thread one casing onto a sausage stuffer (this can be manual or electric, or even a pastry bag with a large opening). Put the sausage into a meat grinder (minus the cutting blade) with the sausage stuffer attached. Tie a knot at the end of the casing with cotton string. As you hold it and let the meat grind through, leave 2 inches of casing unstuffed to allow for shaping and expansion. The sausage should be about 1 inch thick and evenly filled throughout. You can use your hands to gently shape the sausage as it is formed. When the casing is almost full, tie a knot at the end, again allowing 2 inches unstuffed for shaping and expansion. You can let the sausage coil naturally and store it flat on a rack, or you can use the string to tie it off into 4-inch links, twisting each time before tying. Repeat with the remaining mixture. The sausages are best when allowed to air-dry for about 2 hours: either hang them in a cool, well-ventilated place, or place them on racks in the refrigerator. Then store in plastic bags in the refrigerator or freezer.

4. To cook the sausages, place them in a single layer in a heavy, ungreased skillet over low heat. Cook, turning several times, until deep golden brown, crusty, and cooked through, 20 to 30 minutes. Serve hot.

VARIATION

Substitutions: I don't recommend reducing the fat content of this recipe because I have already pared it way back from traditional versions. Most sausage recipes contain two or three times the fat called for here. You may, however, replace half the ground pork with ground chicken or turkey. You can also make the sausage hot and spicy by adding 1 tablespoon dried red pepper flakes or cayenne pepper. If you want to eliminate the wine, replace it with water.

Sichuan Bean Curd with Spicy Pork Sauce

This is a variation of the classic *ma po* bean curd from Sichuan province in China—hot and spicy comfort food at its best. The sauce contains a hefty dose of cornstarch because it is supposed to be creamy and custardy. Soft bean curd is used for this because of its wonderful consistency. This recipe features fiery spiciness from two different sources: the chili–hot bean paste and the Sichuan peppercorns. Have all of the ingredients ready before you start to cook. This can be a meal by itself, or serve it with plain white rice.

MAKES 4 SERVINGS

- 10 large dried Chinese black mushrooms
- 4 cups cubed soft bean curd (tofu), in ¾-inch pieces
- 8 ounces lean ground pork
- ¼ cup plus 1 tablespoon dry sherry
- 2 tablespoons soy sauce
- 2 teaspoons Oriental sesame oil
- 2 tablespoons cornstarch
- ¼ cup canned tomato sauce
- 1½ tablespoons peanut or other vegetable oil
- 2 tablespoons minced fresh ginger
- 1 large garlic clove, minced or crushed through a press
- 2 tablespoons Sichuan hot bean paste
- ⅔ cup sliced whole scallions
- ⅔ cup Chicken Stock (page 73) or canned broth
- ¼ teaspoon ground Sichuan pepper or other pepper

1. Place the dried mushrooms in a small bowl and pour in ¾ cup of boiling water; soak until softened, 30 to 60 minutes. Drain, reserving the soaking liquid. Slice off the tough stems from the mushrooms, cut the caps into fine slivers, and reserve. Strain the soaking liquid through a fine sieve; let cool or chill.
2. Meanwhile, bring a large pot of water to a boil over high heat. Add the bean curd and immediately drain in a colander. (This will slightly firm up the bean curd.) Set aside.
3. Crumble the pork into a medium bowl; add 1 tablespoon of the sherry, 1 tablespoon of the soy sauce, and 1 teaspoon of the sesame oil. Mix with your hands; set aside to marinate for up to 30 minutes. Refrigerate if marinating longer.
4. In a small bowl, combine the cornstarch, remaining ¼ cup sherry, and ¼ cup of the mushroom soaking liquid; stir to dissolve the cornstarch. Stir in the remaining 1 tablespoon soy sauce and the tomato sauce. Set aside.

5. Place a large, heavy wok or skillet over moderately high heat. When very hot, spoon in the oil and swirl to coat the pan. Add the ginger and garlic and stir-fry until very fragrant, about 10 seconds. Crumble in the pork mixture and stir-fry until cooked, 1 to 2 minutes. Add the hot bean paste and stir-fry for 1 minute. Add ½ cup of the scallions and the mushrooms; cook for 30 seconds. Add the stock or broth and bean curd; bring to a boil over high heat. Stir the sauce, pour it in, and cook, stirring, until thickened. Stir in the remaining 1 teaspoon sesame oil and the Sichuan pepper. Turn out onto a platter and sprinkle with the remaining scallions. Serve hot.

SICHUAN PEPPERCORNS

Pungent peppercorns from Sichuan Province in China provide the first burst of flavor when you dip your spoon into Sichuan Hot and Sour Soup. A dusting of the powdery crushed pepper provides punctuation for such a marvelously complex soup.

The reddish brown peppercorn is not related to our familiar black peppercorn. The Sichuan type is open, like a flower with a little husk. Sometimes it is called *fagara*, wild pepper, or flower pepper.

Sichuan peppercorns are more aromatic than spicy, their bark bigger than their bite, but they do contribute a slight numbing sensation on the tongue.

The flavor of the pepper becomes fuller after a light roasting, so toss them in a small dry skillet over low heat for a couple minutes before grinding.

When shopping for Sichuan peppercorns, take a good whiff. Rub some of them together with your fingers. Even through a plastic bag they should have a strong fragrance. The fresher they are, the more potent they will be. Store them in a jar as you would any peppercorns.

Lamb Vindaloo with Potatoes

Vindaloo is a hot and sour Indian curry with deep, complex flavors. I like to add potatoes for balance. The lamb becomes very tender from the long marination. Serve the vindaloo with basmati rice, mango chutney, raita, dal, and Indian flatbread, if desired.

MAKES 6 TO 8 SERVINGS

    2 pounds trimmed boneless lamb, cut into 1-inch cubes
    2 tablespoons vegetable oil
    2 teaspoons dry mustard
    2 teaspoons ground cumin
    2 teaspoons ground coriander
    2 teaspoons homemade Curry Powder (page 385) or store-bought
    1 teaspoon cayenne pepper
  ½ teaspoon ground cardamom
  ½ teaspoon turmeric
  ½ teaspoon ground cinnamon
  ¼ teaspoon ground cloves
    2 medium onions, quartered
    6 garlic cloves, peeled
    2 tablespoons chopped fresh ginger
  ¼ cup cider vinegar

Vindaloo

    6 tablespoons vegetable oil
    3 onions, chopped
 2½ teaspoons salt
    1 to 2 large fresh jalapeño chilies, minced, with seeds
    1 tablespoon minced fresh ginger
    1 large garlic clove, minced or crushed through a press
    1 teaspoon homemade Curry Powder or store-bought
  ½ teaspoon ground cumin
    3 cups Chicken Stock (page 73) or canned broth
  ½ cup canned tomato sauce
    2 pounds red-skinned potatoes
    1 to 2 tablespoons fresh lemon juice

1. Pat the lamb cubes dry with paper towels.
2. Spoon the oil into a small, heavy skillet. Add the dry mustard, cumin, coriander, curry powder, cayenne, cardamom, turmeric, cinnamon, and cloves. Place over moderately low heat and stir for about 1 minute after the mixture begins to bubble around the edges and becomes very fragrant. Do not

let it darken too much. Immediately scrape the mixture into a bowl and set aside to cool.

3. In a food processor or blender, combine the onions, garlic, ginger, and vinegar and process to a smooth puree. Scrape the marinade into a large bowl, then add the sautéed spice mixture and the lamb. Toss to combine. Cover and marinate in the refrigerator for 12 to 24 hours.

4. Make the vindaloo. Spoon 2 tablespoons of the oil into a Dutch oven or large skillet set over moderately high heat. Add the chopped onions and ½ teaspoon of the salt and cook, stirring almost constantly, for 12 to 15 minutes. This technique is a classic Indian brown-frying technique, and it must take about 15 minutes to turn into a dark, caramel-brown paste, or the flavor will not be right. If at any time during the cooking the mixture seems dry, add 1 to 2 tablespoons water and continue cooking until it achieves the dark color. Remove and reserve the caramelized onions; do not wash the pan.

5. Scrape the excess marinade from the lamb cubes and reserve it. Spoon 1 tablespoon of the remaining oil into the reserved pan and add about one-third of the meat. Brown well on one side over moderately high heat, 3 to 5 minutes. Turn and brown the other sides, about 2 minutes. Remove the meat and reserve on a platter. Add 1 tablespoon more oil for each batch of lamb until all is browned.

6. Add the remaining 1 tablespoon oil to the pan and set over moderately high heat. Add the jalapeño(s), ginger, garlic, curry powder, and cumin and cook for 1 minute. Stir in the reserved marinade (you will have about ½ cup) and sauté for 1 minute. Return the onions to the pan and stir in the stock or broth and tomato sauce; bring to a boil. Add the browned lamb and the remaining 2 teaspoons salt; bring to a boil over moderate heat. Reduce the heat to low, partially cover, and simmer gently for about 15 minutes.

7. Peel the potatoes and cut them into eighths. Add to the vindaloo, cover partially, and simmer gently until the meat and potatoes are tender, 45 to 60 minutes longer.

8. Stir in 1 tablespoon of the lemon juice and taste for seasoning. Set aside to cool to room temperature. When reheating the vindaloo, an additional 1 tablespoon of lemon juice may be needed, depending on your taste. Serve the vindaloo hot, with the suggested accompaniments.

Seafood, Fish,

and Shellfish

Malaysian Tiger Prawns

Shanghai Flash-Fried Shrimp

Poppy-Crusted Tuna Steaks with Wasabi-Soy Dipping Sauce

Ginger-Fried Oysters

Hot-and-Sour Shrimp with Watercress and Walnuts

Gorgeous Flavor Crab Cakes

Spanakopita Sole

Ceviche la Playa

Aromatic Grilled Swordfish

Grilled Swordfish Brochettes with Bay and Scallion Oil

Gingered Scrod Fillets

Red Snapper Veracruzano

Crunchy Louisiana Catfish

Bonus Recipes

Poached Shrimp   Scallion Oil

Malaysian Tiger Prawns

Tiger prawns are now farm-raised and more available than ever. If you can't find them, though, just substitute jumbo shrimp. Serve with rice.

MAKES 4 SERVINGS

- 1 tablespoon dried tiny shrimp
- 3 tablespoons Thai or Vietnamese fish sauce (*nam pla* or *nuoc mam*)
- 1 tablespoon dark soy sauce
- 1 tablespoon rice vinegar
- 2 teaspoons Oriental sesame oil
- 5 tablespoons peanut oil
- 1½ pounds large tiger prawns or jumbo shrimp, shelled, deveined, and rinsed
- 1 or 2 hot chili peppers, such as jalapeños, partially seeded, if desired, and cut into slivers
- 2 teaspoons minced fresh ginger
- 1 large garlic clove, minced or crushed through a press
- 4 ounces lean ground pork
- 1 large red bell pepper, cut into ¼ × 2-inch strips
- 1 large green bell pepper, cut into ¼ × 2-inch strips
- 1 large onion, cut lengthwise into ¼-inch-wide slivers

1. Put the dried shrimp in a cup or small bowl and add ½ cup hot water. Set aside to soak until softened, about 30 minutes. Drain, rinse, drain again, and finely mince the tiny shrimp; reserve.

2. In a small bowl, stir together the fish sauce, soy sauce, rice vinegar, and sesame oil. Set the sauce aside.

3. Heat a large, heavy wok or skillet over high heat. Spoon in 2 tablespoons of the peanut oil and heat until smoking hot. Add the prawns and stir-fry for 2 minutes; do not fully cook them at this stage. Scoop out and reserve on a platter. Clean the wok.

4. Spoon 1 tablespoon of the remaining oil into the wok and set over high heat. Add the chili pepper, ginger, garlic, and the minced dried shrimp; stir-fry for 20 to 30 seconds. Crumble in the pork and stir-fry until no longer pink, 1 to 2 minutes. Scoop out and reserve in a small bowl.

5. Spoon the remaining 2 tablespoons peanut oil into the wok, still over high heat. Add the bell peppers and onion and stir-fry for 1 minute. Add 2 tablespoons of water and stir-fry until crisp-tender, about 1 minute. Return the pork mixture to the wok, pour in the sauce mixture, and bring to a boil. Add the prawns and stir-fry briefly until cooked through and opaque. Transfer to a large warm platter and serve hot.

Shanghai Flash-Fried Shrimp

This is an outrageously delicious and simple recipe. Be sure to have all of the ingredients ready before you start to cook. Also have ready some rice or noodles and a vegetable side dish. Once you start to cook this really is ready in a flash. A cool fruit dessert like Passion Fruit Pineapple Sorbet (page 312) will bring your menu to a fresh climax.

MAKES 2 SERVINGS

- 1 pound large shrimp, shelled and deveined
- 1 tablespoon cornstarch
- 1 egg white
- 2 tablespoons dry sherry or Chinese rice wine
- 1 tablespoon light soy sauce
- ½ teaspoon sugar
- ¼ teaspoon salt
- 1½ cups peanut or other vegetable oil
- 1 tablespoon minced fresh ginger
- 1 garlic clove, minced or crushed through a press
- ½ teaspoon dried red pepper flakes
- 2 whole scallions, minced
- 1 teaspoon rice vinegar

1. In a medium bowl, stir together the shrimp, cornstarch, egg white, 1 table-spoon of the sherry, the soy sauce, sugar, and salt. Set aside to marinate at room temperature for 30 minutes.
2. Pour the oil into a large wok and place over high heat; it will be hot enough at the appearance of the first wisp of smoke. Add the shrimp and stir-fry for exactly 15 seconds. Remove with a slotted spoon or strainer and drain on paper towels.
3. Place a skillet or wok over high heat and add 1 tablespoon of the oil. When very hot, add the ginger, garlic, pepper flakes, and scallions and stir-fry for 10 seconds. Add the remaining 1 tablespoon sherry and the vinegar; cook for 10 seconds. Add the shrimp and cook until cooked through and opaque, about 10 seconds. Turn out onto a serving plate or individual plates and serve hot.

Poppy-Crusted Tuna Steaks with Wasabi-Soy Dipping Sauce

Fresh tuna steaks are juicy and meaty when cooked just right. A thick coating of poppy seeds forms a good crust when the steaks are seared in a fire-hot skillet. They are best when just slightly pink in the center. If you can find some Japanese pickled pink ginger, it is a refreshing condiment alongside. You may also want to serve an extra ball of wasabi on the plate. Baked potatoes, noodles, or rice make good accompaniments, as does broccoli or asparagus.

MAKES 2 SERVINGS

> 2 **fresh tuna steaks, cut 1½ inches thick**
> 1 **large egg**
> ½ **cup poppy seeds**
> **Vegetable oil**
> **Wasabi-Soy Dipping Sauce (page 369)**

1. Place a large cast-iron skillet over moderately high heat and preheat for at least 5 minutes before cooking the steaks.
2. Slice off and discard any skin from the steaks; pat dry on paper towels. Stir the egg in a shallow dish and put the poppy seeds in another. After the skillet has preheated, pour in ¹⁄₁₆ inch of vegetable oil.
3. Dip 1 tuna steak into the egg and turn several times to coat. Dredge in the poppy seeds, turning several times to coat. Roll the edges in the seeds to coat. Place in the hot skillet; coat the second steak. Sear the steaks over moderately high heat until well crusted, 4 to 5 minutes. Turn and reduce the heat to moderately low. Cook until just slightly pink in the center, 5 to 6 minutes longer, or to taste. Serve hot, with small shallow dishes of the Wasabi-Soy for dipping. Serve pickled pink ginger and extra wasabi on the side, if desired.

VARIATION

Substitutions: **Use swordfish, mahi-mahi, or mako shark steaks in place of the tuna.**

WASABI

This hot, head-clearing, green "horseradish" is the most intense seasoning used in Japanese cooking. It is so piercingly strong that it is dubbed *namida* (tears), for the tears that it brings to the eyes. But you can just call it sabi, as they do in sushi bars. Of course it always accompanies sushi and sashimi, but it also makes a delicious dip for seafood and gives punctuation to hamburgers with mayonnaise and tomato slices.

Wasabi is a small knobby root, *not* related to Western horseradish, though often compared to it because both volatilize on the tongue, enraging taste buds and opening sinuses. Wasabi is more fragrant and less harsh than white horseradish; it has a pure clean taste that sharpens the appetite.

The plant grows only along the marshy edges of cold streams on the northern sides of shaded mountain valleys in Japan, and it cannot be cultivated. It also takes 2 to 3 years for the precious root to mature to a mere 4 to 5 inches. Fresh wasabi roots command a high price, even in Japan.

You can buy powdered wasabi in small cans or prepared wasabi in tubes. I recommend the powder. All of the prepared wasabi I have sampled had an odd consistency and flavor. Besides, it takes only a few seconds to prepare it from powder. To make about 1½ teaspoons of paste, measure 2 packed and leveled teaspoons of powdered wasabi into a cup and stir in 1 teaspoon of hot water. Let the paste stand for 10 to 15 minutes before using.

Because of the scarcity of wasabi, manufacturers often cut pure wasabi powder by adding mustard or horseradish, or both. But the powder remains an excellent product. You might, however, keep your eyes peeled (and your pocket full of money) for a real fresh wasabi root while shopping for Japanese ingredients.

Buy wasabi powder in the smallest size tin you can find and store it in a cool dry place. It will stay fresh for a year or two.

Poached Shrimp

Here is my favorite way of poaching shrimp for anytime I need cooked shrimp.

Shell and devein 1 or 2 pounds of medium or large shrimp. Put them in a heavy, medium pot with about 4 cups of cold water. Place over moderate heat and bring slowly to a simmer. As the water begins to jiggle, just before it comes to a simmer, remove 1 shrimp and cut through the thickest part. When done, it will be barely opaque to the center. Do not let the water boil. Immediately drain the shrimp and rinse them under cold running water.

Place the shrimp in a large bowl with about 4 cups of ice cubes, ¼ cup dry white wine, and 2 teaspoons salt. Toss and let chill for 10 to 15 minutes. Take shrimp from the ice (really, drain and pick out any remaining ice). Cover and chill until serving time.

Ginger-Fried Oysters

Two unique things about this recipe are the use of the special Japanese bread crumbs called *panko* (they are slivered crumbs), which offer a lot of crunch, and freshly squeezed ginger juice, which contributes a decidedly big flavor to oysters. These delicacies make a special hors d'oeuvre or first course.

MAKES 4 SERVINGS

- 2 **dozen large freshly shucked oysters**
- 3 **tablespoons ginger juice (page 14)**
  Vegetable oil, for frying
- ⅓ **cup all-purpose flour**
- 2 **large eggs**
- 2 **cups *panko* (Japanese bread crumbs) or plain, dry bread crumbs**
  Salt
  Wasabi-Soy Dipping Sauce (page 369) or lemon wedges

1. Drain the oysters, add them with the ginger juice to a medium bowl, toss, and set aside to marinate at room temperature for 30 minutes.
2. Place a large wok over moderate heat. When very hot, reduce the heat to low and keep hot. Pour in about 1 inch of vegetable oil.
3. Put the flour in a small bowl. Whisk the eggs in a medium bowl with 2 tablespoons of water. Put the *panko* in a medium bowl. Drain the oysters.
4. Increase the heat under the wok to moderate (as you cook it will be necessary to regulate the heat to keep the oil very hot but just below the smoking point). Working with 2 at a time, lightly coat each oyster in the flour, dip into the egg, and dredge in the *panko* to coat thoroughly. As they are coated, put them in the hot oil. Continue cooking oysters and fry them, without crowding the wok (4 to 6 at a time), until deep golden brown, 1 to 1½ minutes on the first side. Turn and fry on the other side for about 1 minute longer. Drain on paper towels. Sprinkle lightly with salt. Serve hot with the dipping sauce or lemon wedges.

PANKO—A SPECIAL CRUMB COATING

These delicate white Japanese bread crumbs are special because they are pointed, like crystals, rather than crumb-shaped. When you use them to coat foods to be fried, such as the Ginger-Fried Oysters, the points stick out in all directions, increasing crispiness and texture. Fried foods with a *panko* coating remain crisp after cooling.

Panko is readily available from Japanese grocers. Store the crumbs in a jar with a tight-fitting lid or other airtight container on your pantry shelf and they will keep fresh for about a year. If you cannot find *panko,* substitute coarse dry bread crumbs.

GINGER

Fresh ginger has a warm, clean taste that suggests half spice, half citrus. It has a fresh spicy aroma, tastes hot on the tongue, is relatively high in essential oils, and soothes the digestive system.

Ginger is not a root as some describe, but a rhizome, or ground stem, that grows in handlike formations just below the surface of the soil. The plant grows to four feet tall and thrives in moist climates that get lots of sunshine.

Choose "hands" that are shiny and hard, not soft and shriveled. Although softer ginger can still be used, its flavor will be less potent, almost bland, so use more than a recipe calls for. Although some recommend storing ginger in the refrigerator I have always stored it with my potatoes and it is happy there. But you can also peel it and store it in a jar, covered with dry sherry, in the refrigerator.

Spring ginger or young ginger (available mostly in the spring and fall) has pink sprouts and pale green edges. It is juicier and less fibrous than mature ginger. It is also more delicate and more perishable. I suggest wrapping this ginger in a paper towel and then enclosing it in a plastic bag and storing it in the vegetable drawer of your refrigerator. It has a clean, light, fresh fragrance and you can use it more freely than older ginger. It is juicy like a white rose potato.

• POWDERED GINGER. To make this favorite gingerbread and pumpkin pie spice, "hands" of ginger are cleaned, washed, scraped, boiled, peeled, and dried in the sun before pulverizing.

• GINGER JUICE. You can add the essence of ginger without adding the fibrous bulk by grating fresh ginger onto several layers of dampened cheesecloth, then wringing out the juice into a bowl. The yield will depend on the juiciness of the ginger (see page 14).

• CANDIED OR CRYSTALLIZED GINGER. Slices of fresh ginger are cooked in simple syrup and then packed with sugar crystals. The sugar acts as a preservative and the ginger will keep for several years. Crystallized ginger purchased from Chinese grocers is much less expensive than the bottled type from spice manufacturers.

• PICKLED PINK GINGER. When young spring (and fall) ginger is sliced thin and pickled, it turns a lovely shade of coral pink. It is sweet and sour and hot all at the same time. A requisite condiment to accompany sushi and sashimi, it is available vacuum-packed in pouches wherever Japanese ingredients are sold. Transfer it to a jar and store it in the refrigerator.

Hot-and-Sour Shrimp with Watercress and Walnuts

A light marinade of sherry and ginger flavors jumbo shrimp, which are stir-fried with red bell peppers and scallions. Watercress makes a colorful bed for the shrimp while adding a peppery bite that complements the spicy hot-and-sour sauce. Serve with steamed white rice.

MAKES 4 SERVINGS

- 1 pound large or jumbo shrimp, shelled and deveined
- 4 tablespoons dry sherry
- 1 tablespoon grated, peeled fresh ginger
- ½ cup chicken stock or canned broth
- 2 tablespoons soy sauce
- 2 tablespoons ketchup
- 1 tablespoon cornstarch
- 1 tablespoon rice vinegar or cider vinegar
- 1 tablespoon sugar
- 2 teaspoons Oriental sesame oil
- ½ teaspoon dried hot red pepper flakes or ¼ teaspoon cayenne pepper
- 3 tablespoons peanut oil
- ⅓ cup coarsely chopped walnuts
- 3 bunches watercress, trimmed of large stems
- 2 medium red bell peppers, trimmed and cut into 1-inch squares
- 2 large garlic cloves, minced or crushed through a press
- 8 whole scallions, cut diagonally into 1-inch-long pieces

1. Combine the shrimp, 2 tablespoons of the sherry, and the grated ginger in a bowl. Cover and refrigerate until needed.
2. In a small bowl, mix together the remaining 2 tablespoons sherry, chicken stock, soy sauce, ketchup, cornstarch, rice vinegar, sugar, sesame oil, and red pepper flakes.
3. Heat a large wok or heavy nonreactive skillet over high heat. Add 1 tablespoon of the peanut oil and the walnuts; stir-fry for 1 minute. Transfer with a slotted spoon to a plate. Add the watercress to the wok and stir-fry just until wilted, about 1 minute. Arrange the watercress as a bed on a platter.
4. Add 1 tablespoon of the peanut oil, bell peppers, and garlic to the wok; stir-fry about 1 minute. Add the remaining 1 tablespoon peanut oil, shrimp mixture, and scallions; stir-fry for 1 minute. Stir the stock mixture and add it to the wok and cook, stirring frequently, until the sauce thickens and becomes clear, 1 to 2 minutes. Spoon the shrimp over the watercress and sprinkle with walnuts. Serve hot.

Gorgeous Flavor Crab Cakes

Ears perk, eyes widen, and mouths water when crab cakes are mentioned. Serve them as a main course with lemon wedges and Tartar Sauce or Creole Rémoulade (page 368), or make them tiny and serve as an appetizer.

MAKES 8 TO 12 (2½- TO 3-INCH) OR 18 (1½-INCH)

- 3 tablespoons butter
- 1 medium onion, finely chopped
- 2 large eggs
- ¼ cup mayonnaise
- ¼ cup minced whole scallions
- ¼ cup chopped fresh parsley, plus more, for garnishing
- 2 tablespoons fresh lemon juice
- 1 teaspoon Tabasco sauce
- 1 teaspoon dry mustard
- ½ teaspoon salt
- ¼ teaspoon black pepper
- 1 cup fine soda cracker crumbs (from about 28 crackers)
- 1 pound fresh "high-quality" lump crabmeat, picked over carefully
- 2 tablespoons vegetable oil

1. Melt 1 tablespoon of the butter in a small skillet over moderate heat. Add the onion and sauté until softened and lightly browned, about 5 minutes. Let cool to room temperature.

2. In a large bowl, whisk together the eggs and mayonnaise. Stir in the scallions, parsley, lemon juice, Tabasco, mustard, salt, pepper, and ¼ cup of the cracker crumbs. Gently stir in the sautéed onion and the crabmeat, keeping the crab pieces as large as possible. Taste for seasoning.

3. Put the remaining ¾ cup cracker crumbs in a medium bowl. To make 3-inch cakes, use ⅓ cup of the mixture for each; for 2½-inch cakes, use ¼ cup; and for 1½-inch cocktail cakes, use a generous 2 tablespoons. Measure the crab mixture and shape it into patties. One at a time, put them in the cracker crumbs, turning once to coat. Reshape if necessary and place on a platter or a sheet of waxed paper. If making ahead, cover and chill.

4. Place a large, heavy skillet over moderate heat. Add 1 tablespoon of the remaining butter and 1 tablespoon of the vegetable oil. Add half of the crab cakes and cook until crusty and deep golden brown on one side, 3 to 5 minutes (tiny ones will take only 2 to 3 minutes per side). Turn and brown for 3 to 4 minutes longer. Drain on paper towels. Add the remaining 1 tablespoon each butter and oil to the pan and cook the remaining crab cakes. Drain briefly. Sprinkle lightly with chopped parsley before serving.

Spanakopita Sole

When delicate fillets of sole are stuffed with feta cheese and spinach filling, flavored with dill, a pleasant new seafood entrée is the happy result.

MAKES 6 SERVINGS

> 6 large fillets of sole (each 6 to 8 ounces)
> 1½ cups cooked chopped spinach, drained
> 1 cup crumbled Greek feta cheese (about 4 ounces)
> 2 tablespoons olive oil
> 2 tablespoons butter
> 1 large garlic clove, minced
> 4 whole scallions, chopped
> 2 tablespoons chopped fresh dill
> 1 tablespoon fresh lemon juice
> 2 teaspoons cornstarch
> ½ teaspoon salt
> ⅛ teaspoon black pepper
> 6 thin lemon slices

1. Preheat the oven to 400° F. Lightly butter a 12 × 9-inch baking dish. Pat the fish dry with paper towels.
2. In a large bowl, combine the spinach and feta cheese.
3. In a small, heavy skillet, combine the olive oil and butter and place over moderate heat until the butter melts. Pour off half of this mixture and reserve it for brushing the stuffed sole. Reduce the heat to low and add the garlic, scallions, and dill and sauté until softened, 1 to 2 minutes. Transfer to the bowl of spinach and feta cheese. Stir in the lemon juice, cornstarch, salt, and pepper.
4. Place the fillets, smooth side up, on a cutting board or platter. Brush lightly with half of the reserved olive oil–butter mixture. Divide the filling among the fillets, using about ⅓ cup for each. Spread the filling into an even layer. Starting from the wide end, roll up to enclose the filling; place, seam side down, in the prepared baking dish. Brush with the remaining melted olive oil–butter mixture. Bake until cooked to the center, about 30 minutes. Top with lemon slices and serve hot.

Ceviche la Playa

In Mexico, I learned the trick of adding the water from inside a fresh coconut to ceviche to impart a wonderful flavor. Don't confuse the clear liquid in a coconut with the creamy coconut milk, which is made from the grated flesh of the coconut. And remember that the coconut water *is* optional.

MAKES 8 SERVINGS (ABOUT 5 CUPS)

- 1½ cups very fresh fish fillets, such as sole, halibut, flounder, or king mackerel, cut into ½-inch cubes
- ½ cup fresh lime juice
- ½ cup fresh lemon juice
- 1 cup coconut water (see Note; optional)
- ¼ cup extra-virgin olive oil
- 1½ teaspoons salt
- ½ teaspoon dried oregano, crumbled
- ¼ teaspoon black pepper
- 2 fresh jalapeño chilies, seeded and minced
- 1 cup finely diced tomato
- ½ cup sliced whole scallions
- ⅓ cup sliced pimiento-stuffed green olives
- ¼ cup plus 2 tablespoons chopped fresh cilantro
- Lettuce leaves or avocado halves, for serving

Note: Buy a coconut that's heavy for its size and shake it to make sure it's full of liquid. Pierce the 3 "eyes" of 1 or 2 coconuts with a nail and hammer and drain upside down over a bowl. Taste the liquid: it should not taste sour. If it does, don't use it. The water should have a sweet, fresh fragrance and flavor.

1. In a large bowl, combine the fish cubes with the lime juice, lemon juice, and ½ cup of the coconut water. Cover and marinate in the refrigerator for 6 to 8 hours, tossing once or twice. Drain the fish, reserving the marinade if serving in avocado halves.

2. In a large bowl, combine the remaining ½ cup coconut water with the olive oil. Add the salt, oregano, and pepper and whisk to combine. Add the jalapeños, tomato, scallions, olives, and the ¼ cup cilantro. Add the drained fish cubes and toss; cover and chill for 1 or 2 hours. Taste for seasoning and add more salt and pepper, if needed.

3. To serve, mound the ceviche on lettuce leaves, or pit the avocado halves and use the reserved marinade to coat the avocado flesh to avoid discoloring. Mound the ceviche in the avocado halves. Garnish with the remaining 2 tablespoons chopped cilantro.

Aromatic Grilled Swordfish

Cilantro and parsley add fragrance and flavor to these smoky seafood steaks. Cool Sesame Noodles with Jade Cucumbers (page 130) and Sake-Soaked Mushrooms (page 160) make good accompaniments.

MAKES 4 SERVINGS

$\frac{1}{3}$ cup chopped fresh cilantro

$\frac{1}{3}$ cup chopped fresh parsley

1 large garlic clove, minced or crushed through a press

2 teaspoons sweet paprika

$\frac{1}{2}$ teaspoon ground coriander

$\frac{1}{2}$ teaspoon ground cumin

$\frac{1}{4}$ teaspoon cayenne pepper

$\frac{1}{4}$ cup fresh lime or lemon juice

3 tablespoons olive oil

4 swordfish steaks, cut 1 inch thick
   Salt

2 cups hardwood chips, such as hickory or mesquite, soaked for 30 to 60 minutes

1. In a food processor, make the marinade by combining the cilantro, parsley, garlic, paprika, coriander, cumin, cayenne, and lime juice. With the machine on, add the olive oil.
2. Spread half the marinade into a shallow dish just large enough to hold the steaks in one layer. Add the swordfish steaks and top with the remaining marinade. Cover tightly and marinate in the refrigerator for 1 to 2 hours.
3. Light a charcoal fire. While the coals are catching, remove the swordfish from the refrigerator. When the coals are glowing and covered with gray ash, preheat the grill for 5 minutes.
4. Remove the steaks from the marinade and season lightly with salt. Drain the hardwood chips. Remove the grill rack, scatter the wood chips over the coals, and set the rack back in place. Grill the fish just until opaque throughout, 4 to 5 minutes per side. Serve hot.

VARIATIONS

Substitutions: **Use halibut, tuna, or mako shark steaks in place of the swordfish.**

Indoors: **The marinated steaks can be broiled if a charcoal fire is not possible.**

Grilled Swordfish Brochettes with Bay and Scallion Oil

Fresh bay leaves have much more flavor than dried ones. If you can locate some, the results will be extraordinary. Otherwise, substitute dried ones.

MAKES 4 SERVINGS

    2 pounds trimmed swordfish steaks, cut about 1¼ inches thick, cubed
   16 fresh or dried bay leaves, halved crosswise
    ½ cup Scallion Oil
    3 tablespoons fresh lemon juice
       Salt and pepper
       Lemon wedges, for serving

1. Soak eight 12-inch bamboo skewers in warm water for 30 minutes. Using 2 bamboo skewers for each brochette, thread the swordfish cubes onto the double skewer (this keeps them from twisting around), spacing them ½ inch apart and interspersing the cubes with half of a bay leaf. There should be a bay leaf at each end.

2. Marinate the swordfish brochettes in ¼ cup of the scallion oil and the lemon juice for about 1 hour.

3. Meanwhile, fill a hibachi or barbecue with hardwood chunks or charcoal and ignite. When the charcoals are glowing but covered with gray ash, the fire is ready for grilling. Preheat the grill rack over the charcoals for about 5 minutes before adding the brochettes. Put the brochettes on the hot grill and grill, turning frequently every 3 to 4 minutes, until cooked to the center, 12 to 15 minutes. If flames flare up, spritz them with water.

4. As soon as the fish is cooked through, put the brochettes on dinner plates and drizzle with the remaining ¼ cup scallion oil. Sprinkle lightly with salt and pepper and serve with lemon wedges. Seafood brochettes are also good at room temperature.

Scallion Oil

Although this delicious green oil is served here with swordfish, it is also especially complementary to monkfish. And who could resist cold shrimp dipped into scallion oil with Chinese Chili-Ginger Sauce alongside (page 378)?

To make about ½ cup

In a food processor combine 1 cup sliced scallion—green parts only—with ½ cup vegetable oil and ½ teaspoon salt and process to puree. Place several layers of cheesecloth in a sieve set over a bowl. Pour in the scallion mixture and let drain for about 10 minutes. Gather up the ends of the cheesecloth and squeeze to extract more of the oil. Serve, or transfer to a small jar; tightly cover and store for a week.

Gingered Scrod Fillets

Fragrant, light, and luscious, these broiled fillets are easy to prepare and low in calories. You will need a large quantity of fresh ginger to make the ginger juice. Sole, flounder, or red snapper fillets can be substituted for the scrod; the recipe is easily doubled.

MAKES 2 SERVINGS

½ **cup coarsely grated fresh ginger**
1 **tablespoon soy sauce**
1 **tablespoon dry sherry**
1 **tablespoon fresh lemon juice**
1 **teaspoon sugar**
2 **scrod fillets (8 ounces each)**
1 **tablespoon vegetable oil**
1 **teaspoon Oriental sesame oil**
  Salt

1. Dip a 10-inch triple layer of cheesecloth in water and wring it out. Place in a bowl and add the ginger. Gather up the edges of the cheesecloth and wring out the juice over a bowl. You will need about 2 tablespoons.
2. Reserve 1 teaspoon of the ginger juice for the top of the broiled fish. Put the remainder in a shallow dish and add the soy sauce, sherry, lemon juice, and sugar to make a marinade. If you can feel any bones in the scrod, pull them out with tweezers. Put the fillets into the marinade; turn and let marinate at room temperature, turning occasionally, for 15 to 20 minutes.
3. Preheat the broiler for about 10 minutes.
4. Meanwhile, brush a broiling pan with 1 teaspoon of the vegetable oil. Take the fillets from the marinade and arrange them side by side on the pan. Brush 1 teaspoon of the vegetable oil over the tops. Broil just until cooked through, 4 to 5 minutes; do not turn. With a spatula, transfer the fillets to plates.
5. Drizzle ½ teaspoon of the ginger juice and ½ teaspoon of the sesame oil over each fillet; sprinkle lightly with salt. Serve hot.

Red Snapper Veracruzano

Although usually made with a large, whole red snapper in Veracruz, I have used red snapper fillets in this recipe because they are usually a better bargain at the fish market. If you want to use a whole red snapper, see the Variation that follows. The cooking style of Veracruz, on the Gulf of Mexico, has a strong Spanish influence. In this seductive sauce, you will find olive oil paired with green olives, capers, and parsley, all flavored with cinnamon sticks, cloves, and cumin. Pickled jalapeños add a hint of heat. The sauce can be made well ahead of time.

MAKES 4 SERVINGS

- 8 small or 4 large red snapper fillets (1½ to 2 pounds total weight)
- 2 tablespoons fresh lime juice
- 2 tablespoons olive oil
- 1 large onion, finely chopped
- ½ cup chopped fresh parsley
- 2 large garlic cloves, minced or crushed through a press
- 2 bay leaves
- 1 teaspoon dried oregano, crumbled
- ½ teaspoon ground cumin
- 1 cinnamon stick, 3 inches long
- 3 whole cloves
- 1 teaspoon all-purpose flour
- 1½ pounds ripe tomatoes (4 to 6 medium), peeled (page 15), seeded, and coarsely chopped, with juices reserved
- 1 bottle (8 ounces) clam juice
- ¼ cup dry white wine
- 1 teaspoon salt
- ½ cup sliced pimiento-stuffed green olives
- 2 tablespoons drained capers
- 1 pickled jalapeño chili, minced

1. In a nonreactive shallow dish, combine the fish fillets and lime juice. Cover and marinate in the refrigerator for 30 to 60 minutes.
2. Meanwhile, make the sauce. Heat the olive oil in a nonreactive medium saucepan over moderate heat. Add the onion and sauté until softened and lightly colored, 5 to 7 minutes. Add ¼ cup of the parsley, along with the garlic, bay leaves, oregano, cumin, cinnamon stick, and cloves. Sauté for 2 minutes. Stir in the flour and cook for 1 minute. Add the tomatoes and their juices, along with the clam juice, wine, and salt. Bring to a boil over moderate heat. Reduce the heat to low and simmer for about 10 minutes. Remove and discard the bay leaves, cinnamon stick, and cloves. Add the

olives, capers, and jalapeño; simmer for 5 minutes longer. (The sauce can be prepared ahead to this point.)

3. Preheat the oven to 350° F. Drain the fish fillets and arrange them, skin side down and close together, in a large, shallow glass or ceramic baking dish just large enough to hold them in a single layer. Spoon the sauce over the fish.

4. Bake just until the fish is cooked through, 10 to 15 minutes. Sprinkle each serving with 1 tablespoon of the remaining parsley and serve hot, with crusty bread or steaming hot corn tortillas.

VARIATIONS

Substitution: Two pounds of large, whole, shelled and deveined shrimp can be used in place of the fish fillets. Bake only until the shrimp are cooked to the center.

Whole Fish: To cook a whole red snapper, choose one that weighs about 3 pounds. Have it cleaned, leaving the head and tail intact. Using the tip of a sharp knife, prick the fish about 15 times on each side. Rub 2 tablespoons lime juice into the fish and marinate it in the refrigerator for 1½ hours.

Preheat the oven to 350° F. Place the fish in a large, shallow casserole, just large enough to hold it; pour the sauce over the top. Bake, uncovered, for 15 minutes. Remove the casserole from the oven and, using a large spatula, carefully turn the fish. Spoon the pan sauces over the fish and drizzle with 1 tablespoon olive oil. Bake until the flesh is cooked to the bone, 30 to 40 minutes longer. Serve hot or warm.

Crunchy Louisiana Catfish

Although the bacon fat is optional, adding just a little to the vegetable oil brings out tremendous flavor. Serve these fish with Creole Rémoulade (page 368), Tartar Sauce (page 368), lemons, and/or Tabasco sauce.

MAKES 6 SERVINGS

> **Vegetable oil**
> 2 **tablespoons bacon fat (optional)**
> 2 **pounds catfish fillets**
> 3 **large eggs**
> ½ **cup dry white wine**
> 3 **tablespoons spicy brown mustard or Creole mustard**
> 1 **cup all-purpose flour**
> 1 **teaspoon cayenne pepper**
> 1½ **teaspoons salt**
> 1¼ **cups coarse yellow cornmeal**
> 1 **teaspoon dried oregano, crumbled**
> 1 **teaspoon dried basil, crumbled**
> 1 **teaspoon ground cumin**

1. Pour ¼ inch of vegetable oil into a large, heavy skillet set over moderately high heat. If using, add the bacon fat. Preheat the oil to 360° F.
2. Cut the catfish into strips about 1 to 1½ inches wide and 3 to 4 inches long.
3. In a shallow dish, whisk together the eggs, wine, and mustard. Add all of the catfish strips and set aside.
4. In another shallow dish, mix the flour with the cayenne and ½ teaspoon of the salt. Stir to combine.
5. In a third shallow dish, stir together the cornmeal, the remaining 1 teaspoon salt, the oregano, basil, and cumin. Take 2 strips of catfish from the egg mixture and dredge them in the seasoned flour. Dip them back into the egg and then dredge them in the cornmeal mixture, tapping off the excess. Immediately put them into the hot oil and continue dipping and coating more catfish strips to fill the pan without crowding. Regulate the heat, as necessary, between high and moderately high, and fry until deep golden brown and crunchy on one side, 3 to 4 minutes. Turn with tongs and fry for about 2 minutes longer. Drain on paper towels. Repeat, frying the remaining catfish strips. Sprinkle lightly with salt and serve.

Savory and Sweet

Seed-Crusted Whole Wheat Bread Sticks

Pizza with Pesto, Sausage, and Mushrooms

Goat Cheese Focaccia with Wild Mushrooms and Herbs

Pissaladière Niçoise

Fresh Herb Biscuits

Bacon Corn Bread

Cowboy Corn Bread

Breads

Sourdough Cheddar Potato Bread

Smoked Gouda Bread

Sun-Dried Tomato-Ricotta Muffins

Mango-Macadamia Muffins

Bacon and Onion Corn Muffins

Candied Ginger-Almond Muffins

Amaretto French Toast

American Sourdough Pancakes

Sour Cherry Coffee Cake

Raspberry-Buttermilk Scones

Bonus Recipes

Flavored Butters   Home-Churned Butter   Sourdough Starter

Seed-Crusted Whole Wheat Bread Sticks

An explosion of flavors and textures is created when fresh whole wheat bread sticks are encrusted with tasty toasted seeds. Serve them with soup or salad, as a snack or a party nibble.

MAKES 1 DOZEN

- 1 cup warm water (105° to 115° F.)
- 2 tablespoons sugar
- 1 envelope (¼ ounce) active dry yeast
- 1½ cups bread flour or all-purpose flour
- 1½ cups whole wheat flour
- 2 tablespoons olive oil
- ½ teaspoon salt
- 1 large egg white
- ½ cup sesame seeds
- ½ cup poppy seeds
- 2 tablespoons cumin seeds
- 1 tablespoon coarse (kosher) salt (optional)

1. In a small bowl, combine ¼ cup of the warm water with the sugar. Sprinkle the yeast over the surface, wait a few seconds, and then stir to dissolve. Let proof in a warm, draft-free place until foamy, about 5 minutes. If the mixture does not foam, start over with fresh ingredients.

2. Combine the bread flour and whole wheat flour in a food processor or large bowl (if mixing dough by hand). Add the olive oil, salt, the remaining ¾ cup warm water, and the proofed yeast. Process or stir to make a soft dough. Knead in processor for 1½ to 2 minutes. Remove and knead by hand, working in a little bread flour if the dough is too sticky, until smooth, about 2 minutes. If mixing by hand, knead until smooth, about 10 minutes. Place the dough in an oiled bowl and turn once to oil the top. Cover and let rise in a warm, draft-free place until doubled in bulk, about 1½ hours.

3. Punch down the dough and knead for 1 minute. Set aside to rest for 5 minutes.

4. On a lightly floured surface, pat or roll out the dough into a 12 × 8-inch rectangle. Cut into 12 strips, each 8 inches long. Cover and let rise until puffy, 30 to 45 minutes.

5. Meanwhile, preheat the oven to 375° F. Lightly grease 2 baking sheets.

VARIATION

Substitutions: **Use all sesame seeds or all poppy seeds, if desired, and eliminate the cumin seeds or replace with caraway seeds.**

SESAME SEEDS

Sesame seeds may be the oldest condiment known to man. Records show production in the Tigris and Euphrates valleys that dates back to 1600 B.C.

The tiny, flat, pointed seeds contain about 50 percent oil and are available hulled or unhulled. Toasting greatly enhances their flavor. You can toast them by shaking them in an ungreased skillet over moderate heat until they pop and turn golden brown. There are special sesame-seed toasting pans available in Japanese markets that have screened lids to keep the seeds from popping out.

Sprinkle toasted sesame seeds freely over salads and sandwiches and toss with pasta. If you sprinkle untoasted sesame seeds over an open-face cheese sandwich and run it under the broiler, the seeds will toast as the cheese melts.

The oil from untoasted sesame seeds is nearly flavorless and is an important ingredient in margarine. Roasted sesame seeds are pressed to make the big-flavored, dark-colored Oriental sesame oil. Untoasted sesame seeds are ground to make Middle Eastern tahini.

You can buy the little jars of sesame seeds in the grocery, but the price will be outrageously high. Instead, buy a big bagful in a Middle Eastern or Chinese market and store the seeds in the refrigerator in a jar with a tight-fitting lid.

POPPY SEEDS

These tiny slate-blue seeds are especially appealing when sprinkled over baked goods, such as kaiser rolls and hamburger buns. It's because of their rich (50 percent) oil content that they make such a beautiful crust on bread. My mother used to buy them by the bagful and grind them to make a rich filling for coffee cakes and sweet rolls.

Indigenous to the Eastern Mediterranean, Asia Minor, and Central Asia, poppy seeds are the seeds of the notorious opium poppy. But, luckily, the seeds have absolutely no narcotic properties (because the seeds do not form until the flower has lost its opium-producing qualities).

Roasting, baking, and toasting the seeds brings out their rich nutty flavor and crunchy texture.

Buy poppy seeds in bulk and store them in the refrigerator.

6. In a shallow dish or pie plate, whisk the egg white with 1 tablespoon water. In a rectangular pan (such as a 12 × 8-inch baking pan), combine the sesame seeds, poppy seeds, cumin seeds, and coarse salt. Stir to blend well.

7. Pick up 1 strip of dough and dip it into the egg white. Roll it in the seed mixture to coat all over. Pick up the dough and stretch it until 12 to 14 inches long. Twist it by turning one end 6 to 8 times; place it on one of the baking sheets. Repeat, placing the bread sticks 1 to 1½ inches apart, 6 to a sheet.

8. Bake for 25 to 30 minutes, reversing the sheets halfway through the baking, until lightly browned and crusty. Transfer to a rack.

9. Serve warm or at room temperature. The bread sticks can be reheated at 350° F. for 10 minutes or dried in a 250° F. oven for 45 minutes.

Pizza with Pesto, Sausage, and Mushrooms

You can make good pizzas at home on a baking sheet (see Variations) but you can make really great pizzas on a baking stone. I confess that I didn't have one until a couple years ago and I thought my pizzas were fine. But once I got one, I realized just how invaluable they are. If you frequently make homemade pizza you should buy one; if not, simply follow the instructions listed under the Variations.

By the way, the tomato is added to the top of this pizza so it doesn't make the dough soggy and the mushrooms are added raw, cooking as quickly as the pizza bakes. Use homemade sausage (page 258) or store-bought.

MAKES 2 TO 4 SERVINGS

Dough

- ¾ cup warm water (105° to 115° F.)
- 1 teaspoon sugar
- 1 envelope (¼ ounce) active dry yeast
- About 2 cups bread flour or all-purpose flour
- 1 tablespoon olive oil
- ½ teaspoon salt

Topping

- 3 tablespoons Pesto (page 361)
- 8 ounces whole-milk or part-skim mozzarella, coarsely shredded (2 cups)
- 1½ tablespoons olive oil
- 4 to 6 ounces Italian fennel sausage or turkey sausage
- Coarse yellow cornmeal
- 6 medium mushrooms (4 ounces), thinly sliced
- ½ teaspoon dried oregano, crumbled
- ¼ teaspoon salt
- ⅛ teaspoon pepper
- 2 tablespoons freshly grated Parmesan cheese
- ½ cup canned crushed tomatoes

1. Make the dough. Combine ¼ cup of the warm water and the sugar in a small bowl. Sprinkle on the yeast, wait a few seconds, and then stir to dissolve. Set aside to proof until foamy and doubled in bulk, about 5 minutes. If this does not happen, start over with fresh ingredients.

2. Measure 2 cups of the flour into a food processor or large bowl (if mixing by hand). Add the olive oil and salt. Add the remaining ½ cup lukewarm water and the proofed yeast. Process or stir to make a soft, slightly sticky dough. If necessary, add a little more flour. Knead in the processor for about 2 minutes. Remove and knead by hand for 2 to 3 minutes longer,

until smooth. If mixing entirely by hand, knead for about 10 minutes. Put the dough in a large, lightly oiled bowl and turn once to oil the top. Cover and let rise in a warm, draft-free place until doubled in bulk, 1 to 1½ hours.

3. Punch down the dough and knead for a few seconds. Return to the bowl, cover, and let rest for 10 to 15 minutes.

4. Meanwhile, prepare the topping. Have the pesto ready ahead of time. In a bowl, combine the mozzarella and olive oil and let marinate until needed.

5. Place a small skillet over moderate heat. Slit the sausage casing and crumble the sausage into the skillet; sauté until no longer pink, 3 to 5 minutes. Drain and set aside.

6. Sprinkle a wooden pizza peel with the cornmeal. On a lightly floured surface, roll out the dough into a 14 × 10-inch rectangle or 12-inch round. Pick up the dough and place it on the peel. Cover with a sheet of plastic wrap and let it rise until puffy and almost doubled in bulk, about 30 minutes.

7. Place a pizza stone or quarry tiles in the lower third of your oven. Preheat the oven to 450° F. for at least 30 minutes.

8. Uncover the dough and sprinkle it with half of the mozzarella. Arrange the mushroom slices over the cheese and sprinkle with the sausage. Spoon dabs of the pesto all over. Sprinkle with the oregano, salt, and pepper.

MOZZARELLA

There are two basic types of mozzarella cheese: the familiar, commercial one, sealed in plastic, and found at any supermarket, and the fresh, softer, whiter, round balls that are stored in water or wrapped in plastic with a little water trapped inside to keep them wet. The fresh one has the higher moisture content and is best eaten shortly after purchase. Within these two categories there are many variations, skim, part-skim, lightly salted, or unsalted.

In Italy, the best mozzarella cheese is made from the milk of water buffalo and is never refrigerated (which changes its soft, supple texture). It is made fresh daily and has a good creamy consistency, sweet buttery-milk flavor, and gentle mildness. In this country, commercial mozzarella is almost always made from cow's milk, and often contains binders and additives to "enhance" its melting qualities, making it somewhat rubbery (you can tell when the cheese on that slice of pizza snaps back at you).

In recent years, fresh mozzarella has become increasingly more popular and so more widely available. Sometimes I grate fresh mozzarella and marinate it in a little olive oil to enhance its flavor. Then I use it to top pizzas or casseroles—it's an improvement since most mozzarellas made in this country are not as buttery-rich as those made in Italy.

Scatter the top with the remaining mozzarella and the Parmesan cheese. Spoon the crushed tomatoes over the top.

9. Open the oven door and carefully pull out the shelf with the stone. Hold the peel over the stone, almost parallel to it, and use short jerking motions to shake the pizza free, letting it slide onto the hot stone as you pull away the peel. Slide the shelf back in and close the oven. Bake for 10 to 12 minutes, or until lightly browned on the bottom and bubbly on top. Serve hot, cut into squares or wedges.

VARIATIONS

Substitutions: **Use ground beef or chicken in place of the sausage, adding ¼ teaspoon crushed fennel seeds when you sauté it. Sliced pepperoni can replace the sausage, but do not cook it first.**

Lower calorie: **You can eliminate the 1½ tablespoons of olive oil used to marinate the mozzarella (though you will lose some tenderness and delicacy).**

Additions: **Black olives and anchovies can be added as well.**

To make the pizza on a baking sheet: **Lightly oil a large baking sheet and lightly coat it with cornmeal. Roll out the dough to fit the pan, making a slightly raised edge, if desired. Let the dough rise for about 30 minutes before topping and bake as above. To make the crust extra crispy, move the baking sheet to the oven floor for 2 to 3 minutes after the pizza has baked.**

Goat Cheese Focaccia with Wild Mushrooms and Herbs

Fragrant homemade flatbread is always greatly appreciated. When the cheese is put into the dough, a tender yet crisp, flavorful crust develops. This is great as an appetizer or as bread with a meal.

MAKES 6 TO 8 SERVINGS

1 cup warm water (105° to 115° F.)

1 teaspoon sugar

1 envelope (¼ ounce) active dry yeast

ROSEMARY

The strong, fragrant leaves of rosemary—which resemble small pine needles—have a pleasantly piney and agreeably bitter pungency with undertones of mint and ginger. They grow on an evergreen shrub belonging to the mint family that is native to the Mediterranean.

Rosemary's vigorous fresh aroma and flavor complement roasted meats and potatoes and harmonize with chicken, pork, and lamb. Always buy whole leaves. The flavor of ground rosemary diminishes rapidly.

Ancient Greeks thought that rosemary fortified the brain and refreshed the memory, so students braided rosemary into their hair before taking exams. Rosemary bushes can grow up to five feet tall.

I've often been disappointed by the flavor and fragrance of dried rosemary, so now I keep a plant in my window year-round. But if you need to use dried, the old rule of one-third dried to fresh is a good one to follow.

3½ to 3¾ cups bread flour or all-purpose flour

4 tablespoons extra-virgin olive oil

1 teaspoon coarse salt

6 ounces mild goat cheese, such as Montrachet, at room temperature
Coarse yellow cornmeal

8 ounces portobello mushrooms or fresh porcini, cut into ⅛-inch slices

1 tablespoon snipped fresh oregano

2 teaspoons snipped fresh rosemary

½ teaspoon black pepper

1. In a small bowl, combine ¼ cup of the warm water, the sugar, and yeast. Let the yeast soften for 1 minute; stir to dissolve. Set aside to proof in a warm, draft-free place until foamy and doubled in bulk, about 5 minutes.

2. Put 3 cups of the flour in a food processor or large bowl. Add 2 tablespoons of the olive oil, ½ teaspoon of the coarse salt, and the remaining ¾ cup lukewarm water and process or stir to make a soft dough. Knead in the food processor for 1 minute. Remove the dough and knead on a board until smooth and elastic, 5 to 10 minutes. Shape the dough into a ball and place in an oiled bowl, turning it once to oil the top. Cover and let rise in a warm, draft-free place until doubled in bulk, 1 to 1½ hours.

3. Punch down the dough and let rest for 5 minutes. Crumble the goat cheese over the dough and work it in with your hands. Knead briefly to distribute the cheese. Return the dough to the bowl, cover, and let rise until puffy, about 30 minutes.

4. Meanwhile, preheat the oven to 400° F. If you have them, place a pizza stone or quarry tiles on the top rack to preheat. To use a baking sheet, see Variation on page 290.

5. Sprinkle a pizza peel generously with coarse yellow cornmeal. Depending on your pizza stone, shape the dough into a 12-inch round or 10 × 14-inch rectangle. Using your fingers, make indentations all over the dough. Cover with a sheet of plastic wrap and let rise until puffy, about 20 minutes.

6. Add the mushroom slices and sprinkle with the herbs, the remaining ½ teaspoon salt, and the black pepper. Drizzle the remaining 2 tablespoons olive oil over the focaccia.

7. When the pizza stone is thoroughly preheated, jerk the pizza peel in your hand to see if the focaccia moves. You will have to slide it off the peel onto the pizza stone in the oven, so give it a couple of good jerks. Open the oven, slide the foccacia onto the stone, and bake for 20 to 25 minutes, until crusty and golden brown. Cut into wedges or squares and serve hot.

VARIATION

To make the focaccia on a baking sheet: Lightly oil a large baking sheet (10 × 15-inch) and lightly coat it with cornmeal. Roll the dough to fit the pan and continue with step 5 above. Bake on the sheet 20 to 25 minutes. To make the crust extra crispy, move the baking sheet to the oven floor for 2 to 3 minutes after the focaccia has baked.

Pissaladière Niçoise

This is a rich French cousin to Italian pizza. The great flavor comes from *herbes de Provence*, anchovies, olives, tomatoes, and onions. The yeast crust is enriched with butter, egg, and Parmesan cheese, so it takes longer to rise than simple yeast doughs. It's a good centerpiece for a simple lunch, an eye-catching appetizer.

MAKES 4 TO 8 SERVINGS

¼ cup warm water (105° to 115° F.)
1 teaspoon sugar
1 envelope (¼ ounce) active dry yeast
1½ cups all-purpose flour
⅓ cup freshly grated Parmesan cheese
2 tablespoons butter, at room temperature
1 teaspoon black pepper
1 teaspoon salt

    1 large egg, at room temperature
    3 tablespoons extra-virgin olive oil
    1 pound onions (2 large or 4 medium),
        halved lengthwise and thinly sliced crosswise
  ½ teaspoon dried oregano, crumbled
  ¼ teaspoon dried thyme, crumbled
  ¼ teaspoon dried rosemary, crumbled
    2 large ripe tomatoes, halved lengthwise and thinly sliced
    8 large oil-cured black olives, halved, pitted, and quartered
        lengthwise, or 32 Niçoise olives, pitted
    1 can (2 ounces) flat anchovy fillets, drained and halved crosswise

1. In a small bowl, combine the warm water, sugar, and yeast. Let the yeast soften for 1 minute; stir to dissolve. Set aside to proof in a warm, draft-free place until foamy and doubled in bulk, about 5 minutes.

2. In a food processor, combine the flour, Parmesan, butter, pepper, and ½ teaspoon of the salt. Add the egg and the yeast mixture and process to make a soft, sticky dough. Knead in the food processor for 2 minutes. Remove and knead with your hands for 1 minute. Place in an oiled bowl, turning once to oil the top. Cover and let rise in a warm place until doubled in bulk, 1½ to 2 hours.

3. Meanwhile, spoon 2 tablespoons of the olive oil into a large, heavy skillet set over moderate heat. Stir in the onions, oregano, thyme, rosemary, and the remaining ½ teaspoon salt. Reduce the heat to low, cover, and cook until the onions are soft and translucent but not browned, about 20 minutes. Uncover, increase the heat to moderate, and stir to evaporate any liquid, 1 to 2 minutes; do not brown. Turn the mixture into a bowl and let cool to room temperature.

4. After the dough has doubled in bulk, punch it down and knead it with your hands for 1 minute; let rest for 5 minutes.

5. On a lightly floured surface, pat out the dough with your hands and then use a rolling pin to make a 14 × 10-inch oval about ¼ inch thick. Transfer to a large, oiled baking sheet, reshaping if necessary.

6. Using a fluted pastry cutter, trim off ½ inch from all around the edge. Moisten the bottom of the ½-inch strip and position on top, around the circumference, to make a slightly raised edge. Cover with plastic wrap placed directly on the dough and let rise in a warm, draft-free place until puffy, 20 to 30 minutes.

7. Meanwhile, move an oven shelf to the lower third of the oven. Preheat the oven to 425° F., about 30 minutes.

8. To top the pissaladière, scatter the onions all over the dough. Starting around the outside edge, arrange the tomato slices close together in concentric circles. Top each tomato slice with a bit of olive and a piece of the anchovy. Drizzle the remaining 1 tablespoon olive oil over the top.

9. Bake in the bottom third of the oven for 15 minutes. Reduce the oven temperature to 350° F. and bake for 15 minutes longer, until golden brown. Cut into wedges and serve hot or warm.

Fresh Herb Biscuits

Beautifully high and light, these puffy biscuits have a good herb flavor and a fine crumb, contributed by the cake flour.

MAKES 10 TO 12 BISCUITS

> 1 **cup all-purpose flour**
> 1 **cup cake flour (not self-rising)**
> 1 **tablespoon baking powder**
> $\frac{1}{2}$ **teaspoon salt**
> $\frac{1}{3}$ **cup vegetable shortening**
> $\frac{2}{3}$ **cup milk**
> 2 **tablespoons snipped fresh herbs, such as a combination of oregano, thyme, and basil**
> 1 **tablespoon melted butter or bacon fat**

1. Preheat the oven to 450° F. Lightly grease a baking sheet.

2. In a large bowl, stir together the all-purpose flour, cake flour, baking powder, and salt. With a pastry blender or 2 knives, cut in the shortening until the particles are the size of peas. Add the milk and herbs and stir quickly, just to combine. Knead very briefly by folding over and pushing with the heel of your hand 3 or 4 times. Pat the dough into a 7 × 5-inch rectangle. Cut in half and very lightly dust 1 piece of the dough with a little flour. Put the other piece on top and quickly pat into a 6- or 7-inch round slightly less than 1 inch thick.

3. Using a 2-inch round biscuit cutter, cut out as many biscuits as possible. Place them 1 inch apart on the baking sheet. Gather the scraps and pat out about 1 inch thick and cut out 2 to 4 more biscuits.

4. Quickly brush the biscuits with the melted butter. Bake for about 14 minutes, or until puffy and golden brown. Serve hot, with pats of butter.

Flavored Butters

- **CHOCOLATE BUTTER.** Soften 1 cup butter to room temperature. Place it in a mixing bowl and stir in 2 tablespoons unsweetened cocoa powder and 2 tablespoons confectioners' sugar. Stir in ¼ teaspoon vanilla extract. Taste for sweetness and stir in 1 tablespoon more sugar, if desired. Turn out onto a sheet of waxed paper and shape into a 5-inch log. Roll up to enclose, twisting the ends of the paper to make a tight, compact log. Refrigerate until firm.

- **TOMATO-BASIL BUTTER.** In a food processor, combine 1 cup softened butter with ½ cup fresh basil leaves, 2 tablespoons tomato paste, and ¼ teaspoon salt. Process to chop the basil into fine pieces. Turn the mixture out onto a sheet of waxed paper and shape into a 5-inch log. Roll up tight and twist the ends of the paper to make a compact log. Chill.

- **CARAWAY BUTTER.** If you like rye bread toast with caraway seeds, you'll love this on any kind of toast. Also, shave wafers of it over hot steamed carrots, cabbage, or potatoes. In a mixing bowl, stir 1 cup softened butter with 1 tablespoon slightly crushed or lightly pounded caraway seeds, ¼ teaspoon salt, and ¼ teaspoon black pepper. Turn the mixture out onto a sheet of waxed paper and shape into a 5-inch log. Roll up tightly and twist the ends of the paper to make a compact log. Chill until firm, and then slice.

- **TARRAGON BUTTER.** In a medium bowl, beat ½ cup butter and ¼ cup finely chopped fresh tarragon with a fork to blend. Stir in 1½ teaspoons fresh lemon juice, ¼ teaspoon salt, and ¼ teaspoon pepper. Shape into a 5-inch log on a sheet of waxed paper and roll up to enclose, twisting the ends to hold the shape. Chill.

- **TABASCO BUTTER.** Combine ½ cup softened butter, 1 tablespoon Tabasco sauce, ¼ teaspoon salt, and ¼ teaspoon pepper in a medium bowl and beat with a fork to blend. Shape into a 5-inch log on a sheet of waxed paper and roll up tightly to enclose, twisting the ends to hold the shape. Chill.

Bacon Corn Bread

This corn bread has a rustic appearance and a great crunchy crust. It's baked in a cast-iron skillet.

MAKES 8 SERVINGS

8	slices hickory-smoked bacon, cut into small squares
2	tablespoons melted bacon fat or butter
1½	cups coarse yellow cornmeal
¼	cup all-purpose flour
1	teaspoon salt
1	teaspoon baking soda
1	large egg
1	cup plain yogurt
¾	cup milk

1. Preheat the oven to 450° F.
2. Put the bacon in a 9- to 10-inch cast-iron skillet and cook slowly over moderately low heat until crisp and golden brown, about 12 minutes. Scoop out with a slotted spoon and drain on paper towels. Pour off most of the fat, leaving behind just enough to grease the skillet. Reserve 2 tablespoons, if desired, for the batter. (Otherwise, use melted butter.) Preheat the skillet in the hot oven.
3. In a large bowl, stir together the cornmeal, flour, salt, and baking soda. Make a well in the center of the dry ingredients.
4. In a medium bowl, whisk together the egg, yogurt, milk, and melted bacon fat or butter. Pour into the dry ingredients and stir just to blend; the batter should be lumpy.
5. Carefully remove the skillet from the oven and pour in the batter. Return to the oven and bake until deep golden brown and the edges begin to pull away from the pan, about 20 minutes. Cut into 8 wedges. Split and serve.

Cowboy Corn Bread

This big skillet corn bread was inspired by a trip to the Pitchfork Ranch in Guthrie, Texas. The corn flavor is bigger than in most other versions because you combine three forms of corn: coarse yellow cornmeal, masa harina, and fresh sweet corn kernels cut from the cob. And you brown the corn kernels to intensify the flavor. (You can substitute vegetable oil for the bacon fat to lower the cholesterol.) It is best made in a preheated cast-iron skillet so it bakes up extra crunchy.

MAKES 8 SERVINGS

> 8 slices hickory-smoked bacon, cut into small squares
> 1½ cups fresh or frozen corn kernels, thawed
> 1 fresh jalapeño chili, minced with seeds
> ¾ cup coarse yellow cornmeal
> ¾ cup masa harina or all-purpose flour
> ¾ cup all-purpose flour
> 1 tablespoon baking powder
> ½ teaspoon baking soda
> 1 teaspoon salt
> 3 large eggs
> ¾ cup plain yogurt
> ¾ cup milk
> 1 cup coarsely shredded sharp cheddar cheese (4 ounces)

1. Preheat the oven to 400° F. Have ready a well-seasoned, 10-inch cast-iron skillet.
2. Place a heavy, medium skillet over moderate heat. Add the bacon and cook until crisp and golden brown. Scoop out with a slotted spoon and drain on paper towels. Let 1 tablespoon of the fat remain in the skillet and reserve the rest for the batter. (Or discard the fat and spoon 1 tablespoon oil into the pan and use 3 tablespoons in the batter.)
3. Add the corn and sauté over moderately high heat until browned, 3 to 5 minutes. Add the jalapeño and sauté for about 2 minutes. Let cool to room temperature.
4. Generously oil the cast-iron skillet and place it in the hot oven to preheat while you prepare the batter.
5. In a large bowl, stir together the cornmeal, masa harina, flour, baking powder, baking soda, and salt. Make a well in the center.
6. In a large bowl, combine the eggs, yogurt, milk, and the reserved 3 tablespoons bacon fat or vegetable oil; whisk to blend evenly. Stir in the corn, cheddar, and bacon. Pour into the dry ingredients and stir quickly just to blend. Do not overmix; the batter should be lumpy.
7. Pour the batter into the hot skillet and bake for about 30 minutes, or until the edges begin to pull away from the pan and a toothpick inserted in the center has no crumbs clinging to it when pulled out. Carefully loosen all around the edge with a knife and shake the pan to make sure the corn bread isn't stuck. Invert a plate over the top and unmold so the crisp side is up. Cut into wedges and serve hot, with butter, if desired.

Home-Churned Butter

I'm a modern man so my version of home-churned butter is beaten with an electric mixer or whirled in a food processor. It will be the best butter you can find because it's so sweet, and fresh, and clean-tasting. Have it plain or salted or use it to make any of the flavored butters. Ultra-pasteurized cream will take longer to whip into butter than pasteurized.

To make about 1 cup:

Combine 2 cups cold heavy cream with 1 teaspoon salt in a large, deep bowl. Beat with an electric mixer at medium speed until stiff like whipped cream and then continue beating until the mixture appears curdled and then masses together as the butter separates from the liquid (whey). Regular pasteurized cream will take 4 to 5 minutes; ultra-pasteurized will take 8 to 12 minutes. It is interesting to note that most of the salt will leave the butter with the whey, but will give the butter a pleasant, not overly salty taste. If using a food processor, simply process until the butter separates from the whey. Turn the butter into a sieve placed over a bowl. Squeeze the mass of butter to release more of the liquid. Wrap it in plastic and refrigerate for several hours before using.

Sourdough Cheddar Potato Bread

This recipe is for bakers who love a challenge. The bread has a great sour tang and a big cheddar cheese flavor. You can make two crusty loaves or two dozen shiny round rolls. I usually make one loaf and one dozen rolls (because I love to make hamburgers and serve them on cheddar rolls, so the cheese flavor is in the roll rather than on the burger). Yeast loves potato starch, and that is why this bread is nice and puffy. The recipe is, however, time-consuming: you must first have a Sourdough Starter on hand, and then make the sponge and let it rise for as long as 24 hours before making the bread dough, which then must go through two more risings. Also, I must warn you that sourdough starters are unpredictable and temperamental. Although a good sourdough starter requires no additional yeast for leavening, I have added some to ensure success here. If you want an even bigger challenge, eliminate the yeast, and experiment on your own. The dough can be frozen and thawed for future use.

MAKES 2 LOAVES, 24 ROLLS, OR 1 LOAF AND 12 ROLLS

> 1 **russet baking potato**
>
> *Sponge*
>
> 1 **cup Sourdough Starter (page 296)**
> 1 **tablespoon sugar**
> 2 **cups all-purpose flour**
>
> *Bread*
>
> 1 **tablespoon sugar**
> 1 **envelope (¼ ounce) active dry yeast**
> 1 **tablespoon butter, softened**
> 1 **teaspoon salt**
> 3 **to 4 cups all-purpose flour**
> 12 **ounces sharp cheddar cheese, 8 ounces coarsely**
> **grated, plus 4 ounces cut into ¼-inch cubes**
> 1 **large egg, for glazing**

1. Pour 3 cups of cold water into a medium saucepan and add a big pinch of salt. Peel the potato and cut into 1-inch chunks, dropping them into the water as they are cut. Bring to a boil over high heat, partially cover, and boil until tender when pierced with a fork, about 15 minutes. Strain the potato, reserving all of the liquid; you will need 1¼ cups for this recipe. When the potato has cooled, mash it with a fork. You will need ½ cup of mashed potato for this recipe. (If making the potato and the potato water ahead of time, cover and refrigerate for as long as a day; let return to room temperature before using.)

2. Make the sponge. In a large bowl, stir together the sourdough starter, ¾ cup

Sourdough Starter

Sourdough starter adds a big tangy flavor to bread. A great American tradition, sourdough breads became extremely popular during the early California gold rush. Chuckwagon cowboy cooks are famous for their sourdoughs too.

Basically, a sourdough starter is a living mass of dough that will leaven bread while contributing great flavor. When making bread you always save a wad for the next batch. Then you feed and care for the perpetual starter as if it were your child.

I have had a lifelong fascination with sourdough. There are always two or three dormant in my refrigerator and one or two alive and bubbling away on my kitchen counter. One of my favorites is well over 100 years old, given to me by a chuckwagon cook on a Texas ranch.

You'll need sourdough starter for some of the breads in the chapter. Might as well make it right now because it won't be ready to use for at least three days. After a week it will taste even better. And a hundred years from now . . . well, that's how traditions are started.

Here's a good formula to make about 3 cups of starter: Peel a medium all-purpose potato and cut it into ½-inch dice. Add 3 cups cold water in a saucepan, partially cover, and bring to a boil over high heat. When the potatoes are very tender, about 20 minutes, remove the pan from the heat and let cool in the liquid. Drain, saving the potato water. Mash enough of the potato to make ¼ cup and reserve the remainder for another use.

In a large glass bowl or ceramic crock, stir together 2 cups of all-purpose flour, 2 tablespoons sugar, and 1 teaspoon active dry yeast. In a small saucepan, combine 1 cup of the reserved potato water with 1 cup water; warm over moderate heat to about 100° F. Pour it over the flour mixture, add the mashed potato, and whisk together until smooth.

Top with a sheet of waxed paper and a sheet of aluminum foil. Crimp the foil around the edge to cover. Don't seal it too tightly because the starter must breathe. Leave it at warm room temperature for 2 days.

Uncover and stir in 2 tablespoons of flour. Re-cover and let stand at least one day longer before using. After that, keep it alive by stirring in a little flour, a pinch of sugar and a little water every 2 or 3 days. You can stir in as little as 2 tablespoons flour or as much as ½ cup each time, depending on how frequently you want to use it. Each time that you add flour, add a pinch of sugar and just enough warm water to keep the consistency like thick pancake batter.

If you want the starter to go dormant, transfer it to a jar or plastic container and cover it tightly. Refrigerate for up to 6 months. Bring it back to room temperature, add flour and water as before, and begin feeding and caring for it as you did.

of the lukewarm potato water (reheat if necessary to 105° F.), and the sugar. Stir in the flour to make a very thick batter (or a very sticky dough). Cover loosely with plastic—not so tightly that air cannot get in—and set aside at room temperature in a draft-free place until doubled in bulk, 12 to 24 hours (most sourdough starters seem to take the full 24 hours, but it will be ready when it has doubled).

3. Make the bread dough. Make sure that the remaining ½ cup of potato water is warmed to 105° F. Pour the warm potato water into a small bowl and stir in the sugar. Sprinkle the yeast over the surface and stir to dissolve. Set aside to proof in a warm, draft-free place until foamy and doubled in bulk, about 5 minutes.

4. Uncover the sponge after it has doubled and add the proofed yeast. Stir in the ½ cup mashed potato, the butter, salt, and 1 cup of the flour. Stir to combine the ingredients. Continue stirring and add as much more flour as needed to make a soft dough that is just slightly sticky. (Do not add too much flour or the bread might become dry.) Sourdough should be slightly stickier than traditional bread dough. Knead the dough on a lightly floured surface or by stretching it in your hands, pulling and folding this way and that to activate the gluten in the flour, until it is satin-smooth. Pat out the dough on a work surface and sprinkle with the grated cheddar cheese. Roll up the dough and knead briefly to distribute the shreds. Place the dough in a lightly oiled large bowl, turning once to oil the top. Cover and let rise in a warm, draft-free place until doubled in bulk, about 1½ hours.

5. Punch down the dough and knead for 1 minute. Set aside to rest for 5 minutes. Add the cubed cheddar and knead briefly to distribute evenly.

6. Divide the dough in half. *To make a loaf,* on a floured surface, roll or pat out

VARIATIONS

Other uses: **This dough makes sensational focaccia. After the first rising, divide the dough into 4 equal pieces. On a baking sheet, pat out 1 piece of dough into a 9-inch round. Thinly slice 3 plum tomatoes and arrange them all over the dough. Lightly sprinkle with salt and pepper and top with 2 ounces (½ cup) of grated sharp cheddar cheese. Cover with plastic and let rise until puffy, 20 to 30 minutes. Bake for 15 to 20 minutes, or until deep golden brown. Remove and cool on a rack or serve hot. Use the remaining dough in whatever way you want.**

half of the dough into a 10 × 8-inch oval. Starting at one long side, roll up tightly. Place the dough on an oiled baking sheet. Using a single-edged razor blade or a very sharp knife, make 5 diagonal slashes about ¾ inch deep across the top of the loaf. Cover the loaf with plastic wrap and let rise in a warm, draft-free place until doubled in bulk, 30 to 60 minutes.

To make rolls, shape half of the dough into a thick, 12- to 14-inch-long rope. Cut into 12 equal pieces. One at a time, dust each piece with flour and shape into a ball. Place the balls, smoothest side up, about 1 inch apart on an oiled baking sheet. Cover loosely with plastic wrap and let rise in a warm, draft-free place until doubled in bulk, 30 to 60 minutes.

7. Preheat the oven to 400° F. before the bread has fully risen.

8. After the dough has risen, beat the egg with 1 teaspoon water. Brush the glaze generously over the loaves or rolls. Bake the loaves for 35 to 40 minutes and the rolls for about 20 minutes, until deep golden brown and they sound hollow when tapped on the bottoms. Transfer to racks and let cool to room temperature. Serve or store in plastic bags after they have cooled.

Smoked Gouda Bread

The smoky flavor of the Gouda is noticeable in every bite of this bread, and greatly enhanced when toasted. So making a grilled cheese sandwich, perhaps with pickled jalapeños and Monterey Jack cheese, is a smart way to use Gouda bread.

MAKES 1 LARGE LOAF, 2 MEDIUM LOAVES, OR 12 ROLLS

- 2 tablespoons sugar
- ¼ cup warm water (105° to 115° F.)
- 1 envelope (¼ ounce) active dry yeast
- ¾ cup milk
- 3 tablespoons butter
- 3 large eggs, at room temperature
- 1 teaspoon dry mustard
- 1½ teaspoons salt
- ¼ teaspoon cayenne pepper
- 4½ to 5 cups all-purpose flour
- 1 cup grated smoked Gouda cheese, plus ½ cup diced Gouda (6 ounces total)

1. In a small bowl, combine 1 tablespoon of the sugar with the warm water; stir

to dissolve the sugar. Sprinkle the yeast over the top and stir to dissolve the yeast. Set aside to proof until foamy and doubled in bulk, about 5 minutes.

2. In a small saucepan, combine the milk, butter, and the remaining 1 tablespoon sugar over low heat. Heat just until the butter melts, but do not let the mixture simmer. Let cool to lukewarm.

3. In a food processor, combine 2 of the eggs with the mustard, salt, cayenne, yeast mixture, and the warm milk-butter mixture. Add 4 cups of the flour and process until you have a soft dough, 1 to 2 minutes. Turn out into a floured large bowl and knead in about ½ cup more flour or enough to make a soft, slightly sticky dough. Knead until smooth and elastic, about 10 minutes. Knead in the grated Gouda. Put the dough in a large oiled bowl, turning once to oil the top. Cover and let rise in a warm, draft-free place until doubled in bulk, 1 to 1½ hours.

4. Punch down the dough and let rest for 5 minutes. Add the diced Gouda and knead in to evenly distribute.

5. Lightly grease a large baking sheet. To make 1 large loaf, divide the dough into 3 equal pieces; on a lightly floured surface, roll each into an 18-inch rope. Pinch the ends together and place it on the baking sheet, braiding the remaining strands over each other to make a traditional braid. Pinch the ends together and tuck both ends under the loaf. Cover and let rise in a warm, draft-free place until doubled in bulk, 45 to 60 minutes.

To make 2 medium loaves, divide the dough in half and place each half into an 8 × 4-inch loaf pan. Set aside to rise until doubled in bulk, 45 to 60 minutes.

To make 12 rolls, divide the dough into 12 equal pieces. Roll each into a smooth ball; place the balls 1 inch apart on 2 greased baking sheets, flattening them slightly. Set aside to rise until doubled in bulk, 45 to 60 minutes.

6. Fifteen minutes before the rising is complete, preheat the oven to 375° F.

7. To make the glaze, combine the remaining egg in a cup with 1 tablespoon water; stir with a fork until blended. Generously brush the loaf with the glaze. Bake the large loaf of bread for 40 to 45 minutes, or until deep golden brown and the bottom sounds hollow when tapped. (Bake 2 medium loaves for 30 to 35 minutes. Bake 12 rolls for 20 to 25 minutes.) Let cool on a rack for at least 1 hour before serving. The loaves or rolls may then be put into plastic bags to keep fresh.

Sun-Dried Tomato-Ricotta Muffins

I am particularly fond of savory muffins. This is a recipe that just seemed to create itself as I experimented in the kitchen. The dry-packed sun-dried tomatoes can be very salty, so no salt may be needed in the moist ricotta batter. With the carefully chosen seasonings and the slight smoky quality of the tomatoes, many people will think that these muffins contain sausage or pepperoni. They are perhaps even better the second day, when they become crunchier upon reheating and remain moist inside. The muffins are great with chowders, soups, and salads, or all by themselves.

MAKES 1 DOZEN

> 1½ ounces (¾ cup lightly packed) dry-packed
>   sun-dried tomatoes or ⅓ cup finely chopped well-
>   drained sun-dried tomatoes packed in olive oil
> 2 tablespoons plain, dry bread crumbs
> 2 cups all-purpose flour
> 1 tablespoon baking powder
> ½ teaspoon baking soda
> 1 teaspoon sugar
>   Salt, if needed
> ½ teaspoon crushed or ground fennel seed
> ½ teaspoon dried oregano, crumbled
> ½ teaspoon dried basil, crumbled
> ¼ teaspoon black pepper
> 1 large egg
> 1 cup whole-milk ricotta cheese (8 ounces)
> ½ cup milk
> 2 tablespoons butter, melted
> 1 tablespoon olive oil
> 2 tablespoons fresh lemon juice
> ½ cup plus 2 tablespoons freshly grated Parmesan cheese

1. If using the dry-packed sun-dried tomatoes, place them in a small heatproof bowl and add 1 cup boiling water. Let soak until softened, 3 to 4 minutes. Drain and let cool; finely chop. If using sun-dried tomatoes packed in oil, simply drain well on paper towels and finely chop to yield ⅓ cup.
2. Preheat the oven to 375° F. Lightly grease a 12-cup muffin tin. Spoon ½ teaspoon of the bread crumbs into each and tilt to coat the bottoms and sides; tap out any crumbs that don't adhere.
3. In a large bowl, stir together the flour, baking powder, baking soda, and sugar. Taste the sun-dried tomatoes; if they taste salty, do not add any salt

to the flour. If they do not, add ½ teaspoon salt (the Parmesan will also contribute saltiness). Stir in the fennel seed, oregano, basil, and pepper.

4. In another large bowl, whisk together the egg and ricotta; whisk in the milk, butter, oil, and lemon juice. Pour the mixture over the dry ingredients, then the sun-dried tomatoes and ½ cup of the Parmesan cheese. Stir quickly but thoroughly just to blend the ingredients; the batter will be stiff.

5. Using a large spoon, fill the muffin cups to the tops. Quickly sprinkle each with ½ teaspoon of the remaining Parmesan. Bake the muffins for about 25 minutes, or until deep golden brown and a toothpick pushed halfway into the center comes out clean. Loosen the muffins from their cups and let cool on their sides for 5 minutes before serving. When cool, store in a plastic bag. To reheat the muffins, place directly on the shelf of a 350° F. oven until hot and crunchy, about 15 minutes.

Mango-Macadamia Muffins

These exotic contemporary muffins have an old-fashioned appeal—delicate, tender, moist, and altogether wonderful. I like to use nonstick muffin tins so paper liners aren't needed. Not only do the muffins come out easily, they brown better, too. A firm, ripe mango weighing 1¼ pounds will yield about 1½ cups diced fruit.

MAKES 1 DOZEN

Topping

- ⅓ **cup finely chopped unsalted macadamia nuts (see Note)**
- ¼ **cup all-purpose flour**
- ¼ **cup firmly packed light brown sugar**
- ¼ **teaspoon ground cinnamon**
- 2 **tablespoons butter, softened**

Batter

- 1 **large egg**
- ½ **cup sour cream**
- ½ **cup milk**
- 1 **teaspoon vanilla extract**
- 4 **tablespoons (½ stick) butter, melted and cooled**
- 1½ **cups diced ripe mango**
- 2 **cups all-purpose flour**
- ½ **cup granulated sugar**
- 1 **tablespoon baking powder**

¼ **teaspoon baking soda**
¼ **teaspoon salt**

1. Make the topping. In a small bowl, combine the macadamia nuts, flour, brown sugar, cinnamon, and butter. Mash in the butter with a fork or rub in with your fingertips. Chill until needed.
2. Make the batter. Preheat the oven to 400° F. Grease a 12-cup muffin tin; be sure to lightly grease the area around the muffin wells so they won't stick as they rise over.
3. In a large bowl, whisk together the egg, sour cream, milk, vanilla, and melted butter. Fold in the mango.
4. In another large bowl, stir together the flour, granulated sugar, baking powder, baking soda, and salt. Make a well in the center of the dry ingredients and add the mango mixture. Fold together just to moisten and evenly blend; the batter will be lumpy.
5. Using a large spoon, quickly fill the muffin tins to the tops. Crumble the topping over the tops. Bake for 25 to 30 minutes, or until a toothpick inserted into the center emerges with just a few crumbs clinging to it. Cool in the pan for 5 to 10 minutes. Loosen the muffins and tilt each on its side to cool further. Serve warm or at room temperature.

Note: If only salted macadamia nuts are available, put them in a sieve and rinse off the salt. Dry briefly, shaking them in a small, dry skillet over low heat.

VARIATIONS

Lower calorie: **To cut some calories and cholesterol, use yogurt in place of the sour cream or 1 cup of buttermilk in place of the milk and sour cream. Vegetable oil can replace the butter.**

Substitutions: **Diced peaches, apricots, or nectarines can be used in place of the mango. Walnuts can replace the macadamia nuts.**

Bacon and Onion Corn Muffins

Savory muffins such as these are great for breakfast or brunch and also a good solution for soup and salad menus. These have a smoky bacon and sweet onion flavor punctuated with crunchy cornmeal. Another attractive quality is their ability to reheat in a delicious way—you can make them up to 2 days ahead!

MAKES 1 DOZEN

- ½ cup plus 2 tablespoons coarse yellow cornmeal
- 6 to 8 slices lean hickory-smoked bacon
- 1 tablespoon butter or bacon fat
- 1 medium onion, finely chopped
- 1½ cups all-purpose flour
- 2 teaspoons sugar
- 2 teaspoons baking powder
- ½ teaspoon baking soda
- ½ teaspoon salt
- ¼ teaspoon grated nutmeg
- 1 large egg
- 1 cup buttermilk
- ¼ cup vegetable oil
- 2 ounces coarsely grated sharp cheddar cheese (½ cup)

1. Preheat the oven to 400° F. Lightly grease a 12-cup muffin tin. Put ½ teaspoon of the cornmeal into each well and tilt the pan to coat the bottoms and sides of each cup. Tap out any excess.
2. In a large, heavy skillet, cook the bacon over moderate heat until crisp and golden brown. Drain and let cool. Crumble or chop with a knife; you should have ⅓ to ½ cup.
3. Melt the butter in a heavy, medium skillet over moderate heat. Add the onion and sauté until softened and lightly colored, about 5 minutes. Let cool.
4. In a large bowl, stir together the remaining ½ cup cornmeal, the flour, sugar, baking powder, baking soda, salt, and nutmeg.
5. In another bowl, whisk the egg to blend and then whisk in the buttermilk and oil. Make a well in the center of the dry ingredients and pour in the egg-buttermilk mixture. Add the bacon, onion, and cheddar. Stir just to combine the ingredients; do not overmix.
6. Using a large spoon, fill the muffin cups to the tops. Bake for 20 minutes, until golden brown and a toothpick pushed partially into the center comes out clean. Cool in the tins for 3 to 5 minutes. Serve hot or warm, or let cool completely and reheat directly on the oven shelf at 350° F. for about 15 minutes.

Candied Ginger-Almond Muffins

The big sweet-hot flavor of crystallized ginger is boosted with powdered ginger while ground almonds are boosted with almond extract. The two flavors complement each other and contribute great texture to these moist, buttery muffins. They hold up well and can be made a day ahead. Chinese crystallized ginger is much less expensive than that offered by spice manufacturers.

MAKES 1 DOZEN

- 1¾ cups all-purpose flour
- ⅓ cup sugar
- 1 tablespoon baking powder
- ½ teaspoon baking soda
- 1 teaspoon ground ginger
- ¼ teaspoon salt
- ½ cup blanched almonds, finely ground
- ½ cup finely minced crystallized (candied) ginger (3 ounces)
- 1 cup buttermilk
- 1½ tablespoons fresh lemon juice
- 1 large egg
- ¼ cup melted butter
- 2 teaspoons vanilla extract
- ½ teaspoon almond extract

Topping

- 1 tablespoon sugar
- ½ teaspoon ground cinnamon

1. Preheat the oven to 400° F. Grease a 12-cup muffin tin or line with paper cupcake liners.
2. In a large bowl, stir together the flour, sugar, baking powder, baking soda, ground ginger, and salt. Add the ground almonds and minced ginger to the dry ingredients. Make a well in the center.
3. In a medium bowl, whisk together the buttermilk and lemon juice. Whisk in the egg, melted butter, vanilla, and almond extract. Add the liquids to the dry ingredients and stir quickly just to blend (the batter will be slightly lumpy with the dry ingredients moistened). Working quickly, spoon the batter into the muffin tins, generously filling each.
4. In a cup, combine the sugar and cinnamon; quickly sprinkle over the tops of the muffins. Bake the muffins for 18 to 20 minutes, or until deep golden brown and a toothpick inserted in the center comes out clean. Let the muffins cool in the tin for a few minutes, then loosen and tilt each muffin on its side and allow to cool further. Serve warm, with butter, if desired.

Amaretto French Toast

Big, thick slices of challah (egg bread) or homemade-style white bread are drenched with milk and Amaretto, coated with sliced almonds, and then browned in butter for a marvelous breakfast or brunch treat. Get the bread at least a day ahead so it is slightly stale.

MAKES 6 SERVINGS

> 5 **large eggs**
> ¾ **cup milk**
> ⅓ **cup Amaretto liqueur**
> 3 **tablespoons granulated sugar**
> 1 **teaspoon vanilla extract**
> 3 **tablespoons butter**
> 6 **slices challah or firm white bread, each cut 1 inch thick**
> ⅔ **cup sliced almonds (wafer-thin)**
> **Confectioners' sugar, for serving**

1. Preheat a large, heavy nonstick griddle or skillet over moderate heat. When hot, reduce the heat to low to keep hot.
2. In a large, shallow bowl, whisk together the eggs, milk, Amaretto, granulated sugar, and vanilla.
3. Coat the griddle with ½ tablespoon of the butter. One at a time, dip 2 slices of the bread into the egg mixture for about 20 seconds to saturate. Sprinkle each slice with about 1½ tablespoons of the sliced almonds and invert onto the hot griddle. Repeat to coat the second slice. Cook until deep golden brown, about 3 minutes. Add ½ tablespoon of the remaining butter to the pan, turn the slices, and cook until golden brown on the second side, about 2 minutes. For each batch of 2 slices of French toast, you will use about 1 tablespoon butter. Repeat to cook all 6 slices, sprinkling with sliced almonds each time. Serve hot, sifted with a little confectioners' sugar.

American Sourdough Pancakes

I always have two or three different sourdough starters dormant in my refrigerator. That way all I have to do is take one out, let it come to room temperature, and spike it with some fresh flour and a pinch of sugar to make it lively again. These pancakes are especially delicious made ahead and then reheated in the microwave.

MAKES 12 TO 14 PANCAKES

1 **cup lively Sourdough Starter (page 296)**
¾ **cup milk**
2 **tablespoons sugar**
1 **cup all-purpose flour**
1 **teaspoon baking powder**
½ **teaspoon baking soda**
½ **teaspoon salt**
1 **large egg**
2 **tablespoons vegetable oil or melted butter**
  Butter and pure maple syrup, for serving

1. Preheat a large, heavy griddle for about 10 minutes before you cook the pancakes.
2. In a large bowl, stir together the starter with ½ cup of the milk and the sugar.
3. On a sheet of waxed paper or in a bowl, stir together the flour, baking powder, baking soda, and salt.
4. In a small bowl, combine the egg, oil, and remaining ¼ cup milk. Add the dry ingredients and the liquid ingredients to the starter mixture and stir to make a medium-thick batter. If it is too thick, a little milk can be stirred in, but do this after making a test pancake to see how the batter spreads.
5. When the griddle is hot, adjust the heat from low to moderate as required to brown the pancakes. Dip a paper towel in a little vegetable oil and lightly coat the griddle; recoat between batches. Ladle on about 3 tablespoons batter to test the heat and the consistency of the batter. (It is easiest to use a ¼-cup measure, not quite filling it.) The batter should spread out easily into a 4-inch pancake. Cook until bubbles appear all over and the edge begins to lose its sheen and appears slightly dry, about 1½ minutes. Turn with a spatula and cook for about 45 seconds longer. Repeat to use up all of the batter. If making ahead, cool the pancakes in a single layer, and then stack and refrigerate or freeze. To reheat 3 pancakes, arrange them in a single layer on a plate and microwave on full power for 30 to 40 seconds. Serve hot, with butter and maple syrup.

VARIATIONS

Additions: **For fruit pancakes, fold in about ¾ cup of finely diced peeled apple or banana or whole fresh blueberries.**

Serving: **Sprinkle the cooked pancakes with cinnamon after buttering them but before pouring on the maple syrup.**

Sour Cherry Coffee Cake

The big flavor of bright red sour cherries is a treat reserved for a brief season. Their flavor is perhaps best contrasted with brown sugar, as it is in this easy coffee cake.

MAKES 6 SERVINGS

2 cups fresh sour cherries, rinsed and stemmed

½ cup chopped walnuts (2 ounces)

¼ cup firmly packed light brown sugar

1 cup all-purpose flour

½ teaspoon baking powder

¼ teaspoon salt

¼ teaspoon ground cinnamon

2 large eggs

4 tablespoons (½ stick) butter, melted and cooled

½ cup granulated sugar

1 teaspoon vanilla extract

½ teaspoon almond extract

2 teaspoons confectioners' sugar

1. Cut or tear the cherries in half and remove the pits. You should have about 1½ cups pitted cherry halves. Drain them in a sieve for 5 minutes. Spread out on several layers of paper towels until needed.
2. Preheat the oven to 325° F. Grease a 9-inch springform pan or round cake pan with soft butter or shortening.
3. In a small bowl, combine the walnuts and brown sugar.
4. In a large bowl, stir together the flour, baking powder, salt, and cinnamon.
5. In a medium bowl, whisk together the eggs, melted butter, granulated sugar, vanilla, and almond extract. Add the mixture to the dry ingredients and stir quickly just to moisten and blend evenly. Pour half the batter into the prepared pan and spread evenly. Arrange all of the drained cherries over the batter. Sprinkle with the walnut mixture. Spoon on the remaining batter but do not spread out.
6. Bake for 40 to 45 minutes, or until golden brown and beginning to pull away from the sides of the pan. Cool in the pan for 15 minutes before serving. If using a springform pan, remove the sides. Sift the confectioners' sugar over the top and cut into wedges.

Raspberry-Buttermilk Scones

These delicate scones are slightly crisp around the edges, and the tender cakey centers are polka-dotted with raspberries. They taste best hot and fresh, yet they reheat beautifully. If you want to add jam, I recommend peach. These scones won't work with frozen berries.

MAKES 8

1½ **cups plus 2 tablespoons all-purpose flour**
¼ **cup sugar**
2 **teaspoons baking powder**
¼ **teaspoon baking soda**
¼ **teaspoon salt**
3 **tablespoons cold butter, thinly sliced**
½ **cup buttermilk**
1 **large egg**
2 **teaspoons vanilla extract**
1 **teaspoon pure raspberry extract (optional)**
½ **teaspoon almond extract**
1 **cup fresh raspberries**

1. Preheat the oven to 400° F. Lightly grease a baking sheet with shortening or softened butter.
2. In a large bowl, stir together 1½ cups of the flour with the sugar, baking powder, baking soda, and salt. Cut in the butter until the mixture resembles coarse meal. Make a well in the center and pour in the buttermilk. Add the egg, vanilla, and raspberry and almond extracts. Stir quickly just to blend the ingredients. Toss the raspberries with 1 tablespoon of the remaining flour; quickly stir in the soft dough.
3. Turn out the dough onto the prepared baking sheet and pat lightly into an 8-inch round. Dip a sharp knife in flour and cut into 8 equal wedges, cutting through all the way to the baking sheet. Do not separate the pieces. Sift the remaining 1 tablespoon flour over the top.
4. Bake for 15 to 18 minutes, or until golden brown. Serve hot or warm. To reheat the scones, place in a 350° F. oven for 5 to 10 minutes.

VARIATION

Substitutions: **Use blackberries or blueberries in place of the raspberries. The top can be dusted with cinnamon sugar instead of flour; just stir together 1 tablespoon sugar with ½ teaspoon ground cinnamon.**

Fruit and Desserts

Passion Fruit–Pineapple Sorbet

Sour Cherry Sorbet

Sangrita Sorbet

Cinnamon-Peach Ice Cream

Cherry-Amaretto Ice Cream with Chocolate Chips

Georgia Peach Freeze

Carmen Miranda Frozen Yogurt

Banana-Bourbon Ice Cream with Toasted Pecans

Chocolate Chunk Ice Cream Sandwiches

Berry-Berry Shortcake

Banana-Bourbon Chiffon Cake

Plum-Nuts Upside-Down Cake

Mile-High Peach Melba Cake

Blueberry-Cassis Cobbler

Dutch Apple Pie

Walnut-Pecan Pie

Strawberry-Chocolate Cream Pie

Milk Chocolate–Banana Cream Pie

Lemon-Lime Meringue Pie

Flaky Pastry

Cinnamon Crumb Shell

Chocolate-Cinnamon Crumb Shell

Milk Chocolate–Mocha Brownies

Chocolate Cream Frosting

Fudge Frosting

Fudge Brownies

Naughty Chocolate Mousse Cake

Espresso Fudge Mousse with Whipped Cream

Bonus Recipes

Roasted Pineapple   Easy, Crispy Homemade Ice Cream Cones

Brown Sugar   Baking Pastry Blind

Mocha-Cinnamon Iced Cappuccino

Passion Fruit-Pineapple Sorbet

Sweet, tart, and tropical, this icy velvet sorbet is a cinch to make when you use the frozen passion fruit juice that comes in 14-ounce bags and is available at Latin American grocery stores.

MAKES ABOUT 5 CUPS

> 1 cup sugar
> 1½ cups pure passion fruit juice with pulp
> 1 cup pineapple juice
> 2 teaspoons vanilla extract

1. In a saucepan, combine the sugar and 2½ cups water and stir over moderate heat until the sugar dissolves. Let the syrup cool to room temperature.
2. In a bowl, combine the sugar syrup with the passion fruit juice, pineapple juice, and vanilla. Cover and chill thoroughly.
3. Freeze the sorbet in an ice cream maker according to the manufacturer's instructions. Transfer to a container and freeze until solid.

Roasted Pineapple

Slow-roasting a whole pineapple intensifies the flavor and sweetness and makes it juicier. You let it cool completely in the oven after it has roasted.

Preheat the oven to 325° F. With a large, heavy knife, slice off most of the leafy top of a medium pineapple (ripe but not overly ripe), leaving just 1 inch of green intact. (You don't want to cut into the flesh or the juice will escape.) Place on its side in a nonreactive shallow roasting pan just large enough to hold it. Roast for 1 hour (if using a large pineapple, roast for 1½ hours). Do not open the oven door; just turn off the heat and let the pineapple cool for 1 to 1½ hours.

Slice off the top and bottom. Quarter the pineapple lengthwise and cut off the skin and eyes. Slice off the core from each wedge and cut the wedges lengthwise in half. These are especially delicious broiled with Louisiana Cane Sugar and allowed to cool and chill in the syrup that results.

To make cane sugar–broiled pineapple, preheat the broiler. Place the roasted pineapple wedges on an unslotted broiler pan, arranging them close together (you can also cut them into thinner wedges, halving them again if desired). Sprinkle with about ¼ cup of Louisiana Cane Sugar. Broil until speckled and browned, 3 to 4 minutes. Although they can be served hot, they are especially delicious chilled in the syrup.

PASSION FRUIT

The first thing that strikes you when digging into a passion fruit is a strong burst of sweet tropical fragrance. The center is full of seeds and pulpy juice that has an intense sweet-tart tropical flavor with floral undertones of lemon-lime. Because it is so strong, passion fruit juice is often used to flavor other fruit juices.

When buying the fruit fresh, look for dark purple wrinkled fruit that feels heavy for its size. Some varieties are pink-yellow or red-violet. In general, the smaller varieties are more intensely flavored. The juice yield of passion fruit is low, so you might consider buying blocks of the frozen pulp in a Latin American grocery store.

You can store passion fruit in the crisper drawer for a week or freeze them—whole—in a plastic bag for up to six months. Once thawed, they will be easy to puree.

Sour Cherry Sorbet

This is refreshing, tart, and tangy with a big sour cherry flavor, enhanced with sugar and spice. Either you have to make it during the short sour cherry season or pit the cherries when they're fresh and freeze them for later use.

MAKES ABOUT 1 QUART

3 cups pitted sour cherries
1 cup sugar
1/8 teaspoon ground cinnamon
1/4 cup kirsch
3 tablespoons fresh lemon juice
2 teaspoons vanilla extract
1/2 teaspoon almond extract

1. In a blender, combine the cherries, sugar, and cinnamon and process to a puree. Force through a medium sieve, discarding any bits of skin that remain behind.
2. Put the puree in a nonreactive medium saucepan and add 1 cup water and the kirsch. Bring to a boil, stirring frequently, over moderate heat. Reduce the heat and simmer for 2 minutes. Set aside to cool to room temperature.
3. Stir in the lemon juice, vanilla, and almond extract. Cover and refrigerate until chilled.
4. Transfer the mixture to an ice cream maker and freeze according to the manufacturer's instructions. Transfer to a freezer container, cover, and freeze until serving time.

Sangrita Sorbet

Not to be confused with sangria, *sangrita* (which translates as "little blood") is the popular Mexican spicy tomato-orange chaser for tequila. At first, this may sound like a strange combination, but the tomato is really a fruit, so it does make sense. Serve as a dessert or between the courses of a Mexican dinner.

MAKES ABOUT 3 CUPS

- 1 can (6 ounces) frozen orange juice concentrate, thawed slightly
- ¼ teaspoon grated orange zest
- 1 cup fresh orange juice
- ½ cup canned tomato puree
- ¼ cup fresh lime juice
- ¼ cup sugar
- 2 tablespoons tequila
- 1 tablespoon grenadine syrup
- 4 drops hot pepper sauce

1. In a large bowl, combine all of the ingredients with ½ cup water. Stir to dissolve the sugar.
2. Pour the mixture into an ice cream maker and freeze according to the manufacturer's instructions. Transfer the sorbet to a covered container and freeze until firm.

Cinnamon-Peach Ice Cream

This is a special ice cream reserved for the height of the summer peach season. It's a ritual in my house. The creamy custard base should be cooked well in advance so it is thoroughly chilled on ice cream–making day.

MAKES ABOUT 6 CUPS

- 1 cup milk
- 1 cup light cream
- 1 vanilla bean, or 2 teaspoons vanilla extract
- 3 large egg yolks
- 1 cup sugar
- 1 cup heavy cream
- 1½ pounds ripe peaches (4 large), peeled (page 16), pitted, and chopped
- 1 teaspoon ground cinnamon
- ½ teaspoon almond extract

1. In a heavy saucepan, combine the milk and light cream. Split the vanilla bean, if using, and scrape the seeds from inside; add the pod and seed pulp to the milk mixture and place over moderately low heat. If using vanilla extract, add it in step 2. Scald until bubbles appear around the edges; remove from the heat.

2. Put the egg yolks in a large bowl and whisk or beat with ½ cup of the sugar for 1 minute. Slowly whisk in the hot milk mixture. Return the mixture to the saucepan and stir over low heat until the custard just begins to simmer and becomes thick enough to lightly coat a spoon. Do not let the custard boil or it will curdle. Immediately transfer to a bowl set in a larger bowl of cold water and ice cubes. Stir to cool the custard quickly. If using vanilla extract, stir it in now. Cover with plastic wrap placed directly on the surface of the custard and chill for 6 hours or overnight.

3. Remove the vanilla bean, if using, scraping off any custard and seed pulp. Stir in the heavy cream. Return the custard to the refrigerator.

4. In a bowl, combine the peaches with the remaining ½ cup sugar, the cinnamon, and almond extract. Stir to dissolve the sugar. Cover and chill for 1 hour, stirring occasionally.

5. In the container of an ice cream maker, combine the cream mixture with the fruit mixture. Freeze according to the manufacturer's directions. Transfer the ice cream to the freezer for at least 2 hours before serving.

CINNAMON

What we buy in this country as cinnamon is almost always cassia, not *true* cinnamon. Both are the bark of tropical trees. Cassia has a more intense aroma and sharper cinnamon flavor because it contains more essential oil. But many aficionados choose true cinnamon (Ceylon cinnamon) because it has a more delicate, subtle flavor. A U.S. Food and Drug act of 1938 allowed the two types and terms to be interchangeable.

Cinnamon is sweet and pungent. It gives a sharp, pleasant burn to the tongue and contributes a sweet, spicy flavor unlike anything else. Nothing whets the appetite on a cold morning in quite the same way as a panful of homemade cinnamon rolls baking in the oven.

Cinnamon is an important ingredient in the savory cooking of India and Mexico. Mexican cooks use true cinnamon. Since it is often difficult to find, I sometimes substitute the commonly available ground cinnamon from spice shelves everywhere, using just a fraction, however, so there is just a background hint of flavor. It can easily overpower a savory sauce.

Cherry-Amaretto Ice Cream with Chocolate Chips

There's a big cherry flavor here, enhanced with Amaretto and chocolate. Just be sure to make it at the height of Bing cherry season during the summer. The fruit must macerate for at least 8 hours or overnight, so plan accordingly.

MAKES ABOUT 6 CUPS

1 **pound large, ripe, firm Bing cherries, stemmed, halved, and pitted**
¼ **cup Amaretto liqueur**
⅔ **cup sugar**
1 **teaspoon vanilla extract**
¼ **teaspoon almond extract**
2 **cups light cream**
1 **cup heavy cream**
4 **ounces semisweet chocolate, coarsely chopped**

1. In a large bowl, lightly mash the cherries with the Amaretto, sugar, vanilla, and almond extract. Cover and chill for 8 hours or overnight to macerate the fruit and dissolve the sugar.
2. Add the creams to the macerated fruit mixture; mix well. Put into an ice cream maker and freeze according to the manufacturer's instructions. When soft mounds form, add the chocolate. Transfer to a freezer container, cover, and freeze until solid.

Georgia Peach Freeze

This is thick like a milkshake or a malt, but with a fabulous peach flavor and smooth consistency. What could be simpler?

MAKES ABOUT 3½ CUPS (2 SERVINGS)

2 **large ripe peaches, peeled (page 16), pitted, and coarsely chopped**
¼ **cup Amaretto liqueur**
1 **tablespoon fresh lemon juice**
1 **teaspoon vanilla extract**
¼ **teaspoon ground cinnamon**
1 **pint vanilla ice cream**

1. In a food processor or blender, combine the peaches, Amaretto, lemon juice, vanilla, and cinnamon. Puree until smooth.
2. Add the ice cream and process to a creamy consistency. Pour into soda fountain glasses and serve right away.

Easy, Crispy Homemade Ice Cream Cones

Brittle-crisp homemade ice cream cones are full of toasty caramelized flavor. They are easy to make—toastier and tastier than commercial cones. They can be dipped in chocolate and dunked in chopped nuts for even more flavor and texture.

Although there are special cone-making machines on the market, you really don't need one. You might find, however, that an inexpensive artist's palette knife comes in handy for spreading the batter onto the baking sheets and for coating the insides of the cones with chocolate. (A small, flexible metal spatula will work almost as well for spreading the batter, and a pastry brush can be used to coat the insides of the cones with chocolate.)

To make 8 cones, preheat the oven to 425° F. Lightly grease and flour 2 baking sheets, tapping off the excess flour. Using a 6-inch pan lid or bowl as a pattern, trace rounds on the sheets with a knife tip.

In a medium bowl, whisk 2 large eggs with ¼ cup sifted confectioners' sugar until smooth. Stir in ½ teaspoon vanilla extract, ⅛ teaspoon ground cinnamon, ⅛ teaspoon salt, and ½ cup plus 2 tablespoons all-purpose flour to make a smooth batter.

Spoon 2 level tablespoons (a ⅛-cup measure if you have one) of the batter onto the center of each circle. Spread out the batter to completely coat the circles in an even layer. If desired, sprinkle each with about 2 teaspoons finely chopped nuts, such as hazelnuts, pecans, walnuts, peanuts, or macadamia nuts.

Bake the cones for 4 to 6 minutes, or just until the circles are golden brown around the edges and beginning to change color in the center. If they are browning too quickly, reduce the oven temperature by 10° to 25° F. It is important to watch the wafers as they bake at such a high temperature because they should not become too dark.

Working quickly, run a thin-bladed knife under 1 wafer and roll it into a narrow cone shape, rolling the plain ones so that the underside becomes the outside of the cone and the nut-coated ones so the nuts are on the outside. As they are shaped, place each upright in a small, narrow glass to cool. You must work quickly because the cookies are soft while warm but become crisp and unrollable upon cooling.

When cool, if you like, coat the entire inside of the cones with melted chocolate, or dip just the edges into chocolate and then into chopped nuts, coconut, or jimmies.

Start by melting about 1 pound of semisweet chocolate, stirring until smooth. Spoon a generous tablespoon of the chocolate into 1 cone and tilt. Use a palette knife or pastry brush to spread the chocolate into a thin, even layer. Return upright to its glass and repeat with the remaining cones.

To coat the edges, dip the open end of a cone into melted chocolate to form a scant ½-inch-wide band of chocolate around the edge. Roll the edge in chopped nuts, sprinkles, or shredded coconut. Return to the glass to harden. Fill the cones with ice cream and serve in tall stemmed glasses or wrap in waxed paper and eat out of hand.

VANILLA

The sweet, seductive fragrance and flavor of vanilla is so familiar to all of us that we might not even notice it—that is, unless it were taken away. Although vanilla is not a big flavor all by itself, it is so wonderfully complex that many of our favorite desserts would taste empty and weak without it. It is a building block to big flavor.

The flavor of vanilla (and here, the aroma is tremendously more important than the taste on the tongue) can range from fruity and flowery (even sharp and winey or musky) to heavy and robust. It is also delicately soft and sweet.

• MEXICAN VANILLA. This lovely, flavorful vanilla is soft and sweet with a good floral bouquet and well-rounded taste. It is good for both hot and cold dessert preparations.

• TAHITIAN VANILLA. Interestingly, originally this vanilla was developed for the perfume industry, so it is no surprise that it has a more fragrant floral bouquet than the other varieties. It has a strong aroma and is best when used in cold desserts, such as ice creams, pastry creams, and ganaches, where the fragrance comes through. It does not hold up well to heat, so is not the best choice for baking.

• MADAGASCAR VANILLA. Also called Bourbon vanilla beans, these have a heavy, robust flavor and deep, sweet aroma. The vanilla flavor is sharper, even winey, compared to the others. It is an excellent choice for baking because its flavor holds during heating.

• JAVA VANILLA. These beans generally are not of a very high quality. They are less expensive than the other varieties. Many extracts are made from Java beans and have a weaker, almost watery flavor. In general, if vanilla beans are not labeled as to origin, it is most likely they are from Java.

• HOMEMADE VANILLA EXTRACT. I think the very best vanilla extract is homemade. My favorite is a large, catchall jar that contains various vanilla beans from all over the world. I originally started it by steeping half a dozen vanilla beans in 2 or 3 cups of vodka with 1 cup of commercial vanilla extract. I have continued adding beans and extracts over the past ten years. Each time I scrape the pulp from a vanilla pod for a dessert, I add the pod to the jar. Sometimes I add whole slit pods As the supply depletes, I replenish it with some commercial extract or more vodka.

• COMMERCIAL VANILLA EXTRACTS AND ESSENCES. There are many types of vanilla extract and essences on the market. Essences have the best flavor. If you want to experiment with the specific brands of extracts, La Cuisine, Vann's Spices, and Nielsen-Massey produce high-quality extracts made from Mexican, Tahitian, and Madagascan vanilla beans.

Carmen Miranda Frozen Yogurt

Tangy and sweet, fragrant and fresh, are good phrases to describe this sensibly seductive treat. When choosing strawberries, pick the ones that have the sweetest strawberry aroma.

MAKES ABOUT 5 CUPS

> 1 pint ripe strawberries, quickly rinsed and hulled
> 1 large banana, peeled
> 1 can (6 ounces) frozen orange juice concentrate, thawed
> ½ cup sugar
> 2 teaspoons vanilla extract
> 1½ cups low-fat plain yogurt
> 1 cup light cream

1. In a food processor, combine the strawberries, banana, orange juice concentrate, sugar, and vanilla; process to a smooth puree. Cover and chill for at least 1 hour or as long as overnight.
2. In the container of an ice cream maker, combine the fruit puree with the yogurt and cream. Freeze according to the manufacturer's directions. Place in the freezer for at least 2 hours before serving.

Banana-Bourbon Ice Cream with Toasted Pecans

This ice cream was designed to go with the Banana-Bourbon Chiffon Cake (page 324), but it is absolutely delicious all by itself. Fresh pecans are toasted to bring out their fullest flavor, and you can add chunks of chocolate, if desired (see Variations). Make the custard base the day before you want to make the ice cream so it can chill thoroughly.

MAKES ABOUT 1½ QUARTS

> 3 cups milk
> 1 cup heavy cream
> 6 egg yolks
> 1 cup sugar
> 1 teaspoon vanilla extract
> 1 cup pecan halves (about 4 ounces)
> 1½ cups mashed ripe bananas
> 2 tablespoons Bourbon
> 1 tablespoon fresh lemon juice

1. In a large, heavy saucepan, combine the milk and cream over low heat. Scald until bubbles form around the edge. Set aside.

2. In a large bowl, combine the egg yolks and sugar and beat with an electric mixer until light in color, 2 to 3 minutes. Gradually beat in the hot milk mixture. Return the mixture to the saucepan and set over moderately low heat. Stirring constantly, cook until the custard is thick enough to lightly coat a spoon. It should be thick enough just as the mixture begins to simmer; do not let it boil or it will curdle. Immediately turn it out into a large bowl and set the bowl in a larger bowl that's partially filled with water and ice cubes. Stir the custard to cool quickly. Stir in the vanilla. Cover with plastic wrap placed directly on the surface of the custard and refrigerate until well chilled, at least 2 hours.

3. Preheat the oven to 325° F. Place the pecans in a small baking pan and toast, shaking the pan once or twice, until lightly toasted, about 15 minutes. Let cool, then coarsely chop.

4. In a food processor, combine the bananas, Bourbon, and lemon juice. Process to a smooth puree. Whisk the puree into the chilled custard base.

5. Transfer the mixture to the container of an ice cream maker and freeze according to the manufacturer's directions. Fold in the pecans and then transfer to the freezer and freeze until solid.

DISTILLED FLAVOR ESSENCES

Essences are pure, highly concentrated flavorings. Those made in France through the same distillation procedure used to make perfume are light-years ahead of any flavor extract you can buy in the supermarket here.

Because fresh fruit available in supermarkets can be less than flavorful, a few drops of a distilled essence will make the flavor blossom and taste sensational.

Dozens of flavors are available, such as wild strawberry, passion fruit, Key lime, framboise, apricot, raspberry, peach, pistachio, pineapple, caramel, coffee, cocoa, and vanilla.

They are available in two-ounce bottles from:

La Cuisine
323 Cameron Street
Alexandria, Virginia 22314
800-521-1176
Fax: 703-836-8925

Vann's Spices
1238 E. Joppa Road
Baltimore, Maryland 21286
410-583-1643
Fax: 410-583-1783

Both sources carry a complete line of high-quality flavorings, herbs, and spices.

Chocolate Chunk Ice Cream Sandwiches

Although you can eat the cookies all by themselves, the recipe included here is to make ice cream sandwiches. All of the homemade ice creams on pages 314 to 320 make fresh fillings for these cookies.

MAKES 7 TO 10 SANDWICHES

2 bars (3 ounces each) dark chocolate
1 cup all-purpose flour
½ teaspoon baking soda
½ teaspoon ground cinnamon
¼ teaspoon salt
8 tablespoons (1 stick) lightly salted butter, at room temperature
¾ cup firmly packed light brown sugar
2 teaspoons vanilla extract
1 large egg
1 cup chopped walnuts
1½ quarts ice cream, slightly softened

1. Preheat the oven to 350° F. Very lightly grease 1 to 3 baking sheets.
2. Break the chocolate bars into squares along the dividing lines, then coarsely chop, cutting each piece approximately in half on the diagonal.
3. In a large bowl, stir together the flour, baking soda, cinnamon, and salt.
4. In another large bowl, beat the butter with an electric mixer until fluffy, about 30 seconds. Beat in the brown sugar, ¼ cup at a time. Add the vanilla and the egg and beat until light in color, 1 to 2 minutes. Stir in the dry ingredients until blended, and then add the chocolate and walnuts to make a

stiff dough. (The dough can be prepared ahead of time and chilled, or used right away.)

5. To make 3-inch cookies, measure the cookie dough into 2-tablespoon portions and arrange on the prepared baking sheets, 6 to a sheet. Dip your fingers in water and pat each portion into a 2-inch round. (For 3½-inch cookies, use about 3 tablespoons of dough and pat them into 2½-inch rounds.)

6. Bake for 9 to 12 minutes, or until golden brown and set, reversing the sheets halfway through if necessary. Remove from the oven and let the cookies cool on the sheets for about 2 minutes. Remove with a spatula and let cool completely on racks.

7. Repeat with cooled baking sheets, lightly greasing again before shaping. Let the cookies cool thoroughly before assembling the sandwiches.

8. To assemble the ice cream sandwiches, spread ½ to ⅔ cup of the softened ice cream over the underside of 1 cookie and invert another cookie over that. Wrap individually in plastic and store in the freezer.

Berry-Berry Shortcake

This is a big old-fashioned dessert, updated to add more flavor. Grated lemon zest and nutmeg add their aromas to the shortcakes, while pureed raspberries double up the berry flavor with the strawberries. The luscious sauce is a beautiful deep ruby-red color that will surely leave its mark on anything you splash or drip it on.

MAKES 4 LARGE SERVINGS

Berries

- 2 pints small, ripe strawberries, rinsed and hulled, or large berries, halved
- ½ pint red raspberries
- ¼ cup orange liqueur, such as Grand Marnier, Cointreau, or Triple Sec
- ¼ cup granulated sugar
- 2 teaspoons vanilla extract
- 1 teaspoon fresh lemon juice
- ¼ teaspoon almond extract

Shortcakes

- ½ cup milk
- 1 teaspoon grated lemon zest
- ½ teaspoon grated nutmeg
- 1½ cups all-purpose flour

    2 tablespoons granulated sugar
    2 teaspoons baking powder
    ¼ teaspoon salt
    ¼ cup vegetable shortening
    2 tablespoons cold butter, thinly sliced

For Serving
    ½ cup heavy cream
    1 tablespoon confectioners' sugar
    ½ teaspoon vanilla extract

1. In a food processor, combine ½ cup of the strawberries, the raspberries, orange liqueur, granulated sugar, vanilla, lemon juice, and almond extract; puree. Force through a medium sieve; discard the seeds. Add the remaining strawberries to the sauce. Taste for sweetness; if desired, add 1 to 2 tablespoons more sugar. Cover and chill for at least 1 hour.

2. Make the shortcakes. Preheat the oven to 400° F. Have ready an ungreased baking sheet.

3. In a cup, combine the milk, lemon zest, and nutmeg.

4. In a large bowl, stir together the flour, granulated sugar, baking powder, and salt. Cut in the shortening and butter with a pastry blender or 2 knives until the particles are the size of peas. Spoon on half of the milk mixture and stir quickly just to blend. Spoon on the remaining milk and stir to form a dough that is moist enough to hold together.

5. Turn out the dough on a lightly floured surface and knead by folding over 5 or 6 times. Dust very lightly with flour, fold over the dough, and quickly pat into a 5-inch square. Cut lengthwise and crosswise into equal quarters and arrange the squares about 2 inches apart on the baking sheet. Bake until golden brown, 12 to 15 minutes. Let cool for at least 10 minutes before serving.

6. To serve, set a deep bowl and electric beaters in the freezer for about 10 minutes. Pour the cream into the bowl and beat with the cold beaters until fluffy. Add the confectioners' sugar and vanilla and beat briefly.

7. Split the shortcakes and place the bottom half on each of 4 dessert plates. Spoon half of the berries and sauce over the bottoms and set the tops in place. Spoon the remaining berries and sauce over and top with the whipped cream. Serve right away.

Banana-Bourbon Chiffon Cake

This is a gorgeous, golden-brown cake with a moist, delicate crumb. The big flavors of banana and Bourbon come through in every bite. It sports a mouthwatering Bourbon glaze and is double delicious when served with the Banana-Bourbon Ice Cream with Toasted Pecans on page 319. While the oven preheats, measure the dry ingredients and mash the bananas.

MAKES 10 TO 12 SERVINGS

Cake

8 large egg whites (1 cup)
½ teaspoon cream of tartar
2¼ cups sifted cake flour (not self-rising)
1¼ cups granulated sugar
1 tablespoon baking powder
½ teaspoon salt
5 large egg yolks
1 cup mashed very ripe bananas
½ cup vegetable oil
3 tablespoons Bourbon
1 teaspoon vanilla extract

Glaze

2 tablespoons Bourbon
1 tablespoon milk
1½ cups sifted confectioners' sugar

1. Preheat the oven to 325° F. Have ready an ungreased 10-inch tube pan with a removable bottom; *do not* use one that has a nonstick surface.
2. In a large, deep bowl, combine the egg whites and cream of tartar. Using an electric mixer, beat at moderately high speed until stiff peaks form; do not overbeat. Do not wash the beaters.
3. In a large bowl, stir together the flour, granulated sugar, baking powder, and salt. Sift into another bowl; sift back into the large bowl. Make a well in the center and add the egg yolks, mashed bananas, and oil. Spoon the Bourbon into a measuring cup and add enough water to measure ⅓ cup. Add to the well along with the vanilla. Using the electric mixer, beat the ingredients in the center of the well, gradually taking the dry ingredients in from around the edge as you beat, just until smooth. Pour one-third of this batter over the beaten whites and fold together quickly but thoroughly. Repeat twice more.
4. Pour the batter into the cake pan. Bake in the center of the oven for 55 minutes; *do not* open the oven door while the cake bakes or it may fall.

5. Increase the oven temperature to 350° F. and bake for 10 to 15 minutes longer, or until a wooden pick inserted in the center comes out clean. Immediately hang the pan upside down (most angel food cake pans have legs for this or a long neck in the center; if yours does not, hang upside down over the neck of a sturdy bottle). Let cool completely.

6. Invert the pan and run a thin-bladed long knife around the sides, pressing close against the pan so as not to cut into the cake. Remove the cake, still attached to the removable bottom, and run the knife underneath and around the neck. Invert, bottom side up, onto a large serving plate.

7. Prepare the glaze. In a small, heavy saucepan, bring the Bourbon and milk to a simmer. Add the confectioners' sugar and stir to dissolve. Immediately spread the glaze over the top of the cake with a long metal cake spatula. It looks nice to let the glaze drip down. Let cool until the glaze sets. Use a long serrated knife to slice the cake into wedges.

Plum-Nuts Upside-Down Cake

Slices of luscious red plums in a setting of caramelized walnuts crown this fragrant cardamom-scented cake. Especially delicious served slightly warm, it is a delightful choice for brunch, coffee break, or tea party.

MAKES 6 TO 8 SERVINGS

- 5 tablespoons butter
- ⅓ cup firmly packed light brown sugar
- 1 pound firm red plums, such as Santa Rosas (6 to 10 medium)
- ¾ cup chopped walnuts or pecans
- 1 cup all-purpose flour
- 1 teaspoon baking powder
- ⅜ teaspoon ground cardamom
- ¼ teaspoon ground cinnamon
- 3 large eggs
- ⅛ teaspoon salt
- ⅔ cup sugar
- ⅓ cup milk
- 2 teaspoons vanilla extract

Brown Sugar

You can make your own brown sugar. For 1 cup, packed, stir ¼ cup unsulphured molasses into 1 cup granulated sugar. Store in a zippered plastic bag, plastic container, or jar.

1. Preheat the oven to 325° F. This cake can be baked in a 9- to 10-inch cast-iron skillet or a 9-inch round cake pan. If using a cast-iron skillet, melt the butter directly in it over moderate heat (otherwise melt it in a medium skillet).

CARDAMOM

My mother used to take the seeds from white cardamom pods, easily prying them open with her fingernails, and wrap them in a linen napkin, and then pound them with a hammer until pulverized. She was a Finn, and *nisua*, a Finnish cardamom bread, has always been a tradition in our house.

Later I learned that Asian Indians add cardamom to curries, stews, and vegetable dishes, and even chew on the seeds as a breath freshener.

With a strong aromatic flavor reminiscent of airy ginger and pine, this tropical seed is the world's third most costly spice, after saffron and vanilla. It is so powerful and distinctive that just a little goes a long way.

White or buff-colored cardamom pods are mature and sun-dried, while the green pods are unripe and artificially dried. The green pods are not as strongly flavored, so use twice as many.

Always buy whole cardamom pods. If you buy them from an Indian store you will pay a fraction of the price fetched in supermarkets.

Since they are so soft they are easy to split and remove the seeds. Crush them in a mortar and pestle just before using for their biggest flavor and fragrance.

Store them in a sealed jar in a cool dark place.

Remove and reserve 2 tablespoons of the butter for the batter. Add the brown sugar and 1 teaspoon water to the pan and sizzle until foamy and caramelized, 2 to 3 minutes. (If using a cake pan, pour the mixture into it.) Let cool while you prepare the plums.

2. Cut the plums in half, following the natural indentation. Twist and pull the halves apart. Pry out the pits. Cut each half into 4 wedges.

3. Sprinkle 2 to 3 tablespoons of the chopped nuts into the center of the pan and sprinkle the remaining nuts around the edge. Starting around the outer edge, arrange the plum slices, skin sides down, in 2 tight concentric circles.

4. In a medium bowl, stir together the flour, baking powder, cardamom, and cinnamon.

5. Separate the eggs, putting the egg whites in a large, deep bowl and the yolks in a cup. Add the salt to the whites and beat with an electric mixer at medium speed until soft peaks form. Gradually beat in the sugar and beat until stiff glossy peaks form. Beat in the yolks and then the milk and vanilla. Add the flour mixture and reserved melted butter; beat just until blended.

6. Pour the batter over the prepared fruit and nuts, spreading it evenly. Bake for 40 to 45 minutes, or until deep golden brown and a toothpick inserted in the center comes out clean.

7. Run a knife around the edge of the cake to loosen it from the pan. Invert a serving plate over it and carefully invert to unmold the cake. Reposition any plums or nuts, if necessary, and let cool slightly. Serve warm or cool.

Mile-High Peach Melba Cake

This dramatically tall cake is luscious to look at and even better to eat. It's perfect for a summer party when both peaches and raspberries are in season. Of course, it's best to use tree-ripened peaches. This cake is, indeed, a full six to eight inches tall, so make sure there's room in the refrigerator, because the whipped cream must be chilled. It should be served on the day it's made.

MAKES 8 TO 12 SERVINGS

Cake

- 2 cups sifted cake flour (not self-rising)
- 2 teaspoons baking powder
- ¼ teaspoon salt
- 1 cup milk
- 2 tablespoons butter
- 4 large eggs, separated
- 1¼ cups granulated sugar
- 2 teaspoons vanilla extract

Filling

- 7 to 8 large ripe peaches (2½ to 3 pounds), peeled (page 16), pitted, and cut into ¾-inch slices
- 2 tablespoons fresh lemon juice
- 2 cups fresh raspberries, picked over but not rinsed
- 3 cups heavy cream
- 1 cup sifted confectioners' sugar
- ½ teaspoon vanilla extract
- ½ teaspoon almond extract
- ¾ cup seedless raspberry preserves
- ¼ cup brandy or Cognac

1. Make the cake. Evenly space 2 racks in the oven and preheat to 350° F. Grease and flour two 9-inch round cake pans, tapping out the excess flour.
2. In a large bowl, sift together the cake flour, baking powder, and salt.
3. In a small saucepan, combine the milk and butter and place over low heat until scalded.

4. Put the egg whites in a large, deep bowl. Beat with an electric mixer at medium speed until stiff peaks form. Beat in the egg yolks and then gradually beat in the granulated sugar. Add the vanilla and beat until blended. Sift half of the dry ingredients over the egg white mixture and fold in with a rubber spatula. Sift the remaining dry ingredients over and fold together quickly and thoroughly.

5. Divide the batter between the prepared pans. Bake for 28 to 30 minutes, or until the top springs back when lightly touched. When done, the edges of the cake will begin to pull away from the pans and a toothpick inserted in the center will come out clean. Cool the cakes in the pans on racks for 10 minutes. Run a sharp knife around the edge of each cake and turn out. Cool on racks, placing one layer right side up and the other upside down.

6. Make the filling. In a bowl, toss the peaches with the lemon juice. Choose the 12 best peach slices for the top of the cake; reserve. Choose the 12 best raspberries; reserve with the 12 peach slices.

7. Pour the heavy cream into a deep medium bowl and beat until half stiff. Sift in the confectioners' sugar, ¼ cup at a time, and beat until stiff peaks form. Beat in the vanilla and almond extract.

8. In a nonreactive small saucepan, combine the raspberry preserves and brandy over low heat. Bring to a simmer, stirring. Remove from the heat and keep warm or reheat when needed.

9. Assemble the cake. Using a long, serrated knife, split each cake layer horizontally in half. Starting with the layer that cooled upside down, place the top half upside down on a serving plate. Spread the layer with about ¼ cup of the raspberry preserve mixture. Arrange one-third of the peach slices and ½ cup of the raspberries over it. Spoon on about 1½ cups of the whipped cream. Add the next half cake layer and repeat the layering 2 more times. Top with the remaining layer and spread or pipe with the remaining whipped cream, making decorative swirls. Decorate the center and the top edges, alternating the peaches and raspberries. Chill until serving time.

Blueberry-Cassis Cobbler

This exciting cobbler, with its deep, purple-crimson filling and light, cakey topping, has a crisp sugar coating. It holds up well, so making it hours ahead of time is fine.

MAKES 6 TO 8 SERVINGS

    2 pints blueberries, rinsed, picked over, and drained
  ½ cup blueberry preserves
    2 tablespoons cornstarch
    1 tablespoon sugar
    1 teaspoon grated orange zest
  ¼ cup Crème de Cassis
    2 tablespoons fresh lemon juice
    1 tablespoon butter, cut into bits

Topping

  1½ cups all-purpose flour
  ⅓ cup plus 1 tablespoon sugar
    2 teaspoons baking powder
  ¼ teaspoon baking soda
  ¼ teaspoon salt
  ⅔ cup milk
    3 tablespoons butter, melted
    1 tablespoon fresh lemon juice
    1 teaspoon vanilla extract
       Heavy cream, for serving (optional)

1. Preheat the oven to 400° F. Butter a shallow 12 × 8-inch baking dish. Add the blueberries and blueberry preserves to the prepared dish and stir together.
2. In a cup, combine the cornstarch, sugar, and zest. Sprinkle over the blueberry and preserve mixture and toss to combine. Add the cassis, lemon juice, and bits of butter; toss again. Spread out evenly in the dish.
3. Prepare the topping. In a large bowl, stir together the flour, ⅓ cup of the sugar, the baking powder, baking soda, and salt. Make a well in the center. Add the milk, melted butter, lemon juice, and vanilla and stir just to blend into a slightly lumpy batter. Spoon the batter unevenly over the blueberry mixture; do not try to cover completely. Sprinkle the top with the remaining 1 tablespoon sugar.
4. Bake the cobbler for 25 to 30 minutes, or until bubbly and golden brown. Let stand for 20 to 30 minutes before serving. Serve hot or warm, topped with heavy cream, if desired.

Dutch Apple Pie

Here is a perfect apple pie for fall or any of the winter holidays. It has just one crust but there is plenty of the crunchy crumb-nut streusel topping to make everyone happy.

MAKES 6 TO 8 SERVINGS

> **Flaky Pastry (page 337)**
> 5 **large tart green apples, such as Granny Smiths or Greenings**
>   **(2½ pounds), peeled, cored, and cut into ½-inch slices**
> 2 **tablespoons fresh lemon juice**
> ⅔ **cup granulated sugar**
> ¼ **cup all-purpose flour**
> 1 **teaspoon ground cinnamon**
> ½ **teaspoon grated nutmeg**
> ¼ **teaspoon salt**
> ½ **cup sour cream**
> ⅓ **cup dark raisins (optional)**

Streusel Topping
> ½ **cup firmly packed dark brown sugar**
> ½ **cup all-purpose flour**
> ½ **cup chopped walnuts (4 ounces)**
> ½ **teaspoon ground cinnamon**
> ¼ **teaspoon baking powder**
>   **Pinch of salt**
> 4 **tablespoons (½ stick) butter, softened**

1. Preheat the oven to 425° F. On a lightly floured surface and using a lightly floured rolling pin, roll out the pastry to a 12-inch round. Loosely drape it into a 9-inch pie pan and fit against the bottom and sides of the pan without stretching the dough. Roll under the overhanging pastry all around to form a raised edge. Crimp decoratively.

2. Line the pastry with a sheet of aluminum foil, pressing lightly so it conforms; fill with pie weights, dried beans, or rice to keep the sides from slumping. Place on a baking sheet. Bake for 8 to 10 minutes, or until the edges are set. Carefully remove the weights and foil. Continue baking, pricking the bottom with a fork if it bubbles up, until set, about 5 minutes. Remove to a rack; reduce the oven temperature to 375° F.

3. In a large bowl, toss the apple slices with the lemon juice. Add the granulated sugar, flour, cinnamon, nutmeg, and salt; toss to coat. Stir in the sour cream and raisins. Turn the filling into the prepared shell and place on a baking sheet. Bake for 30 minutes while you prepare the topping.

4. In a medium bowl, stir together the brown sugar, flour, walnuts, cinnamon, baking powder, and salt. Stir in the butter with a fork, or better yet, use your fingers to rub it into the dry ingredients. Chill until needed.

5. When the pie has baked for 30 minutes, carefully remove it and crumble the streusel all over the top. Bake for about 20 minutes longer, or until golden brown. Cool on a rack. Serve slightly warm or at room temperature, cut into wedges.

VARIATIONS

Bigger flavor: **For a refreshing flavor enhancement, add 2 teaspoons grated orange zest to the apple filling and 2 teaspoons more to the streusel topping.**

Substitution: **Replace the raisins with diced dried apricots.**

Walnut-Pecan Pie

Chopped walnuts and spices add excitement to this rich, gooey filling with its crusty topping of pecans. It is a pie suitable for holidays and celebrations. Just be sure to use the freshest nuts you can find.

MAKES 8 SERVINGS

 Flaky Pastry (page 337), unbaked
1 cup coarsely chopped walnuts (about 4 ounces)
¼ cup honey
1½ teaspoons ground cinnamon
¼ teaspoon ground cloves
¾ cup firmly packed light brown sugar
¾ cup light corn syrup
4 tablespoons (½ stick) unsalted butter, melted and cooled
 to room temperature
4 large eggs, lightly beaten
¼ teaspoon salt
1 cup pecan halves (about 4 ounces)
 Whipped cream (optional)

1. On a lightly floured surface, roll out the pastry to a 12-inch round. Loosely drape it into a 9-inch pie pan and fit it into the pan without stretching the

dough. Trim the overhanging pastry so there is only ½ inch all around. Tuck it under, then use the tines of a fork to press all around. Chill the shell until needed.

2. Preheat the oven to 350° F.

3. In a small bowl, stir together the walnuts, honey, cinnamon, and cloves. In a large bowl, stir the brown sugar with the corn syrup until blended. Stir in the melted butter, eggs, and salt. Stir in the nut mixture until blended.

4. Pour the filling into the prepared pie shell and smooth the surface. Starting around the outside top edge, arrange the pecan halves, flat sides down, in concentric circles, placing them directly on the filling. Set the pie on a baking sheet. Bake for about 1 hour, or until the filling is puffed in the center and the edges are light golden brown. Cool the pie on a rack. As it cools it will level. Serve at room temperature, garnished with softly whipped cream, if desired.

Strawberry-Chocolate Cream Pie

I used to think that I liked only vanilla pastry cream with strawberries, until I realized how much I enjoy chocolate-dipped strawberries. The flavor combination is exciting and this recipe combines two favorite pies in one. The wild strawberry essence (page 320) is not a necessary addition, but it does contribute a bigger strawberry flavor. Make the shell and pastry cream well in advance. The first slice of a glazed pie is always difficult to remove, but it's easier if you start off by cutting 2 slices. You can also make individual pies (see Variation).

MAKES ONE 9-INCH PIE

Chocolate-Cinnamon Crumb Shell (page 338)
Chocolate Pastry Cream
- ⅓ cup sugar
- 2 tablespoons all-purpose flour
- 2 tablespoons cornstarch
- ⅛ teaspoon salt
- 1¼ cups milk, scalded and kept warm
- 2 egg yolks
- 3 ounces semisweet or bittersweet chocolate, finely chopped or grated
- 2 tablespoons butter
- 1 teaspoon vanilla extract

Glazed Strawberries

4 pints perfectly ripe strawberries, rinsed and hulled

⅔ cup sugar

2 tablespoons cornstarch

1 tablespoon fresh lemon juice

1 teaspoon vanilla extract

¼ teaspoon distilled essence of wild strawberry (optional)

Lightly sweetened vanilla whipped cream, for serving

1. Make the crumb shell well ahead of time and let cool to room temperature.

2. Prepare the chocolate pastry cream. In a heavy saucepan, stir together the sugar, flour, cornstarch, and salt. Whisk in the scalded milk all at once, blending thoroughly. Set over moderately low heat and, stirring constantly, bring to a boil. Simmer for 2 to 3 minutes, or until very thick.

3. Whisk the egg yolks in a large bowl. Off the heat, whisk the yolks into the thickened pastry cream. Return to low heat and simmer, stirring constantly, until *slightly* thickened, 2 to 3 minutes. Remove from the heat and stir in the chocolate, butter, and vanilla; stir until the chocolate melts. Transfer to a bowl set in a larger bowl containing ice water. Stir frequently to cool quickly. Pour the filling into the prepared pie shell. Cover with a sheet of waxed paper placed directly on the surface and chill until set, several hours or overnight.

4. Prepare the glazed strawberries. Reserve three-fourths of the best-looking berries for the shell; drain well on several layers of paper towels. Coarsely chop the

VARIATION

Single-serving pies: **You will need six 5-inch pie pans (which can be foil). Butter the inside bottom of each (not the sides). After mixing up the crumb shell ingredients, place ¼ cup into each pan, then divide any remainder evenly. Press into shells as you would for a large pie and bake on a sheet for 8 to 10 minutes. Fill each with a slightly mounded ¼ cup of chocolate filling. Save 18 of the best medium-sized berries for the tops, then place one of the largest berries in the center of each pie and surround with 6 or 7, placing them on their sides, star fashion. Glaze the berries, top with the three reserved berries for each pie, and glaze again. Chill as with the large pie.**

remaining berries. In a medium saucepan, combine the chopped berries with ¼ cup water over moderate heat and bring to a boil. Reduce the heat to moderately low and mash the berries with a potato masher as they simmer. Place a medium sieve over a bowl and pour in the sauce. Strain, pushing on the solids; discard the pulp. You will have 1 cup of thick juice.

5. In a large bowl, stir together the sugar and cornstarch. Whisk into the strawberry juice until blended. Transfer to a nonreactive medium saucepan and set over moderate heat. Stir in the lemon juice and bring to a boil, stirring constantly. Reduce the heat to low and simmer, stirring, until thick, 1 to 2 minutes. Remove from the heat and stir in the vanilla and strawberry essence. Use the glaze while it is hot or it will set.

6. Remove the chilled pie from the refrigerator and peel off the waxed paper. Saving the best half of the strawberries for the top, arrange the remaining berries over the chocolate. Spoon half of the hot glaze over them, napping each berry with a light coat of the glaze. Top with the remaining strawberries and nap with the remaining glaze. Refrigerate for at least 1 hour, or until well chilled. Cut into wedges and serve cold, with vanilla whipped cream.

Milk Chocolate-Banana Cream Pie

This chocolate version of a classic vanilla pastry cream filling is decidedly big in flavor, though rich, creamy, and comforting. The pie is a good slicer, too. The milk chocolate is made by combining semisweet chocolate with milk and sugar.

MAKES 8 SERVINGS

Cinnamon Crumb Shell (page 338)
⅔ cup granulated sugar
¼ cup all-purpose flour
¼ cup packed, leveled cornstarch
¼ teaspoon ground cinnamon
¼ teaspoon salt
2¼ cups milk, scalded and kept warm
2 large egg yolks
2 ounces semisweet chocolate, finely chopped or grated
2 tablespoons cold butter
1 teaspoon vanilla extract
½ teaspoon almond extract
3 large bananas

Topping

   1½ **cups heavy cream**
   3 **tablespoons sifted confectioners' sugar**
   ¼ **teaspoon vanilla extract**

1. Make the crumb shell well ahead of time so it has time to cool.
2. In a heavy saucepan, stir together the granulated sugar, flour, cornstarch, cinnamon, and salt. Pour in the scalded milk and stir or whisk constantly to make sure that all of the dry ingredients are dissolved around the edges of the pan. Cook the mixture over low heat, stirring constantly, until thick and boiling. Reduce the heat to very low and simmer, stirring, for 5 to 7 minutes until very thick.
3. In a large bowl, whisk the egg yolks. Gradually whisk in about half of the hot mixture until blended. Return the mixture to the pan and cook, stirring, until very thick, about 5 minutes longer. Remove from the heat and stir in the chocolate, butter, vanilla, and almond extract. Turn into a large bowl and let cool to room temperature, stirring frequently. This is best done over a bowl of ice water so the pastry cream cools quickly.
4. Peel the bananas and cut half of them into ¼-inch slices, letting the slices fall directly into the pie shell. Spread with half of the milk chocolate filling. Slice the remaining 1½ bananas over the top of the filling; spread with the remaining filling. Cover with plastic or waxed paper and chill until set, about 4 hours.
5. Make the topping. Pour the heavy cream into a deep medium bowl and beat until soft peaks form. Add the confectioners' sugar and beat until stiff, adding the vanilla just as the cream becomes stiff.
6. Remove the plastic wrap from the pie and spread the whipped cream over the top. It will look best if you save a spoonful and make a slightly raised swirl in the center. Cut the pie into wedges and serve cold.

VARIATIONS

Serving: **For a fancier pie, use 2 cups of heavy cream and an extra tablespoon of sugar. Use some of the whipped cream to make rosettes with a pastry bag fitted with a star tip. You can also decorate the top with chocolate shavings.**

Lemon-Lime Meringue Pie

The creamy citrus filling in this light-but-rich pie is tart and tangy and topped with clouds of meringue. Be sure to grate the zest before you squeeze the lemons and limes.

MAKES 8 SERVINGS

> Flaky Pastry (page 337)
> 1 cup sugar
> 5 tablespoons cornstarch
> 1/4 teaspoon salt
> 1/4 cup fresh lemon juice
> 1/4 cup fresh lime juice
> 4 egg yolks
> 1 teaspoon grated lemon zest
> 1 teaspoon grated lime zest
> 3 tablespoons butter
> 1/2 teaspoon vanilla extract
> 1 drop of green food coloring (optional)

Meringue

> 4 large egg whites
> 1/4 teaspoon cream of tartar
> 1/4 teaspoon salt
> 1/2 cup sugar

1. Bake the shell according to the instructions on page 339 and let it cool completely.
2. In a nonreactive medium saucepan, stir together the sugar, cornstarch, and salt. Stir in the lemon juice, lime juice, and egg yolks. Stir in 2 cups cold water. Place over moderate heat and bring the mixture to a full boil, stirring or whisking constantly. Reduce the heat to low and cook, stirring, for 1 minute. Remove from the heat and stir in the lemon zest, lime zest, butter, vanilla, and food coloring; stir until the butter melts. Pour the filling into the pie shell, place a round of waxed paper directly on the surface, and set aside on a rack to cool to room temperature.
3. Adjust an oven shelf to the lower third of the oven and preheat to 350° F.
4. Make the meringue. In a large, deep bowl, combine the egg whites, cream of tartar, and salt. Beat with an electric mixer at medium speed until soft peaks begin to form. Gradually beat in the sugar and continue beating until stiff and glossy, increasing the speed as the whites stiffen. Do not overbeat.
5. Remove the waxed paper from the pie filling and pile on the meringue, spreading it to slightly overlap the fluted edge of the piecrust (this is

important, or the meringue will shrink inward over the filling as it bakes or cools). Make decorative swirls with the back of a spoon.

6. Bake for 12 to 14 minutes, or until the top of the meringue is pale golden brown. Place on a rack and let cool to room temperature. Refrigerate just until chilled and set, 2 to 3 hours.

7. To serve, use a long, sharp knife dipped into hot water between each cut to keep the meringue from sticking.

Flaky Pastry

The key to successful pastry making is using ice-cold ingredients and blending the flour quickly so you do not activate the gluten and toughen the pastry.

MAKES ENOUGH PASTRY FOR 1 SINGLE-CRUST 9-INCH PIE

- 1½ cups all-purpose flour
- ¼ teaspoon salt
- 4 tablespoons (½ stick) cold butter, thinly sliced
- ¼ cup vegetable shortening
- 3 to 4 tablespoons ice water

1. In a large bowl, stir together the flour and salt. Add the sliced butter and spoon in the shortening in bits. With a pastry blender or 2 knives, cut in the butter and shortening until the particles are the size of oats. Sprinkle

on half of the ice water and stir quickly with a fork. Stir in about 1 table-spoon more ice water and then add drops of the remaining water to make a dough that will hold together.

2. On a sheet of waxed paper or plastic wrap, pat out the dough into a 5- to 6-inch round. Wrap and chill for at least 1 hour. If making farther ahead, seal in a plastic bag. If making more than 2 days ahead, freeze.

Cinnamon Crumb Shell

Adding ground cinnamon to vanilla cookie crumbs gives an extra dimension of flavor. This is a snap to put together and can be made well ahead of time.

MAKES ONE 9-INCH SHELL

> 1⅓ cups finely crushed vanilla cookie crumbs, such as
> vanilla wafers, ground in a food processor
> 2 tablespoons sugar
> ½ teaspoon ground cinnamon
> 5 tablespoons butter, melted

1. Preheat the oven to 350° F. Butter just the bottom of a 9-inch pie pan (do not butter the sides or the shell will slump).
2. In a large bowl, combine the cookie crumbs, sugar, and cinnamon. Drizzle half of the melted butter over the mixture and toss. Drizzle on the remaining butter and toss to moisten evenly. Dump the mixture into the pan. With fingertips, pat out the crumbs in a light even layer that is thicker toward the sides.
3. Bake for 8 to 10 minutes, until lightly browned. Cool in the pan on a rack.

Chocolate-Cinnamon Crumb Shell

Cocoa gives graham cracker crumbs a good deep chocolate flavor. The shell is perfect for the Strawberry-Chocolate Cream Pie (page 332) or the Milk Chocolate–Banana Cream Pie (page 334).

MAKES ONE 9-INCH SHELL

> 1⅓ cups fine graham cracker crumbs (from about 12
> whole graham crackers, ground in a food processor)
> 3 tablespoons sugar

3 tablespoons unsweetened cocoa powder
2 teaspoons ground cinnamon
5 tablespoons butter, melted

1. Preheat the oven to 350° F. Generously butter the bottom of a 9-inch pie pan (not the sides, or the shell will slump).
2. In a large bowl, combine the crumbs, sugar, cocoa, and cinnamon. Drizzle half of the melted butter over the mixture and stir to blend. Drizzle on the remaining butter and mix thoroughly. Turn into the prepared pie pan. With your fingers, scatter the crumbs all over to distribute evenly. First, establish the sides by pressing lightly, then the bottom. Once the thickness is even, press more firmly.
3. Bake for 8 to 10 minutes, or until lightly browned. Cool on a rack.

Baking Pastry Blind

When a pie shell is baked without a filling it is baked blind.

Position an oven rack in the center of the oven and preheat to 425° F.

On a lightly floured surface, roll out the pastry with a lightly floured rolling pin to a thin round about 12 inches in diameter. Fold it carefully in half (or in quarters, if you like) and pick up the round and place it in a 9-inch pie pan. Unfold it and ease it to fit the sides of the pan without stretching the dough (pie pastry has a memory and if you stretch it it will return to its old shape as it bakes). Roll the overhanging pastry tightly under all around and crimp the edges to make a decorative fluting all around.

Line the pastry shell with a sheet of aluminum foil, pressed to conform to the shape. Fill with pie weights or dried beans or rice (this keeps the shell from slumping). Place on a baking sheet and bake 10 to 12 minutes, until the edge has set. Carefully remove the foil and weights (picking all up together from the corner points of foil). Return the shell to the oven for about 5 minutes, until the bottom is firm and golden brown. After the first minute, check to see if it has bubbled up; if it has, tap with a long fork, then continue baking. Cool on a rack before filling. The shell can be made a day or two in advance.

NOTE: If the pastry should tear or break while you are working with it, simply moisten the area surrounding the tear with water and press another piece of dough on top.

Milk Chocolate-Mocha Brownies

Just a pinch of cinnamon is added to the chocolate and coffee to give background flavor to these brownies. They're rich and thin and can be spread with fudge frosting, if desired.

MAKES 16

> 8 ounces milk chocolate, coarsely chopped
> 1 tablespoon powdered instant coffee
> 4 tablespoons (½ stick) butter, at room temperature
> ½ cup sugar
> 2 large eggs, at room temperature
> 2 teaspoons vanilla extract
> ⅛ teaspoon ground cinnamon
>   Pinch of salt
> ½ cup all-purpose flour
>   Chocolate Cream or Fudge Frosting (page 340; optional)

1. Preheat the oven to 350° F. Lightly butter an 8-inch square baking pan. Line the bottom with a sheet of aluminum foil so it extends up 2 sides. Lightly butter the foil.
2. In the top of a double boiler, combine the chocolate and powdered coffee. Place over (not touching) simmering water and stir until melted and smooth. Remove the top of the double boiler from the heat and reserve.
3. In a large bowl, beat the butter with an electric mixer until fluffy. Beat in the sugar. One at a time, beat in the eggs, beating well after each addition. Beat for about 2 minutes longer, or until light in color. Blend in the vanilla, cinnamon, and salt. Add the chocolate mixture and the flour and beat quickly, just until blended.
4. Turn the batter into the prepared pan; smooth the top with a spatula. Bake for 20 to 25 minutes, or until a toothpick pushed into the center comes out with crumbs clinging to it. Cool in the pan on a rack for about 4 hours.
5. Run a sharp knife around the edges of the brownie to loosen it from the pan. Lift it out with the extended foil edges; peel off the foil. Cut into 2-inch squares or return to the pan and spread with the fudge frosting. Refrigerate until set, about 30 minutes. Cut into squares.

Chocolate Cream Frosting

This not-too-sweet, simple frosting is a cinch to put together. It tastes great on either of the brownie recipes on pages 340 and 344.

MAKES ABOUT 1 CUP

- $\frac{1}{2}$ **cup heavy cream**
- 8 **ounces semisweet chocolate, coarsely chopped**

1. In a small saucepan, combine the cream and chocolate over very low heat. Stirring constantly, heat just until the chocolate melts. Remove from the heat and allow to cool slightly, about 5 minutes.
2. Spread the warm frosting over the top of an 8-inch square pan of cooled brownies. Let set at room temperature for at least 3 hours before cutting, or chill for about 1 hour before cutting.

Fudge Frosting

Fabulously fudgy but not as sinful or wicked as the Chocolate Cream Frosting, this frosting is like fudge because it is cooked. It doesn't need to be chilled. Use it with either of the brownie recipes on pages 340 and 344.

MAKES ABOUT 1 CUP

- $\frac{3}{4}$ **cup sugar**
- $\frac{1}{2}$ **cup evaporated milk**
- 3 **ounces unsweetened chocolate**
- 1 **tablespoon butter**
- 1 **teaspoon vanilla**

1. Combine the sugar and evaporated milk in a heavy, medium saucepan. Place over moderate heat and stir until the mixture comes to a full boil. Immediately reduce the heat to low and boil gently for exactly 10 minutes. During the first minute dip a pastry brush in cold water and brush down the sides of the pan. This will prevent sugar crystals from forming and your frosting will remain creamy. Repeat again after 5 minutes.
2. As soon as the 10 minutes are up, remove from the heat and stir in the chocolate, butter, and vanilla. Stir until smooth and then spread over the top of an 8-inch square pan of cooled brownies. Let cool.

CHOCOLATE TIPS

UNSWEETENED (OR BAKING) CHOCOLATE

• Pure ground roasted cocoa beans in a solid state, also called pure chocolate liquor.

• Contains 50 to 60 percent cocoa butter.

• Flavor nuances vary from brand to brand, depending on the quality of the cocoa bean, roasting temperature, refining process, and blend of roasted varieties. Also, vanilla, roasted nuts, and extracts may be added.

• Substitute 3 tablespoons unsweetened cocoa powder plus 1 tablespoon butter or shortening for 1 ounce unsweetened chocolate.

• Good brands to try are Baker's, Callebaut, Ghirardelli, Hershey's, Peter's Jewel (Nestlé), Valrhôna, and Van Leer Family American.

SEMISWEET CHOCOLATE

• This category also includes chocolates called bittersweet, extra bittersweet, dark, and sweet.

• A blend of chocolate liquor, sugar, vanilla, or other flavorings, and sometimes additional cocoa butter. The level of sweetness varies from brand to brand.

• Blending chocolates for fragrance, flavor, and consistency is a fine art. The best chocolate combines flavor nuances that range from rich and nutty to deep-roasted and robust, with a bitter edge of chocolate flavor enhanced by just the right degree of sweetness and a pleasant, lingering aftertaste.

• To store chocolate, wrap tightly and keep in a cool (60° F.), dry place for up to two years. If stored too warm, it will "bloom." If stored too cold, it will "sweat."

• Good brands to try are Baker's, Callebaut, Droste, Ghirardelli, Hershey's, Lindt, Nestlé, Tobler, Valrhôna.

MILK CHOCOLATE

• Made from at least 10 percent pure chocolate liquor blended with sugar, milk solids, milk fat, cocoa butter, lecithin (a soybean-based emulsifier), and flavorings, such as vanilla.

• Sweeter, lighter, softer, and smoother than dark chocolate.

• Creamy-sweet with a fresh-milk or cooked-milk flavor and subtle flavor nuances of caramel, roasted nuts, and vanilla, depending on the roasting of the cocoa beans.

• More delicate than dark chocolate and must be treated more gently during cooking.

- Requires more flavor enhancement than dark chocolate.

- Store, tightly wrapped, in a cool (60° F.) place for about one year. Because of its high milk-fat content, it is more sensitive to heat and moisture and has a shorter shelf life than darker chocolates.

- Good brands to try are Ghirardelli, Hershey's, Lindt, Nestlé, Tobler, Valrhôna, and Van Leer.

WHITE CHOCOLATE

- Technically not really a chocolate since it contains no cocoa solids.

- Consists of approximately one-third each fat (cocoa butter and butterfat), milk solids, and sugar.

- Should be cream-colored or ivory; pure white color indicates that it was made from hardened vegetable fat, used as a confectionery coating.

- White chocolate is extremely sweet.

- Delicate, it lacks strength and stability and is sensitive to heat and moisture.

- Tightly wrapped and stored at 60° F., it will keep for up to one year.

- Good brands to try are Droste, Lindt, and Tobler.

UNSWEETENED COCOA POWDER

By using cocoa powder you can add intense chocolate flavor without adding the fat contained in solid chocolate. Because of its low fat content, cocoa will keep indefinitely when sealed in a tin and stored in a cool place.

DUTCH-PROCESS OR ALKALIZED COCOA

- Chocolate process perfected by the Dutch, to neutralize the natural acidity in chocolate.

- Has smoother flavor.

- Has deep, rich color.

- If a recipe calls for Dutch-processed cocoa (or European-style, or Dutched, or alkalized), you shouldn't add baking soda, since the acidity has already been neutralized.

- Good brands to try are Droste, Lindt, Poulain, Valrhôna, and Van Houten.

NONALKALIZED COCOA (UNSWEETENED COCOA)

- This is the most popular common type of cocoa, Hershey's being the most popular brand.

- Other good brands to sample are Baker's, Ghirardelli, and Nestlé's.

Fudge Brownies

Rich and chewy brownies become even fudgier when spread with frosting.

MAKES 16

> 8 tablespoons (1 stick) unsalted butter
> 3 ounces unsweetened chocolate, coarsely chopped
> 2 large eggs, at room temperature
> Pinch of salt
> 1 cup sugar
> 2 teaspoons vanilla extract
> ½ cup all-purpose flour
> ¼ teaspoon cinnamon
> 1 cup (4 ounces) coarsely chopped walnuts
> Chocolate Cream or Fudge Frosting (page 341; optional)

1. Preheat the oven to 325° F. Lightly butter an 8-inch square baking pan. Line the bottom with a sheet of aluminum foil so it extends up 2 sides. Lightly butter the foil.
2. In a small, heavy saucepan, melt the butter over low heat. Remove from the heat and add the chocolate. Leave it undisturbed for 5 minutes to melt and then stir until smooth. Reserve until needed.
3. In a large mixing bowl, combine the eggs and salt. Beat with an electric mixer for about 30 seconds, until frothy. Gradually beat in the sugar and continue beating until light in color, about 2 minutes longer. Add the vanilla and the melted chocolate mixture and beat until smooth. Add the flour and cinnamon and quickly beat, just until blended. Stir in the walnuts.
4. Turn the batter into the prepared pan; smooth the top with a spatula. Bake for 25 to 30 minutes, or until a toothpick inserted near the center comes out with a few crumbs clinging to it. Cool in the pan on a rack for about 4 hours. Run a sharp knife around the edge to loosen the brownie from the pan. Using the extended foil, pull out and peel off the foil. Cut into 16 small squares, or return to the pan and spread with fudge frosting. Let set for about 30 minutes, and then cut into squares.

Naughty Chocolate Mousse Cake

Here is the decadent dessert that I make when my certified chocoholic friends need a fix. It is made with close to 2 pounds of chocolate and only 2 tablespoons of flour! The divinity-smooth mousse filling is twice as thick as the fudgy layers. *Sinful* and *naughty-but-nice* are words that come to mind when I indulge.

MAKES 12 SERVINGS

Cake

- 8 ounces semisweet chocolate, coarsely chopped
- 4 tablespoons (½ stick) unsalted butter
- 4 large eggs, separated
- ¼ teaspoon salt
- ½ cup sugar
- 1 teaspoon vanilla extract
- 2 tablespoons all-purpose flour

Filling

- 1½ cups heavy cream
- 2 tablespoons sugar
- ⅛ teaspoon salt
- 12 ounces semisweet chocolate, coarsely chopped
- 8 tablespoons (1 stick) unsalted butter, sliced
- 2 egg yolks
- 2 teaspoons vanilla extract

- ½ cup seedless raspberry preserves
- 2 teaspoons brandy or rum

Milk Chocolate Glaze

- ¼ cup milk, scalded
- 8 ounces milk chocolate, coarsely chopped

Dark Chocolate Glaze (optional)

- 2 ounces semisweet chocolate, coarsely chopped
- 2 tablespoons hot water

Fresh raspberries and whipped cream, for serving (optional)

1. Make the cake layers. Preheat the oven to 350° F. Grease two 9-inch round cake pans. Line the bottoms with rounds of parchment or waxed paper; grease the paper.
2. Combine the chocolate and butter in the top of a double boiler over (not touching) barely simmering water. Stir occasionally until melted and

smooth. Remove the top of the pan and let cool slightly, until just slightly warm, 10 to 15 minutes.

3. Meanwhile, in a large, deep bowl, combine the 4 egg whites with the salt. Beat with an electric mixer until soft peaks begin to form. Gradually beat in ¼ cup of the sugar and beat until almost stiff. Reserve; do not rinse beaters.

4. In a large bowl, combine the egg yolks with the remaining ¼ cup sugar. Beat with the same beaters at high speed until thickened and light in color, 2 to 3 minutes. Beat in the vanilla; beat in the melted chocolate mixture. Quickly stir in about one-third of the beaten whites to lighten. Sift the 2 tablespoons flour over the top and fold in gently. Fold in the remaining beaten egg whites.

5. Divide the batter between the 2 pans, spreading it quickly but evenly. Bake for about 20 minutes, or until a toothpick inserted in the center comes out clean; when the surface is touched lightly it will spring back when done. Cool in the pans on wire racks for 10 minutes.

6. Run a knife around the edges of each cake layer to loosen from the pans. Invert a plate or cardboard round over each and turn out the layers, tapping firmly, if necessary, to free. Peel off the paper and set aside to cool completely. If a layer should break, do not worry, the pieces can be put together and the filling will hold them in place. (The layers can be made well in advance; wrap tightly and freeze.)

7. Make the filling. In a medium saucepan, combine the cream, sugar, and salt over low heat. Bring to a simmer and keep warm.

8. Put the chocolate in a food processor and finely grind. Add the butter, egg yolks, and vanilla and pulse to blend. Add the hot cream mixture and blend until smooth. Turn out into a medium bowl and let cool to room temperature, stirring occasionally. Chill the filling, stirring occasionally, until firmed up and thickened but not set, about 1 hour.

9. Beat the filling with an electric mixer at high speed until fluffy, 20 to 30 seconds.

10. Assemble the cake. In a small bowl, stir together the raspberry preserves and brandy. Place 1 cake layer upside down on a serving plate. Spread the top with half of the raspberry glaze. Turn all of the chocolate filling onto the cake and spread into an even layer. Spread the remaining raspberry glaze over the bottom of the second layer. Invert the layer over the chocolate filling. Holding a spatula vertically, even the filling all around the edge. Cover the cake with plastic wrap and chill until set, 1 to 2 hours, or as long as overnight.

11. Make the milk chocolate glaze. Combine the milk and milk chocolate in the

top of a double boiler and place over (not touching) barely simmering water. Stir occasionally until melted and smooth.

12. Remove the plastic wrap from the cake. Spread all of the warm milk chocolate glaze over the top and let it run down the sides, smoothing with a spatula to coat evenly. Chill until set, or add the optional dark chocolate glaze and chill until set.

13. Make the dark chocolate glaze. Combine the semisweet chocolate with 2 tablespoons hot water in the top of a double boiler. Let stand until the chocolate melts and then stir until smooth. Turn the chocolate into a small plastic zip-lock bag or make a small, parchment paper cone and fill with the chocolate. Snip a $1/16$-inch hole at one corner of the plastic bag or at the tip of the cone. Beginning in the center of the cake, decorate the top with a tight spiral design. Make small chocolate dots all around the outer edge and one in the center. Chill until set.

14. To serve, cut into 12 wedges and lift off slices with a spatula. If desired, decorate each with fresh raspberries and a dollop of whipped cream.

VARIATIONS

Substitutions: Use apricot preserves (heated and sieved before measuring) in place of the raspberry preserves and edge the top of the cake with toasted hazelnuts or walnut halves

Replace the raspberry preserves with orange marmalade, and if desired, replace the brandy with Grand Marnier. Use toasted pecans to top the cake.

Espresso Fudge Mousse with Whipped Cream

This is one of those desserts so rich and creamy that even a dab for dessert will fix any chocoholic. It's also one of the easiest desserts imaginable to put together, requiring only a good folding technique.

MAKES ABOUT 5 CUPS (8 SERVINGS)

Mousse

- 4 tablespoons (½ stick) unsalted butter, sliced
- 6 ounces semisweet or bittersweet chocolate, cut up
- 1 tablespoon powdered instant espresso coffee
- ¼ teaspoon ground cinnamon (optional)
- 1½ teaspoons vanilla extract
- ¼ teaspoon almond extract
- 3 large eggs, separated
  Pinch of salt
- 3 tablespoons granulated sugar
- ½ cup heavy cream

Topping

- ½ cup heavy cream
- 1 to 2 tablespoons confectioners' sugar
- ¼ teaspoon vanilla extract

1. Make the mousse. Set a 4-cup bowl or soufflé dish in the freezer to chill. Combine the butter and chocolate and place over barely simmering water until melted. Stir until smooth and remove from the heat. Spoon the coffee powder and optional cinnamon into a cup and add 1 tablespoon of boiling water. Stir to dissolve, then stir into the chocolate along with the vanilla and almond extract. Cool to room temperature. Whisk in the egg yolks.

2. In a large, deep bowl combine the egg whites and salt. Beat with an electric mixer until soft peaks begin to form; gradually beat in the sugar and beat until stiff glossy peaks form.

3. In a large, deep bowl, whip the heavy cream with an electric

ICED COFFEE

I wasn't a fan of iced coffee until I moved to New York City twenty years ago. It wasn't that I didn't like it; it was just that I had never been around anyone who drank it, so the whole concept sounded odd. But when that first hot and horribly humid summer weather arrived that year, and everyone around me was drinking iced coffee in the morning, hot coffee lost its appeal until fall.

Although I always drink hot coffee black, I find that iced coffee needs milk and sugar.

mixer until soft peaks form.

4. Gently stir a spoonful of the whites into the chocolate mixture to lighten it. Turn the mixture out over the remaining whites and fold together quickly but carefully. Fold in the whipped cream. Mound into the frozen bowl, cover, and place in the freezer for an hour.

5. Make the topping. Pour the cream into a deep medium bowl and beat until soft peaks form. Add 1 tablespoon of the sugar and beat to blend. Taste and add a little more sugar, if desired. Beat in the vanilla.

6. To serve, scoop the mousse into stemmed glasses and top with a dollop of whipped cream.

Mocha-Cinnamon Iced Cappuccino

Make this the night before you want to serve it.

Brew 4 cups of strong coffee, adding 1 tablespoon of ground cinnamon to the coffee grounds. I like a mixture of half French roast, half Colombian. Meanwhile, scald 2 cups of milk in a saucepan. Remove from the heat and stir in 3 ounces of chopped semisweet chocolate and ¼ cup sugar, until melted.

Combine the coffee with the chocolate milk and let cool to room temperature. Cover and chill. Stir in 2 teaspoons vanilla extract and shake vigorously in a jar until frothy. For a richer flavor and creamier consistency, add ¼ cup heavy cream before shaking. Serve cold, over ice.

ESPRESSO

It must have been the beatnik coffeehouses in this country during the 1950s that were responsible for the early misspelling of "espresso." The term actually refers to the "pressing out" of flavor from finely ground, Italian-roast coffee beans, rather than anything quick or "express."

Espresso is a dark, bitter, concentrated Italian coffee served in small cups. In Italy it is often enjoyed at stand-up espresso bars or at sidewalk cafés. Here at home it is most often served after dinner with the American additions of lemon rind and liqueur.

Because it is so intense, espresso makes a great flavoring for desserts and chocolates.

Sauces

Raspberry Applesauce

Leta Jo's Pineapple Cranberry Sauce

Fragrant Raspberry Sauce

Spiced Peach Sauce

Parmesan White Sauce

Simple Fragrant Tomato Sauce

Fresh Tomato Sauce with Bacon

Red-Hot Bolognese Sauce

Sausage and Mushroom Sauce

Hearty Wine-Braised Beef Sauce

Pesto

Creamy Pesto

Arugula Pesto

Rus's Own Barbecue Sauce

Cool, Creamy Dill Sauce

Curried Mayonnaise

Basil Mayonnaise

Jalapeño Mayonnaise

Avocado Mayonnaise

Chipotle Mayonnaise

Hoisin Mayonnaise

Tartar Sauce

Creole Rémoulade

Vietnamese Dipping Sauce (Nuoc Cham)

Wasabi-Soy Dipping Sauce

Soochow Black Vinegar Dipping Sauce

Hoisin Peanut Dipping Sauce (Nuoc Leo)

Taratoor Sauce

Plum Sauce

Tamarind Sauce

Bonus Recipe

Pork Chops with Plum Sauce

Raspberry Applesauce

Raspberries add great flavor and color to applesauce, but since the two fruits are not in season at the same time, I have used frozen raspberries here. This ruby-red sauce will taste best if you make it at least 6 hours ahead. It makes a fine accompaniment to poultry, pork, and cheese, and also a refreshing breakfast side dish.

MAKES ABOUT 4 CUPS

1 cup apple cider or juice
¼ cup sugar
2 tablespoons fresh lemon juice
1 cinnamon stick, 3 inches long
7 whole cloves
3 pounds (8 to 10 medium) McIntosh apples
1 package (10 ounces) frozen raspberries in light syrup, thawed
¼ cup dry sherry

1. In a nonreactive large saucepan, combine the cider, sugar, lemon juice, cinnamon stick, and cloves. One at a time, peel, quarter, core, and dice (¾ inch) the apples, dropping the pieces into the pot as they are cut. Bring to a boil over moderate heat. Reduce the heat to low, cover, and simmer for 20 minutes.

2. Place a medium sieve over a bowl and add the raspberries in syrup. Force through with a stiff whisk or rubber spatula. Discard the seeds. Add the raspberry puree and the sherry to the applesauce, and simmer, uncovered and stirring frequently, until thick as applesauce, 20 to 30 minutes. Let cool. Cover and chill, leaving the whole spices in the sauce. Remove the spices just before serving.

VARIATIONS

Substitutions: If available, ½ pint fresh berries may be used. Blackberries can replace the raspberries. For strawberry applesauce, hull and quarter 1 pint of strawberries. Cook, mashing, with ¼ cup sugar; force through a sieve and add to the applesauce in place of the raspberry puree.

Leta Jo's Pineapple Cranberry Sauce

My cousin's tart and tangy cranberry sauce cooks in 10 minutes, but should chill for at least a day to allow the flavors to blossom. It makes a great punctuation point on a plate of roast turkey, chicken, duck, pork, or beef.

MAKES ABOUT 2⅓ CUPS

> 3 cups (12 ounces) fresh or thawed frozen cranberries, rinsed and picked over
> 1 can (8 ounces) pineapple chunks in juice
> ½ cup sugar
> 1 large orange
> 1 teaspoon vanilla extract

1. In a food processor, combine the cranberries, pineapple chunks and juice, and the sugar. Pulse on and off until coarsely chopped. Transfer to a non-reactive medium saucepan.
2. Grate the zest from the orange and reserve it. Squeeze the orange; add ¼ cup of the juice to the saucepan. Bring to a boil over moderate heat. Reduce the heat to low and simmer, stirring occasionally, until thick and translucent, 8 to 10 minutes.
3. Remove the mixture from the heat and stir in the reserved orange zest and the vanilla. Set aside to cool to room temperature. Cover and refrigerate for at least 24 hours. Serve cold.

Fragrant Raspberry Sauce

I love the perfume and flavor of this simple luscious sauce.

MAKES ABOUT 1½ CUPS

> 2 cups fresh raspberries
> ½ cup sugar
> 1 teaspoon vanilla extract

1. In a small saucepan, combine the raspberries and sugar with ¼ cup water. Bring to a boil over moderate heat. Reduce the heat to low and simmer until softened, about 2 minutes.
2. Pour the raspberry mixture through a medium sieve set over a bowl. Force through with a stiff whisk or the back of a spoon; discard the seeds. Stir in the vanilla. Set aside to cool to room temperature; cover and chill. The syrup can be made a day or two ahead.

Spiced Peach Sauce

This is a cool summer sauce that requires tree-ripened peaches. Serve this over yogurt, ice cream, or sponge cake.

MAKES 4 SERVINGS

> 1½ pounds ripe peaches (3 large or 6 medium),
> peeled (page 16), pitted, and cut into ½-inch slices
> 2 tablespoons fresh lemon juice
> ⅓ cup honey, such as orange blossom or clover
> 2 teaspoons unsulphured molasses
> ½ teaspoon ground cinnamon
> ¼ teaspoon grated nutmeg
> 1 teaspoon vanilla extract
> ¼ teaspoon almond extract

In a large bowl, combine the peaches, lemon juice, honey, molasses, cinnamon, nutmeg, vanilla, and almond extract. Toss gently. Serve, or cover and chill for 30 to 60 minutes.

Parmesan White Sauce

You can use this simple white sauce for just about any recipe calling for plain white sauce. Parmigiano Reggiano adds the richness.

MAKES ABOUT 4 CUPS

> 4 tablespoons (½ stick) butter
> 1 tablespoon olive oil
> 1 garlic clove, minced or crushed through a press
> ½ cup all-purpose flour
> 4 cups milk, scalded
> ⅜ teaspoon freshly grated nutmeg
> ¾ teaspoon salt
> ¼ teaspoon black pepper
> ¼ cup dry white wine
> ½ cup grated Parmesan cheese, preferably Parmigiano Reggiano

In a heavy, medium saucepan, combine the butter, oil, and garlic over moderate heat. When the butter melts, sauté the garlic for 1 minute, then add the flour and cook, stirring constantly, until thick, about 1½ minutes. Pour in the hot milk and add the nutmeg, salt, and pepper. Stir constantly until the sauce comes to a boil and thickens. Pour in the wine, reduce the heat to low, and simmer, stirring, for about 3 minutes. Remove from the heat; stir in the Parmesan until melted. Put a paper towel over the top of the pan and add the pot lid to keep warm and stop condensation from dripping into the sauce. Stir occasionally and reheat if necessary.

Simple Fragrant Tomato Sauce

Try to find fresh, supple, bright green bay leaves for this sauce. They will remain intense even after drying, so when you find a source—perhaps a friend with a California bay laurel plant—stock up. Otherwise, obtain the most fragrant dried ones you can find.

MAKES ABOUT 5 CUPS (ENOUGH FOR 2 POUNDS OF PASTA)

- 1 tablespoon olive oil
- 1 tablespoon butter
- 1 medium onion, finely chopped
- 1 carrot, peeled and finely chopped
- 1 large garlic clove, minced or crushed through a press
- 3 bay leaves
- ½ teaspoon dried oregano or thyme, crumbled
- 1 carton (35 ounces) strained Italian tomatoes, such as Pomi, or 1 can (28 ounces) crushed tomatoes
- ½ cup dry white wine
- 1 teaspoon salt
- ¼ teaspoon pepper

1. Combine the olive oil and butter in a nonreactive heavy saucepan set over low heat. When the butter melts, add the onion and carrot and sauté gently until softened, about 5 minutes. Add the garlic, bay leaves, and oregano or thyme and cook for 2 minutes.
2. Add the tomatoes (if using canned crushed tomatoes, force them through a medium sieve with a stiff whisk), wine, salt, pepper, and 1 cup water. Bring to a boil over moderate heat. Reduce the heat to low and simmer, uncovered and stirring occasionally, for about 30 minutes, or until thickened slightly and intensified in flavor. Discard the bay leaves. Use right away, or cool to room temperature, cover, and refrigerate for up to a week.

Fresh Tomato Sauce with Bacon

Sliced smoky bacon adds a wonderful flavor to fresh, juicy summer tomatoes. Be sure to buy lean, hickory-smoked bacon for the best flavor.

MAKES ABOUT 5 CUPS (ENOUGH FOR 2 POUNDS OF PASTA)

- 6 to 8 slices lean, hickory-smoked bacon, cut into $\frac{1}{2}$-inch pieces
- 1 large onion, chopped
- 2 large garlic cloves, minced or crushed through a press
- 1 teaspoon dried basil, crumbled
- $\frac{1}{2}$ teaspoon diced oregano, crumbled
- 3 pounds ripe summer tomatoes (10 to 12 medium or 6 large beefsteak), peeled (page 15), seeded, and coarsely chopped with the juices reserved
- $\frac{1}{4}$ cup tomato paste
- $\frac{1}{2}$ cup dry white wine
- 2 teaspoons sugar
- 1 teaspoon salt
- $\frac{1}{8}$ teaspoon black pepper
- 1 bay leaf

1. In a nonreactive large saucepan over moderate heat, cook the bacon until crisp. Spoon off and discard all but 1 tablespoon of the fat.
2. Add the onion to the skillet and sauté until softened, 3 to 5 minutes. Add the garlic, basil, and oregano and cook for 1 minute. Add the tomatoes and their juices, the tomato paste, wine, sugar, salt, pepper, and bay leaf. Bring to a boil over moderate heat. Reduce the heat to low and simmer until slightly thickened and the flavors are blended, about 30 minutes. Taste for seasoning and add a little more salt, if necessary. Remove the bay leaf. Set aside to cool to room temperature. Cover and chill for up to a week.

VARIATIONS

Bigger flavor: Omit the dried basil and add $\frac{1}{2}$ cup slivered fresh basil during the last 5 minutes of cooking.

Addition: To make a marinara sauce, a 2-ounce can of drained chopped anchovy fillets can be added in the last 5 minutes.

Red-Hot Bolognese Sauce

The layering of flavors from herbs and wine and the reduction of wine and cream add intensity and richness. This sauce is complex and addictively delicious with subtleties, complexities, and undertones that you can taste on different levels at different times. Of course, you can add as little of the hot pepper as you like. You can finely chop the onions, carrots, and celery in a food processor. This sauce is delicious with lasagne, fettuccine, linguine, spaghetti, ziti, and rigatoni. And I've been known to eat it on top of *Bruschetta* (page 27). This recipe makes a lot, but it freezes well. And you will need 3 cups for the cannelloni on page 114.

MAKES ABOUT 12 CUPS (ENOUGH FOR 3½ POUNDS OF PASTA)

- 3 to 4 tablespoons olive oil
- 2 large onions, finely chopped
- 2 carrots, finely chopped
- 2 celery ribs, finely chopped
- 3 large garlic cloves, minced or crushed through a press
- 2 or 3 fresh jalapeño chilies, minced with the seeds
- 2 pounds lean ground beef sirloin or chuck
- 1 tablespoon salt
- 2 cups dry white wine
- 1½ cups half-and-half
- ½ teaspoon grated nutmeg
- 2 bay leaves
- 3 teaspoons dried basil, crumbled
- 3 teaspoons dried oregano, crumbled
- 2 teaspoons fennel seeds
- 1 teaspoon dried rosemary, crumbled
- ½ teaspoon dried red pepper flakes
- ½ teaspoon black pepper
- 1 can (28 ounces) whole tomatoes, with their juices, coarsely chopped
- 1 can (28 ounces) crushed tomatoes
- ¼ cup tomato paste

1. Spoon 3 tablespoons of the oil into a nonreactive large saucepan or casserole set over moderate heat. Add the onions, carrots, and celery and sauté until translucent, 8 to 10 minutes. Add the garlic and 2 of the jalapeños and sauté for 2 to 3 minutes.
2. Push the vegetables to the side of the pan and crumble in the beef. Sprinkle with the salt, increase the heat to moderately high, and sauté until half-cooked (the meat will be slightly pink), 3 to 5 minutes. Pour in 1½ cups of the wine, increase the heat to high, and boil until the liquid completely evaporates, 10

to 15 minutes (when this happens, the meat will begin to sizzle rather than simmer, so you will notice a difference in sound as the wine boils away).

3. Pour in the half-and-half and add the nutmeg, bay leaves, 2 teaspoons of the basil, 2 teaspoons of the oregano, the fennel seeds, rosemary, red pepper flakes, and pepper. Bring to a boil over high heat. Reduce the heat to moderate and boil, stirring occasionally, until the half-and-half is absorbed and/or evaporated, about 10 minutes.

4. Stir in the whole tomatoes and their juices and the crushed tomatoes. Stir in the tomato paste and 2 cups water and bring to a boil over moderate heat. Reduce the heat to low, partially cover the pot, and simmer very gently, stirring occasionally, for 3 hours. (If the sauce becomes too thick or dry, add a little water as it cooks. This probably will not happen, though, since the pot is partially covered.)

5. Uncover the pot and taste for heat intensity; add the remaining jalapeño, if desired. Pour in the remaining ½ cup wine and add the remaining 1 teaspoon basil and 1 teaspoon oregano. Partially cover again and simmer, stirring occasionally, until thick and rich, 1 hour longer. Remove the bay leaves. If making ahead, allow to cool to room temperature. Store in tightly covered containers in the refrigerator for up to a week or in the freezer for up to 6 months.

Sausage and Mushroom Sauce

You can make this with homemade sausages, or with commercial sausages. It will taste best if you make it a day ahead and reheat it, adding an extra ¼ cup of wine and ½ teaspoon each of basil and oregano. This robust sauce is especially suitable for hearty pasta shapes like orrechiette and cavatelli.

MAKES ABOUT 10 CUPS (ENOUGH FOR 3 POUNDS OF PASTA)

½ ounce dried porcini
1 pound sweet Italian sausages (page 258) or store-bought
2 large onions, finely chopped
3 large garlic cloves, minced or crushed through a press
1 tablespoon dried basil, crumbled
2 teaspoons dried oregano, crumbled
1 teaspoon dried thyme, crumbled
1 teaspoon fennel seeds
2 bay leaves
1 pound lean ground beef

2 pounds fresh mushrooms, stems trimmed and
   mushrooms finely chopped
1 can (6 ounces) tomato paste
1 can (28 ounces) crushed tomatoes
1½ cups full-bodied dry red wine
2 teaspoons salt
½ teaspoon black pepper
½ teaspoon dried red pepper flakes

1. Soak the porcini in ½ cup boiling water for about 30 minutes. Drain and finely chop; strain the soaking liquid through a fine sieve and reserve it. Set the
   porcini aside.
2. Place a nonreactive large saucepan or Dutch oven over moderate heat. Slit the
   sausage casings, if necessary, and crumble in the meat. Cook until lightly
   browned and no longer pink, 3 to 5 minutes. Tilt the pan and spoon out all
   but 1 tablespoon of the fat. Add the onions, garlic, basil, oregano, thyme,
   fennel seeds, and bay leaves and sauté until the onions soften slightly, 3 to
   5 minutes. Crumble in the ground beef and sauté for 4 minutes.
3. Add the fresh mushrooms to the pan and increase the heat to moderately high. Cook, stirring frequently, for about 10 minutes.
4. Stir in the tomato paste until blended; add the crushed tomatoes, wine, and 2 cups water. Add the porcini and their soaking liquid, along with the salt, pepper, and red pepper flakes. Bring to a boil over moderate heat. Reduce the heat to low and simmer, stirring occasionally, until thick and rich, about 1½ hours. Remove the bay leaves. If making ahead, allow to cool to room tempera-ture. Store in tightly covered containers in the refrigerator for up to a week or in the freezer for up to 6 months.

BAY LEAVES

There are two popular kinds of bay leaf: the subtle and sophisticated Turkish bay leaves—with their pale olive green color and wide shape—and the strong, pungent California bay laurel leaves—with their glossy dark green color and elongated shape.

Bay leaves give authority to sauces, stocks, and stews. Although Turkish bay leaves can be left in while stocks and sauces simmer for hours, California bay leaves have such a strong spicy-bitterness that you may want to leave them in for just a short time. Of course, this is a matter of personal taste.

If you chew on a bay leaf you will taste the penetrating qualities of pepper, mint, basil, and clove with perhaps a bit of cardamom thrown in. Remove bay leaves before serving dishes because the leaves are sharp and can cut the throat or stomach.

Hearty Wine-Braised Beef Sauce

The rich, deep flavor of this special sauce comes from the beef stock, red wine, and the well-browned little cubes of beef. This is not supposed to be a thick sauce, rather a saucy or soupy one that is perfect for pappardelle or fettuccine.

MAKES ABOUT 8 CUPS (ENOUGH FOR 2 POUNDS OF PASTA)

> 3 tablespoons olive oil
> 2 pounds lean beef chuck, cut in ¾-inch cubes
> 2 medium onions, finely chopped
> 3 large garlic cloves, minced or crushed through a press
> 1 teaspoon dried thyme, crumbled
> 1 teaspoon dried oregano, crumbled
> 1 teaspoon dried basil, crumbled
> 2 bay leaves
> 1 can (28 ounces) whole tomatoes, drained, seeded, and chopped
> 3 tablespoons tomato paste
> 4 cups Rich Brown Beef stock (page 74), Quick Beef Stock (page 75), or canned broth
> 1½ cups full-bodied dry red wine
> 1 teaspoon salt (optional)

1. Spoon 1 tablespoon of the olive oil into a nonreactive large casserole or Dutch oven and place over moderately high heat. Add half the beef cubes and stir quickly just once to coat with the oil and distribute evenly. Brown very thoroughly, without stirring, increasing the heat to high, if necessary, about 5 minutes. Turn the pieces and brown for 2 to 3 minutes longer. Remove the cubes and reserve. Add 1 tablespoon olive oil and brown the remaining beef. Remove and reduce the heat to moderate.

2. Add the remaining 1 tablespoon olive oil and the onions. Sauté until softened and lightly colored, about 5 minutes. Stir in the garlic, thyme, oregano, basil, and bay leaves and cook for 2 minutes. Stir in the tomatoes, tomato paste, beef stock, and red wine. Bring to a boil over moderate heat. Reduce the heat to low, partially cover, and simmer until the beef is very tender, about 2½ hours. If necessary, add a little water to prevent reduction and concentration. (The sauce is even better made a day ahead. Consider simmering it for 2 hours the first day, then adding ½ to 1 cup water and simmering it for about 30 minutes longer when reheating.) Taste for seasoning and add salt, if needed. Remove the bay leaves. Serve hot. If making ahead, cool to room temperature. Store in tightly covered containers in the refrigerator for up to a week or in the freezer for up to 6 months.

Pesto

There are hundreds of pesto recipes around, and most of them qualify as a big flavor, but this favorite version of mine has a couple of subtle variations: it's made with walnuts instead of the more costly pine nuts and the garlic is lightly sautéed instead of being the harsher, almost hot, raw garlic. This sauce is particularly good with linguine, fettuccine, and spaghetti, but is also great on gnocchi, in lasagne, and on pizza (see pages 120 and 286).

MAKES ABOUT 1¼ CUPS (ENOUGH FOR 1 POUND OF DRIED PASTA)

> 5½ tablespoons extra-virgin olive oil
> 2 large garlic cloves, minced or crushed through a press
> 3 cups lightly packed fresh basil leaves, rinsed and dried
> ½ cup chopped walnuts
> ½ cup freshly grated Parmigiano Reggiano
> 2 tablespoons grated Pecorino Romano cheese (optional)
> ½ teaspoon salt
> ¼ teaspoon pepper

1. Spoon 2 tablespoons of the oil into a small, heavy skillet set over low heat. Add the garlic and sizzle until soft and fragrant but not browned, about 1 minute. Remove from the heat and cool quickly, so the garlic does not continue to cook, by holding the bottom of the pan in cold water.
2. In a food processor, combine the basil, the remaining 3½ tablespoons olive oil, garlic oil, walnuts, Parmigiano Reggiano, Pecorino Romano, salt, and pepper. Pro-cess to a puree, scraping down the sides occasionally. Turn into a small bowl or container. If making ahead, pour a film of olive oil over the top to keep the pesto from darkening.
3. To serve with fettuccine, linguine, or spaghetti, spoon 3 to 4 tablespoons of the hot pasta cooking water into the pesto before draining the pasta. Then drain and toss the hot pasta with the sauce and serve right away.
4. To store any remaining pesto, cover with a film of olive oil and store, covered, in the refrigerator, where it will keep for a week.

Creamy Pesto

Often, when I am in the mood for pesto with pasta, this lighter, creamier version is the one I make. It's not at all like the richer traditional pesto from Genoa. The sauce is a vibrant, bright green color.

MAKES ABOUT 2 CUPS (ENOUGH FOR 1 POUND OF DRIED PASTA)

    4 ounces cream cheese
    ¼ cup olive oil
    2 large garlic cloves, minced or crushed through a press
    1 cup sour cream
    3 cups lightly packed fresh basil leaves, rinsed and dried
    ½ cup freshly grated Parmesan cheese
    ½ teaspoon salt
    ¼ teaspoon pepper

1. Cut the cream cheese into bits and put them in a food processor. Let come to room temperature while you continue.
2. Pour the olive oil into a small, heavy skillet set over low heat. Add the garlic and sizzle until soft and fragrant but not browned, about 1 minute. Pour the mixture over the cream cheese.
3. Add the sour cream, basil, Parmesan, salt, and pepper. Process to a puree. Transfer to a bowl or other container.
4. To serve, boil fresh or dried pasta until al dente. Drain and toss with the sauce. Serve right away, with more grated Parmesan for topping.

Arugula Pesto

The good peppery bite of arugula works well in a sauce when tossed with thin linguine and topped with Parmesan cheese.

MAKES ABOUT 2 CUPS (ENOUGH FOR 1 POUND OF DRIED PASTA)

    1 pound arugula, washed, stemmed, and dried
    1 cup peeled, seeded, and chopped fresh or canned tomatoes
    1 teaspoon salt
    ¼ teaspoon black pepper
    ⅓ cup extra-virgin olive oil

1. In a food processor or blender, combine the arugula leaves with the tomatoes, salt, and pepper. Process to a puree. With the motor running, gradually pour in the olive oil in a steady stream and process until smooth.
2. Boil the pasta until al dente; drain well and toss with the pesto. Serve topped with freshly grated Parmesan cheese. Cover any remaining pesto with a thin film of olive oil and refrigerate.

Rus's Own Barbecue Sauce

My good friend Rus cooks up this damn good barbecue sauce and gives it out to his friends. The sauce can be stored in the refrigerator for several months.

MAKES 6 CUPS

    2 tablespoons vegetable oil
    1 large onion, finely chopped
    4 large garlic cloves, minced or crushed through a press
    1 teaspoon dried red pepper flakes
    1 teaspoon dried basil, crumbled
  ½ teaspoon dried oregano, crumbled
  ½ teaspoon dried thyme, crumbled
  ½ teaspoon ground cumin
  ½ teaspoon celery seeds
  ¼ teaspoon ground cloves
    1 tablespoon chili powder
    1 teaspoon dry mustard
    2 teaspoons salt
    1 teaspoon coarsely cracked black pepper
    4 cups Beef Stock (page 74) or canned broth
    2 cans (6 ounces each) tomato paste
    2 cans (8 ounces each) tomato sauce
  ½ cup unsulphured molasses
  ¼ cup firmly packed dark brown sugar
  ¼ cup cider vinegar
  ¼ cup Worcestershire sauce
    2 tablespoons Kitchen Bouquet or caramel coloring
1½ tablespoons Liquid Smoke
  ¼ cup prepared brown or yellow mustard

1. In a nonreactive large saucepan or casserole, combine the oil and onion over moderate heat. Sauté, without browning, until softened, about 5 minutes. Add the garlic, red pepper flakes, basil, oregano, thyme, cumin, celery seeds, and cloves and cook for 1 minute. Add the chili powder, dry mustard, salt, and black pepper and cook for 1 minute.
2. Pour in the stock or broth and bring to a boil, stirring. Stir in the tomato paste, tomato sauce, molasses, and brown sugar. Add the cider vinegar, Worcestershire sauce, Kitchen Bouquet, and Liquid Smoke and bring to a boil, stirring frequently. Reduce the heat to low and simmer, stirring occasionally, until thick enough to coat a spoon and reduced to about 6 cups, about 1½ hours. Watch carefully during the last 30 minutes and do not let

the sauce scorch. (If the sauce should begin to scorch, immediately pour it into another pot without scraping the bottom of the pan.) Stir in the prepared mustard. The consistency of the sauce is really up to you: Some people like a thin barbecue sauce and some like it as thick as ketchup.

3. Let the sauce cool to room temperature. Cover and chill for at least 12 hours or as long as 2 or 3 months.

Cool, Creamy Dill Sauce

Serve this fragrant, tangy dill sauce with cold seafood, such as fish fillets, shrimp, mussels, scallops, lobster, and crab. It is also sensational with cold sliced chicken.

MAKES ABOUT 1½ CUPS

½ cup sour cream
½ cup low-fat plain yogurt
⅓ cup prepared mayonnaise
¼ cup chopped fresh dill
1 tablespoon fresh lemon juice
2 teaspoons Dijon mustard
¼ teaspoon salt
¼ teaspoon white or black pepper

Combine all of the ingredients in a medium bowl and whisk until blended. Cover and chill for at least 1 hour before serving.

Curried Mayonnaise

This is delicious on almost anything. It will taste best made at least a day ahead. But I expect you to know your own mind on egg safety.

MAKES ABOUT ¼ CUP

¼ cup rice vinegar
2 tablespoons dry sherry or rice wine
About ⅓ cup coarsely grated fresh ginger
2 large garlic cloves, minced or crushed through a press
⅔ cup peanut or other vegetable oil (not olive oil)
1 teaspoon homemade Curry Powder (page 385) or store-bought
1 large egg yolk

  ⅛ teaspoon cayenne pepper
   About ¼ teaspoon salt

1. In a nonreactive small saucepan, combine the rice vinegar, sherry, 2 table-spoons of the ginger, and the garlic over moderate heat. Boil until syrupy, 2 to 3 minutes. Strain through a sieve, pressing on the solids; you should have 1 tablespoon of liquid; discard the solids.
2. Spoon 2 tablespoons of the oil into a small pan and add the curry powder. Place over low heat and sizzle for 1 minute to intensify the flavor. Let cool.
3. Whisk the egg yolk in a large, deep bowl. Add the 1 tablespoon reduced vine-gar and whisk until frothy. Add 1 drop of the remaining peanut oil and whisk for 30 seconds. Whisk in the first teaspoon of oil drop by drop to make sure that the emulsion has taken. Then progress, adding more drops and then in a trickle, whisking all the while until the mixture is very thick. Gradually whisk in the curry-flavored oil and then the cayenne.
4. Put the remaining 3½ tablespoons grated ginger on several layers of damp-ened cheesecloth and wring out over a bowl to extract the ginger juice. Whisk 1 teaspoon (or a little more to taste) of the juice into the mayonnaise. Tightly cover and refrigerate for a day before using.

Basil Mayonnaise

One thing you should do with this fresh and fragrant mayonnaise is slather it over toasted kaiser rolls and add a big juicy grilled hamburger and a thick slice of beefsteak tomato. Another is to concoct a potato salad, adding a few other fresh herbs to play up the color and flavor: parsley, tarragon, and chervil should do it (and add a little sour cream to lighten the dressing).

MAKES ABOUT ¾ CUP

  ½ cup packed fresh basil leaves, rinsed and dried
  ⅔ cup prepared mayonnaise
  1 teaspoon extra-virgin olive oil
  ½ teaspoon fresh lemon juice

Combine all of the ingredients in a small food processor and process to a smooth puree. Transfer to a bowl and serve, or scrape into a jar and cover and chill for a couple days.

Jalapeño Mayonnaise

You can use commercially bottled pickled jalapeños for this fiery spread, but I encourage you to make a batch of homemade Pickled Jalapeños (page 384) the next time the chilies are on sale.

MAKES ABOUT ½ CUP

- ⅓ **cup prepared mayonnaise**
- 2 **to 3 tablespoons finely chopped pickled jalapeños**
- 1 **teaspoon extra-virgin olive oil**

In a small bowl, fluff up the mayonnaise with a fork by whipping it. Stir in 2 tablespoons of the jalapeños and the olive oil. Taste for heat and add a little more chili if serving to fire-eaters. Cover and store in the refrigerator for up to 1 week.

Avocado Mayonnaise

This rich, cool, green mayonnaise with its luscious flavor and consistency is lovely slathered in chicken and tomato sandwiches or tortas. In fact, it's perfect on BLTs and roast beef sandwiches as well.

MAKES ABOUT 1¼ CUPS

- 1 **perfectly ripe California avocado, such as Haas or Fuerte,**
     peeled and pitted
- ⅓ **cup prepared mayonnaise**
- 1 **to 2 tablespoons fresh lemon or lime juice**
- ½ **teaspoon salt**

In a food processor or blender, combine the avocado pulp, mayonnaise, 1 tablespoon of the lemon juice, and the salt. Puree until smooth. If desired, add more lemon juice to taste. Cover and chill. Serve cold. Use this within 2 or 3 days.

Chipotle Mayonnaise

Chipotle chili peppers have a big smoky flavor that carries beautifully through mayonnaise. Spoon this over any sandwich or burger that you like. If you can find the tiny (100-gram) cans of Bufalo Chipotles en adobo, I suggest that you stock up. A little goes a long way.

MAKES ABOUT ¼ CUP

> About ¼ cup canned chipotles in adobo, or 2 tablespoons
>   Chipotle Salsa (page 393)
> ⅔ cup prepared mayonnaise

1. Force the chilies and some of their sauce through a medium sieve. You will need about 2 tablespoons of puree for this recipe.
2. In a small bowl, stir together the mayonnaise and pureed chipotle. Cover and refrigerate for up to several weeks or use right away.

Hoisin Mayonnaise

Bottled Chinese hoisin sauce is made from fermented soybeans. It is slightly sweet and thick as jam. When added to mayonnaise, its full flavor and subtleties can be appreciated. Use this for sandwiches of roast pork or as a dip for cold sliced chicken breast and shrimp.

MAKES ⅔ CUP

> ½ cup prepared mayonnaise
> 2 tablespoons hoisin sauce
> 1 teaspoon fresh lemon juice
> ¼ teaspoon Oriental sesame oil

In a small bowl, stir together the mayonnaise and hoisin sauce to blend smoothly. Stir in the lemon juice and sesame oil. Cover and refrigerate until needed.

HOISIN SAUCE

Technically, hoisin sauce is a variation on brown bean sauce, with a distinct personality of its own. Its name translates to "sea freshness." It is thick and rich, strong, sweet, piquant, and complex, made from fermented mashed soybeans, sugar, rice vinegar, chilies, garlic, sesame oil, and wheat flour. Sometimes pumpkin is added.

Hoisin sauce is most often used as a dipping sauce or condiment for Peking duck, mu shu pork, and roast suckling pig. Koon Chun is a good label to look for. There is no substitute. Sometimes hoisin sauce is called barbecue sauce. Sealed in a jar and stored in the refrigerator, it will keep for a year or two.

Tartar Sauce

This delicious tartar sauce has a good, sharp flavor and tastes best after chilling. It is hot, sweet-and-sour, and pungent with mustard and olives.

MAKES ABOUT 1 CUP

> ⅔ cup prepared mayonnaise
> 2 tablespoons spicy brown mustard
> 1 tablespoon fresh lemon juice
> 1 teaspoon Tabasco or other hot pepper sauce
> ¼ cup finely chopped sweet pickles
> 3 tablespoons finely chopped pimiento-stuffed green olives
> 2 tablespoons finely chopped dill pickles

In a medium bowl, stir together the mayonnaise and mustard. Stir in the lemon juice and Tabasco. Fold in the sweet pickles, olives, and dill pickles. Cover and refrigerate for up to 2 weeks or chill and serve right away.

Creole Rémoulade

This bold sauce explodes with flavor and is luscious as a dip for cold shrimp or when spooned over seafood. I love it on the Rich-Boy Po' Boys on page 186. Creole mustard, especially Zatarain's, is well worth locating.

MAKES ABOUT 1¼ CUPS

> ½ cup prepared mayonnaise
> 2 tablespoons tomato paste
> 2 tablespoons Creole mustard
> 2 tablespoons extra-virgin olive oil
> 1 teaspoon red wine vinegar
> 1 teaspoon Worcestershire sauce
> 1 teaspoon Tabasco or other hot pepper sauce
> ½ cup minced celery heart
> ¼ cup minced scallion or white onion
> ¼ cup minced fresh parsley
> ¼ teaspoon salt

In a medium bowl, stir together the mayonnaise, tomato paste, and mustard with a fork until smooth. Gradually stir in the olive oil and then all of the remaining ingredients. Cover and refrigerate for up to 2 weeks or chill and serve right away.

Vietnamese Dipping Sauce (Nuoc Cham)

This addictively delicious, intriguing orchestration of flavors is deep and complex. The punctuation comes from Vietnamese fish sauce. It is perfect for anything Vietnamese and is especially delicious with Fresh Vietnamese Spring Rolls (page 32) and soft Fresh Vietnamese Spring Rolls (page 30). The sauce keeps well for weeks in the refrigerator.

MAKES ABOUT 1 CUP

- ⅓ cup Vietnamese or Thai fish sauce (*nuoc mam* or *nam pla*)
- ¼ cup rice vinegar
- 1 large garlic clove, minced or crushed through a press
- ½ teaspoon dried red pepper flakes
- 1 tablespoon sugar
- 1 tablespoon fresh lime or lemon juice
- 1 small carrot, peeled and cut into fine slivers, about ¹⁄₁₆ × ½ inch

1. In a nonreactive small saucepan, combine the fish sauce, rice vinegar, garlic, red pepper flakes, and ⅓ cup water. Bring to a full boil; remove from the heat. Stir in the sugar. Transfer to a small bowl and let cool to room temperature.
2. Stir in the lime juice and carrot. Transfer the sauce to a jar, tightly cover, and refrigerate for at least 12 hours before using. The spiciness can be increased by adding more pepper flakes. If you prefer raw garlic, add it after the initial liquid has cooled.

Wasabi-Soy Dipping Sauce

Serve this flavorful dipping sauce with the Poppy-Crusted Tuna Steaks on page 268, with the Ginger-Fried Oysters on page 270, or with cold shrimp.

MAKES ABOUT 3 TABLESPOONS

- 1 teaspoon prepared wasabi (page 269)
- 2 tablespoons Japanese soy sauce

In a cup, stir together the wasabi and soy sauce until smooth. Stir in 1 tablespoon cold water. If making ahead, store in a covered jar in the refrigerator.

Soochow Black Vinegar Dipping Sauce

The Chinese city of Soochow is famous for dim sum that are "as delectable and desirable as its women." So it's no wonder they serve such a delicious dipping sauce as this with their dumplings. There is no substitute for the black Chinkiang rice vinegar, but it is readily available in Chinese grocery stores and once you locate some it will keep for years. Make this sauce at least 1 day ahead. It will keep for a month in the refrigerator.

MAKES ABOUT ²/₃ CUP

> 2 tablespoons black Chinkiang rice vinegar
> 2 tablespoons clear rice vinegar
> 2 tablespoons light soy sauce
> 1 tablespoon dry sherry or Chinese rice wine
> 1 tablespoon grated fresh ginger
> 1 tablespoon sugar
> 2 whole scallions, thinly sliced

In a medium bowl, stir together the vinegars, soy sauce, sherry, and 3 tablespoons water. Stir in the ginger, sugar, and scallions. Cover and refrigerate for at least 1 day before serving in shallow dishes.

BLACK VINEGAR

Chinese black rice vinegar has a unique, deep, fermented flavor and concentrated sweetness. It makes a distinctive dark dipping sauce for dumplings (see page 135) that cannot be duplicated with any other vinegar. The best black vinegar comes from Chinkiang (just north of the Fukien province), so look for that name on the label. Black vinegar is relished by the Chiu Chow and Hakka peoples of China.

Hoisin Peanut Dipping Sauce (Nuoc Leo)

This is a simplified version of the classic Vietnamese dipping sauce, usually made with fresh peanuts. I have opted for peanut butter to make it simpler. Of course, hoisin sauce is a bottled Chinese condiment that will keep fresh in your refrigerator for a year.

MAKES ABOUT 1 CUP

> ¼ cup hoisin sauce
> ¼ cup smooth peanut butter

1   **tablespoon vegetable oil**
1   **large garlic clove, minced or crushed through a press**
¼   **teaspoon cayenne pepper**
⅓   **cup Chicken Stock (page 73) or canned broth**
1   **tablespoon Vietnamese or Thai fish sauce (*nuoc mam* or *nam pla*)**
1   **tablespoon chopped peanuts (optional)**

1. In a medium bowl, blend together the hoisin sauce and peanut butter. Stir in the oil, garlic, and cayenne. Gradually stir in the stock and fish sauce. Cover and chill until needed.
2. Transfer the sauce to a bowl and sprinkle with the chopped peanuts. Serve cold.

Taratoor Sauce

This quintessential Middle Eastern sauce—creamy, rich sesame sauce, tart and tangy with zesty lemon juice—is for spooning over falafel sandwiches (page 198), salads, and slices of roasted chicken. It is also a great dip for raw vegetables. If you prefer the flavor of raw garlic, skip the initial sautéing in step 1. Serve it cold or at room temperature.

MAKES ABOUT 1 CUP

1   **tablespoon Oriental sesame oil**
1   **large garlic clove, minced or crushed through a press**
½   **cup tahini (Middle Eastern sesame paste)**
¼   **cup fresh lemon juice**
½   **teaspoon salt**
¼   **teaspoon black pepper**

1. Spoon the sesame oil into a small skillet and add the garlic. Sizzle gently over low heat until fragrant but not browned, 1 to 2 minutes. Turn into a large bowl and let cool.
2. Add the tahini and stir with a fork. Gradually stir in ⅓ cup cold water and the lemon juice (the mixture will at first seize and thicken and then become creamy as you stir in more of the liquid) until creamy and emulsified. Stir in the salt and pepper. If the sauce is too thick, add a little more cold water. Serve or cover and refrigerate for up to a week or more. If the sauce thickens too much upon chilling, stir in a little more cold water.

Plum Sauce

With a deep, reddish-purple plum color and a fresh sweet-and-sour flavor, this simple sauce tastes even better a week after you make it. Slices of ginger and garlic add dimension and enhance the plum flavor but do not overpower because they are removed after making their contribution. This sauce is perfect for pork chops, but it also makes a great dip for shrimp. A dab on a plate next to roast duck is heavenly.

MAKES ABOUT 1½ CUPS

> 3 cups (1½ pounds) unpeeled, pitted, coarsely chopped purple, black, or blue plums
> ¼ cup firmly packed dark brown sugar
> ¼ cup rice vinegar
> ¼ cup dry sherry
> 8 large thin slices fresh ginger
> 1 large garlic clove, sliced crosswise into thirds
> 1 tablespoon soy sauce
> 1 teaspoon Oriental sesame oil

1. In a nonreactive medium saucepan, combine the chopped plums, brown sugar, vinegar, sherry, ginger, garlic, and soy sauce. Bring to a boil, stirring frequently, over moderate heat. Cook until slightly thickened, 8 to 10 minutes. Reduce the heat to low and simmer gently, stirring frequently, until thick as jam, about 5 minutes.
2. Place a medium sieve over a bowl and add the sauce. Fish out the garlic and ginger slices. Force the sauce through with a stiff whisk or rub through with a spatula; discard any solids. Stir the sesame oil into the sauce and let cool to room temperature. Cover and refrigerate for up to 2 weeks.

Tamarind Sauce

Sour with sweet undertones, simple and addictive, this sauce offers a burst of flavor with every lick. Tamarind is one of my favorite big flavors. You can buy chunks of tamarind pulp in Asian, Indian, and Chinese markets and it will keep well, wrapped, in the cupboard for years. I often spoon it over pork chops or roast chicken, and it is delicious with fried fish and shrimp. You can sauté fillets of sole or flounder that have been dusted with flour and browned, and then spoon this sauce over them.

MAKES ABOUT 1 CUP

¼ cup (about 2½ ounces) tamarind pulp

2 to 3 tablespoons honey

2 teaspoons finely grated fresh ginger

½ teaspoon salt

1. Break up the tamarind, pulling it apart into marble-size pieces; put them in a heatproof bowl. Pour in 1 cup of boiling water. Set aside to soak for at least 2 hours or overnight.
2. Place a medium sieve over a bowl and pour in the tamarind mixture. Push through with a whisk; discard any solids. You will have about 1 cup.
3. Transfer the sauce to a small bowl and stir in 2 tablespoons of the honey, the ginger, and salt. If too thick, stir in 1 to 2 tablespoons water. Taste for sweetness and add 1 tablespoon more honey, if desired. Transfer to a covered container and store in the refrigerator or serve right away.

Pork Chops with Plum Sauce

In a bowl, stir together ¼ cup each of spicy brown mustard, honey, soy sauce, rice vinegar, and minced fresh ginger. Stir in 2 large minced garlic cloves and ½ teaspoon each of cinnamon, ground cloves, black pepper, and cayenne pepper. In a large zippered plastic bag combine 4 to 6 1-inch thick pork chops with the marinade. Let marinate in the refrigerator for 6 to 24 hours then let come to room temperature 30 to 45 minutes before cooking.

Preheat a broiler or light a charcoal grill. Lightly oil a broiler pan or grill rack. Take chops from marinade and broil or grill until cooked through; broiling should take about 15 minutes and grilling about 20 minutes, although this can vary significantly depending on the heat source. Cook until the juices run clear.

To serve, spoon 2 to 3 tablespoons of plum sauce on each dinner plate and top with a pork chop. Spoon a little plum sauce over the top and a dab of Chinese mustard to one side. Serve hot. Singapore Rice Noodles (page 128) makes a great accompaniment.

Quick and Easy
and

Hot and Spicy Ketchup

Quick Chili Sauce

Hot Chinese Mustard

Chinese Ginger-Chili Sauce

Oriental Apricot Sauce

Fresh Horseradish

Honey-Mustard Pickle Chips

Condiments, Pickles, Relishes

Refrigerator Dill Pickles

Quick Kim Chee

Pickled Jalapeños

Avocado Salsa Verde

Salsa Verde

Jicama-Orange Salsa

Chunky Dill-Cucumber Salsa

Salsa Ranchera

Summer Salsa

Winter Salsa

Chipotle Salsa

Bonus Recipes

Curry Powder   Garam Masala   Huevos Rancheros
Macho Nachos

Hot and Spicy Ketchup

If you've ever made ketchup the old-fashioned way, from scratch, you know that you start with a bushel of ripe summer tomatoes that need skinning, chopping, and straining and a very long simmer—not to mention all those canning jars and sterilizing. In short, it's a full day's work. But not with this version. This is a quick and easy refrigerator ketchup that begins with canned tomato paste and requires just 15 to 20 minutes of cooking! And since it is kept in the refrigerator, you don't have to bother with old-fashioned canning procedures that are necessary for storing foods in a cupboard. Serve it liberally over hamburgers and the Cajun Fries on page 175 or use it to make Russian Dressing (page 99).

MAKES ABOUT 3 ½ CUPS

> 3 cans (6 ounces each) tomato paste
> ½ cup sugar
> 2 teaspoons salt
> 1½ teaspoons celery salt
> 1 to 1½ teaspoons cayenne pepper
> ½ teaspoon ground cinnamon
> ¼ teaspoon ground cloves
> ⅔ cup cider vinegar
> 1½ tablespoons Worcestershire sauce
> 2 teaspoons Angostura bitters

1. Decide what you are going to put the ketchup in after cooking: small or large jars or bottles with screw caps. (I save commercial chili sauce bottles because they have wide necks and are easy to fill, and look so beautiful filled with homemade ketchup.) Wash the containers in hot soapy water and rinse well.

2. In a nonreactive large saucepan, preferably nonstick, combine the tomato paste, sugar, salt, and celery salt. Add 1 teaspoon cayenne for a moderately hot ketchup or 1½ teaspoons for a very hot ketchup. Stir in the cinna-

ANGOSTURA BITTERS

This most popular of bitters is a strong concentrated liquid made from the bitter bark of one of two South American Citrus trees (*Galipea Officinalis* or *G. Gusparia*), which contain the intensely bitter angosturin. It is named for the old Venezuelan town of Angostura, though it is made in Trinidad. In addition to the bark, it contains cinnamon, cloves, nutmeg, mace, orange and lemon rind, and prunes that have been crushed with their pits.

Of course a splash adds a great flavor to cocktails and drinks, but a dash of bitter also adds complexity to cooked dishes, cutting sweetness and adding mystery. Try it with red beans.

mon and cloves; gradually stir in the vinegar. Add 1½ cups water along with the Worcestershire sauce and bitters. Bring to a boil, stirring frequently, over moderate heat. Reduce the heat to low and simmer, stirring frequently, until thick and rich, 15 to 20 minutes. (It is helpful to use a spatter screen because this stuff can spit scorching hot tomato balls at you as it boils.)

3. Using a wide funnel and a ladle, fill the containers. Let cool to room temperature. Cover and refrigerate for at least 2 days before using. Because of the high vinegar content, the refrigerated ketchup will keep for several months.

Quick Chili Sauce

It's easy and inexpensive to make your own chili sauce at home. This is stored in the refrigerator so there's no canning involved. Spoon it liberally over charcoal-grilled hamburgers or use it to top a meat loaf, such as the Harlem Meat Loaf on page 226.

MAKES ABOUT 4 CUPS

> 1 can (16 ounces) crushed tomatoes
> 1 can (6 ounces) tomato paste
> ½ cup firmly packed dark brown sugar
> 1 small onion, grated or ground in a food processor
> 1½ teaspoons celery salt
> 1 teaspoon salt
> 1 teaspoon ground cinnamon
> 1 teaspoon cayenne pepper
> ½ teaspoon ground cloves
> 1 cup cider vinegar
> 1 tablespoon Worcestershire sauce

1. In a large nonstick saucepan, stir together the crushed tomatoes, tomato paste, and brown sugar. Add the onion, celery salt, salt, cinnamon, cayenne, cloves, vinegar, and Worcestershire sauce and stir to combine. Bring to a boil, stirring frequently, over moderate heat. Reduce the heat to low and simmer, stirring frequently (if you have a spatter screen, use it, otherwise cook uncovered, but the chili sauce will spatter as it cooks), until very thick, 15 to 20 minutes.

2. Remove from the heat and let cool to room temperature. Then pour into jars, cover, and refrigerate.

Hot Chinese Mustard

Here's my favorite formula for a sinus-clearing hot mustard dipping sauce. Serve with the dumplings on page 135 or with spring rolls (pages 30 to 32). For double dipping (and twice the tingling), serve alongside the Chinese Ginger-Chili Sauce (below). This is an easy recipe to cut in half should you want only 2 tablespoons of the powerful stuff. Make it at least an hour ahead.

MAKES ABOUT ¼ CUP

> ¼ cup Colman's dry mustard
> 1 tablespoon rice vinegar
> ½ teaspoon salt

In a small heatproof bowl or cup, combine the mustard, vinegar, and salt. Add 2 tablespoons of boiling water and stir until smooth. Cover and refrigerate for at least 1 day before serving. If the mustard becomes too thick, stir in 1 or 2 teaspoons water before serving. Serve in shallow bowls for dipping.

Chinese Ginger-Chili Sauce

This is a hot dipping sauce for dim sum and dumplings that has plenty of flavor, thanks to the ginger, garlic, chili, soy sauce, and sesame oil. Make this at least 1 day ahead; it will keep in the refrigerator for several weeks.

MAKES ABOUT ⅔ CUP

> 2 tablespoons vegetable oil
> 2 tablespoons minced fresh garlic
> 1 tablespoon dried red pepper flakes
> 1 large fresh green jalapeño chili, minced with the seeds
> ¼ cup minced peeled fresh ginger
> 3 tablespoons rice vinegar
> 1 tablespoon soy sauce
> 2 teaspoons sugar
> ½ teaspoon salt
> 1 teaspoon Oriental sesame oil

1. In a nonreactive small saucepan, combine the vegetable oil, garlic, red pepper flakes, and jalapeño over moderate heat. Sizzle, stirring, until softened and fragrant but not browned, about 2 minutes. Turn into a medium bowl.
2. Stir in the ginger, vinegar, soy sauce, sugar, salt, and sesame oil. Cover and refrigerate for at least 1 day before serving. Serve in shallow dipping dishes.

Fresh Horseradish

Fresh horseradish has so much more flavor than bottled varieties that it is well worth making. Make this at least an hour before you want to use it.

MAKES ABOUT ½ CUP

> 1 piece fresh horseradish root 3 to 4 inches long, peeled
> ⅓ cup rice vinegar or white vinegar
> ½ teaspoon salt
> ½ teaspoon sugar

Finely grate the horseradish into a small bowl until you have ½ cup lightly packed. Stir in the vinegar, salt, and sugar. Cover and let stand for 1 hour, or cover and refrigerate until needed.

HORSERADISH

This 12- to 15-inch fleshy white root with its nubby brown skin belongs to the mustard family. It has virtually no aroma until you scratch its skin, and then it will emit a sharp, penetrating scent similar to mustard oil. Horseradish enrages the taste buds and nostrils with its powerful, highly volatile oils and hot, pungent flavor. It also clears the sinuses.

Freshly grated horseradish is folded into whipped cream to make a classic accompaniment to roast beef. It is also a favorite flavoring for shrimp cocktails, oysters, vinegars, and mustards. It is a perky condiment to add to potato salad or serve with cold chicken or beets.

Oriental Apricot Sauce

Here is a fragrant sweet and sour dipping sauce for Oriental dumplings and spring rolls. I like to serve it alongside Hot Chinese Mustard for a good contrast of flavors.

MAKES ABOUT ⅔ CUP

> ½ cup apricot preserves, heated and served before measuring
> 1 tablespoon soy sauce
> 1 tablespoon rice vinegar or white vinegar
> 2 teaspoons Oriental sesame oil

In a small bowl, mash the apricot preserves with a fork. Stir in the soy sauce, vinegar, and sesame oil. If making ahead, cover and refrigerate. Serve in shallow bowls for dipping.

Honey-Mustard Pickle Chips

Here's another of my no-can canning recipes. You make a batch of crunchy pickle slices and bathe them with a silky honey-mustard dressing. They are a cinch to put together and you just store them in the refrigerator, where they remain crisp and crunchy. Serve alongside sandwiches and hamburgers with potato chips.

MAKES ABOUT 5 CUPS

- 2 pounds medium Kirby cucumbers (8 to 12)
- 4 cups ice cubes
- 2 onions, peeled, halved lengthwise, and thinly sliced
- 3 tablespoons coarse (kosher) salt or sea salt
- 1 teaspoon powdered alum (available with the spices in supermarkets)
- ¼ cup firmly packed brown sugar
- 3 tablespoons all-purpose flour
- 1 tablespoon dry mustard
- 1 teaspoon ground turmeric
- 1 teaspoon ground ginger
- ½ teaspoon ground cinnamon
- ½ teaspoon celery seeds
- 7 whole cloves
- ¾ cup cider vinegar
- ½ cup honey
- 2 tablespoons prepared brown mustard or Dijon mustard

1. Rinse the cucumbers and brush them with a vegetable brush to dislodge any grit. Trim off the ends and cut the cucumbers into ¼-inch slices. Combine them in a large bowl with the ice cubes, onions, salt, and alum; toss and let stand for 2 hours, tossing occasionally. Drain. Rinse well with cold water and drain again.

2. In a nonreactive heavy saucepan, rub the brown sugar, flour, and dry mustard together with your fingertips to combine. Add the turmeric, ginger, cinnamon, celery seeds, and cloves. Whisk in the vinegar and the honey.

3. Place over moderate heat and bring to a boil, stirring constantly. Simmer until thickened, about 2 minutes. Remove from the heat and stir in the prepared mustard.

4. Pour the hot pickling sauce over the cold vegetables and toss. Set aside to cool to room temperature. Cover and chill for at least 1 day before serving. They will keep for up to several months in jars in the refrigerator. Serve cold.

TURMERIC

Turmeric still has the unfortunate reputation that paprika had a couple decades ago: a spice to be used merely as coloring and not for flavor.

Not so. This robust tropical herb of the ginger family contributes its strong yellow color, to be sure, but it also gives a distinct pepper-mustard-cardamom flavor with a fragrant, earthy-clay dimension that I find addictive. It contributes an edge of bitterness, too.

The turmeric plant has rhizomes, or swollen stems, that grow just beneath the surface of the soil, similar to ginger. The rhizomes are dried and then finely ground into powder. Turmeric combines the properties of both spice and dye.

Turmeric is sometimes used as an inexpensive substitute for saffron and is occasionally regarded as the poor cousin of ginger. But in Asia it is highly esteemed, and rightfully so.

Turmeric adds its bright yellow color to hot dog mustard and curry powder. It is also an important ingredient in bread-and-butter pickles and pickled cauliflower.

Store it in a dark, cool place to avoid discoloration.

Refrigerator Dill Pickles

Crunchy, juicy, sour dill pickles are especially good on charcoal-grilled hamburgers with sliced summer tomatoes and mayonnaise. Making these pickles takes just a few minutes of your time each day for 2 days, and the result can be enjoyed after just 1 additional day. There is no canning involved and the pickles will keep well for at least 6 months in the refrigerator.

MAKES ABOUT 2 QUARTS

> 2 pounds medium Kirby cucumbers (8 to 12)
> ½ cup plus 1 tablespoon coarse (kosher) or pickling salt
> 2 bay leaves
> 2 teaspoons coriander seeds
> ½ teaspoon dried red pepper flakes
> 1 cup cider vinegar
> 3 large garlic cloves, sliced
> ½ cup fresh dill sprigs, or 1 tablespoon dried dill
> 1 spray dill seed, or 1 teaspoon dried dill seeds

1. Rinse the cucumbers and lightly brush them with a vegetable brush to dislodge any sand. In a nonreactive crock or large bowl, combine 5 cups of

cold water with ½ cup salt; stir to dissolve the salt and add the whole cucumbers. Submerge them with a plate or a ceramic lid and weight down with bricks or heavy cans. Let stand at room temperature for 2 days, checking occasionally to make sure that the cucumbers are submerged in the brine. Drain, rinse well, and drain again.

2. In a medium saucepan, combine 1 cup water with the remaining 1 tablespoon salt, bay leaves, coriander seeds, and red pepper flakes. Bring to a boil. Remove from the heat and let cool to room temperature.

3. In a large bowl, combine 2 cups cold water with the vinegar, garlic, dill sprigs, dill seeds, and cooled bay leaf mixture. Choose a bowl, crock, or wide-mouthed jar that will hold the pickles (I have a cookie jar that is perfect), and combine the brine and cucumbers. Weight them down, if necessary, to submerge. Refrigerate for at least 24 hours before serving. Keep stored in the refrigerator.

CORIANDER SEEDS

The coriander plant gives us two flavors in one: the spicy dried seeds, called coriander seeds; and the fresh, fragrant leaves called cilantro, fresh coriander, or Chinese parsley (page 61). (The roots can be eaten too, and they have a similar flavor to the leaves but with a nutty dimension.)

The seeds have a warm, distinctive aroma and mild sweet flavor that suggest a combination of lemon and sage. They contribute a very slight numbing sensation on the tongue.

The flavor of coriander works well with other seeds, and it is an important ingredient in curry powder. Its flavor and aroma improve with slight aging, though as with all spices, coriander diminishes after reaching its peak.

Experiment a little, adding coriander seed to dips, sauces, and stuffings. Lightly toast the seeds in a dry skillet over moderate heat for a minute or so. Then crush them in a mortar or pulverize in a spice grinder.

The best bargain is a large bag of seeds from an Asian or Indian market. Store in a jar in a cool, dark place.

Quick Kim Chee

Classically, the spicy pickled Korean cabbage called kim chee is naturally fermented and takes at least 3 to 4 weeks to make. In this quick version I have cheated to speed things up, adding vinegar instead of waiting for nature to sour the cabbage. Kim chee is delicious with grilled beef (burgers or *bue goki*) and poultry dishes.

MAKES ABOUT 5 CUPS

1 medium napa cabbage (about 2 pounds)
2 medium pickling cucumbers, such as Kirbys (4 ounces each)
¼ cup coarse (kosher) salt
1 tablespoon grated fresh ginger
1 large garlic clove, minced or crushed through a press
1 tablespoon sugar
1 tablespoon sweet paprika
¼ to ½ teaspoon cayenne pepper
1 to 2 tablespoons soy sauce
¼ cup rice vinegar
⅓ cup sliced whole scallions

1. Trim away and discard any wilted or bruised outer cabbage leaves. Cut the head crosswise into 1½-inch slices. Discard the core end.
2. Trim the ends from the cucumbers, halve them lengthwise, and spoon out any seeds. Cut crosswise into ¼-inch slices.
3. Combine the cabbage and cucumbers in a large bowl. Sprinkle 3 tablespoons plus 1 teaspoon of the salt over the vegetables; toss. Let stand for 1 hour, tossing occasionally.
4. Fill the bowl with cold water, swish the vegetables in the water, and drain. Repeat to rinse off all of the salt.
5. In a medium bowl, combine the ginger, garlic, sugar, paprika, ¼ teaspoon of the cayenne, 1 tablespoon of the soy sauce, and the remaining 2 teaspoons salt. Stir in the vinegar and 1½ cups cold water. Add the cabbage, cucumbers, and scallions. Toss together; cover with plastic wrap placed directly on the surface. Refrigerate for several hours or overnight before serving. Taste and add ¼ teaspoon more cayenne and 1 tablespoon more soy sauce, if desired.

VARIATION

Kim chee burger: For each 4 ounces of ground beef, fold in about ¼ cup chopped kim chee. Grill, broil, or pan-fry the burger as you usually would (see page 185).

Pickled Jalapeños

I always have some of these in my refrigerator. I put them on hamburgers, club sandwiches, and tuna salad sandwiches. Sometimes I even add them to potato salad or macaroni salad. They have a good oregano-spiced flavor, good heat, and good sharpness from the vinegar. They are also easy to make and keep well in the refrigerator for months.

MAKES 3 TO 4 CUPS

- 1½ **pounds medium to large fresh jalapeño chilies**
- 2 **tablespoons coarse (kosher) salt or sea salt**
- 3 **tablespoons vegetable oil**
- 3 **large garlic cloves, sliced**
- 1 **teaspoon dried oregano, crumbled**
- 1 **teaspoon cumin seeds**
- 10 **black peppercorns**
- 5 **whole cloves**
- 3 **bay leaves**
- 1 **tablespoon sugar**
- ½ **cup cider vinegar**

1. Chilies contain volatile oils that can irritate or burn. (You may want to wear protective gloves when you work with them. I never bother with this practice myself, since I seem to lose all my sensitivity when I put on a pair of gloves. In any case, avoid rubbing sensitive areas, such as your eyes, after working with them.) Slice off the stem ends and cut the jalapeños lengthwise into quarters. Slice off as much or as little of the seeds and ribs as you want. The more you leave on, the hotter they will be. Combine the jalapeños and salt in a large bowl. Let stand for 2 hours, tossing occasionally. Drain through a sieve set over a bowl; reserve all of the liquid.

2. Spoon the oil into a nonreactive large skillet or sauté pan set over moderate heat. Add the garlic, oregano, cumin seeds, peppercorns, cloves, and bay leaves. Sauté to bring out the flavor, 2 to 3 minutes. Add the drained jalapeños and the sugar and sauté, tossing until softened, about 5 minutes. Pour in the vinegar, the reserved liquid, and ½ cup water. Bring to a boil; remove from the heat.

3. Transfer the mixture to a bowl or large jar; set aside to cool to room temperature. Cover and chill for at least 1 or 2 days before serving.

CUMIN SEEDS

Part of the parsley family, with seeds of a similar shape and size to caraway, cumin is a strongly scented spice with a flavor that is decidedly earthy and sweet. Although cumin seeds have a certain balanced bitterness, they do not produce the same numbing effect on the tongue as does caraway.

Cumin is a flavoring that we associate with Mexico and India. In Mexico, however, Diana Kennedy recommends that it be used judiciously: "The amounts used in the United States would be totally unacceptable to the Mexican palate," she once told me.

Large quantities of cumin alone taste unpleasant. Although cumin is used in large quantities as an important component in blending curry powder, other flavors are used to balance it.

The flavor of cumin is bigger and better when the seeds are lightly toasted before grinding. It's not a good idea to buy preground seeds, as the flavor begins to diminish quickly after grinding.

Curry Powder

Here is my favorite blend of spices to make great fresh-tasting curries and curried dishes. Toasting the whole seeds brings out their flavors and makes them more fragrant. All the ingredients are available where Indian groceries are sold. Once you grind and blend the spices, store the powder in a tightly sealed jar in a cool place; it will keep reasonably fresh for 4 to 6 months.

To make about ¾ cup:

In a heavy, medium skillet, combine 3 tablespoons coriander seeds, 2 tablespoons cumin seeds, and 1 tablespoon each black peppercorns, mustard seeds, fenugreek (optional), and fennel seeds. Add a 3-inch stick of cinnamon and 1 teaspoon whole cloves. Place over moderate heat and toast, shaking the pan constantly, until fragrant, 2 to 3 minutes. Let cool to room temperature.

To grind the spices, I highly recommend using an electric spice grinder, but you can also do it the old-fashioned way, in a mortar with a pestle. Before grinding, combine all the toasted spices with 3 tablespoons ground turmeric, 1 tablespoon ground ginger, and 1 teaspoon cayenne pepper or hot paprika; grind to a powder. Pack firmly into a jar, tightly seal, and store in a cool place.

Garam Masala

There is no spice blend quite as fresh and fragrant as homemade garam masala—the important Indian seasoning.

To make about ½ cup:

In a heavy, medium skillet, combine 3 tablespoons cumin seeds, 2 tablespoons coriander seeds, a 3-inch cinnamon stick cracked with a mallet, 2 teaspoons whole cloves, and 2 teaspoons cardamom seeds (about 3 tablespoons pods). Place over moderate heat and stir constantly until fragrant, about 2 minutes. Turn into a bowl and add 1 teaspoon freshly grated nutmeg. Let cool to room temperature. Pulverize the spices in an electric spice grinder or in a mortar with a pestle. To store, pack in a small jar, tightly seal, and store in a cool, dark place.

Avocado Salsa Verde

When I have this salsa on hand in the refrigerator, I spoon it over just about everything in sight—from meat loaf sandwiches or cold shrimp to hard-cooked eggs or charcoal-grilled hamburgers. Of course, you can spoon it liberally over tacos, Totopos (page 46), and burritos.

MAKES ABOUT 2½ CUPS

> 8 ounces fresh tomatillos (5 medium), husks removed
> 1 large, perfectly ripe California avocado, such as Haas
> 1 large, fresh jalapeño chili, chopped, with the seeds
> ½ cup sliced whole scallions
> 1 cup loosely packed fresh cilantro
> ¼ cup sour cream
> 1 teaspoon salt

1. In a nonreactive small saucepan, combine the tomatillos and 1 cup water. Bring to a boil over moderate heat. Reduce the heat to low and simmer, stirring several times, until soft, 5 to 7 minutes. Remove the tomatillos with a slotted spoon and let cool; reserve the liquid. When cool, put the tomatillos in a food processor.
2. Cut the avocado lengthwise in half and discard the pit. Spoon out the flesh and add it to the processor, along with the jalapeño, scallions, cilantro, and sour cream. Add ½ cup of the reserved cooking liquid and the salt. Process until well blended and smooth.

3. Serve the salsa right away or cover and refrigerate. The acidity of the tomatillos will delay the darkening of the avocado. Serve cold.

TOMATILLOS

Although called *tomate verde* in Mexico (where it is indigenous), this big berry cloaked in a papery husk is *not* related to the tomato. Once the husk is removed, however, it resembles an immature green tomato in appearance but has a unique flavor all its own—simple acidic-tart flavor vaguely reminiscent of green apple. Once cooked, the flavor mellows and its consistency softens. Its simple flavor screams out for garlic, cilantro, chilies, and salt to make it blossom.

Fresh tomatillos are best, but canned will do in a pinch (they are labeled *"tomatillo entero"* and, in general, a 13-ounce can can be substituted for 8 ounces of fresh).

Store fresh tomatillos in the refrigerator and they will keep for several weeks, sometimes even longer, until they soften. Just before using, remove the husks and rinse the tomatillos. They are most frequently cooked into sauces, but also can be blended raw.

Salsa Verde

This fresh green salsa with its light, bright taste is especially good spooned liberally over tostadas; to make them, spread tostada shells (flat, crisp, fried corn tortillas, commercial or homemade) with hot cheese-enriched refried beans, then add meat or chicken if desired and top with shredded lettuce, diced tomato, Salsa Verde, and shredded Cheddar or crumbled queso cotija cheese. Spoon on a dollop of sour cream and sprinkle with chopped cilantro. One of the nice things about tostadas is that you can have everything ready and arranged on a buffet table, with beans and meat kept hot in chafing dishes; guests assemble their own to taste.

MAKES ABOUT 2½ CUPS

    1   pound fresh tomatillos (12 to 16 medium), husks removed; or 2 cans
        (each 13 ounces) tomatillos, drained
    2   fresh jalapeño chilies, minced with ½ teaspoon or more seeds
        reserved, to taste
    1   tablespoon vegetable oil
    1   large garlic clove, minced or crushed through a press
    ¼   cup chopped fresh cilantro
    1   teaspoon salt

1. In a nonreactive heavy saucepan, combine the fresh tomatillos with 1½ cups cold water. Bring to a boil over medium heat. Reduce the heat to low and simmer until soft but not bursting, 8 to 10 minutes. Drain the tomatillos in a strainer set over a bowl; reserve the liquid. Let cool to room temperature. If starting with canned tomatillos, simply drain and discard the liquid.

2. In a blender or food processor, combine the tomatillos, jalapeños and seeds, and ½ cup of the reserved cooking liquid (or water, if using canned). Process to a puree.

3. Spoon the oil into a nonreactive small saucepan. Add the garlic and sauté gently for 10 to 20 seconds. Pour in the sauce and cook for 5 minutes. Remove from the heat and let cool to room temperature. Stir in the cilantro and salt.

4. If making ahead, chill. Upon chilling, salsa verde becomes gelatinous, so allow it to warm to room temperature and stir in a little water, if needed.

Jicama-Orange Salsa

In Mexico, cool and crisp jicama is served with a squeeze of lime and a sprinkle of red hot pepper—the inspiration for this fresh salsa. It is simple and bright with festive colors of red, white, and orange. Serve with Totopos (page 46) and grilled seafood.

MAKES ABOUT 3 CUPS

> 2 cups peeled, finely diced (¼ inch) jicama
> 3 to 4 navel oranges, cut into segments (see page 17)
> 3 tablespoons fresh lime juice
> ¾ teaspoon salt
> ¼ teaspoon cayenne pepper
> 1 large ripe tomato, peeled (page 15), seeded, and diced

Put the jicama in a large bowl. Cut the orange segments into ½-inch pieces and add them, along with all of their juices, to the jicama. (You will have about 1 cup orange pieces with juice.) Stir in the lime juice, salt, cayenne, and tomato. Toss and taste for seasoning. Cover and chill until serving. Serve cold.

Chunky Dill-Cucumber Salsa

Great with grilled fish and seafood and with chicken and lamb, this approach to salsa is closely related to a relish. I like to serve sliced summer tomatoes along one side of a broiled scrod with this chunky salsa on the other.

MAKES ABOUT 2½ CUPS

- 4 medium Kirby cucumbers or 2 large regular cucumbers, trimmed and peeled
- ½ cup sliced whole scallions
- 3 to 4 tablespoons snipped fresh dill
- 1 fresh or pickled jalapeño chili, seeded, if desired, and minced
- 3 tablespoons fresh lime juice
- 2 tablespoons vegetable oil
- 1 tablespoon cider vinegar
- 1 teaspoon salt
- ¼ teaspoon black pepper

1. Halve the cucumbers lengthwise and use a small spoon to scoop out any seeds. Cut the cucumber lengthwise into thin strips and then chop into ¼-inch dice; you will have about 2 cups.
2. In a bowl, combine the cucumbers, scallions, 3 tablespoons of the dill, the jalapeño, lime juice, oil, vinegar, salt, pepper, and 2 tablespoons cold water.
3. Cover and chill for about 2 hours, tossing occasionally. Taste and add a little more dill, if desired.

SALSA SAAVY

Salsas aren't just for corn chips. Consider serving them over steamed fish fillets, grilled chicken, or with cold poached shrimp (page 269). Besides spooning salsa over traditional dishes like tacos, tostadas, taquitos, quesadillas, and burritos, try adding them to omelets, burgers, or pita bread pocket sandwiches. One great way to save calories and avoid fat is to serve salsa instead of butter with hot crusty bread. Also try them on Crostini and Bruschetta (page 26).

Salsa Ranchera

This is best made with fresh ripe tomatoes and poblano chilies. But in a pinch, use canned tomatoes and canned peeled green chilies.

MAKES ABOUT 2½ CUPS

> 4 slices lean hickory-smoked bacon, cut into small squares
> 1 medium onion, finely chopped
> 1 or 2 fresh jalapeño chilies, seeded and minced
> 2 pounds (4 large) ripe tomatoes, peeled (page 15),
>   seeded, and chopped, with juices reserved
> 8 ounces (2 to 3 large) fresh poblano chilies, roasted (page 17),
>   peeled, and cut into ½-inch dice; or 1 can (4 ounces)
>   peeled mild green chilies, drained and chopped
> 1½ teaspoons salt
> ¼ teaspoon black pepper
> ¼ cup chopped fresh cilantro leaves

1. In a nonreactive heavy skillet, fry the bacon over moderate heat, stirring frequently, until crisp and golden brown, 5 to 7 minutes. Push the bacon to one side and tilt the pan; spoon off all but 1 tablespoon of the fat.
2. Add the onion and jalapeños to the skillet and sauté until softened, about 3 minutes. Stir in the tomatoes, roasted chilies, salt, and pepper and bring to a boil. Reduce the heat to low and simmer gently until thickened slightly and reduced to 2½ cups, 15 to 20 minutes. Remove from the heat and cool for 20 to 30 minutes.
3. Stir in the cilantro; reheat if making ahead.

VARIATIONS

Substitution: Omit the bacon and sauté the onion in 1½ tablespoons vegetable oil or olive oil.

Addition: Add ¼ cup sliced scallions with the cilantro.

Huevos Rancheros

This famous ranch-style breakfast is as simple as fried eggs on corn tortillas with tomato-chili sauce spooned over and sprinkled with a little cheese. The 2½ cups Salsa Ranchera is enough for 6 to 8 eggs.

Pour ⅛ inch vegetable oil into a medium skillet and place over moderate heat. When very hot (touch an edge of a tortilla to the oil and it should sizzle loudly upon contact), add 1 corn tortilla and cook to soften without letting become crisp, 3 to 5 seconds. Turn once. Drain on a paper towel. You will need 1 tortilla softened for each egg. They can be kept hot in a warm oven.

In a medium or large skillet over moderate heat, using 1 teaspoon butter for each egg, fry the eggs sunny-side up, or over lightly, flipping once. Slide one onto each tortilla (if serving 2 per guest, arrange the tortillas slightly over-lapping on the same plate). Spoon ⅓ cup Salsa Ranchera over each egg and sprinkle with about 1 tablespoon crumbled queso cotija or farmer cheese and 1 teaspoon chopped cilantro. You can dress them up with a garnish of 2 thin strips roasted and peeled poblano chili, made into an X over each yolk.

Summer Salsa

In Mexico you can get ripe juicy tomatoes all year long, but here they are good only during the summer. When such tomatoes are not available, use the recipe for Winter Salsa that follows. The sauce carries the perfume of cilantro and has the energetic vitality of a hot tamale.

MAKES ABOUT 3 CUPS

  3 cups diced ripe juicy summer tomatoes
  ½ cup finely chopped white onion
  ½ cup chopped fresh cilantro
  1 or 2 fresh jalapeño chilies, chopped, with ½
      teaspoon seeds, if desired
  2 teaspoons fresh lime or lemon juice
1½ to 2 teaspoons salt

In a medium bowl, combine the tomato, onion, cilantro, jalapeños, lime juice, and salt. Taste and add more seeds if a hotter salsa is desired. Serve right away or cover and chill.

Winter Salsa

This is a good, juicy salsa because canned tomatoes are combined with the firmer winter tomatoes found in the market much of the year. The scallions and cilantro add freshness and fragrance. Of course, you can make this year-round.

MAKES ABOUT 3 CUPS

- 2 ripe winter tomatoes, finely diced
- ⅓ cup chopped fresh cilantro
- ¼ cup chopped whole scallions
- 1 or 2 fresh jalapeño chilies, minced with ½ teaspoon seeds reserved, if desired
- 1½ teaspoons salt
- 1 can (28 ounces) whole tomatoes, chopped and drained
- ¼ cup tomato sauce

In a medium bowl, combine the tomatoes, cilantro, scallions, jalapeños, salt, tomatoes, and tomato sauce. Stir well. Serve right away or cover and chill.

Macho Nachos

A delightful offering for small get-togethers or large parties is a platterful of Macho Nachos. You can make them as "macho" as you desire by the amount of homemade Chipotle Salsa that you spoon over them or serve alongside. This recipe will serve 6 to 8, but it's easily doubled.

Although I recommend that you make a batch of Totopos (page 46), you can also achieve excellent results by starting with 48 large round nacho chips or corn chips. If you like meat atop your nachos, make the chicken filling from the recipe for Enchiladas Verde (page 210). You will also have to decide if you want guacamole or sour cream (or both). Half of the recipe for Chunky Guacamole (page 38) will be enough for 48 nachos as will 1 cup of sour cream.

Preheat the oven to 400°F. and position an oven shelf to the top third. Spread each of 48 totopos or corn chips with ½ tablespoon of refried beans (canned or homemade as you like; 1½ cups will be needed) and arrange them on two baking sheets. Top each with a slightly mounded teaspoon of chicken filling (optional), 1 thin slice of Pickled Jalapeño (page 384), 1 teaspoon finely diced tomato (1 cup total), a few sliced scallions, and 1 teaspoon each of grated Monterey Jack and Cheddar cheeses (4 ounces of each needed).

One tray at a time, bake the nachos in the top third of a very hot oven for 5 to 7 minutes, until the cheese melts. Remove from the oven and top each with about 1 teaspoon of guacamole and/or sour cream. Splash on Chipotle Salsa to taste, from a drop or two to ½ teaspoon. Serve right away.

Chipotle Salsa

I am fond of Mexican sauces flavored with smoky chipotle chilies. For this smooth salsa, it is tamed a little with tomato, but the sauce is still hot enough to satisfy fire-breathers. The initial toasting of the chilies makes the kitchen fragrant like Mexico. Spoon the sauce over tacos, burritos, tostadas, and eggs. A dollop of sour cream alongside helps to tame the flame.

MAKES 1½ TO 2 CUPS

> 2 ounces (20 to 30) small dried chipotle chilies
> 1½ tablespoons vegetable oil
> 2 large garlic cloves, minced or crushed through a press
> 1 teaspoon ground cumin
> 1 teaspoon dried oregano, crumbled
> ¼ teaspoon ground cinnamon
> ½ to 1 cup canned tomato sauce
> ½ cup cider vinegar
> 1 tablespoon sugar
> 1½ teaspoons salt

1. Put the chilies in a heavy, medium skillet over moderate heat and toast lightly, tossing and turning, until soft and fragrant, 2 to 3 minutes. Working over a bowl to catch the seeds (and using rubber gloves if desired to protect the skin—these chilies *are* hot), pull out the stems and tear open the chilies so the seeds fall out. Tear the chilies into large pieces (halves or quarters) and place them in a small heatproof bowl; discard the seeds and stems. Pour 1 cup of boiling water over the chilies and soak, stirring occasionally, for 1 hour. Do not drain.

2. Spoon the oil into a heavy, medium skillet set over low heat. Add the garlic, cumin, oregano, and cinnamon and sizzle to soften but not brown the garlic, 1 to 2 minutes. Add the chilies with their soaking liquid, ½ cup of the tomato sauce, the vinegar, sugar, and salt. Bring to a boil. Remove from the heat and set aside to cool to room temperature.

3. Puree the salsa in a food processor. Strain through a medium sieve; discard the solids. If the sauce is too thick, stir in 2 to 3 tablespoons water. Taste for the heat to tomato ratio and stir in the remaining ½ cup tomato sauce, if desired. Cover and store in a jar in the refrigerator. It will keep well for several months.

Index

Conversion Chart
Equivalent Imperial and Metric Measurements

American cooks use standard containers, the 8-ounce cup and a tablespoon that takes exactly 16 level fillings to fill that cup level. Measuring by cup makes it very difficult to give weight equivalents, as a cup of densely packed butter will weigh considerably more than a cup of flour. The easiest way therefore to deal with cup measurements in recipes is to take the amount by volume rather than by weight. Thus the equation reads:

1 cup = 240 ml = 8 fl. oz.   ½ cup = 120 ml = 4 fl. oz.

It is possible to buy a set of American cup measures in major stores around the world.

In the States, butter is often measured in sticks. One stick is the equivalent of 8 tablespoons. One tablespoon of butter is therefore the equivalent to ½ ounce/15 grams.

Liquid Measures

Fluid Ounces	U.S.	Imperial	Milliliters
	1 teaspoon	1 teaspoon	5
¼	2 teaspoons	1 dessert spoon	7
½	1 tablespoon	1 tablespoon	15
1	2 tablespoons	2 tablespoons	28
2	¼ cup	4 tablespoons	56
4	½ cup or ¼ pint		110
5		¼ pint or 1 gill	140
6	¾ cup		170
8	1 cup or ½ pint		225
9			250, ¼ liter
10	1¼ cups	½ pint	280
12	1½ cups or ¾ pint		340
15		¾ pint	420
16	2 cups or 1 pint		450
18	2¼ cups		500, ½ liter
20	2½ cups	1 pint	560
24	3 cups or 1½ pints		675
25		1¼ pints	700
27	3½ cups		750
30	3¾ cups	1½ pints	840
32	4 cups or 2 pints or 1 quart		900
35		1¾ pints	980
36	4½ cups		1000, 1 liter
40	5 cups or 2½ pints	2 pints or 1 quart	1120
48	6 cups or 3 pints		1350
50		2½ pints	1400
60	7½ cups	3 pints	1680
64	8 cups or 4 pints or 2 quarts		1800
72	9 cups		2000, 2 liters

Solid Measures

U.S. and Imperial Measures		Metric Measures	
Ounces	Pounds	Grams	Kilos
1		28	
2		56	
3½		100	
4	¼	112	
5		140	
6		168	
8	½	225	
9		250	¼
12	¾	340	
16	1	450	
18		500	½
20	1¼	560	
24	1½	675	
27		750	¾
28	1¾	780	
32	2	900	
36	2¼	1000	1
40	2½	1100	
48	3	1350	
54		1500	1½
64	4	1800	
72	4½	2000	2
80	5	2250	2¼
90		2500	2½
100	6	2800	2¾

Oven Temperature Equivalents

Fahrenheit	Celsius	Gas Mark	Description
225	110	¼	Cool
250	130	½	
275	140	1	Very Slow
300	150	2	
325	170	3	Slow
350	180	4	Moderate
375	190	5	
400	200	6	Moderately Hot
425	220	7	Fairly Hot
450	230	8	Hot
475	240	9	Very Hot
500	250	10	Extremely Hot

Equivalents for Ingredients

all-purpose flour—plain flour
cheesecloth—muslin
confectioners' sugar—icing sugar
cornstarch—cornflour
granulated sugar—caster sugar

shortening—white fat
sour cherry—morello cherry
unbleached flour—strong, white flour
vanilla bean—vanilla pod
zest—rind

light cream—single cream
heavy cream—double cream
half and half—12% fat milk
buttermilk—ordinary milk

Jim Fobel is the author of seven books, including *Jim Fobel's Old-Fashioned Baking Book*, which was cited as one of the Best Cookbooks of the Year by the James Beard Foundation, and *Jim Fobel's Diet Feasts*. Test kitchen director of *Food & Wine* magazine from 1979 to 1983, Fobel is now a contributing editor for *Cooking Light* magazine.